Questions on German History

Ideas, forces, decisions from 1800 to the present.

Historical Exhibition
in the Berlin Reichstag
Catalogue, 3rd (updated) Edition

The Exhibition is organised by the German Bundestag under the auspices of the President of the German Bundestag.

by the German Bundestag
Publications' Section, Bonn

English Edition

CIP-Titelaufnahme der Deutschen Bibliothek

Questions on German history: ideas, forces, decisions from 1800 to the present; histor. exhibition in the Berlin Reichstag; catalogue/(the exhibition is organised by the German Bundestag. Publ. by the German Bundestag, Publ. Sect., Bonn). – Engl. ed., 3rd (updated) ed. – Bonn: German Bundestag, Publ. Sect., 1989
Parallelt.: Fragen an die deutsche Geschichte. – Dt. Ausg. u. d. T.: Fragen an die deutsche Geschichte. – Franz. Ausg. u. d. T.: Interrogeons l'histoire de l'Allemagne
ISBN 3-924521-25-5
NE: Deutschland <Bundesrepublik>/Bundestag: PT

Source of Supply for Catalogues and Cassettes in German, English and French: Historical Exhibition in the Reichstag Building and Publishers.
The Exhibition is open Tuesday–Sunday from 10.00–17.00, holidays included.
Educational Groups visiting the Exhibition should ring prior to their arrival: Tel. Nr. (030) 39772141.
Individuals visiting the Exhibition can make use of a tape-recorded guide, available in German, English and French for DM 2.

Table of Contents

Appendix

Supplements

Introduction to the 3rd Edition of the Exhibition Catalogue "Questions on German History"

Opened in 1971 and expanded in 1974, the historical exhibition in Berlin's Reichstag building reflects that period of German history when essential foundations were laid for our nation's current governmental, social, and economic system and illustrates the forces, ideas, and decisions from which this system developed. The exhibition points out the far-reaching changes which were occurring throughout the world in which people lived at that time, and the political situations which decisively affected Germany's historical development during the 19th and 20th centuries are analysed in detail. In keeping with its fundamental significance for the present time, the historical development of parliamentary democracy with its high and low points receives particular emphasis.

The steady stream of visitors which has continued for more than a decade and the brisk demand for the exhibition catalogue testify to a widespread and lively interest in knowing more about this period of German history, understanding it better and, last but not least, in coming to grips with it. In response to advances in historical research and to current developments in government, the exhibition has been continually expanded and developed further, especially the section concerning the Federal Republic of Germany.

The third edition of this book about the exhibition, which has been enlarged and supplemented, is intended to fulfil the function it has already performed so well in the past: providing an introduction to the exhibition as well as a coherent, vivid, and multi-faceted picture of German history from 1800 to the present, whether it be for the purpose of following up on a visit to the exhibition or as reading material independent of it.

Prof. Dr. Rita Süssmuth
President of the German Bundestag

Note on the Catalogue

This catalogue does not attempt to list and describe each individual exhibit numerically. Such an undertaking would not just have been totally unrealistic, considering the great number of vastly differing exhibits, it would also, in view of the character of the exhibition, have been irrelevant. This exhibition does not simply aim to consider each era by means of reports and illustrations, rather it aims to stress certain points, to provide guidelines, to point out links which provoke a series of questions, which refer to the political and social decisions of the German history of the last 190 years and the ideas and forces which lay behind them. Thus each individual exhibit has only a functional purpose. Apart from one or two key documents, the exhibit's individual value is less than its function of illustrating and elucidating certain historical processes. It therefore seemed more important to describe again the major issues and the links between them, by referring briefly to the individual picture-boards and by stressing the particularly important, characteristic or graphic illustrations or written documents (a selection of which is included in the catalogue), than to provide the usual detailed chronological detail. In this way a more general and thorough insight should be gained into the complexity of questions which are connected with the theme, which should serve as a good pre-visit guide to the exhibition and also provide more detailed supplementary reading.

Introduction

by Lothar Gall

Before attempting to consider around 190 years of German history by means of an exhibition, a whole series of preliminary questions must be raised. Firstly there is the highly topical general problem of whether historical facts and knowledge are of any real significance for our understanding of the present, or indeed, of whether they provide us with any guidelines for the shape of the future. Furthermore, and closely linked with the previous question, one must consider the practical aims of such an exhibition and ask whether the chosen theme of German history is not in itself a limiting factor, since it implies a continuity of national development (in the positive or negative sense) which was broken in 1945 by the division of Germany. In other words we must ask whether or not one is attempting to create an artificial tradition for the Federal Republic, whose 25th anniversary was the reason for this exhibition, or to embed it in certain traditions.

Doubtless, these are legitimate questions. They basically concern the purpose of such an exhibition and additionally the fundamental question of what modern historical science should seek to achieve by presenting its results in the form of an exhibition.

Any attempt to answer these questions will have to start from the quite indisputable fact that the approach to the 'advantages and disadvantages of history' and our appraisal of its function for the individual and society have changed considerably in the last few decades. Things have evolved to such an extent that occasionally the conclusion has been drawn that knowledge of historical processes and an insight into the factors determining them are, objectively and subjectively speaking, of but secondary importance in terms of understanding the present and of providing guidelines for the future. Therefore, it has been claimed that there is no longer any need for the government and its educational institutions to make any special effort to foster such knowledge and insight. The implication of such assertions must undoubtedly be taken seriously and not dismissed with noncommittal phrases about the educational value of history. It is the notion that the rapidly changing environment, living and working conditions, as well as fundamental changes in political, economic and social structures resulting from that process, have detached the individual and society as a whole, with its many institutions, from any historical background both on a national and continental level. This assumes that they are therefore subject to development trends and forces which can only be identified by analysing existing highly complicated sociological, economic and positive political criteria; rarely are historical criteria relevant or useful.

Such a critical view of the role and function of historical insights and knowledge in considering the present, is in itself based on unrealistic suppositions and, moreover, ignores the trends and pressures of the past, which have unavoidably influenced the institutions of the state and society and the economic structure as well as regional and national cultural patterns; the aforegoing can only realistically be assessed historically. Furthermore, this critical view bases its claims on what is really a very traditional and outdated understanding of the role of history as a scientific discipline, which is no longer accepted by modern historians themselves. Above all there is a tendency, said to be still prevalent, to link inextricably the present and the past and, in particular, as is tacitly presumed, to a 'chosen' past, characterised by certain traditions, which have been emphasised for generations, notably by German historians. However, this is hardly the case nowadays and one of the main objectives of the modern historian, who consciously sees his task as not merely to consider things retrospectively but as to promote an understanding of history and to help to provide a guide for future action, is to make the individual and the public as a whole aware of the fact that social behaviour and fundamental political decisions, ideologies and economic and political systems, patterns of thought and decision-making criteria, are all conditioned by history. In his critical exploration and presentation of the history therefore, the historian, pursuing such an undoubtedly demanding objective, is mainly interested in arousing and fostering a basic mental attitude to the present and future which encourages the individual, when formulating his own plans, not simply to consider these plans superficially but to try to study their background and to realise that there are limits to his plans. In this way the individual can become free to make responsible decisions. To some, such a fundamental attitude is difficult to accept because it is clearly irreconcilable with too nonchalant a belief in progress in that it does not easily allow them to avoid a confrontation between what is rationally desirable and what is actually possible. But to hold the historian and his allegedly conservative mind responsible for this is to mistake cause for effect.

On the other hand, this approach to history may also be critically regarded by those who think that the object should be to demonstrate how well the present compares with the past and how much has been achieved in the interim. It is time to say that the historian should, indeed may, not offer blind praise of the past; in this respect the positive changes in social relations, economic conditions and the political system, will always attract his special attention. However, considering his understanding of his own role he cannot concentrate his criticism exclusively on the past and should not, therefore, offer blind praise of the present. On the contrary, the basic mental attitude which he seeks to impart is, by nature, inevitably critical of the present also. Throwing light on the historical background of present-day systems and actions means relating one to the other and thus providing a basis for future changes and fundamental decisions, though without mapping out a specific programme – an erroneous expectation which no serious historian can attempt to fulfil.

The aforegoing is essentially, in abstract form, a reflection of the concept behind this exhibition which covers the last 170 years of German history since the epoch-making French Revolution and all its consequences. On the one hand "Questions on German History" concerns the main conditions, i.e. the background to the development of our present governmental, social and economic system as well as the most important forces, ideas and basic decisions which have facilitated its development. In this context the movement towards a liberal parliamentary democracy, which was repeatedly interrupted and suffered many setbacks, is of central importance. On the other hand they also concern the decision-making processes themselves and an attempt is made to go beyond considering events in isolation and to portray the conditions which both render possible and limit political action.

In so doing, it would not be sufficient simply to pose superficial questions or to provide unclear answers. Another method which has recently become increasingly popular, and which consists of providing one-sided, provocative, exaggerated interpretations, was rejected because it presupposes too much preliminary knowledge and information and because it would turn an exhibition aimed at providing intellectual stimulus into a mere tool of indoctrination. On the contrary, importance is attached here at the exhibition to providing visitors with information that corresponds to their knowledge of this field and an attempt is made to enable them to form a judgement which is not final but remains open for discussion.

Within this framework further preliminary decisions had to be made which have substantially influenced the character of the exhibition. With regard to the theme, it was above all necessary to decide where the emphasis should be placed and, as regards representation, how much importance had to be attached to the individual factors. One of these central points of interest, namely the history of parliamentary democracy in Germany, has already been mentioned. Another focal point had to be the sweeping changes resulting from the development of modern industrial society. It was not only a matter of illustrating this development and of giving a clear idea of its driving forces but of demonstrating the respective political and social consequences of this process and, in so doing, of providing a detailed survey of the situation, its special problems and immediate tasks, its contradictions and political challenges. Against this background the causes, the influencing factors and the short and long-term consequences of the decisions made in the various stages of Germany's historical development in the 19th and 20th centuries had to be analysed: the radical change in the period from 1806 to 1815, the revolution of 1848, the great constitutional conflict in Prussia and the setting up of the German Reich in 1871, the revolution in 1918 and the creation of the Weimar Republic, Weimar's decline and the assumption of power by the National Socialists, the deadly enemies of the liberal democratic parliamentary system and of all its governmental, social and economic foundations, and, finally, the successful attempt to restore and develop this system and to adapt it to modern requirements after 1945. This emphasis on the turning points of the historical process produced several independent sections which can be studied separately and into which it has been possible to incorporate certain factors that had a decisive influence on the character and intellectual atmosphere of a particular era in the field of art, literature and science – in short on the cultural life of the time in the widest sense of the word – but which are in retrospect frequently no longer inter-related.

Naturally, numerous problems arise when certain points are emphasized and when an exhibition is divided into sections: some aspects which the visitor may have considered to be of major importance are not described in detail, some that proved difficult to illustrate could only be included in the text. Moreover, some important inter-relationships could only be touched upon and in some cases there will appear to be no cohesion at all. The division into periods of history, although it considers not only turning points but also decisive radical changes, is certainly open to criticism, but it should be remembered that, apart from the general considerations outlined above, the practical side had to be taken into account. In particular, it was necessary to consider how much time and energy the less well informed visitor could be expected to devote to such an exhibition. The sections had to be arranged in such a way as to facilitate his choice and give him a clear idea of the thematic links and developments of specific periods of history. There was a natural limit to this, especially as this exhibition is mainly geared towards problems and not so much towards events. However, if the objective of such an exhibition is to draw the visitor's attention to the complexity of the factors and conditions determining political actions, such a restriction is likely to challenge him to ask further questions, to make comparisons and to try to trace more connections. The task with which he is expected to cope – in spite of all the guidance offered – is no mean one but is no more difficult than the one with which he is confronted as a present or future voter in a democratic society which is only able to function because he is able to form a political opinion and to take political decisions. There is an inextricable link between the two of them and the organisers of this exhibition have consciously regarded this as a kind of guideline for the degree of concentration and ability to be critical that could legitimately be expected of the visitor.

At the same time this guideline made it clear that there was no point in relating history so closely to the present that it developed into an additional argument for or against a certain policy. This applies to the whole exhibition, but particularly to the sections leading immediately up to the present, above all the section devoted to the history of the Federal Republic. Since source material was still scarce and did not afford an adequate basis for balanced historical judgement, great caution was required and clearly the aim had to be to provide as much information and documentation as possible rather than to attempt a definitive classification and evaluation. This may seem unsatisfactory to some people and evoke discussion and criticism but from the point of view of the individual, who has to participate in the day to day political decision-making process, this is completely legitimate, in fact highly desirable. However, it is one thing to use – as an individual – the most recent past as a basis for one's political judgement and, in so doing, to give it an additional perspective and dimension (the exhibition tries to serve this purpose) and another to suggest – as the organiser – political conclusions on the basis of certain historical judgements.

For the rest, clear judgements will certainly be made where historical findings and scientific discussion permit. In the light of the concepts outlined above, these judgements are obviously not just a question of celebrating the victory of what are supposedly good principles and forces, nor does one simply lament their defeat in naive, if well-meaning picture-book fashion. Rather, an attempt is made to sound out the conflict of differing ideas and interests and to measure the scope for decisions. No attempt is made to state what is desirable. There will obviously be contradictions which will arise in this respect and these are to be welcomed. Indeed, they can even be regarded as an indication of the extent to which the exhibition helps the visitor to judge the political and historical processes. Moreover, they will show how the exhibition revives discussion on the nature and significance of fundamental decisions made in the past and still relevant today.

If those who have organised this exhibition and who are responsible for it had their way, the exhibition would focus on a question the topicality and problematic nature of which is indisputable: the question of the historical background of liberal parliamentary democracy in Germany and the problems faced during its development. What obstacles hindered the introduction of this system, which forces opposed and which supported it, what were its origins and why were its foundations created rather late in Germany and why did they then remain shaky for such a long time? What made it vulnerable both to threats from outside and to a process of self-destruction, to internal crises which were repeatedly a threat from the beginning, and what factors finally made its adversay, the authoritarian state, so attractive for so many years – and to some extent continue to do so even today? This exhibition considers all these questions. The answers provided also have a topical dimension if they are considered more closely and if one is not merely interested in superficial and therefore often misleading parallels. This applies not least to one aspect which, if overlooked, could easily become a threat to the very existence of liberal parliamentary democracy as a whole: the fact that certain forms of expression and organisation in this system and some of its foundations and mechanisms, which are much less significant than is often suggested, are the product of the prevailing circumstances.

Here too, and particularly so, historical analysis can help increase the observer's ability to distinguish between external form and inner substance and to discover the point where form and content begin to become contradictory under different conditions. If this exhibition succeeds in providing an incentive in this respect and thus encourages people to think in historical terms, helping them to overcome rigid forms of life that have developed over the ages and assisting new and better developments, then this will provide full justification and outweigh the call, which is fashionable in certain quarters, for the allegedly false presentation of history to be discarded.

Central Europe at the start of the 19th Century

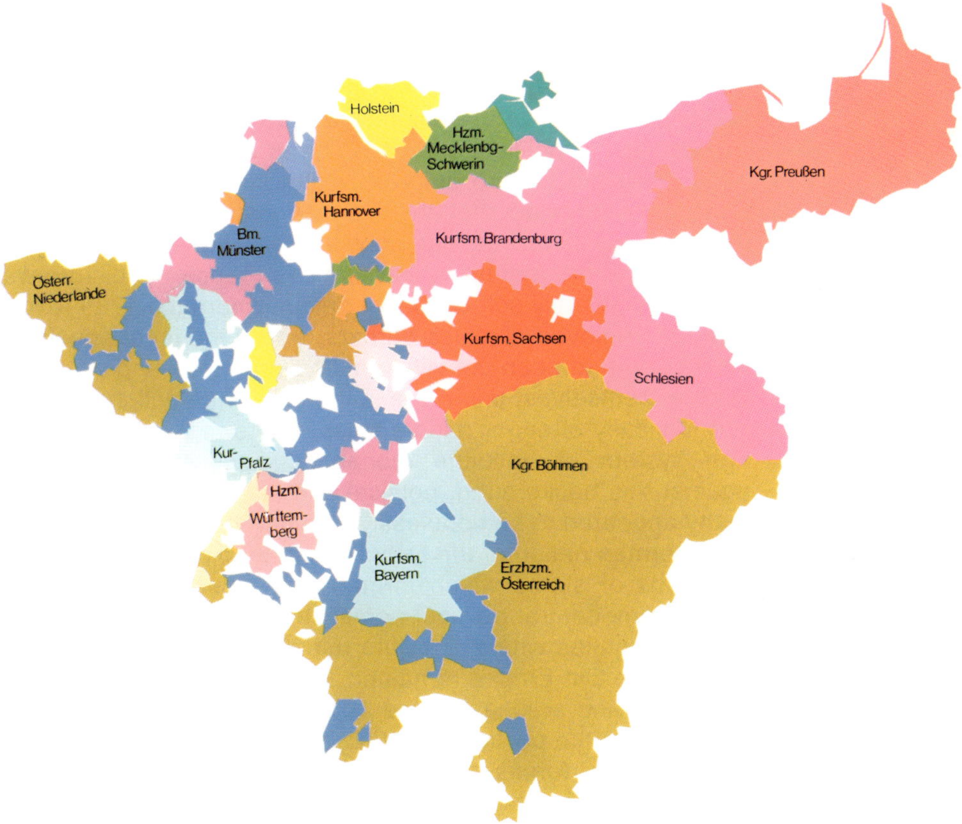

Room I

Political Awakening and Congress of Vienna

Around the end of the eighteenth century a serious crisis threatened the political and social order of Germany. The swift collapse of the Empire before the attacking French revolutionary armies showed that the German nation of the Old Holy Roman Empire lacked not only external but also, and more significantly, internal unity. In victorious France the picture was one of a politically self-confident nation, where the 1789 revolution had removed all class barriers, where the legal equality of the citizen had been constitutionally guaranteed and where the people themselves, under the leadership of an enlightened and economically stronger middle class, had swept away the tutelage system of absolute monarchy. Especially when seen against this background, political and social conditions in Germany appeared to be hopelessly anachronistic.

The German nation of the Holy Roman Empire was divided into hundreds of states which formed only a loose confederation lacking any central political administration. Germany consisted of sovereignties where absolute rule was enforced. Whilst support for the Old Empire remained alive in several of the smaller territories and amongst some constitutional experts, the main influence on the political situation of the Empire was exerted by the opposing forces of the two major powers: Prussia and Austria.

Inside the states strong class divisions between the aristocracy, the middle class and the peasants were blocking social and economic development. There was a lack of any national political awareness both amongst the disenfranchised subjects and their monarchs who pursued narrow-minded, selfprotective, policies. Only amongst intellectuals in the second half of the eighteenth century was support for national unity expressed, which broke down social barriers, and which was summed up by Schiller: "The German Empire and the German Nation are two different concepts . . . whilst the political Empire has wavered, the spiritual one has become stronger and more complete."

Because there was no strong middle class in the economically underdeveloped Germany of the time, the French Revolution, despite its considerable influence upon intellectuals, was politically insignificant for Germany. The revolutionary wars simply exposed the weakness of the old political and social order. The absolute state monarchies collapsed under the attack of the French revolutionary armies, the two major powers of Prussia

and Austria were defeated and, following Napoleon's geographical reshaping of Germany, the Empire crumbled in 1806.
Following this total defeat, several people began to realise that the root cause of the disaster lay primarily in the deep rift between state and society. Social reforms were seen to be a political necessity. Freedom and equality should become the corner-stones of the new state's bourgeois society and thus assist the liberation of the Fatherland. The aim was to enfranchise citizens through state reforms and in so doing to arouse their interest in the state and nation.
Shortly before he was appointed Prussian Prime Minister in 1807 Freiherr vom Stein, still imbued with imperial patriotism, described the aims of social reforms as: "The awakening of public-spiritedness and citizenship, the application of dormant or misdirected forces and misguided knowledge, harmony between the spirit of the nation, its views and requirements and those of the state authorities, the re-awakening of feelings of independence and national honour".
In this respect the link between social reforms and national feeling was apparent and the consequence of this was the demand for a representative constitution. According to Prussian reformers a "representative system" should be introduced "which ensured the effective participation of the nation in law-making, in order to consolidate public-spiritedness and the love of the Fatherland". The fact that these promises were not fulfilled by the reactionary policies pursued after 1815 robbed the Prussian social reform of all credibility. At the same time the drawbacks of the reform became apparent: many peasants and artisans suffered under the liberal economic system and became impoverished. Moreover, education and property remained the privileges of a small élite.
The social reforms in the Confederation of the Rhine, influenced by Napoleon, resembled superficially the Prussian reforms but had a different aim. As with the Prussian reforms, class barriers were broken down, the economic system was modernised and the equality of the citizen was legally guaranteed. However, at the outset, no political rights were granted and the first priority of the reforms was the setting up of a centralised administration. Since the promised Prussian representative system never emerged and since such a system was introduced in Southern Germany after 1815, political emancipation progressed further here prior to the 1848 Revolu-

tion than in Prussia. Austria was still entrenched in an absolutist system.
The nationalist aspirations of the Prussian reformers won considerable support due, to a certain extent, to the pressure of the French occupation. Men such as Fichte and Arndt made a significant contribution, through their writing, to the birth of a new national political awareness and paved the way for the uprising against the Napoleonic rulers. Works such as these were filled with nationalist exaggeration and expressed a basic hatred of the victors, as displayed for example in Kleist's 'Hermannschlacht'. The German monarchs took advantage of this increase in nationalist sentiment to form a short-term alliance between crown and people in the liberation war.
After feelings of nationalism had been further strengthened by the victory over the Napoleonic armies the hopes of the patriots were not fulfilled. At the Congress of Vienna the interests of the monarchs alone determined the fate of Germany. As was the case in the majority of individual states, there was no people's representation in the German Confederation. A nation-state was not created in Germany but a loose Confederation dominated by the monarchies. The main aim of this Confederation was the squashing of all liberals and nationalists who still dared, after the reactionary victory, to express demands for constitutions, national representation and freedom of the press. In external affairs the German Confederation, along with its largest states, was drawn into the Holy Alliance system of the Pentarchy, which favoured the cementing of existing political and social conditions. The monarchs remained absolute sovereigns. The middle classes, though economically better off, due to the social reforms, had made no progress at all in the struggle for political influence.

I/1 Banquet for the Kaiser and the Electors in the Römer Palace, Frankfurt am Main, 1758.

I/2 Reichstag session in Regensburg, 1675.

The Old Empire (Boards 1–36)

Boards 1–6 and 18/19

The Constitution of the Old Empire

Johann Jacob Moser, the German constitutionalist, wrote: "The Roman Empire would still be indisputably the greatest power in Europe if its people, and above all those in the highest positions of power, could reconcile their differences and work more for the common good than for the furtherance of their private interests". Indeed, the fragmentation of the Empire into hundreds of small, almost autonomous, states, the quarrels of the electors, the princes, the knights and towns, and the continual conflict between protestants and catholics, were the real weakness of "the German Nation of the Holy Roman Empire". In contrast to its more centralised neighbouring states the Empire was only a loose confederation of independent, separatist powers. Most sovereigns exerted absolute power over internal affairs and with regard to external matters, because of their conflicting interests they rarely achieved a unified position.

Boards 4–6

The central state institution and the external expression of its continuing unity was the Empire. For a long time, however, the power of the Kaiser had relied solely upon his position of dominance over the Habsburg states. Moreover, neither the glitter of the medieval imperial insignia nor the ceremonious coronation of the Emperor in the Free Imperial City of Frankfurt could hide the truth of the situation *(cat. illustr. 1)*.

A glance at the European map on the eve of the French Revolution shows the many divisions inherent in the territories of the Empire. A common political stance was rendered practically impossible by the mere existence of more than 1,790 independent states. In such a small area as Swabia there were 92 sovereigns and imperial cities. State unity was also often lacking in the territories of the Empire because, as for example in the Archbishopric of Mainz, the dependencies were scattered throughout the entire country. Only the major powers of Austria and Prussia possessed extensive and geographically-concentrated territories, which, moreover, stretched beyond the boundaries of the Empire.

Boards 18/19

From 1663 until the end of the Empire a 'permanent Imperial Diet' met *(cat. illustr. 2)*. It was a gathering of representatives of the princes, dignitaries, electors and imperial cities (Reichsstände), which, having been divided up according to religion, pronounced upon imperial affairs. The Kaiser was the nominal chairman and was bound by the decrees of the Imperial Diet. The decision-making process was laborious because the envoys were mandated by their superiors. In addition, it was rare for the interests of the individual states and classes represented to coincide. Thus, the significance of the Imperial Diet gradually diminished and the fate of the Empire came to depend more and more on the relationship between the two major powers: Austria and Prussia.

Board 20 The weakness of the Empire was also reflected by the absence of central institutions. There was no executive authority, no common tax system and no standing Imperial Army. The Imperial Diet could call for the setting up of an army but the princes could not be relied upon to heed the decisions of the Diet and did not always send their predetermined quota of troops nor their financial contribution. Johann Jacob Moser remarked ironically that the Imperial Army was so weak that it would be in the Empire's best interest to forbid the waging of any war. The truth of these words was demonstrated by the pitiful performance of the Imperial troops in the wars against revolutionary France.

Board 21 The legal unity of the Empire was embodied in the two highest Imperial Courts: the Reichshofsrat in the Emperor's city of residence, Vienna, and the Supreme Court in Wetzlar. It is well known that Goethe – who like many young law students was an assistant at the Supreme Court – complained about the slowness of the legal procedures in Wetzlar. Single cases were known to stretch over more than a hundred years because the government lacked both the money and the personnel to deal with the surfeit of appeals. However, the Imperial Courts did offer some measure of protection against the despotism of the sovereigns. For example, when Johann Jacob Moser was imprisoned by Duke Karl Eugen, as a result of his defence of the rights of the Württemberg middle classes, against the claims of the monarch, a decree issued by the Reichshofsrat secured his release in 1764.

Board 22 One of the few institutions which remained viable was the Imperial Post. The double-headed Imperial eagle could be seen in all areas in post offices and on post carriages *(cat. illustr. 4)*. The Imperial Post, through inheritance in the hands of the princes of Thurn and Taxis, was responsible both for the postal service and for public transport. However, states such as Prussia and Saxony succeeded in breaking the monopoly of the

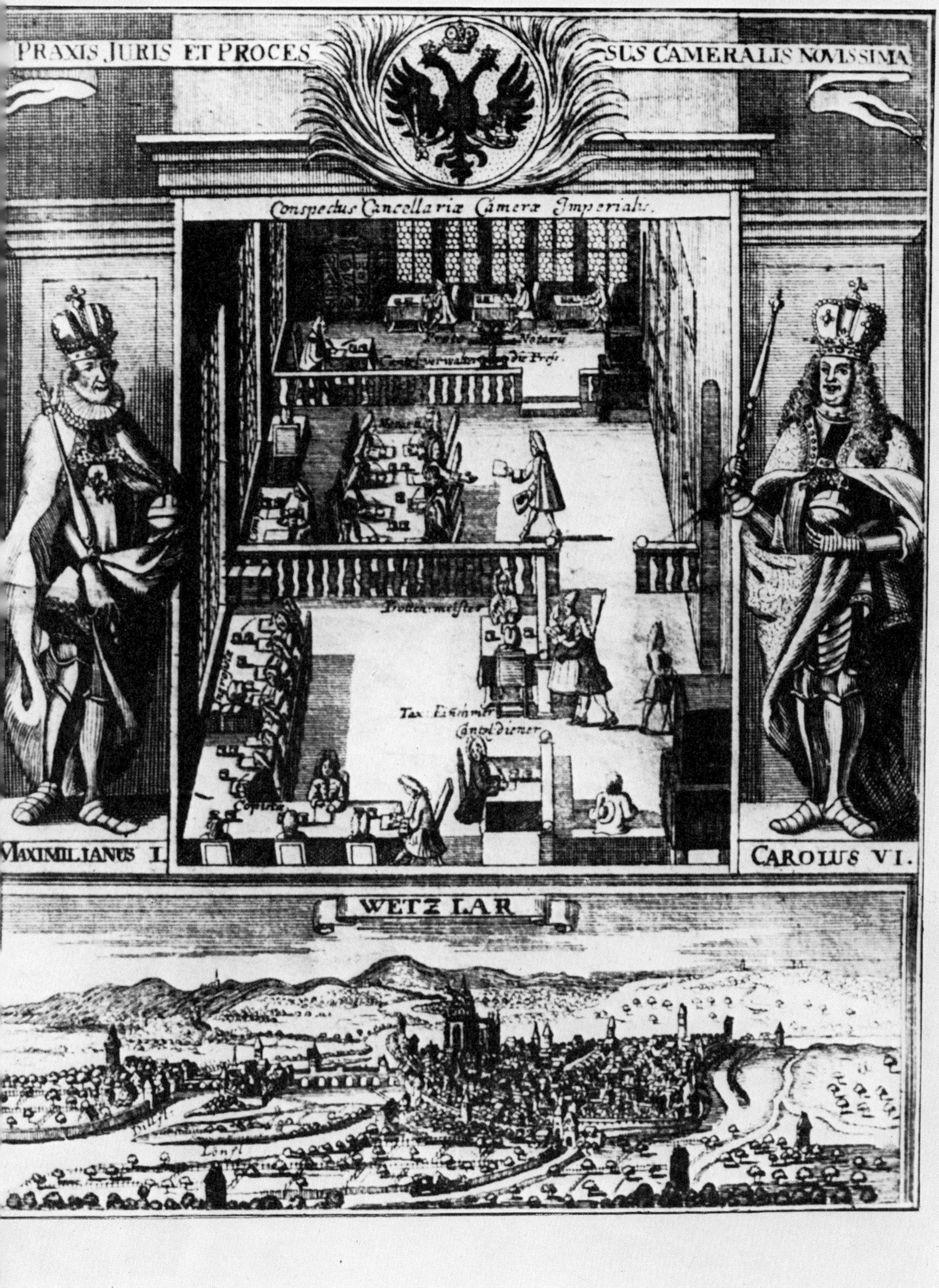

I/3 Supreme Court in Wetzlar.

I/4 Post Office sign of the Imperial Post, mid eighteenth century.

Imperial German Post and secured their independence in this sphere by setting up their own postal service.

Board 23

Although the whole Empire was practically stagnated, the experts of the time did not dismiss it as a dying institution. The small and weak states in particular saw it as a means of protection against the will of the bigger, stronger areas. Judicial experts such as Pufendorf, Pütter, Johann Jacob Moser and his son Friedrich Karl von Moser, still offered support for the Imperial idea. They wanted to carry through political reforms with the help of the Empire. In this respect many liberals later referred to 'Imperial Patriotism'.

Boards 7–15 and 30–36

The Economic and Social Order of the Old Empire

When compared to England and Western Europe at the end of the eighteenth century, Germany lagged a long way behind as far as economic and social development were concerned. The medieval economic and social order remained almost completely intact as did, therefore, the strict division of society into class strata. The peasantry, the middle classes and the aristocracy were clearly differentiated through their speech, dress and customs. Moreover, within these three classes there were further specific subdivisions forming distinct social groupings: earls, knights, landed gentry, patricians, craftsmen, skilled workers and ordinary workers, independent, semi-independent and serf farmers.

The peasantry formed the largest part of the population – $\frac{4}{5}$ of the Empire's inhabitants lived on the land. Here, the feudal conditions of subservience vis à vis goods, property and the legal system ensured that the aristocracy retained the most influential positions in society. In the towns it was the skilled workers organised in guilds who were most powerful. The latter insisted upon their privileges and thus blocked the natural development of economic life. Furthermore, territorial fragmentation impeded the exchange of goods. In addition to the urban middle class, the upper class and the craftsmen, who were organised in guilds, the beginning of a trading middle class was in evidence. In contrast to developments in France, it was the influential civil service, especially those engaged in courts and universities, which became the proponent of enlightening ideas. This civil service represented the new, all but non-existent, 'middle class'.

Boards 7–15 In 1746, an enlightened contemporary complained about the class divisions in the Old Empire, ". . . where there existed no community-feeling between the various ranks and classes of its inhabitants; where no sense of community-spirit existed between the highest aristocrat and the lower classes, between the lower classes and the new classes, between the latter and the bourgeoisie, nor between the bourgeoisie and the peasantry; where each class shut out the others, each class avoided the others, and where each person carved out a position for himself and remained in his own world". Another person commented: "It gave the impression that various different nations were living amongst each other". It was not individual achievement but birth which determined one's social and political position; one was born into a class and remained a member of it for life.

Board 31 The sharpest division in society was that between the aristocracy and the other groups: "The partition which the law and customs have created between the aristocratic class and the non-aristocrats is the largest and most significant division apparent in bourgeois society". The general law applicable in the Prussian states defined the aristocracy as the highest rank in the state, in which was entrusted the defence of the state, the upholding of its dignity overseas and the domestic system of government. Thus, the aristocracy laid claims to all the key positions at court, in the army and in the administration. This dominant position was further enhanced by the aristocrats' land ownership and the authority which accompanied this.

Board 32 In the western parts of the Empire the estate system was still predominant; the peasants were subject to taxation by their feudal lord. A complicated system of payment in money and produce had remained intact from medieval times. On the other hand, in areas to the east of the Elbe, the land owner controlled his goods and the peasants were "bound to him in serfdom", they were tied to his land as "working possessions". Under the estate system the serfs were compelled to work. The smallholder peasants had to provide manual labour. If they possessed a yoke they had to place it at the disposal of the estate for the majority of the year. There hardly remained any time for these peasants to work their own patch of farmland which had been granted to them by their master. Their children served as menial servants and maids. Their villages came under the jurisdiction of the Manor. Moreover, the peasants were subject

I/5 The land-owner's right to inflict corporal punishment at the end of the eighteenth century.

I/6 Running the gauntlet in the army of Frederick the Great; engraving by Daniel Chodowiecki.

I/7 Work certificate for a craftsman, Berlin, 1807.

to the landowner's right to inflict corporal punishment *(cat. illustr. 5).*

Board 33 In wars the peasants served the aristocratic officers as common 'cantonists'. In the army they were considered to be a rabble who could be whipped. The discipline of the Prussian armies was largely based on draconian punishments of whippings on premises such as the fact that the soldier had more to fear from his non-commissioned officer than from his enemy *(cat. illustr. 6).*

Board 34 In the smallest towns of the Empire the guilds were still powerful bodies. The guilds prevented free competition and in so doing therefore blocked economic progress. Each guild master was only permitted to manufacture a limited amount of goods per certain number of workers. Especially in the residential towns, with their high consumption of luxury products, a grotesque sharing-out of work had developed in accordance with the strict guild principles. Stocking-knitters, button-makers, brass-workers, lace-weavers all specialised in a certain product and made absolutely certain that nobody else meddled in their affairs *(cat. illustr. III and 7).*

Board 35 Due to the limited requirements of the people and the corresponding production methods, the most important goods could still be provided by the local area. The sale of goods over greater distances was almost exclusively restricted to materials in high demand. The free circulation of goods was prevented by the territorial divisions of the Empire and by a complicated system of customs duties and levies. Thus, in Prussia, at every town gate an 'excise duty' – a direct consumer tax – was levied: on a dozen coloured ladies' hats 4 Gr. 6 pf. was levied; if one wanted to eat a tub of 9 to 12 herrings a 6 pf. tax had to be paid. In addition, throughout the Empire there were different systems of measure and currency. In short, a dirigist state controlled economic life. Merchants demanded the removal of these barriers.

Board 36 Although the town guilds impeded the expansion of factories and the agricultural laws prevented a free rural exodus, manufacturing production gradually began to gain a foothold at the end of the eighteenth century, firstly in the textile industry. Manufacturing incorporated the division of labour, which had been organised by the guilds, and converted it into a rational distribution of labour at the level of the firm. For example, a pinmaker had about twenty stages of work to complete. Manufac-

turing production divided this process into individual jobs which could be carried out by specialised workers with an increased amount of skill and speed *(cat. illustr. 8).* "Thus, division of labour brings about, in each industry, a proportionate increase in productivity" (Adam Smith).
The next stage of economic development was the mechanisation of the production process. Gradually, machines began to replace trained workers.

The Effects of the French Revolution (Boards 37–51 plus film)

Board 38

The French Revolution also led to fundamental changes in the politics, economics and society of Germany. The results of the 1789 French Revolution, especially the forming of an constituent National Assembly and the storming of the Bastille, the symbol of despotism, by the citizens of Paris, had a considerable effect upon German citizens.
In 1793 German 'Jacobins' established, for a short time, the first republic on German soil in Mainz, under the protection of the French military rulers. However, the support for the Revolution soon dwindled due to its radicalisation and the high cost of the French army of occupation *(cat. illustr. 9).*

Board 39

The territorial structure of Germany was fundamentally reformed under Napoleon. The religious territories were secularised and the Imperial cities and numerous Imperial sovereignties lost their independence. Only a few sovereigns, who openly supported Napoleon, retained their sovereignty over these areas.
The southern and western German states, which had been restructured in this way, left the Imperial Alliance and joined together, under Napoleon's protection, in the 'Rhine League' *(cat. illustr. 10).* The defeat of the German Imperial Crown by Franz II on 6th August 1806 sealed the dissolution of the 'Holy Roman Empire of the German Nation'.

Board 40

Following the French model, and under pressure from France, basic administrative and social reforms were introduced in the states of the Confederation of the Rhine. Their aim was to achieve an egalitarian society. The aristocracy and the church were to lose their privileges. A new centralised administration

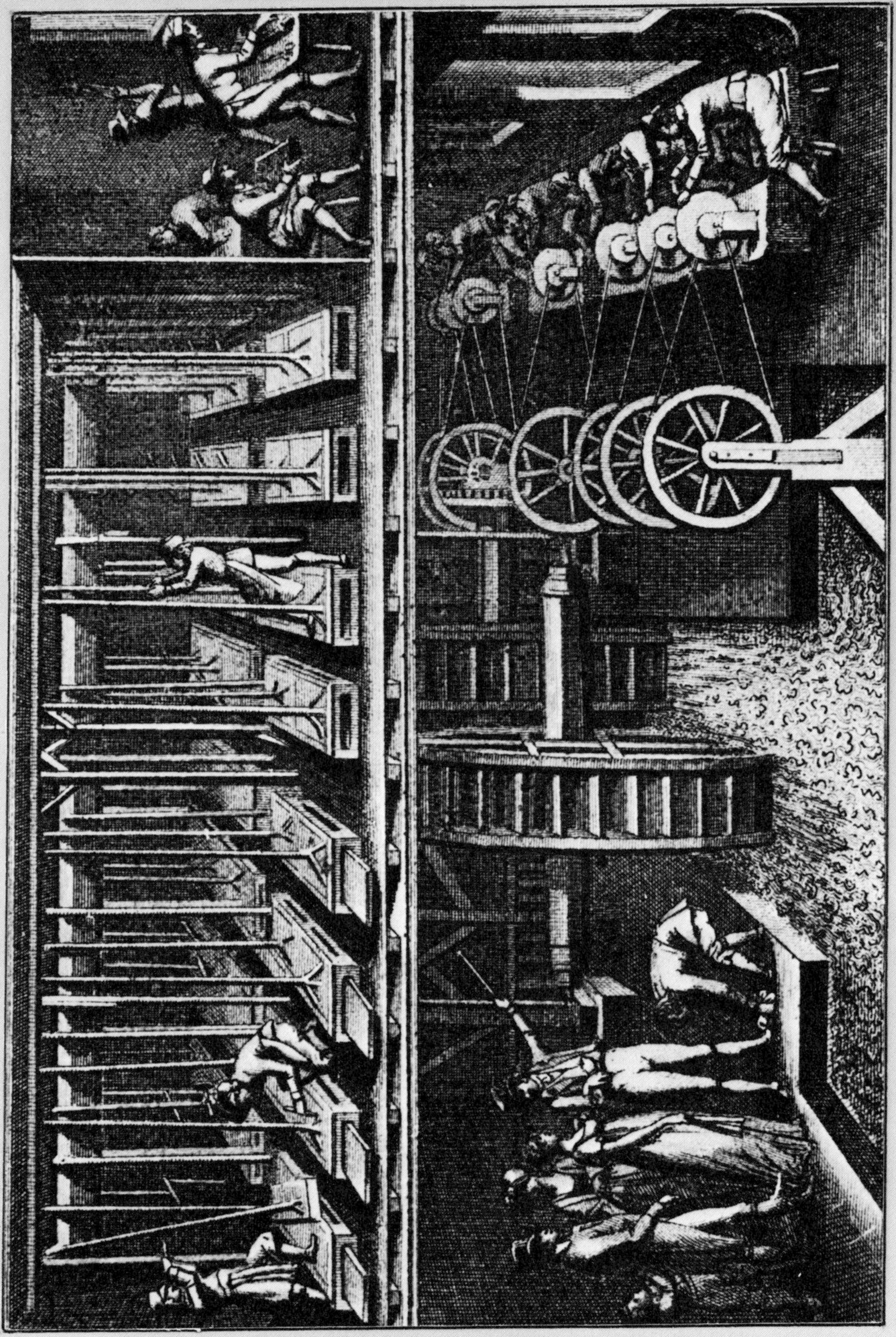

I/8 Manufacturing around 1790: pin production.

Die Franzosen in Nürnberg als Mitarbeiter an der deutschen Freyheit, 1796.

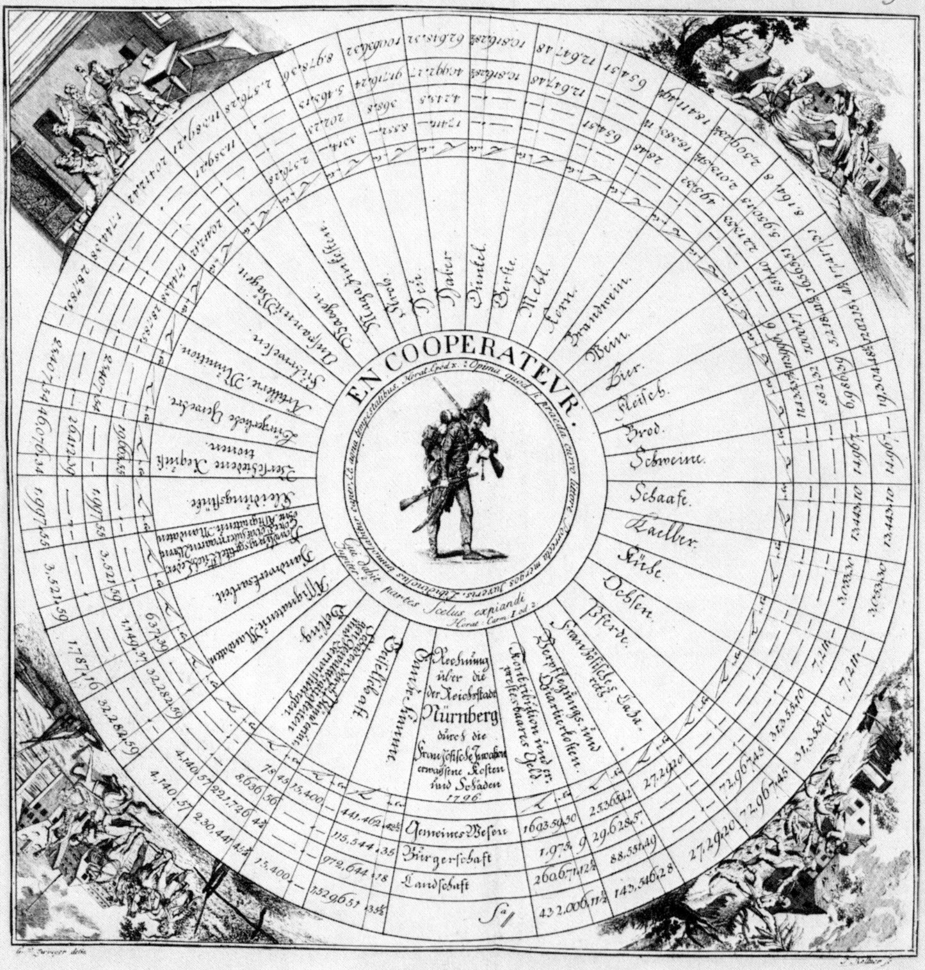

I/9 The Burdens of the French Occupation, Nuremberg, 1796: the diagram shows the levies imposed by the occupying French army in Nuremberg for various products.

I/10 The sovereigns of the Confederation of the Rhine swear allegiance to Napoleon.

would permit, even in Southern Germany, the setting up of modern states. At the same time, the new system should provide the necessary conditions for economic growth. With the introduction of the famous Napoleonic Code in the kingdom of Westphalia and other states of the Confederation, the basic principles of the French Revolution also took effect in Germany: freedom and security of the individual, equality before the law, abolition of class differences, security and inviolability of property, the separation of church and state, the separation of justice from administration. The Napoleonic Code abolished serfdom and made no distinction between the aristocracy and the middle classes. It abolished the dependency of the peasants upon their Lord of the Manor and the privileges of the feudal lords. These regulations would increase the social mobility of the citizens, yet their effects remained small at first since the economic situation in the Confederation of the Rhine was becoming increasingly worse, due to the high material cost of the Napoleonic occupation.

Board 41

After defeat against the Napoleonic Army in 1806 *(cat. illustr. II)* a phase of internal reforms began in Prussia. Frederick William III explained: "The state should replace by spiritual strength those material things which have been lost". He made Freiherr vom Stein *(cat. illustr. 11)* a minister, a man who, in a statement in spring 1807, had demanded a new organisation of state and society, not through revolutionary upheaval but through social reforms. His aim was to provide the state with an entirely new social foundation which would allow the establishment of a bourgeois society based on freedom and equality.

The most important facet of the reform, he wrote, was "the revival of public-spiritedness, the application of dormant or misdirected forces and knowledge, harmony between the spirit of the nation, its views and requirements and those of the state-authorities, the re-awakening of the feelings of independence and national honour" *(cat. illustr. 12)*.

This statement became the manifesto of the Prussian reformers who were striving for reforms to the Prussian state and for the liberation and unification of Germany.

Social reforms enhanced the citizens' prospects of promotion in politics, the economic sphere and in intellectual life. By means of revolutionary agricultural reforms, the re-establishment of self-administration in towns and a liberal economic policy, Prussian statesmen were trying to bring state and society closer together and in so doing to provide the state with more power. On the land, the peasants were freed from their obligation to hand over their produce. Each peasant who possessed a horse and therefore a ploughing beast, was allowed to work independently, provided that he renounced a portion of his land to his former landlord by way of compensation. In the towns the freedom to set up a business was introduced. In this way, the medieval need to belong to a guild, which had prevented competition, was abolished. The limitation placed on the number of workers was discontinued. Moreover, each worker could henceforth, having chosen his job freely, set up his own business. At the same time the introduction of the free sale of property brought an end to the class distinction between the landowning aristocracy and the bourgeoisie.

Later, at the time of the Restoration, however, the drawbacks to the freeing of the peasants and the right to set up a business became apparent. Free competition became the downfall of many small tradesmen who had set up in business independently, because very often their firms were not able to compete. Many peasants who had ceded a portion of their land to their landlord as compensation were not capable of running their smaller plot of land without their former protectorate. A worker and peasant proletariat grew up. The beneficiaries were the aristocratic landowners, who considerably expanded their properties, as did the largescale businessmen, who further asserted themselves by being highly competitive. The first signs of the bourgeois society changing into a classless society, having originally been established under the banner of equality, became apparent. Social conflicts were reinforced by the dawning of the industrial revolution.

Reforms were made to schools and universities in the aim of providing equal opportunities in education. In the place of schools divided on a class basis, such as the aristocratic academies and the secondary schools providing occupational training (Realschulen), secondary schools open to all were established (Volksschulen) along with the grammar schools (Gymnasien) as a preparation for university.

This reform aimed to create an all-round education system operating on the basis of freedom of teaching and research. At the same time the reform aimed to serve national education as portrayed by Wilhelm von Humboldt in his text marking the opening of Berlin University *(cat. illustr. 13/14).*

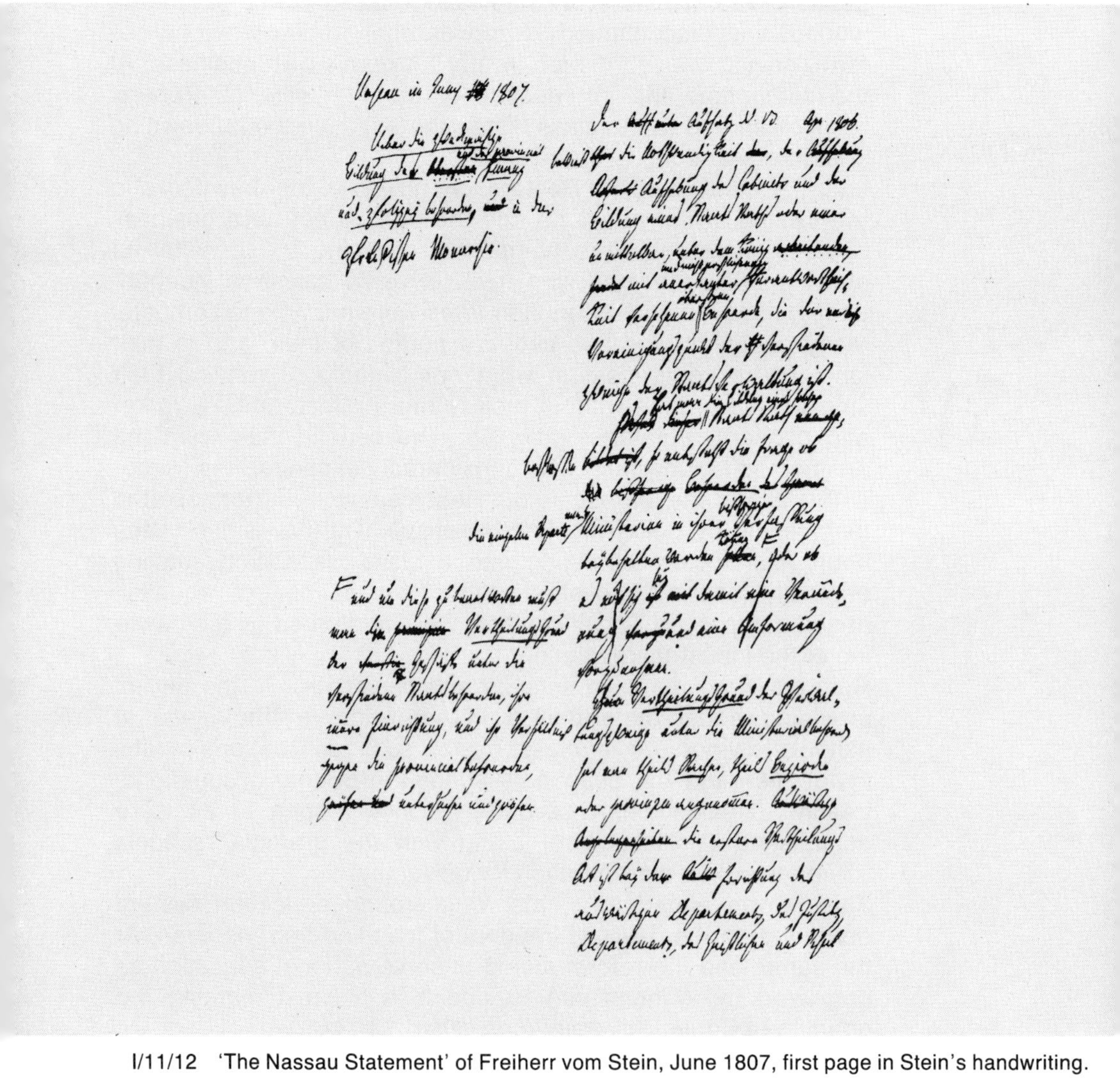

I/11/12 'The Nassau Statement' of Freiherr vom Stein, June 1807, first page in Stein's handwriting.

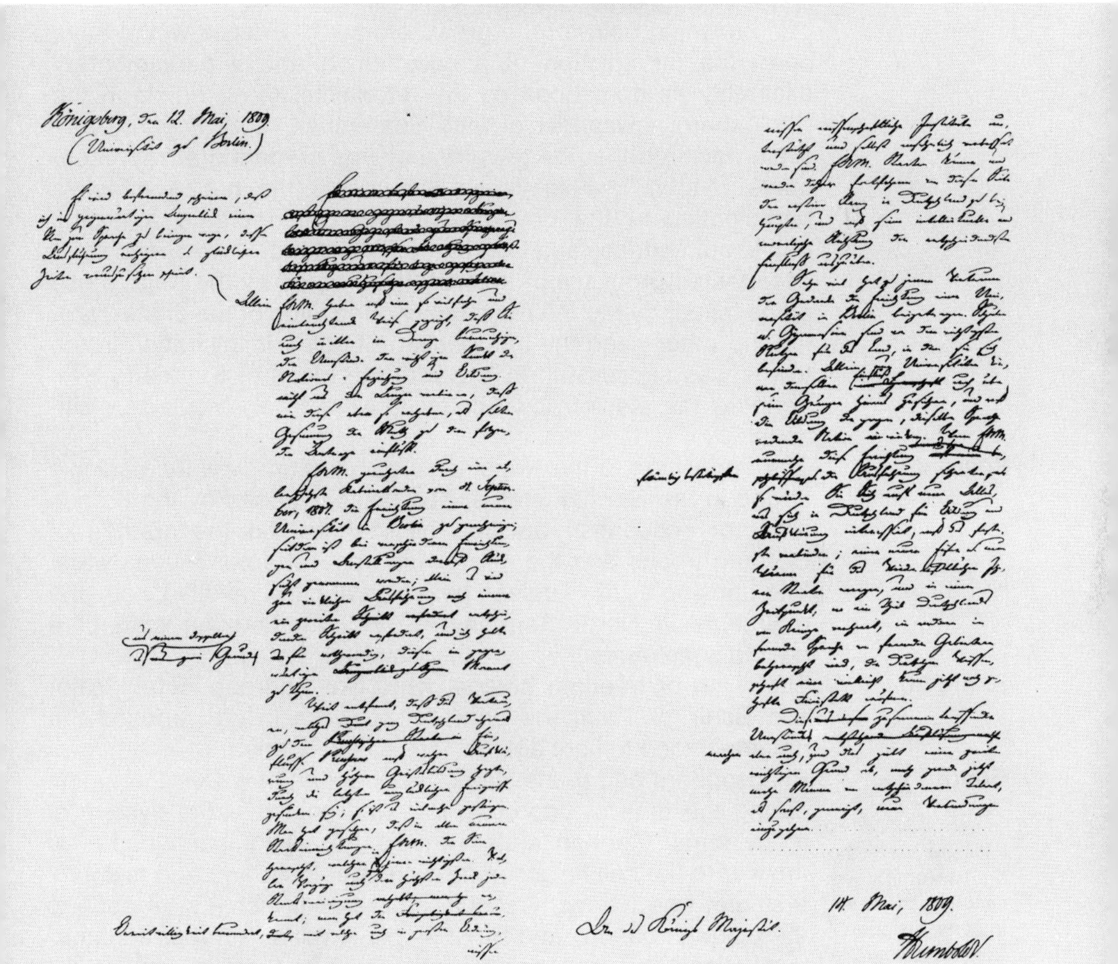
Königsberg, den 12. Mai, 1809.
(Universität zu Berlin.)

14. Mai, 1809.
Humboldt

I/13/14 Wilhelm von Humboldt's statement on the establishment of Berlin University, 12th May 1809, first page in Humboldt's handwriting.

The clearest example of the switch from an authoritarian to a bourgeois state was the reform of the laws governing the armed forces. The introduction of general compulsory military service meant that henceforth the principle of equal obligations and rights would apply to all. The officer ranks were open to all citizens. The standing army was supplemented by public conscription into the reserves (Landwehr). The main priority for the reformers was to rid the army of its class divisions and transform it into a national people's army.

The crowning point of the great reforms in Prussia would have been the introduction of a constitution and a parliamentary assembly as demanded by the reformists. In an article in the Königsberg newspaper of 29th September 1808, Freiherr vom Stein declared that the government was preparing a "representative System" which would ensure for the nation effective participation in the government and would create a lasting public-spiritedness and love of the Fatherland. However, in spite of repeated promises of a constitution made by the King, these plans failed, due to the reactionary opposition of the aristocracy. On the other hand the introduction of self-administration in the towns was successful. In line with the ideas of Stein and Hardenberg the elected town councils were freely elected by citizens.

Board 49

The opposition to the Napoleonic occupation grew increasingly strong in the German states. The taxes imposed by the French army of occupation became harsher as did the drafting of German troops and the misery felt about the continuous wars. The uprising by the Tirolean peasants and the revolts by several regiments in North Germany in 1809 marked the start of a people's movement, which was, however, defeated.

Board 50

The myth of freedom heroes, who, like Andreas Hofer, Major von Schill or Palm the book-seller, were killed, aroused the national mood to fight against foreign domination.

Board 51

Philosophers and poets supported the idea of a German nation during the time of oppression. It was said that the system of many small German states should be relinquished and – in answer to the call for a common culture, language and history – a single, free Germany should be created. Fichte's "speech to the German nation" and Ernst Moritz Arndt's "spirit of the time" symbolised this nationalist sentiment in the same way as did Friedrich Ludwig Jahn with his popular gymnasts' movement.

I Illustration on the right: solemn escorting of the Imperial Insignia from Nuremberg to Frankfurt am Main on 27th September 1790.

The nationalist movement in Prussia obliged the King to join

T. . .

I.P. Wolff. sel. Erbn.

II Battle at Jena and Auerstedt on 14th October 1806.

10.

gezeichnet von A. Gabler. gestochen von G. Vogel. N.

Der Schlosser.

11.

A. Gabler del. Vogel sc.

Der Schriftgiesser.

a. Die eine Haelfte des Schriftgiesser Instruments. b. Ein fertige Letter. c. die Matrice. d. das Besehblech.

14.

V. f.

Der Kupferschmied.

18.

A: Gabler: inv: et del.

Der Sattler u. Riemer.

Der allgemeine Weltfriede, *geschlossen im Jahr 1814.*

Den hohen Verbündeten Mächten bringt der Genius den von den Völkern so lange ersehnten Oelzweig. Frankreich, mit dem Lilienmantel umgethan, hebt seinen rechtmäßigen König wieder auf den Thron. Die feindlichen Krieger umarmen sich nun wie Brüder. Aber der Weltverwüster wird in den Abgrund geschleudert; und mit ihm der Adler samt dem Tieger, welche die deutsche Tapferkeit ferner zu bewachen wissen wird.

forces with the Czar in 1813 and to take up arms against Napoleon *(cat. illustr. 15).* The surge of nationalist sentiment was led by the Freikorps – amongst them the 'Lützowsche Jäger' – bands of volunteers. In the battle of Leipzig of 1813 sections of Napoleon's Confederation of the Rhine troops deserted and rallied under the Prussian flag. The victory of the united Prussian, Austrian and Russian troops hammered the first nail into the coffin of Napoleon's domination of Europe.

The German Confederation (Boards 52–87)

Boards 52–72 The Congress of Vienna and the new European Order

After the defeat of Napoleon the new European order aimed to guarantee peace and stability *(cat. illustr. IV).*

Boards 53/54 Between September 1814 and June 1815 the allied powers: Russia, Great Britain, Austria and Prussia met in Vienna with the French representative and the delegates of various kingdoms and principalities in order to determine the new political and territorial structure of Europe *(cat. illustr. 16).* The nationalist sentiments which had been aroused during the liberation wars expected the Congress to end the fragmentation of Germany and to put an end to the absolute rule by the sovereigns.

Board 55 In numerous statements German statesmen, taking heed of the will of the people, demanded a renewal of the old Empire (Stein), a closer federation (Hardenberg) and the participation of the citizens in the political process.

Board 56 After a general haggling process between the victors at the Congress, where each nation was at pains to ensure an equal distribution, a pentarchic system of five major powers was created, the aim of which was to ensure peace for the coming decades. However, the hopes of the people for unity and freedom were still unfulfilled. The Congress ignored their wishes. Thus the German nation-state, the setting up of which had been the aim of the liberation movement, was not achieved. Neither Prussia nor Austria were prepared to tolerate dominance by one or the other. The South German states, and notably Bavaria and Württemberg, insisted upon their sovereignty, which had been achieved through the German Confederation.

Only the smaller and weak German states favoured the setting

III (illustr. overleaf) From 'portrayal of skills and trades' by Johann von Voit, Nuremberg, 1790:
(1) Locksmith
(2) Type-founder
(3) Copper-smith
(4) Saddler

IV (illustr. left) Portrayal of the Paris Peace Treaty, 30th May 1814.

Schlesische privilegirte Zeitung

No. 34. Sonnabends den 20. März 1813.

Se. Majestät der König haben mit Sr. Majestät dem Kaiser aller Reußen ein Off- und Defensiv-Bündniß abgeschlossen.

An Mein Volk.

So wenig für Mein treues Volk als für Deutsche, bedarf es einer Rechenschaft, über die Ursachen des Kriegs welcher jetzt beginnt. Klar liegen sie dem unverblendeten Europa vor Augen.

Wir erlagen unter der Uebermacht Frankreichs. Der Frieden, der die Hälfte Meiner Unterthanen Mir entriß, gab uns seine Segnungen nicht; denn er schlug uns tiefere Wunden, als selbst der Krieg. Das Mark des Landes ward ausgesogen, die Hauptfestungen blieben vom Feinde besetzt, der Ackerbau ward gelähmt so wie der sonst so hoch gebrachte Kunstfleiß unserer Städte. Die Freiheit des Handels ward gehemmt, und dadurch die Quelle des Erwerbs und des Wohlstands verstopft. Das Land ward ein Raub der Verarmung.

Durch die strengste Erfüllung eingegangener Verbindlichkeiten hoffte Ich Meinem Volke Erleichterung zu bereiten und den französischen Kaiser endlich zu überzeugen, daß es sein eigener Vortheil sey, Preußen seine Unabhängigkeit zu lassen. Aber Meine reinsten Absichten wurden durch Uebermuth und Treulosigkeit vereitelt, und nur zu deutlich sahen wir, daß des Kaisers Verträge mehr noch wie seine Kriege uns langsam verderben mußten. Jetzt ist der Augenblick gekommen, wo alle Täuschung über unsern Zustand aufhört.

Brandenburger, Preußen, Schlesier, Pommern, Litthauer! Ihr wißt was Ihr seit fast sieben Jahren erduldet habt, Ihr wißt was euer trauriges Loos ist, wenn wir den beginnenden Kampf nicht ehrenvoll enden. Erinnert Euch an die Vorzeit, an den großen Kurfürsten, den großen Friedrich. Bleibt eingedenk der Güter die unter

I/15 Appeal by Frederick William III “To my People” – 20th March 1813.

Silesian Privileged Paper.

No. 34. Saturday 20th March 1813.

His Majesty the King has, a short time ago, signed an offensive and defensive alliance with his Majesty the Kaiser.

To My People

Neither my loyal subjects nor those of Germany need an explanation of the causes of the war which is now beginning. The gloom in Europe is plain for all to see.

We were suffering under French domination. The peace agreement, which was forced upon me by half of my subjects, was no saving grace because it inflicted deeper wounds than the war itself. The standing of the Land was diminished, the major garnisons remained occupied by the enemy, agriculture was crippled and the hitherto flourishing cultural life of our towns was stifled. Freedom of trade was restricted and thus the source of competition and prosperity was drained. The Land became impoverished.

By the strictest adherence to my duties and responsibilities, I hoped to provide relief for my people and eventually to convince the French Emperor that it would be to his own advantage to grant Prussia her independence. However, my honest intentions were misinterpreted as disloyal excesses and we saw only too clearly that the Emperor's treaties were gradually inflicting more harm upon us than his wars. Now the moment has arrived where all deception about our status must cease.

Citizens of Brandenburg, Prussians, Silesians, people of Pommerania and Lithuania! You know full well what you have suffered for almost seven years, you are aware of what will be your sad fate should the war not reach an honourable conclusion. Remember the old times, the great princes, the great Friedrich. Bear in mind the goods which . . .

I/16 Meeting of the plenipotentiaries at the Congress of Vienna – portrait by Von Godefroy.

up of a federal German state, but were only allowed to participate in the discussions in the concluding stages.
The result of a vote taken in the German Committee about the draft federal constitution ("The 20 points") revealed a lack of consensus about the future structure of Germany.

Board 57 The result of the Congress of Vienna for Germany was a loose confederation of states without a sovereign. The aim was to ensure the independence of the individual sovereign states and the suppression of the new political and social forces. The only pan German institution was the Parliament in Frankfurt which was not, however, a people's representative assembly but a congress of delegates appointed by the German sovereigns and free cities *(cat. illustr. 17).*

Boards 58/59 The organisation of the confederation was cumbersome and in practice could only operate when the two great powers, Austria and Prussia, cooperated. The result fell short of the expectations of the progressive forces.

Board 60 The political order which had been newly established by the Congress contradicted the demands for citizens' freedom and for the participation of the people in the political decision-making process. Germany was 'recreated' in the mould of the old dynasties of the pre-revolutionary days. The people remained subservient *(cat. illustr. 18).* Democratic and nationalist sentiments were considered to be the "disruptive spirit of the times". The inherited authority of the monarchs and the equilibrium between the five great powers ensured peace in Europe, which soon became a political graveyard.

Boards 64–66 The rulers of Russia, Prussia and Austria joined together to form the 'Holy Alliance' and promised mutual support "at all times and in all places", moreover, demanded that the European states join the Alliance. What was ideologically meant to be a treaty renewing Christian principles, in practice turned out to be an instrument for maintaining the dynastic structure of society and for forcefully suppressing all liberation attempts by the European peoples.

Boards 67–69 At various congresses military intervention was decided upon to put down uprisings in Naples, Piedmont-Sardinia and Spain in order to bring these countries into "the arms of the Holy Alliance".

I/17 Session of the German Parliament in Frankfurt am Main 1817.

I/18 "Germany's recreation or the long awaited return of the Hessian King".

I/19 The State Parliament in Stuttgart, 1883.

I/20 Frederick William IV, "No piece of paper will come between my people and I".

I/21 Kotzebue's murder, 23rd March 1819.

I/22 'The tame press' – portrayal of the press-censorship.

I/23 "The thinkers' club" – portrayal of the suppression of freedom of speech.
"Important question for consideration at today's meeting: how long shall we be allowed to think?"

No. 12. Fürstlich Reuss-Plauisches 1832.

Amts- und Verordnungs-Blatt.

Greiz, Freitags den 23. März 1832.

Publicandum.

Nachdeme die hohe Bundesversammlung in ihrer Sitzung vom 2ten März dieses Jahres nachstehenden Beschluß gefasset hat:

»Die Bundesversammlung hat sich aus den von der Bundestags-Commission in Preßangelegenheiten erstatteten Vorträgen und vorgelegten Artikeln der in Rheinbaiern erscheinenden Zeitblätter: die »Deutsche Tribüne« und der »Westbote«, so wie auch der in Hanau erscheinenden »Neuen Zeitschwingen«, überzeugt, daß diese Zeitblätter die Würde und Sicherheit des Bundes und einzelner Bundesstaaten verletzen, den Frieden und die Ruhe Deutschlands gefährden, die Bande des Vertrauens und der Anhänglichkeit zwischen Regenten und Volk aufzulösen sich bestreben, die Autorität der Regierungen zu vernichten trachten, die Unverletzlichkeit der Fürsten angreifen, Personen und Eigenthum durch Aufforderung zur Gewalt bedrohen, zum Aufruhr anreizen, eine politische Umgestaltung Deutschlands und Anarchie herbeizuführen und staatsgefährliche Vereine zu bilden und zu verbreiten suchen, — sie hat daher, auf den Grund des provisorischen Preßgesetzes vom 20. September 1819, § 1, 6 und 7, welches, nach den einstimmig und wiederholt gefaßten Beschlüssen aller Bundesglieder, so lange in Kraft besteht, bis der Deutsche Bund sich über neue gesetzliche Maßregeln vereinigt haben wird, so wie in pflichtmäßiger Fürsorge für die Erhaltung des Friedens und der Ruhe im Bunde, im Namen und aus Autorität desselben, beschlossen:

1) Die in Rheinbaiern erscheinenden Zeitblätter: die »Deutsche Tribüne« und der »Westbote«, dann das zu Hanau erscheinende Zeitblatt: die »Neuen Zeitschwingen«, so wie diejenigen Zeitungen, die etwa an die Stelle der drei genannten — unter was immer für einem Titel — treten sollten, werden hierdurch unterdrückt und in allen Deutschen Bundesstaaten verboten.

No 12.

Anzeigen des Fürstenth[...] Schaumburg-Lippe.

Sonnabend, den 24. März 1[...]

Höhere Bekanntmachung.

Die hohe deutsche Bundes-Versammlung hat in ihrer neunten dießjährigen Sitzung am 2. d. M. nachstehenden Beschluß gefaßt:

Die Bundesversammlung hat sich aus den von der Bundestags-Commission in Preßangelenheiten erstatteten Vorträgen und vorgelegten Artikeln der in Rheinbayern erscheinenden Zeitblätter: die „Deutsche Tribüne" und der „Westbote", so wie auch der in Hanau erscheinenden „Neuen Zeitschwingen", überzeugt, daß diese Zeitblätter die Würde und Sicherheit des Bundes und einzelner Bundes-Staaten verletzen, den Frieden und die Ruhe Deutschlands gefährden, die Bande des Vertrauens und der Anhänglichkeit zwischen Regenten und Volk aufzulösen sich bestreben, die Autorität der Regierungen zu vernichten trachten[...] Unverletzlichkeit der Fürsten angr[...] Personen und Eigenthum durch A[...]derung zur Gewalt bedrohen, zum [...]ruhr anreitzen, eine politische Umg[...]tung Deutschlands und Anarchie he[...]zuführen und staatsgefährliche Ve[...] zu bilden und zu verbreiten suchen[...] sie hat daher, auf den Grund des [...]visorischen Preßgesetzes vom 20. [...]tember 1819, §. 1, 6 und 7, wel[...] nach den einstimmig und wiederhol[...]faßten Beschlüssen aller Bundesgl[...] so lange in Kraft besteht, bis der [...]sche Bund sich über neue gesetzliche [...]regeln vereinigt haben wird, so w[...] pflichtmäßiger Fürsorge für die E[...]kung des Friedens und der Ruhe [...] Bunde, im Namen und aus Auto[...] desselben, beschlossen:

1., Die in Rheinbayern ersche[...]den Zeitblätter: die „Deutsche [...]

Verordnungs-Sammlung.

№ 6.

Braunschweig, den 23. März 1832.

(6.) Verordnung, das Verbot der in Rheinbaiern erscheinenden Zeitblätter: die »deutsche Tribüne« und der »Westbote«, auch des zu Hanau erscheinenden Zeitblattes: die »Neuen Zeitschwingen« betreffend.
D. D. Braunschweig, den 16. März 1832.

Von Gottes Gnaden, Wir **Wilhelm**, Herzog zu Braunschweig und Lüneburg ꝛc.

fügen hiemit zu wissen:

Demnach von der deutschen Bundesversammlung in der 9ten diesjährigen Sitzung unterm 2ten d. Mts. folgender Beschluß gefasst worden:

„Die Bundesversammlung hat sich aus den von „der Bundestags-Commission in Pressangelegenheiten „erstatteten Vorträgen und vorgelegten Artikeln der in „Rheinbaiern erscheinenden Zeitblätter: die „deutsche „Tribüne" und der „Westbote", so wie auch „der in Hanau erscheinenden „Neuen Zeitschwin„gen", überzeugt, daß diese Zeitblätter die Würde

Kanzelei-Patent,

wodurch

ein fernerer, den Mißbrauch der Presse betreffende[r] Beschluß der Deutschen Bundesversammlung zu[r] öffentlichen Kunde gebracht wird,

für das Herzogthum Holstein.

In der neunten Sitzung der Deutschen Bundesversammlung vom 2ten März d. J. ist hinsichtlich des Mißbrauchs der Presse folgender fernere Beschluß gefaßt:

Die Bundesversammlung hat sich aus den von der Bundestags-Commission in Preßangelegenheiten erstatteten Vorträgen und vorgelegten Artikeln der in Rheinbayern erscheinenden Zeitblätter: die "Deutsche Tribüne," und der "Westbote," so wie auch der in Hanau erscheinenden "Neuen Zeitschwingen," überzeugt, daß diese Zeitblätter die Würde und Sicherheit des Bundes und einzelner Bundesstaaten verletzen, den Frieden und die Ruhe Deutschlands gefährden, die Bande des Vertrauens und der Anhänglichkeit zwischen Regenten und Volk aufzulösen sich be-

I/24 Newspaper bans issued by the German Confederation.

Boards 73–77 Constitutional Development in the German States

Of the expected reforms there remained nothing more than the vague provision of Article 13 of the Federal Acts: "In all federal states a representative constitution will be drawn up". Nothing was said, however, either about the content of the constitutions or about the time of their introduction.

Board 74 Article 13 was even interpreted as forbidding modern representative constitutions. Thus nothing changed with regard to the constitutions of Prussia and Austria. Absolute rule remained in both of the major German states. Petitions presented by Prussian citizens had no success. Royal promises of a constitution were not fulfilled. Frederick William IV of Prussia considered himself King through the grace of God and wished for no constitutional paper to come between him and "his people" *(cat. illustr. 20).*

Board 75 By contrast, constitutions were passed by the monarchs of the South German and several mid-German states, which would involve the citizens in the running of the state. Some constitutions incorporated basic rights. In Baden, though there were certain restrictions, universal suffrage was introduced. In the parliamentary chambers of these states political opinions were, for the first time, articulated from below *(cat. illustr. 19).* The national reform movement found its strongest support in these smaller states.

Boards 76/77 The modern constitutional structure of these states can be most clearly shown by contrasting Baden with Prussia, which was still under absolute rule.

Boards 79–87 The German Confederation as Reactionary Protector

The establishment of a liberal nation-state was not achieved. Pan-German politics were almost exclusively limited to the suppression of all attempts to achieve greater unity and freedom.

Board 80 Karl Ludwig Sand, a student, murdered the poet and statesman Kotzebue, a symbol of reaction *(cat. illustr. 21).* The murder provided a welcome opportunity to attack all liberal, democratic and nationalist supporters through the passing of severe laws.

Board 81 The 'Karlsbad Decrees' were the legal basis for the "witchhunt on demagogues". The status quo was keenly defended by police-state methods.

Boards 82/83 The press and publishers were subject to severe censorship. All printed matter of less than 20 pages had to be approved by the censoring authorities *(cat. illustr. 22, 23).*

The unity of Germany was only expressed in a negative sense: in the suppression of slanderous newspapers. Liberal and democratic newspapers were often individual discussion points for the Federal Parliament. They were censored or banned as dangers to the state.

Board 84 Charters banning newspapers appeared with the same regularity in all German states *(cat. illustr. 24).*

Board 85 There was little opportunity for the press to defend itself. Censored newspapers were printed with gaps replacing the censored articles.

Board 86 Political journals were frequently printed on the smallest possible size of paper, in order to exceed the censorship barrier of 20 pages.

In addition to press censorship personal witchhunts were made against representatives of the opposition. Liberals and democrats were imprisoned. The report produced in 1833 by the Central Commission of Investigation in Mainz, a secret authority set up after 1819, named 1,867 people who had been pursued or imprisoned for political crimes.

Board 87 Political coercion was also evident in universities. Professors who criticised the system lost their jobs and students were sent down from the universities.

Until the 1848 Revolution, the reactionary policies of the Confederation were in full control of the internal affairs of Germany.

The German Confederation after 1815

Room II

Pre-1848

Numerous reformist movements were formed in the decades between 1815 and 1848, in the pre-revolutionary period: the March Revolution of 1848, opposing the system of government in the German Confederation, which operated on the basis of "restoration, legitimacy and solidarity". Although supported by various sections of society, whose aims and political methods differed, all the various movements agreed upon the fact that there was a need for a basic change in the economic, social and political order; they all supported the setting up of a nation-state with a parliamentary system, which would abolish the outdated political structures and unite the fragmented forces.
Nationalist ideas were not only in evidence in Germany but represented a revolutionary force in Europe. Liberation struggles by the Greeks, the Spanish, Italians and Poles were being fought at the same time as the German nationalist movement was active. There arose a solidarity amongst the suppressed and divided peoples against the forces of monarchist legitimacy which were preventing the liberation. Polish and Greek associations in Germany were expressions of the opposition to the reactionary conditions existing in the country. The French July Revolution of 1830 sparked off a whole series of revolutionary uprisings and the German nationalist movement was more active than hitherto. There was a profusion of folk festivals taking place, above all in South West Germany, at which it became obvious that the establishment of a nation-state was not merely the goal of a few theoreticians or interest groups but the wish of the majority of the population. Moreover, the nationstate was rarely seen as a means of gaining political power or for the selfish satisfaction of emotional aims. Nor did it serve to fulfil historic demands, although considerable momentum is gained in modern nationalist thinking from common language and culture and from the memory of a glorified national past. The main arguments of the nationalist movement centred around demands for the abolition of economic, political and social injustices. For all reform movements of the time the nation-state was seen as the integrating factor.
Strong pressures for national unity were aroused, firstly by economic development. After the beginning of industrialisation in Germany the further development of trade and industry suffered, above all from the economic and political fragmentation of Germany, which was exemplified by the abundance of customs barriers and the lack of a common currency or a common

system of weights and measures. Not only were the German states divided from each other by customs barriers but also provinces and cities. Whilst most important neighbouring European states were trying to protect their markets from foreign goods by erecting protective barriers, German states were operating under free trading conditions in their dealings with foreign countries. Foreign goods flooded the German market and threatened to ruin the growing German industry. Therefore, the middle classes, having already endured the liberation wars against Napoleon and having upheld the idea of national unity, also demanded the political unification of Germany for economic reasons.

A first step towards the economic unification of Germany was achieved with the abolition of internal customs duties in Prussia in 1818. Under the influence of this step the 'General German Trade and Commerce Association' was founded in Frankfurt in the following year, which became the centre of those manufacturers and salesmen whose aim was economic unification. Following the mid-German customs union, and the tariff agreement between Prussia and mid and South German states, the German customs union was established in 1833, which, with the exception of Austria, incorporated the majority of the German states. Parallel to this the rail, road and canal constructors took the necessary steps towards forming a unified economic area. The main aim of the customs was the enlargement of the economic market, however, for certain people, for example Friedrich List, political considerations were, from the beginning, given top priority. The economic prosperity of those states incorporated in the customs union seemed highly attractive to other states. The economic agreement made plain the logic of taking matters a state further towards political unity.

However, the main impetus for nationalist feelings came from the tradition of the liberation wars which remained alive, especially amongst the students. The students' associations, which had been established on a pan-German scale, formed the vanguard of the nationalist movement until 1830. In the form of the Wartburg Festival of 1817 they organised the first public demonstration in favour of German unity.

In the "principles of the Wartburg Student Rally" the connection was made clear between the wish for unity: "There is but one Germany and one Germany should exist and endure" – and the demand for social and political emancipation. "Man is only free if he has the means of self determination". Their opposition was expressed by the burning of reactionary symbols and writings. The 'Gießener Schwarzen', the radical wing of the Association, saw the setting up of a republic as their aim, which would only be possible after the forceful removal from power of the monarchs.

On the other hand, the representatives of political liberalism, the most important opposition movement of the time, tried to achieve their aims through legal means and initially in individual states. Their common goal was the winning of personal and political for all subjects, therefore the granting of citizens' rights, such as freedoms of speech, the press and assembly, as well as the participation by the citizens in the political decision-making process.

They favoured a system of government along the lines of the constitutional monarchies of England and France. The liberals concentrated their efforts on the constitutions which had been introduced after 1815 in the mid and southern German states. Indeed, they succeeded in gaining ceratin reforms but failed to achieve any far-reaching changes because of the individual staates' claims to their own sovereignty and because of continued attempts by the governments, which were still semi-absolutist, to make the press and parliament mere tools of the executive.

The restricted freedom in the German states enhanced the nationalist aspirations of liberalism. There were ever increasing demands for national unity made in the state parliaments. The most wellknown of these was the Welcker Motion put before the Second Chamber in Baden, which proposed the setting up of a German Parliament. This was a classic example of the aim for national unity being combined with demands for greater freedom. Public meetings, the press and citizens' associations, in which liberals of all shades of opinion had any influence, became the focal point for agitation in favour of the nation-state.

The political and social demands made by the 'radicals' went beyond those of most other liberals. They did not merely ask for participation by the people butwent as far as demanding self government for the people. And, in addition to favouring the free development of inherited and acquired powers, they vociferously supported the idea of social equality. For them that meant the eradication of all differences, of all forms of preference and privilege and, thus, the acquisition of an improved political and social position for the socially disadvantaged. The main inspiration for the ideas of the 'radicals' was the mass poverty which followed the freeing of the peasants and the onset of industrialisation. Poverty was the central problem of social development in the pre-revolutionary period. The 'radicals' made far-reaching political demands in answer to the situation.

"The lower classes must be granted the right to a dignified existence: free political institutions are worthwhile only as a means to an end" (Johann Jacoby).

The interests of the poor and the disenfranchised were to be embodied in a "people's state" republic. The government and the people would no longer be opposing forces – as under the constitutional monarchy – and the government, as the proponent of the "people's will", would be the only source of all power. The victory of the new would only come about after the total destruction of the old and would not be won by legal means. According to the theory of the 'radicals' the only course of action which would lead to the setting up of a republic was revolution.

Various groups of emigrants, who joined associations abroad, were even more extreme than the 'radicals' in Germany. Because of the laws governing societies in the individual states, most of them were secret organisations. The "league of the lawful" (Bund der Gerechten) and the "league of outlaws" (Bund der Geächteten) developed, under the influence of French theoreticians, early socialist 'communist' programmes, in which they concentrated more on the need for changesin the structure of society than on freedom and political progress. The main ideas of the political opposition, the moderate, liberal wing and the more radical democratic wing, were expressed in the form of two programmes shortly before the outbreak of the 1848 Revolution: "The Heppenheim and Offenburg Programmes". In these programmes the alternative ideas for a new system were laid out, a decision on these being eventually taken in the Revolution.

The German Student Association (Boards 1–4)

German universities were one of the centres of the national and liberal movement in the period preceding the 1848 Revolution. Students and academics led the citizens' opposition to the existing political conditions.
The students, returning from the liberation wars filled with national pride, were disappointed about the ensuing restoration. They demanded the political unity of the nation and the abolition of absolute forms of government. These progressive basic ideas were often combined with irrational germanic, Christian conceptions. For many the old German Empire was glorified as a romantic ideal.

Board 1

In order to make a reality of German unity, at least in universities, the students formed a unified German Students' Association. The first association was founded in June 1815 in Jena. Its motto was: 'Honour, freedom, the fatherland'. Black-Red-Gold, which the students took from the uniforms of the Lützow volunteer corps as those of the association's flag, were to the students the colours of the old Empire and soon became the common symbol of the national and liberal movement. From Jena the Association expanded to include most German universities.

Board 2

In 1817 the Students' Association of Jena summoned the students of Germany to the Wartburg rally. This was a joint celebration of the 300th anniversary of the Reformation and the anniversary of the Battle of Leipzig. About 500 students arrived at Wartburg on 18th October 1817 with their associations' flags and demanded the unification of the fatherland and the introduction of the promised constitutions *(cat. illustr. 25).* Theology student Heinrich Riemann said in his speech: "the German people had expressed great hopes, they have all been disappointed".
An example of the dual character of this student movement was the fact that both symbolic reactionary works and works from the age of enlightenment were burnt at the rally. Amongst the writings were Haller's 'Restoration of political science' but also a copy of the Napoleonic Code *(cat. illustr. 26).*

Board 3

In October 1818 the associations amalgamated to form the 'German Association'.
The 'Gießen Blacks' were the most radical section, so called because of their 'old German' costumes. Their leader, Gießen

II/25 Procession of students to Wartburg, 1817.

II/26 Burning of books at the Wartburg Rally.

Revers
welcher von den Studirenden vor der Immatriculation zu unterschreiben ist.

Nachdem die nachstehenden Auszüge aus den Gesetzen, nämlich:

1) Aus dem Bundestags-Beschlusse vom 20. September 1819 über die in Ansehung der Universitäten zu ergreifenden Maassregeln.

§. 3. „Die seit langer Zeit bestehenden Gesetze gegen geheime oder nicht „autorisirte Verbindungen auf den Universitäten, sollen in ihrer ganzen Kraft und „Strenge aufrecht erhalten, und insbesondere auf den seit einigen Jahren gestifteten, „unter dem Namen der allgemeinen Burschenschaft bekannten Verein und um so be„stimmter ausgedehnt werden, als diesem Verein die schlechterdings unzulässige Vor„aussetzung einer fortdauernden Gemeinschaft und Correspondenz zwischen den ver„schiedenen Universitäten zum Grunde liegt. Den Regierungs-Bevollmächtigten soll in „Ansehung dieses Punktes eine vorzügliche Wachsamkeit zur Pflicht gemacht werden."

„Die Regierungen vereinigen sich darüber, dass Individuen, die nach Bekannt„machung des gegenwärtigen Beschlusses erweislich in geheimen oder nicht „autorisirten Verbindungen geblieben, oder in solche getreten sind, bei kei„nem öffentlichen Amte zugelassen werden sollen."

§. 4. „Kein Studirender, der durch einen von dem Regierungs-Bevollmäch„tigten bestätigten oder auf dessen Antrag erfolgten Beschluss eines akademischen „Senats von einer Universität verwiesen worden ist, oder der, um einem solchen „Beschlusse zu entgehen, sich von der Universität entfernt hat, soll auf einer an„dern Universität zugelassen, auch überhaupt kein Studirender ohne ein befriedigen„des Zeugniss seines Wohlverhaltens auf der von ihm verlassenen Universität von „irgend einer andern Universität angenommen werden."

2) Aus dem Bundestags-Beschlusse vom 14. November 1834, in Betreff der deutschen Universitäten.

Art. 6. „Vereinigungen der Studirenden zu wissenschaftlichen oder geselligen „Zwecken können mit Erlaubniss der Regierung, unter den von letzterer festzusetzen„den Bedingungen, stattfinden. Alle andern Verbindungen der Studirenden, sowohl „unter sich, als mit sonstigen geheimen Gesellschaften, sind als verboten zu betrachten."

Art. 7. „Die Theilnahme an verbotenen Verbindungen soll, unbeschadet „der in einzelnen Staaten bestehenden strengeren Bestimmungen, nach „folgenden Abstufungen bestraft werden:

1. „Die Stifter einer verbotenen Verbindung und alle diejenigen, welche Andere zum „Beitritte verleitet oder zu verleiten gesucht haben, sollen niemals mit blosser „Carcerstrafe, sondern jedenfalls mit dem *Consilio abeundi*, oder, nach Befinden, „mit der Relegation, die den Umständen nach zu schärfen ist, belegt werden."
2. „Die übrigen Mitglieder solcher Verbindungen sollen mit strenger Carcerstrafe, „bei wiederholter oder fortgesetzter Theilnahme aber, wenn schon eine Strafe „wegen verbotener Verbindungen vorangegangen ist, oder andere Verschärfungs„gründe vorliegen, mit der Unterschrift des *Consilii abeundi* oder dem *Consilo* „*abeundi* selbst, oder, bei besonders erschwerenden Umständen, mit der Rele„gation, die dem Befinden nach zu schärfen ist, belegt werden."
3. „Insofern aber eine Verbindung mit Studirenden anderer Universitäten, zur Be„förderung verbotener Verbindungen, Briefe wechselt, oder durch Deputirte „communicirt, so sollen alle diejenigen Mitglieder, welche an dieser Correspon„denz einen thätigen Antheil genommen haben, mit der Relegation bestraft werden."
4. „Auch diejenigen, welche, ohne Mitglieder der Gesellschaft zu sein, dennoch „für die Verbindung thätig gewesen sind, sollen, nach Befinden der Umstände, „nach obigen Straf-Abstufungen bestraft werden."
5. „Wer wegen verbotener Verbindungen bestraft wird, verliert nach Umständen zu„gleich die akademischen Beneficien, die ihm aus öffentlichen Fonds-Kassen, oder „von Städten, Stiftern, aus Kirchenregistern u. s. w., verliehen sein möchten, „oder deren Genuss aus irgend einem andern Grunde an die Zustimmung der „Staats-Behörden gebunden ist. Desgleichen verliert er die seither etwa genos„sene Befreiung bei Bezahlung der Honorarien für Vorlesungen."

II/27 Measures taken against political groupings in universities.

Declaration

To be signed by students before enrollment. After reading the following legal extracts:

1. *From the parliamentary decree of 20th September 1819 concerning the rules to be followed with respect to universities.*

   § 3. The longstanding laws against secret or unauthorised gatherings at universities should be vigorously respected and, in particular, with reference to the German Students' Association which has existed for several years, especially since this society is the root cause of the totally unauthorised links and correspondence between the different universities. Those authorised by the government should, in view of this point, pay the keenest attention, as a matter of duty, to ensure that it is respected.
   The government are agreed that individuals who, having been made aware of the present decree, remain members of or join secret or unauthorised societies, should be barred from all public office.
   § 4. No student, who is sent down because of reports by government authorities or on the recommendation of an academic senate, or who has left university in order to escape such a recommendation, should be allowed entrance to another university, nor should any student, who has left a university without a certificate of satisfactory conduct, be accepted by another university.

2. *From the Parliamentary Decree of 14th November 1834 with reference to German universities.*

   Art. 6. Student societies serving scientific or social ends shall be permitted, their nature having been scrutinised and permission having been given by the government. All other student societies, both internal clubs and those formed together with other secret societies, are forbidden.
   Art. 7. Participation in forbidden societies is punishable, without prejudice to the existing regulations of the individual states, according to the following degrees:
   1. The founders of an outlawed society and all those who have induced or attempted to induce others to join should under no circumstances merely be given a simple term of imprisonment but should be sent down or, after due consideration, be expelled, the severity of the punishment being in accordance with the circumstances.
   2. The remaining members of such societies should be given harsh terms of imprisonment but, in cases of repeated or continued membership, where a punishment for adherence to an illegal society has already been given, or where there are other factors which make the matter more serious, then with the signature of the university senate or, in extremely difficult circumstances, of the chancellor himself, the guilty person should be expelled, the severity of the punishment being in accordance with the circumstances.
   3. As far as someone who associates with students of other universities in order to further the goals of outlawed societies is concerned, or who exchanges letters or communications via delegates, they should be punished by expulsion.
   4. Those who, without being society members, have nevertheless given active service to the society should, after consideration of the circumstances, be punishable in accordance with the above scale.
   5. A person who has been punished because of his association with illegal societies loses, depending on the circumstances of his crime, the academic benefits loaned to him from public funds or by a town, benefactors or church registries etc., or those benefits which he had been granted for any other reason by state authorities. At the same time he loses the exemption which he had hitherto been granted with respect to the payment of lecture fees.

universtiy lecturer Karl Follen, favoured the removal by force of the sovereigns and the establishment of a unified German republic. Karl Ludwig Sand, a pupil of Follen, sought to give reality to what he had been taught and murdered the comedy writer Kotzebue, who, it was claimed, was an agent of the Czar. This was supposed to be the signal for a general uprising.

The murder of Kotzebue in the summer of 1819 gave Metternich the opportunity, for which he had been waiting, to take action against the politically dangerous associations. The latter were banned by the Karlsbad Decrees, in addition to a close watch being placed on university affairs and hundreds of students being sent down and arrested. The commission of investigation which was set up in Mainz worked for decades to expose "revolutionary plots and demagogic connections" *(cat. illustr. 27).* Even as late as the period 1832 to 1838 1,200 students were prosecuted for being association members.

Board 4

Only a minority of students remained politically active. They continued the Association illegally in the form of secret meetings, and proclaimed at an Association gathering in Stuttgart in 1832: "The aim of the Association should henceforth be to incite a revolution in order to achieve the liberation and unification of Germany".

In this respect 1,833 Association members staged a dilettante putsch attempt to overthrow the Parliament (Bundestag). They stormed the main guard in Frankfurt. The putsch failed and was followed by a new wave of arrests.

The Association had no direct political influence though they influenced the thoughts of those academics who assumed the political leadership of the middle classes in the 1848 Revolution and in the period immediately preceding it (Vormärz). Under pressure from the onset of the Revolution, Parliament made the Association's colours 'Black-Red-Gold' the federal German colours.

Economic Development in the Period preceding the 1848 Revolution (Vormärz) (Boards 5–8)

The conditions for the growth of an economically strong middle class had been created at the time of the reforms in Prussia by the freeing of the peasants and the introduction of the right to set up a business. In the countryside the number of propertyless people was growing and in the towns the power of the guilds had been broken. Thus, Prussia was experiencing a growth of manufacturing industries and factories. In the rest of Germany, however, the traditional economic structure persisted and it was the aim of the reformists to change this along the lines of the Prussian and West European models.

Board 5 The problem of the economic fragmentation of Germany had not yet been resolved. Although internal customs' duties had been abolished in most states, the customs' levies at the borders of each federal state still remained a barrier to free trade.

Friedrich List proposed a German 'customs union' – a unitary economic area within the boundaries of the German confederation *(cat. illustr. 28).*

On 1st January 1834 the German customs union, which had been pioneered by Prussia, became operational. It incorporated 18 states with 23 million inhabitants. It was commented: "As midnight struck the barriers were raised and amidst loud cheers the processions of carriages rushed over the border. Everyone felt that the great battle had been won."

Board 6 A precondition of the free movement of goods was an efficient transport system. The road construction, which had been begun in great style by Napoleon, was continued. In the short period between 1817 and 1828 Prussia spent 11 million thaler on road construction *(cat. illustr. 31).* There was also a speeding up of canal construction and steamers took on a more important role in internal water transport *(cat. illustr. 32).* Yet the decisive step forwards was the construction of railway lines *(cat. illustr. VIII).*

Again it was Friedrich List who was the driving-force behind the development. At the same time as expressing his views on the German customs union he proposed a railway network for Germany *(cat. illustr. 29).* In 1835 the first stretch between Nuremberg and Fürth became operational *(cat. illustr. 30).*

Board 7 At first people were sceptical about railway construction but their necessity and profitability were soon recognised: joint-stock companies were formed in order to raise the required capital. In 1842 the Prussian government granted a guaranteed rate of interest of $3\frac{1}{2}$% for railway joint-stock companies. Thus, whoever was willing to invest in railways would make a profit without having to take a risk. For example, the dividends of the Magdeburg to Leipzig Railway Company soared from 4% (1840) to 10% (1843). This trend encouraged the first wave of speculation. The railway network expanded rapidly and in 1846 alone 1100 kms of track were laid.

Board 8

After modern production methods had been largely restricted to textile manufacturing during the first phase of industrialisation, the iron manufacturing industry took precedence following the beginning of railway construction *(cat. illustr. VI).* During the first years of rail construction English and Belgian pig iron had to be imported in order to meet demands. The engines were also mainly imported from England. Nevertheless, by 1844 the customs union was in a position to impose a protective tariff on English iron. The significant progress which had been made in wrought iron production techniques was made possible by the introduction of the puddling process *(cat. illustr. 34).*

With the increasing demand for coal and iron most industrial production became concentrated in the Ruhr area which gradually developed into the first economic and industrial centre of Germany.

Fundamental changes were also made in the textile industry. Considerable improvements were made to spinning machines and weaving looms *(cat. illustr. 33).* Cloths and materials became cheaper because of these more efficient machines and weavers who were still working by hand fell victim to competition.

Ueber

ein sächsisches Eisenbahn=System

als Grundlage

eines allgemeinen

deutschen Eisenbahn=Systems

und insbesondere

über die Anlegung einer Eisenbahn

von

Leipzig nach Dresden.

Von

Fr. List,

Consul der Vereinigten Staaten für das Großherzogthum Baden.

Leipzig,

A. G. Liebeskind.

1833.

II/28/29 Friedrich List, the driving force behind German economic unity. A paper by Friedrich List of the setting up of a railway network in Saxony as the foundation of a German system and concentrating primarily here on a line between Leipzig and Dresden.

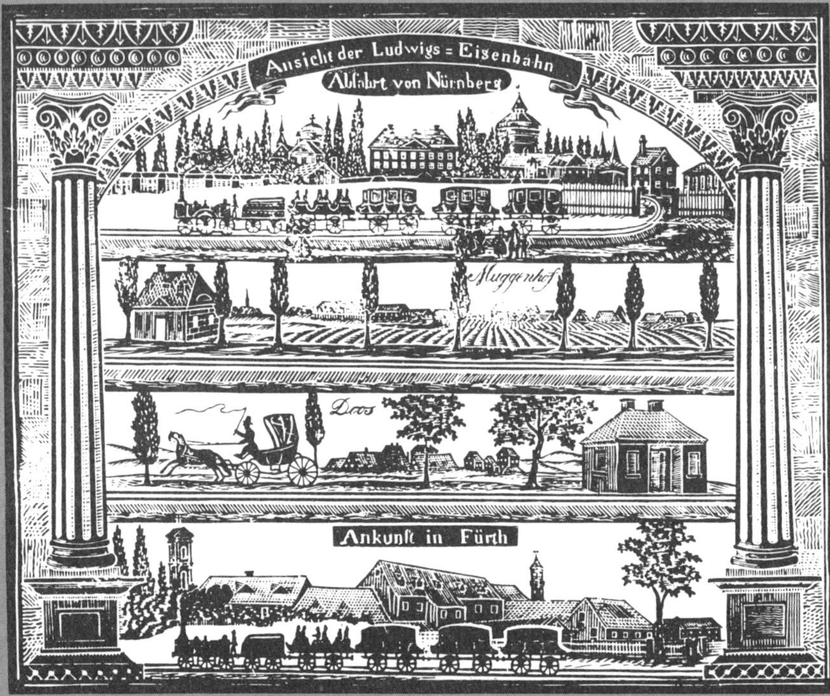

II/30 The first German railway, popular woodcarving, 1835.

II/31 The introduction of modern means of transport (near Erlangen).

II/32 The first German steamship, 1816.

II/33 Machine-shop of a cotton spinning factory around 1830.

II/34 Iron production around 1830 by the puddling process.

Social Developments in the Period preceding the 1848 Revolution (Vormärz) (Boards 9–12)

Board 9 The economic changes caused changes in the social structure of society. In contrast to the petty bourgeoisie organised in guilds the early industrial entrepreneurs gradually grew in number *(cat. illustr. 35, 36).* Many skilled craftsmen succumbed to the competition of the factories. Together with the unemployed ordinary workmen they made up the workers' proletariat. In those states where the freeing of the peasants was accompanied by the requirement to cede a portion of land many peasants could no longer operate their reduced plots at a profit. They were forced to sell their land and become farm labourers. These casual labourers later formed the reservoir for the industrial proletariat. Many of them found work on railway constructions in the first instance.

Board 10 Technical developments meant that in addition to men, women and children were drawn into the production process to carry out the more simple and light jobs *(cat. illustr. 37–39).* In this way competition amongst workers was increased: the lower wages paid for womens' and childrens' work also depressed the mens' wages. Whereas around 1770 a working man could manage to sustain his family, around 1830 his wife and three children had also to work in order to ensure survival on the bread-line.

Board 11 The weavers were hardest hit by the competition of cheap machine production *(cat. illustr. VII and 40).* Flax was now being machine-spun in the same way as cotton. The ruined village flax spinners now sought work in linen weaving but even the scope for expansion in the rural linen weaving industry was limited by the introduction of mechanical weaving looms. There was surplus labour and wages sunk below the bread-line. Despite working hours of 12, 14 even 16 hours per day the majority of the population were living in great misery. A contemporary of the time reported: "For seven or more years the unfortunate have not been able to buy a single item of clothing; their clothes are in rags, their houses decaying because they cannot afford to repair them; because of the failed potato crops of the last two years they have depended for food on the cheaper wild or fodder potatoes and on coarse or animal meal. Only a few of them ate meat, at Easter, Whitsun and Christmas and then for a family of five to six people they had perhaps half a pound!" In 1844 the Silesian weavers revolted. They looted the houses of rich fac-

II/35/36 Self-portrait of the early industrial businessman, painting by Louis Krevel.

II/37 Soap boiling factory.

II/38 Women working in a tobacco factory around 1840.

II/39 Child labour, pre-1848.

Erklärung

der

Menschen- und Bürgerrechte.

Art. 1. Der Zweck der Gesellschaft ist das Glück aller ihrer Glieder.

Art. 2. Um dieses Glück zu sichern, muß die Gesellschaft einem Jeden verbürgen:

Sicherheit der Person;

Die Mittel sich auf eine leichte Weise ein Auskommen zu verschaffen, welches ihm nicht nur die Bedürfnisse des Lebens, sondern auch eine des Menschen würdige Stellung in der Gesellschaft sichert;

Entwicklung seiner Anlagen;

Freiheit;

Widerstand gegen Unterdrückung.

Art. 3. Da alle Bürger, wie groß immer die Verschiedenheit ihrer Kräfte sein mag, ein gleiches Recht auf diese Zusicherung haben, so ist Gleichheit das Grundgesetz der Gesellschaft.

Art. 4. Die Sicherheit entspringt aus der Mitwirkung Aller zum Schutze der Person und der Rechte jedes Einzelnen und zur sichern Bestrafung dessen, der sie beeinträchtigt.

Art. 5. Das Gesetz schützt die öffentliche und persönliche Freiheit gegen die Unterdrückung derer, welche regieren. Es hält das Volk für gut, die Beamten für zugänglich dem Irrthum und der Verführung.

Art. 6. Niemand kann verfolgt, verhaftet, festgehalten oder angeklagt werden, als kraft eines vorherbestehenden Gesetzes und der hierin vorgeschriebenen Formen; jeder Befehl, jede Strenge, welche das Gesetz nicht erlaubt, kann mit Gewalt zurück gewiesen werden; die, welche dazu ermächtigen oder sie ausführen, sind schuldig und müssen somit bestraft werden.

Art. 7. Das Leben des Menschen ist heilig.

Art. 8. Die Strafen können keinen andern Zweck haben, als Verhütung der Verbrechen und die Besserung der Schuldigen; ihre Strenge darf nie die dringendste Nothwendigkeit überschreiten.

Art. 9. Niemand kann angeklagt oder verurtheilt werden, als auf Erklärung eines Geschwornengerichts.

Art. 10. Alle beweglichen und unbeweglichen Güter, seien sie im Gebiete des Staates belegen, oder von Mitgliedern desselben auswärts besessen, gehören der Gesellschaft an, welche allein durch Gesetze die Grenzen bestimmen kann, über die der Besitz des Einzelnen nicht hinausgehen darf.

Art. 11. Eigenthum ist das Recht, welches jeder Bürger auf den Genuß desjenigen Gütertheiles hat, der ihm vom Gesetze zugesichert ist.

II/42 Declaration of human and citizens' rights by the "league of outlaws", 1834.

“Declaration of human and citizens’ rights”

Art. 1. Society aims to ensure the well-being of all its members.

Art. 2. In order to ensure this well-being society must guarantee to each person: the means to ensure comfortably for himself an income which secures for him not only the bare necessities of life but also a position of dignity in society;
the development of his skills;
liberty;
protection against all oppression.

Art. 3. Since all citizens have an equal right to protection, however large the discrepancies in their abilities, equality is the corner-stone of society.

Art. 4. Security is achieved by each citizen cooperating in the protection of the person and rights of the individual, and in ensuring that all who infringe these rights are punished.

Art. 5. The law protects public and personal liberty against oppression by those in government. It protects the people and holds civil servants responsible for mistakes or malpractice.

Art. 6. No individual can be harrassed, arrested, held or accused unless they have violated one of the laws laid down in this declaration; orders and restrictions which are not ordained by law are not enforceable by force. Any person authorising or carrying out such measures is guilty in the eyes of the law and thus punishable.

Art. 7. The life of the individual is sacred.

Art. 8. Punishment must serve no other purpose than the prevention of crime or the reforming of the guilty. Its severity must not exceed the requirements.

Art. 9. No person can be accused or judged except by sworn court of justice.

Art. 10. All movable and immovable objects, whether situated within the territory of the state or possessed by its members abroad, are the property of society, which alone can determine through law the limits beyond which the possessions of an individual may not be taken.

Art. 11. The right of the individual to possess and enjoy his property is protected by law.

II/40 The weavers' misery, woodcarving by Kubitz from the 1840s.

II/41 Pictures from the Munich 'pamphlets'.
Misery in Silesia. – Hunger and Despair. – Official Help.

tory owners. The Prussian military put down the revolt *(cat. illustr. 41)* but the hopeless rebellion drew attention to the need and despair of the lower classes. The 'impoverishment' and the pauperisation of the propertyless was also being recognised as a social problem amongst the middle classes. Many journals concentrated upon social problems.

Board 12 Social distress drove tens of thousands to emigrate. Those who refused to resign themselves to the situation and who took up the struggle for better working conditions faced prison sentences because workers' unions were forbidden by the Prussian industrial regulations of 1845.

Thus the first 'communist' leagues were established beyond the borders of the German Confederation, especially in Switzerland and in France. It was here, in connection with the 'young Europe' of Mazzini and the 'society of the four seasons' of the French revolutionary August Blanemi, that the 'Young Germany' and the 'League of Outlaws' grew up, whose more radical members joined the 'league of the righteous'. By 1834 the 'league of outlaws' had laid down in its programme the need for human and citizens' rights on the basis of social equality *(cat. illustr. 42)*. In the 1840s the tailor Wilhelm Weitling, who was active in Paris, became the leading theoretician on "artisans' communism". This utopian form of communism attracted its support from radical workers and journeymen whose organisations were moulded in the tradition of social-revolutionary secret societies. However, it was not until the Revolution of 1848 that workers and journeymen won the right to form unions and the right to have their interests represented publicly by their own associations.

The Political Reform Movement: Liberals and Democrats (Boards 13–16)

The economic and social changes brought with them political reform movements. The demands ranged – according to social background and political views – from the granting of freedom rights for citizens to fundamental changes in the existing political and social order. The common aim was the resolution of the problem of the fragmentation of Germany and the establishment of a free national-state which should either be a constitutional monarchy or a republic.

Board 13

Liberalism was the most significant new political movement of the period between the Congress of Vienna and the 1848 Revolution.

It demanded modern 'representative constitutions' for each German state. It formed a strong opposition in the state parliaments which already existed. Its aim was the removal of economic barriers and a united Germany based on parliamentary principles. Only in this way did it see liberal citizens' rights as being ensured *(cat. illustr. 43–46).*

The significance of liberalism in the period preceding the 1848 revolution (Vormärz) was more based on the scientific and theoretical than on practical policies. There was an abundance of constitutional writings which laid down the political aims of liberalism.

Rotteck and Welcker, the leading theoreticians of the South German liberals, drew up the liberal political programme in the 'state encyclopaedia'. Rotteck was the first to develop the concept of a modern representative constitution in Germany in his "Ideas about Representative Bodies". The first and most important demand of the liberals was for constitutions which would guarantee basic rights and would ensure for the informed and property-owning citizens participation in the running of the state. In this the liberals saw embodied the criterion of "modern state constitutions which were appropriate for the cultural level of the nation". The majority of liberals were against depriving the sovereigns of power but sought merely a limitation of this power. In spite of this the constitutions had to be fought for because most sovereigns would not willingly grant the right of political participation. In the period following the Congress of Vienna modern constitutions were drawn up in the south- and several mid-German states, as a result of the liberal constitutional movement, into which civil rights were written, for the first time.

Board 14

The liberals aimed to embody these rights, and indeed extend them, in the state parliaments. However, there was in the period preceding 1848 (Vormärz), no liberal 'party'. The unity of the liberals was merely based on their common opposition to the governments of the semi-absolutist states. They saw themselves, if one excludes their conscience, as responsible and free individuals who were in no way subject to party discipline. Thus the 'party' of political liberalism spanned the entire spectrum, from the 'moderates' who did not question the monarchy, whose aims were to reach a settlement by legal means, and who

II/43 Karl von Rotteck.

II/44 Karl-Theodor Welcker.

II/45 Robert von Mohl.

II/46 Arnold Ruge.

II/47 The Second Chamber in Baden, 1845.

V Series of pictures showing the revolutionary events of 1830. "The most memorable days of 1830".

VI The Harkort Factory in Castle Wetter around 1834, painting by Alfred Rethel.

VII The Silesian weavers, painting by Wilhelm Hübner 1844.

were prepared to share governmental responsibilities, under certain circumstances, to the 'radicals' who wished to change the whole structure of state and society by revolutionary means and whose ultimate aim was the establishment of a republic.
Liberalism was primarily a movement of the educated and property-owning middle class. For example, in the Second Chamber of Baden *(cat. illustr. 47)* it was mainly middle class jobs which were represented: administrative officials, judges, mayors and professors as well as the clergy, innkeepers, shopkeepers and manufacturers. The members of parliament of the South German chambers were no longer bound by the instructions of their own class but were representatives of the whole 'Nation'. The liberals understood the 'people' in the abstract sense as the sum of like-minded individuals who enjoyed equal rights. The informed and property-owning middle class person should henceforth be the pillar of the state since he was the most appropriate representative of the interests of the whole people. For the most part the problem of the socially disadvantaged, which was already evident in the pre-1848 period (Vormärz), was left untouched by the liberals.
Baden was the stronghold of pre-1848 liberalism. Its aims can be best understood by considering the motions laid before the Second Chamber of Baden. Since the constitution of Baden did not yet grant the chamber the right to initiate laws, the liberals attempted to steer the government towards a course of constitutional reform by laying down motions. The main emphasis was laid upon social, economic and judicial reform in addition to the transformation of the authoritarian state (Obrigkeitsstaat), through administrative and constitutional reforms, into a parliamentary constitutional state on the lines of the West European model.

VIII (illustration left) Opening of the Munich-Augsburg railway line, 1st September 1839.

The liberals were also extremely active in trying to publicise their aims outside the chambers in critical newspapers. In addition, they did not shy away from direct political confrontations. 'The Göttingen Seven', a group of liberal professors, paid with the loss of their posts for their protest against the absolutist despotism of the King of Hannover who, at his own arbitrary discretion, abolished the constitution *(cat. illustr. 48)*.

Board 15

Liberal national ideas gained impetus from the restricted freedom of the individual states. The hopes of all progressive forces were aimed at German unity and a parliament which would represent all German people. The liberal national state would

combine the divided forces and make possible the political and social emancipation. There were proposals laid down in state parliaments which correspond to these aims. The most famous of these was the Welcker Proposal of 1831 made in the Second Chamber of Baden "for the completion of national developments in the Geram Confederation which would assist, in the best possible way, the promotion of German nationhood and citizens' freedom". The national movement became a people's movement. At meetings and festivals demands were made for a united and free Germany *(cat. illustr. 49)*.
Opinions differed as to how the above aims and demands were to be achieved. The 'moderates' favoured negotiations with the sovereigns. The 'radicals' wanted to organise a liberation struggle and aspired to a unified and free Germany only through revolutionary means.

Board 16 The willingness of the 'moderates' to compromise did not have the expected success. In addition, they took little account of the most socially disadvanted groups. The 'democrats' meanwhile turned primarily to the lower classes. Middle class intellectuals and the proletariat joined forces, mainly abroad, in secret societies and demanded in pamphlets the establishment of a republic. One of the most important secret associations was the 'league of outlaws' which possessed its own press agency. Within Germany the most important voice of the 'democrats' until it was banned in 1843 was the 'Rhineland Newspaper' (Rheinische Zeitung) with its editor Karl Marx. It demanded the uncontitional implementation of the principle of sovereignty of the people. Their main aims were social equality and a German Republic. They saw the reform of Germany as the catalyst for the reform of Europe and the liberation of all oppressed and underprivileged peoples.
Political pressure in the German Confederation and the unsuccessful efforts at compromise resulted in the radical democratic movement gaining more and more support.

The National Cultural Movement (Boards 17–20)

Parallel to the political and economic reform movement there emerged the national cultural movement. Although there was no political unity, Germany was unified culturally. From the common language, poetry and history the concept of a uniform

II/48 The 'Gottingen Seven'.

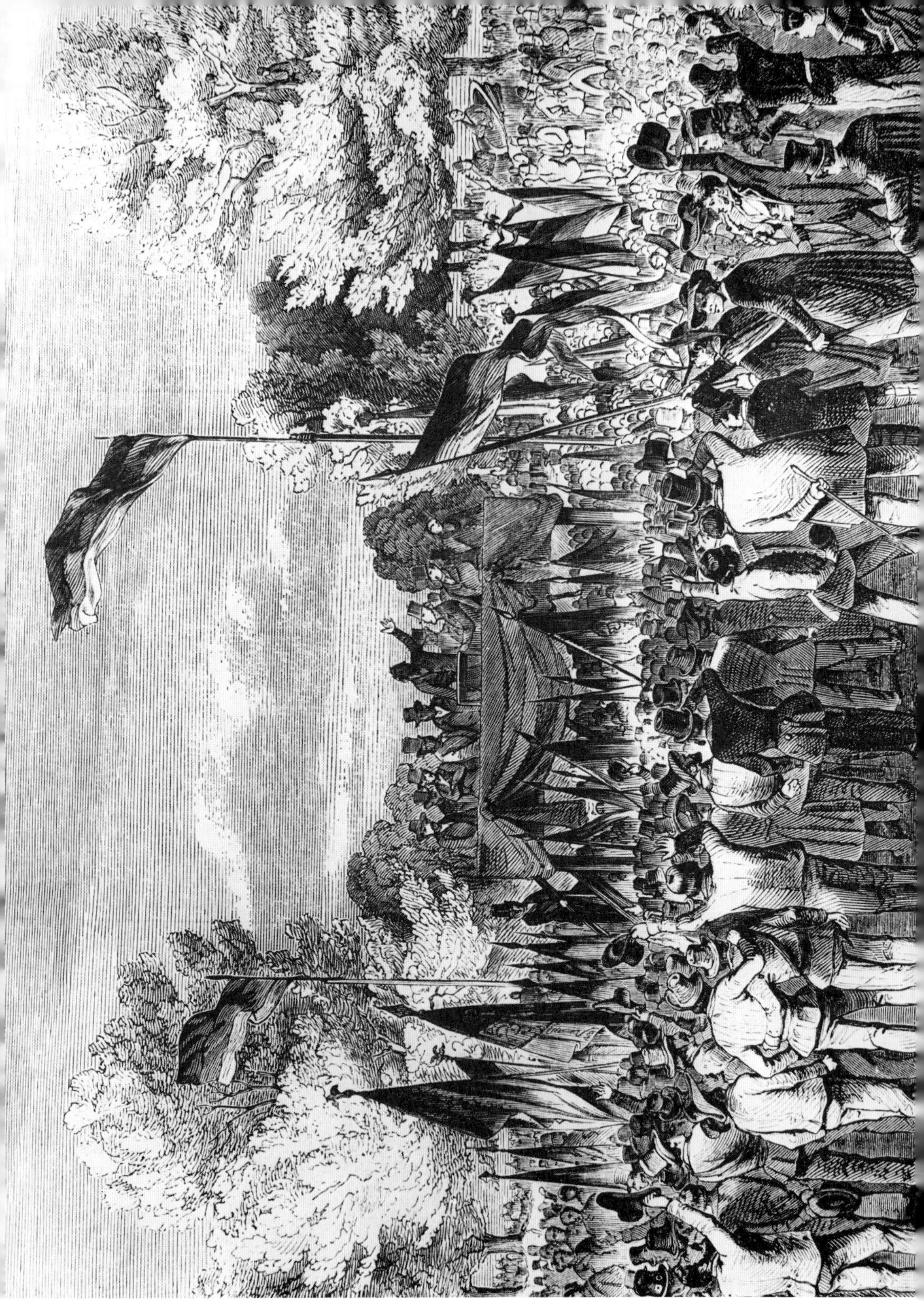

II/49 Peoples' gathering on the hillside, Judenbühl, on 13th March 1849 in Nuremberg.

German national culture was developed. The national consciousness was completed for many by the memory of a romantically glorified past. Leaving aside political reality romanticism discovered the German 'national spirit' (Volksgeist). Not until after the experiences of the French July Revolution of 1830 did democratic writers focus their attention directly on the problems of the present.

Board 17 'Heidelberg Romanticism', a circle of writers centering around Achim von Arnim, Clemens Brentano and Josef Görres, and working in Heidelberg around 1806, was a striking example of this turning away from the present and its problems. Looking back on those years Achim von Arnim noted: "the true history was for me at that time, in view of the sad burden weighing down on Germany, an object of aversion; I tried to forget it through poetry since I found in the latter something which did not borrow its substance from the present but which survived untarnished throughout all periods of history". Thus poetic testimonies of the German 'national spirit' were collected, which were still circulating the lower classes as fables, songs and legends.

Instead of the progressive political ideas of the middle class the virtues of the idealised past were extolled, the testimonies of which, it was hoped, would provide the impetus for a national rebirth. "Whatever may be the wealth of the whole people, whatever may shape its own inner strengths, the product of powerful forces acting over many years, the beliefs and knowledge of the people and the things that accompany them, in the shape of desires and death, songs, legends, customs, proverbs, stories, prophecies and melodies: we want to give everything back to all people . . . to the universal monument of the greatest, new Germany people" (A. v. Arnim). German philosophy was developing at this time and the language was scientifically investigated as a unifying feature of the nation. The brothers Grimm produced an historic 'German grammar' and in so doing founded German philology.

Board 18 The German science of history which was being developed around this time, gained impetus from the recourse made to the romantically glorified past, as contrast to the bleak present. The science's beginnings were given a considerable boost by Freiherr vom Stein, who ordered the collection and publication of historical sources of medieval Germany, the 'Monumenta Germaniae Historica'. The theme took hold not only in historical research but also in poetry and art. 'The Holy Roman Empire of the German Nation', in which German unity, power and greatness were seen to be embodied, was taken as a stark contrast to the fragmentation of the German Confederation of the present day. The myth of the sleeping Emperor in the Kyffhäuser, represented the hope for a future people's empire. This 'Altdeutschtum' became unclearly mixed in with conservative thinking and with ideas for restoring the estate system. Wide sections of the public were impressed by these ideas: the completion of Cologne cathedral as a 'Monument of German Unity', begun in 1842, was praised and greeted by all sides and actively supported *(cat. illustr. 50).*

Board 19

The looking back to the middle ages and the hopes for a return to the old empire were scorned by democratic writers. In particular, Heine continually directed his attacks on these 'Teutschtümelei'. The spiritual centre of the national democratic movement was a group of radical authors: Börne, Freiligrath, Hoffmann von Fallersleben and the 'Young Germany' *(cat. illustr. 51–53).*

They all demanded a democratic people's state, fought against feudalism and clericalism, against bureaucracy and monarchy, against state suppression of the press and of the freedom of speech and of thought. These writers, who gained in influence after the French July Revolution of 1830, were bound by the liberal and democratic 'spirit of the times'.

Board 20

German writers on the left went beyond the publishing of liberal political demands and turned to social criticisms in their writings. Foremost were their complaints about social need, inequality, hunger and misery: "The material pressure facing a high proportion of Germany is just as sad and reproachable as the intellectual; and in my eyes it is far less distressing that this or that liberal is not allowed to express his opinion than the fact that many thousands of families are not in a position to grease their potatoes" (Georg Büchner). The abolition of social inequalities became part of the practical revolutionary programme in the 'Hessian State-message' *(cat. illustr. 54, 55).* The attack made by critical writings no longer merely concentrated on the semi-absolutist governments and on the Metternich police system but also criticised the middle class social structure. "The relationship between the poor and the rich is the only revolutionary principle in the world", wrote Büchner in 1835 in Gutzkow.

The reaction to their work drove these writers into exile or led to their imprisonment. Pastor Weidig, a coauthor of the 'Hessian State-message', was tortured to death in 1837 at his trial, which was never concluded.

II/50 The celebration marking the completion of Cologne Cathedral, 14th August 1848.

II/51/52/53 Heinrich Heine, Georg Herwegh, Ludwig Börne.

Der Hessische Landbote.

Erste Botschaft.

Darmstadt, im Juli 1834.

Vorbericht.

Dieses Blatt soll dem hessischen Lande die Wahrheit melden, aber wer die Wahrheit sagt, wird gehenkt, ja sogar der, welcher die Wahrheit liest, wird durch meineidige Richter vielleicht ge[illegible]aft. Darum haben die, welchen dies Blatt zukommt, folgendes zu beobachten:

1) Sie müssen das Blatt sorg[illegible]ltig außerhalb ihres Hauses vor der Polizei verwahren;
2) sie dürfen es nur an treue Freunde mittheilen;
3) denen, welchen sie nicht trauen, wie sich selbst, dü[illegible]en sie es nur heimlich hinlegen;
4) würde das Blatt dennoch bei Einem gefunden, der es gelesen hat, so muß er gestehen, daß er es eben dem Kreisrath habe bringen wollen;
5) wer das Blatt nicht gelesen hat, wenn man es bei ihm findet, der ist natürlich ohne Schuld.

Friede den Hütten! Krieg den Pallästen!

Im Jahr 1834 siehet es aus, als würde die Bibel Lügen gestraft. Es sieht aus, als hätte Gott die Bauern und Handwerker am 5ten Tage, und die Fürsten und Vornehmen am 6ten gemacht, und als hätte der Herr zu diesen gesagt: Herrschet über alles Gethier, das auf Erden kriecht, und hätte die Bauern und Bürger zum Gewürm gezählt. Das Leben der Vornehmen ist ein langer Sonntag, sie wohnen in schönen Häusern, sie tragen zierliche Kleider, sie haben feiste Gesichter und reden eine eigne Sprache; das Volk aber liegt vor ihnen wie Dünger auf dem Acker. Der Bauer geht hinter dem Pflug, der Vornehme aber geht hinter ihm und dem Pflug und treibt ihn mit den Ochsen am Pflug, er nimmt das Korn und läßt ihm die Stoppeln. Das Leben des Bauern ist ein langer Werktag; Fremde verzehren seine Aecker vor seinen Augen, sein Leib ist eine Schwiele, sein Schweiß ist das Salz auf dem Tische des Vornehmen.

Im Großherzogthum Hessen sind 718,373 Einwohner, die geben an den Staat jährlich an 6,363,364 Gulden, als

1)	Direkte Steuern	2,128,131	fl.
2)	Indirecte Steuern	2,478,264	„
3)	Domänen	1,547,394	„
4)	Regalien	46,938	„
5)	Geldstrafen	98,511	„
6)	Verschiedene Quellen	64,198	„
		6,363,363	fl.

Dies Geld ist der Blutzehnte, der von dem Leib des Volkes genommen wird. An 700,000 Menschen schwitzen, stöhnen und hungern dafür. Im Namen des Staates wird es erpreßt, die Presser berufen sich auf die Regierung und die Regierung sagt, das sey nöthig die Ordnung im Staat zu erhalten. Was ist denn nun das für gewaltiges Ding: der Staat? Wohnt eine Anzahl Menschen in einem Land und es sind Verordnungen oder Gesetze vorhanden, nach denen jeder sich richten muß, so sagt man, sie bilden einen Staat. Der Staat also sind Alle; die Ordner im Staate sind die Gesetze, durch welche das Wohl Aller gesichert wird, und die aus dem Wohl Aller hervorgehen sollen. — Seht nun, was man in dem Großherzogthum aus dem Staat gemacht hat; seht was es heißt: die Ordnung im Staate erhalten!

II/54/55 First page of the ‘Hessian state message’ by Georg Büchner.

Manifestations of the National Movement (Boards 21 – 24)

Differing political conditions in the German States prevented a unified organisation of the national movement. In addition, it was illegal to form associations whose membership spanned more than one state. Thus, the supporters of the national movement were forced to express their wishes at festivals and conventions which were primarily non-political in character.

The French July Revolution of 1830 provided a great impetus for the national people's movement. Especially in South-West Germany many meetings took place which were dominated by democratic demands.

Board 21

The high point of the movement was the Hambach Festival near Neustadt an der Haardt in 1832. It was held to celebrate the anniversary of the Bavarian Constitution of 1818, but turned into a demonstration for unity and freedom, the like of which Germany had never before experienced. Approaching 30,000 people from all over Germany took part – an extraordinarily high number for that period if one considers that the population of a city like Frankfurt am Main was approximately 50,000. The participants were mainly representatives on the urban middle class, tradesmen, students and peasants, the festival beginning with a huge procession of all those present to the ruin of Hambach Castle *(cat. illustr. 56)*. During the procession black-red-gold flags were flown bearing the inscription "Germany's Rebirth" as were the colours of the political liberation struggle.

The organisers of the festival were two journalists, Wirth and Siebenpfeiffer, two of the most courageous representatives of the liberal opposition in South Germany.

In his festival address 'The German May', Siebenpfeiffer wrote that what had already been achieved should not be celebrated; instead this should be a festival of hope, a demonstration of the fight "for the shaking off of internal and external domination, for the struggle for legal freedom and German national honour". The festival became an expression of the opposition to the policies of the German Confederation. Logically, the national movement showed its solidarity with the democratic forces which had been forced into exile because of their opposition to the prevailing political conditions in Germany.

Board 22

More than 20 speeches were delivered at the festival. Common to all of them was their expression of anger at the fragmentation of Germany, their bitterness about the pressure exerted by the sovereigns and the material need of the lower classes. Welfare, freedom and unity should be incorporated into a German nation-state. The main speakers were Wirth and Siebenpfeiffer. Wirth's speech ended with the words "Three cheers for the united free states of Germany! Three cheers for the Republican-European-Confederation!" Their most famous phrase was the 'eternal curse' against the kings as the "traitors of the people and the whole human race". Even stronger was the revolutionary passion in Siebenpfeiffer's speech, who called for the people to strive for "the re-establishment of a fatherland and a free homeland". Nevertheless, the plan to create a solid organisation, which would strengthen the ideas of people's sovereignty, democracy and understanding with other nations, failed because no agreement on a common programme could be reached.

The reply of the reactionary forces to the festival was a new wave of arrests which included many pariticipants and the speakers at Hambach. The German Confederation stepped up its surveillance methods with the draconian "steps for maintaining legal peace and order in the German Confederation". The displaying of the colours 'Black-Red-Gold', the expression of liberal and democratic opposition, was no longer permitted in public.

Board 23 The Hambach Festival was the most significant, but not the only, demonstration in favour of unity and freedom during these years. At numerous academic conferences the spiritual and cultural links in Germany were emphasised. "Here Germany is represented in its spiritual unity": with these words Alexander von Humboldt greeted the participants at the 1828 Berlin convention of the 'Society of German naturalists and doctors' which had been established in 1822 and in so doing expressed the political character of these meetings.

Festivals of song and gymnastics *(cat. illustr. 57)* were also testimony to the national movement. At such occasions people from all over Germany gathered together. Their aim was the establishment of a free nation-state, but they took care to remain unpolitical so as to avoid providing the authorities with any chance to ban them. Especially at gymnastic festivals the national tradition of the liberation wars was upheld.

Board 24 Nevertheless, liberal aims and a general feeling of belonging together were not the only driving forces behind nationalist

II/56 The Hambach Festival, 1832.

II/57 Festival of Song on the Luisenburg near Wunsiedel.

Griechenlands Befreyung vom Türkenjoche.

Ietzt oder nie! – Des Schicksals Würfel liegen;
Ietzt gilt es, sterben oder siegen;
Euch ruft das Vaterland.
Ergreift die Waffen, Söhne der Hellenen!
Ein schöner Sieg wird eure Thaten krönen,
Des Nachruhms Unterpfand.

Ietzt oder nie ... zerbrecht die Sclavenketten.
Setzt alles dran die Freiheit euch zu retten,
Des Lebens höchstes Gut.
Hoch aufgelodert sind der Rache Flammen
Sie schlagen über Mahmeds Thron zusammen,
Löscht sie mit Türkenblut.

Auf Stambuls Wälle pflanzt das Glaubenszeichen!
Der Halbmond muß dem Kreuze weichen,
Dem Griechen der Barbar.
Und wären ihrer auch wie Sand am Meere,
Euch bleibt der Sieg, Gott ist mit eurem Heere.
Drum muthig, tapfre Schaar!

II/58 Pamphlet on the Greek freedom struggle: “Greece’s Liberation from the Turkish Yoke”.

thinking. The national aim often became an end in itself. An emotional nationalism influenced the building of national movements as national shrines; an example of this was the Walhalla, which was opened in 1842 near Regensburg and in which the monuments to the spiritual heroes served to portray the pitiful state of the nation.
The gymnastic movement (Turnerbewegung) of Jahn also upheld similar aims through its uncritical praise for all things German. In the Rhine-cult the naive love of the fatherland spilled over into a hatred of the French. Nicolaus Becker's Rhine song was a popular nation anthem around 1840 and later. In all these respects the two faces of nationalism were revealed.

National Precedents in Europe (Boards 25–28)

The liberal and national movement in Germany formed only a part of a wider European trend. Everywhere people were fighting for national unity and independence, for constitutions and liberal reforms. Hand in hand with this struggle went the fight for national unification and independence. Foreign events provided strong incentives. The nationalist revolt in Greece, the Italian unification struggle, the French July Revolution and the Polish uprising of 1830 urged on the national movement in Germany.

Board 25

When the Greeks rose up against their Turkish rulers in 1821, the Greek freedom struggle was supported in Germany by the pro-Hellenic associations ('Philhellenen') through the dispatch of both money and volunteers *(cat. illustr. 58)*. The Bavarian king Ludwig 1st sent officers to Greece against the will of Metternich who stressed the 'legitimacy' of the Sultan's rule. Lord Byron was the most famous English volunteer to go to Greece. When Russia, France and England recognised the Greek independence in 1827 the 'legitimacy policy' pursued by Metternich suffered its first defeat in its struggle against the national movement.
By contrast the liberal movements were defeated in Spain and Italy because of the intervention of the 'great powers'. The Spanish liberals' revolt in 1820 forced King Ferdinand VII, although only temporaily, to re-introduce the Napoleonic Constitution. However, the intervention of France helped the reactionary forces to achieve victory. Following the Spanish example, the Italian carbonari revolted in the same year and forced

the introduction of a liberal constitution in Naples. The carbonari ('charcoal burners') were members of a secret society which was spreading throughout Italy and which provided the first major impetus for moves towards Italian unification. Metternich had their uprising in Naples and Piedmont put down by ordering his Austrian troops to invade and intervene. Out of the ranks of the carbonari group Giuseppe Mazzini (1805–72) arose as the first major proponent of the Italian national movement. He founded the secret republican organisation Giovane Italia (Young Italy) in exile in 1831. A parallel organisation was created in 1834 in Switzerland by German refugees, mostly travelling artisans, which went under the name of 'Young Germany'. Together with 'Young Poland' these emigrant groups joined forces under Mazzini's leadership to become 'Young Europe'.

Board 26 The 1830 Paris July Revolution had the strongest influence on the political situation in Germany. The overthrow of the king by the middle class acted as a signal to Europe.

Board 27 In Germany, Italy, Belgium and Poland there were uprisings *(cat. illustr. V)*. Riots in Brunswick, Saxony, Hannover and Hessen forced new constitutions. In Brunswick the castle of the absolutist Duke was razed to the ground. The German liberals and democrats won followers and support amongst the mass of the people.

Board 28 A further consequence of the Paris July Revolution was the Polish uprising of 1830/31. The Poles, who were still divided up within Russia, Prussia and Austria, were fighting for the re-establishment of a Polish nation-state. In doing so they shocked the three major powers concerned. Whilst Prussia secured the province of Posem through military occupation, the Czar put down the revolt. Both in Russia and Prussia strongly anti-Polish policies were introduced and thousands of Poles were forced to emigrate. The failure of the uprising and the suffering of the Poles after their surrender aroused the sympathy of all European liberals and democrats. A wave of pro-Polish feeling also swept through liberal Germany. The emigrants were publicly extolled and supported by numerous Polish societies. The latter were banned by the Bundestag out of fear of the increasingly popular national movement. In the same way as the heroic deeds of the Greeks the suffering of the Poles became a favourite subject vor political propaganda *(cat. illustr. 59)*.

II/59 Pamphlet in support of the Polish freedom struggle.

Die Forderungen des Volkes.

Unsere Versammlung von entschiedenen Freunden der Verfassung hat stattgefunden. Niemand kann derselben beigewohnt haben, ohne auf das Tiefste ergriffen und angeregt worden zu sein. Es war ein Fest männlicher Entschlossenheit, eine Versammlung, welche zu Resultaten führen muß. Jedes Wort, was gesprochen wurde, enthält den Vorsatz und die Aufforderung zu thatkräftigem Handeln. Wir nennen keine Namen und keine Zahlen. Diese thun wenig zur Sache. Genug, die Versammlung, welche den weiten Festsaal füllte, eignete sich einstimmig die in folgenden Worten zusammengefaßten Besprechungen des Tages an:

Die Forderungen des Volkes in Baden:

I. Wiederherstellung unserer verletzten Verfassung.

Art. 1. Wir verlangen, daß sich unsere Staatsregierung lossage von den Karlsbader Beschlüssen vom Jahr 1819, von den Frankfurter Beschlüssen von 1831 und 1832 und von den Wiener Beschlüssen von 1834. Diese Beschlüsse verletzen gleichmäßig unsere unveräußerlichen Menschenrechte wie die deutsche Bundesakte und unsere Landesverfassung.

Art. 2. Wir verlangen Preßfreiheit; das unveräußerliche Recht des menschlichen Geistes, seine Gedanken unverstümmelt mitzutheilen, darf uns nicht länger vorenthalten werden.

Art. 3. Wir verlangen Gewissens- und Lehrfreiheit. Die Beziehungen des Menschen zu seinem Gotte gehören seinem innersten Wesen an, und keine äußere Gewalt darf sich anmaßen, sie nach ihrem Gutdünken zu bestimmen. Jedes Glaubensbekenntniß hat daher Anspruch auf gleiche Berechtigung im Staate.

Keine Gewalt dränge sich mehr zwischen Lehrer und Lernende. Den Unterricht scheide keine Confession.

Art. 4. Wir verlangen Beeidigung des Militärs auf die Verfassung.

Der Bürger, welchem der Staat die Waffen in die Hand gibt, bekräftige gleich den übrigen Bürgern durch einen Eid seine Verfassungstreue.

Art. 5. Wir verlangen persönliche Freiheit.

Die Polizei höre auf, den Bürger zu bevormunden und zu quälen. Das Vereinsrecht, ein frisches Gemeindeleben, das Recht des Volkes sich zu versammeln und zu reden, das Recht des Einzelnen sich zu ernähren, sich zu bewegen und auf dem Boden des deutschen Vaterlandes frei zu verkehren — seien hinfüro ungestört.

II. Entwickelung unserer Verfassung.

Art. 6. Wir verlangen Vertretung des Volks beim deutschen Bunde.

Dem Deutschen werde ein Vaterland und eine Stimme in dessen Angelegenheiten. Gerechtigkeit und Freiheit im Innern, eine feste Stellung dem Auslande gegenüber gebühren uns als Nation.

Art. 7. Wir verlangen eine volksthümliche Wehrverfassung. Der waffengeübte und bewaffnete Bürger kann allein den Staat schützen.

Man gebe dem Volke Waffen und nehme von ihm die unerschwingliche Last, welche die stehenden Heere ihm auferlegen.

Art. 8. Wir verlangen eine gerechte Besteuerung.

Jeder trage zu den Lasten des Staates nach Kräften bei. An die Stelle der bisherigen Besteuerung trete eine progressive Einkommensteuer.

Art. 9. Wir verlangen, daß die Bildung durch Unterricht allen gleich zugänglich werde.

Die Mittel dazu hat die Gesammtheit in gerechter Vertheilung aufzubringen.

Art. 10. Wir verlangen Ausgleichung des Mißverhältnisses zwischen Arbeit und Capital.

Die Gesellschaft ist schuldig die Arbeit zu heben und zu schützen.

Art. 11. Wir verlangen Gesetze, welche freier Bürger würdig sind und deren Anwendung durch Geschwornengerichte.

Der Bürger werde von dem Bürger gerichtet. Die Gerechtigkeitspflege sei Sache des Volkes.

Art. 12. Wir verlangen eine volksthümliche Staatsverwaltung.

Das frische Leben eines Volkes bedarf freier Organe. Nicht aus der Schreibstube lassen sich seine Kräfte regeln und bestimmen. An die Stelle der Vielregierung der Beamten trete die Selbstregierung des Volkes.

Art. 13. Wir verlangen Abschaffung aller Vorrechte.

Jedem sei die Achtung freier Mitbürger einziger Vorzug und Lohn.

Offenburg, 12. September 1847.

II/60 Offenburg Programme of 12th September 1847.

The Demands of the People

Our meeting of firm friends of the constitution has taken place. No person can possibly have been present without having been most deeply aroused and stirred. It was a celebration of masculine resolve, a meeting which must produce results. Every word which was uttered expressed the determination and demand for energetic bargaining. We offer neither names nor numbers of those present – since they are of little relevance to the issue. It suffices to say that the meeting, which filled the large festival hall, was unanimous in its agreement on the following statement which was drawn up during the discussions:

The Demands of the People in Baden:
I Restoration of our violated constitution

Art. 1. We demand that our state government disassociates itself from the Karlsbad Decrees of 1819, the Frankfurt Decrees of 1831 and 1832 and the Vienna Decrees of 1834. These Decrees are contrary to our inviolable human rights, the acts of the German Confederation and our State Constitution.

Art. 2. We demand freedom of the press; the inviolable right of a human being to express his thoughts freely can no longer be withheld from us.

Art. 3. We demand freedom of conscience and teaching. The relations of an human being with his God belong to his innermost soul and no external force has the right to intervene or to impose its own opinion. Each confession of faith has therefore the same right to demand equal treatment by the state.

No force should interfere in matters concerning teachers and pupils. There should be no divisions in teaching because of religious differences.

Art. 4. We demand that the military swear an oath of allegiance to the Constitution.

The citizen who is armed by the state should immediately swear his allegiance to the constitution for the good of the remainder of the population.

Art. 5. We demand personal freedom.

Domination and harassment of citizens by the police should cease. The right of association, the right to enjoy a healthy community life, the right of the people to hold meetings and to speak, in public, the right of the individual to a decent existence, the right to move freely and travel anywhere in the German Fatherland should all be henceforth inviolable.

II Development of our Constitution

Art. 6. We demand the people's representation in the German Confederation.

There should be one fatherland for Germans and a voice for them in the running of its affairs. We, as a nation, have a right to freedom and justice at home and a firm policy towards foreign nations.

Art. 7. We demand a national constitution for the military. Only the citizen who is trained in the use of weapons and armed can protect the state.

One should provide the people with weapons and relieve them of the unbearable taxes which standing armies impose upon them.

Art. 8. We demand a just taxation system. Each person should pay taxes to the state according to his means. As a replacement for the tax system which has been hitherto in operation, a progressive system of taxation should be introduced.

Art. 9. We demand that an equal school education should be provided for all citizens.

The whole populations must share the cost of providing this according to their means.

Art. 10. We demand a levelling of the disparities existing between labour and capital.

Society is responsible for providing and protecting a work-force.

Art. 11. We demand laws worthy of free citizens and that they be imposed by enforcement by jury.

The citizen should be judged by fellow-citizens. It is the duty of the people to ensure that justice is upheld.

Art. 12. We demand a popular state administration.

Free institutions are prerequisites of a healthy society. Its forces should not be controlled and determined by a remote bureaucracy. Self-government of the people should replace government by officials.

Art. 13. We demand the abolition of all privileges.

Each person has a right to the respect of his fellow-citizens, to express his own preferences and to a wage.

Offenburg, 12th September 1847.

1. Von der Bundesversammlung, wie sie gegenwärtig besteht, ist für die Förderung der Nationalanliegen nichts Ersprießliches zu erwarten. Sie hat ihre in der Bundesakte vorgezeichnete Aufgabe, soweit sie die Herstellung landständischer Verfassungen, freien Handels und Verkehrs, des freien Gebrauchs der Presse usw. betrifft, nicht gelöst. Dagegen ist die Presse unter Zensurzwang gestellt, sind die Verhandlungen der Bundesversammlung in Dunkel gehüllt, aus welchem von Zeit zu Zeit Beschlüsse zu Tage kommen, die jeder freien Entwicklung Hindernisse in den Weg legen.

2. Das einzige Band gemeinsamer deutscher Interessen, der Zollverein, wurde nicht vom Bunde, sondern außerhalb desselben, durch Verträge zwischen den einzelnen deutschen Staaten geschaffen.

3. Hieran knüpft sich die Frage, ob eine Vertretung der Nation bei der Bundesversammlung Besserung bewirken kann und daher als Ziel der Vaterlandsfreunde aufzustellen ist. Doch die Aussicht auf Verwirklichung dieses Gedankens ist nicht vorhanden: der Bund enthält Glieder, die als zugleich auswärtige Mächte, wie Dänemark und Niederland, sich mit einer deutschen Politik und Stärkung deutscher Macht niemals befreunden werden. Ferner bedingt eine Nationalvertretung auch eine Nationalregierung, ausgerüstet mit den Befugnissen der obersten Staatsgewalt, die bei dem völkerrechtlichen Bunde nicht vorhanden ist.

4. Das Ziel der Einigung Deutschlands zu einer deutschen Politik und gemeinsamen Leitung und Pflege nationaler Interessen, wird wohl eher erreicht, wenn man die öffentliche Meinung für die Ausbildung des Zollvereins zu einem deutschen Vereine gewinnt. Jetzt schon hat der Zollverein die Leitung einer Reihe wichtiger gemeinschaftlicher Interessen in Händen und steht auch in Vertragsverhältnissen zu auswärtigen Staat Durch weitere Ausbildung wird der Zollvere eine unwiderstehliche Anziehungskraft für d Beitritt der übrigen deutschen Länder üben, au den Anschluß der österreichischen Bundesländ herbeiführen und somit eine wahre deutsc Macht begründen.

5. Unbestritten bleibt, daß die Mitwirku des Volkes durch gewählte Vertreter hierbei un läßlich, und unbezweifelt, daß bei dem E wicklungsgang des Jahrhunderts und Deutsc lands die Einigung durch Gewaltherrsch unmöglich, nur durch die Freiheit und mit de selben zu erringen ist.

6. Anträge, welche in allen deutsch Kammern gleichlautend zu stellen sind:

Einführung der Pressefreiheit
Öffentliches und mündliches Gerichtsverfahr mit Schwurgerichten
Trennung der Verwaltung von der Rechtspfle
Befreiung des Bodens und seiner Bearbeiter v mittelalterlichen Lasten
Selbständigkeit der Gemeinden in der Verwa tung ihrer Angelegenheiten
Minderung des Aufwands für das stehende He und Einführung einer Volkswehr.

7. Aus Abgeordneten verschiedener Länd wird eine Kommission gewählt, die im nächst Jahr über das Steuerwesen und die Zustän der ärmeren Klassen berichten und Anträ formulieren soll, wobei besonders die gerech Verteilung der öffentlichen Lasten zur Erleicht rung des kleinen Mittelstands und der Arbeit zu berücksichtigen ist.

(Nach dem Bericht der Heidelber Deutschen Zeitung, Oktober 1847)

II/61 The Demands of the Heppenheim Meeting, 10th October 1847.

1. From the assembly of the Confederation, in its present form, nothing profitable can be expected with regard to the prospects for national unification. It has not carried out its duty, as laid down in the acts of the confederation, in respect of representative governments, free trade and commerce, freedom of the press, etc. The press is censored, the procedures of the Confederal Assembly are cloaked in darkness, out of which decrees are announced from time to time, which place obstacles in the path of all liberal development.

2. The only bond of common, German interests, the customs union, was not created by the Confederation but by agreements reached between the individual German states.

3. The question must be raised as to whether improvements can be gained by achieving the representation of the people in the Confederal Assembly and thus as to whether this should be an aim of those loyal to the Fatherland. Therefore, there are no prospects for the realisation of this aim: the Confederation contains members who, together with external powers such as Denmark and the Netherlands, would never be well disposed towards a German policy or towards a strengthening of German power. Furthermore, national representation depends on a national government equipped with the powers of the highest state-authority, something which is lacking in the Confederation.

4. The aim of German unification, with a German policy and common direction and protection of national interests, will be more easily achieved once public opinion has been won over in support of the extension of the customs union to a German society. The customs union already directs a whole series of common interests and has established treaties with outside states. Through its further development the customs union will act as an irresistible pole of attraction for the participation of the remaining German states and will also bring about unfication with the Austrian states and thus lead to the establishment of true German power.

5. It is indisputable that the participation of the people through elected representatives is absolutely essential and that, in accordance with the trends of the century and developments in Germany, unification can not be achieved through despotism but only through the granting of freedom.

6. The following are proposals which are to be laid before all German chambers alike:
granting of freedom of the press
public and oral legal proceedings before an assize court
separation of the government and the administration of justice
the freeing of land and those who work it from medieval taxes
independence for communities in the administration of their affairs
minimisation of the expenses for the standing army and the introduction of a peoples' army.

7. A Commission will be chosen from parliamentarians from the various states which will, next year, produce a report on the tax system and the conditions of the poorer classes, in which special consideration will be given to the just distribution of the public tax burden, so as to improve the position of the lower middle class and the workers.

(Taken from the report of the Heidelberg German Newspaper, October 1847)

Grouping of the Political Forces (Boards 29–32)

In 1847 the political, economic and social conditions in Germany became even worse. Political groups began to form alliances with their counterparts in other German states. This process highlighted even more clearly the rift between the majority of moderate liberals, who still placed their hopes on reforms and agreements with the sovereigns, and the minority of radical democrats, whose aspirations were still socialist-revolutionary in character.

Boards 29/30 The republicans, who were concentrated in Baden, gathered together, under the leadership of Hecker and Struve, in Offenburg on the 12th September 1847. In the 'Demands of the People in Baden' they demanded the restoration of freedom of the press and freedom of teaching, the abolition of all privileges, the levelling out of "disparities between labour and capital". Moreover they demanded a "people's representation in the German Confederation" *(cat. illustr. 60).*

Boards 31/32 The moderate liberals met on 10th October 1847 in Heppenheim. The gathering was made up mainly of parliamentarians from the South German Chambers but there were also Rhineland liberals present, such as the Rhineland-Prussians Hansemann and Mevissen. The mouthpiece of their aims was the newly established 'German Newspaper' ('Deutsche Zeitung') in Heidelberg. The participants at the meeting expressly rejected German unification through violent means. They also rejected the idea of people's representation in the German Confederation on the grounds that this organisation had no central government structure. By contrast, they developed a plan to extend the scope of customs union gradually until it became an institution which would unite Germany politically. In addition, they discussed the situation of the poorer classes and the "just redistribution of public taxation so as to ease the situation of the lower middle class and the workers" *(cat. illustr. 61).*

The Three Proposals for Solving "The German Question"

Room III

The Revolution of 1848/49

In the middle of the nineteenth century a strong movement of liberal and democratic opposition had developed in Germany. A demand common to all in this movement was the unification of Germany into one nation-state, a demand which was aimed against the ruling state powers and which, at the same time as raising the national problem, highlighted the need for fundamental social changes. National and social problems were inextricably linked, and depending on the political stance adopted by the different movements, the demand for national unity was either a result or a precondition of aims to reform the economic and social structure. Indeed there were occasionally irrational pan-German characteristics inherent in the national idea. However, these were, in comparison with their views on social emancipation, largely insignificant and the majority of the opposition clearly distanced itself from "the arrogance and selfishness of Germanomania" (Deutschtümelei) [Varnhagen]. Before 1848 the nationalist idea united the most wide-ranging reformist views. During the discussions, negotiations and struggles of the revolutionary years of 1848/49, however, it became obvious that, in practical political terms, it was almost impossible to find common ground amongst the different shades of opinion.

Social and political tensions became more serious towards the end of 1847 against the background of a European-wide economic crisis which had begun in 1846: people's gatherings, peasant revolts and petitions presented to the governments, all increased. The March demands, which were drafted firstly in South-West Germany, aimed primarily to establish freedom of the press, trial by jury, constitutional systems of government in all states and the forming of a German parliament. Finally, the example of the Paris February Revolution led to the March uprisings in Vienna and Berlin. The German sovereigns considered themselves obliged to grant concessions: they granted liberal constitutions, appointed liberals to ministries, promised freedom of the press and the freedom to hold meetings and a German Parliament.

Frankfurt was the focal point of the Revolution. This was the meeting place of the National Assembly (Vorparlament) which had been convened by the revolutionary movement. The attempts made by a small group of left-wing republicans to change the Assembly into a kind of permanent Revolutionary Executive Committee failed. The will of the liberal majority prevailed and favoured the election of a National Parliament with the agreement of the state governments. On the 18th May 1848 the official opening took place in the Frankfurt Paulskirche of the National Assembly, which had been elected at the end of April. There were, however, still no political parties in the modern sense of the word, though alliances, which resembled parties, were formed during the course of debates. The middle of the road liberal element formed the majority. From the outset the policies of the National Assembly were characterised by a remarkable willingness to compromise with the governments of the German states.

The Assembly had two major tasks: to draw up a national constitution and to create a centralised government executive. As early as the beginning of June proposals for an Imperial executive were being discussed and the Assembly formed, on its own authority, a temporary Imperial Government. The composition of this government reflected the problems of relations between a unified German state and the individual states, especially the most powerful amongst them, whilst the election of the Austrian Arch Duke Johann to the position of Imperial Administrator was seen as some protection for Austrian interests, the Prussian influence was still overwhelming in the newly-formed Imperial Ministry. Nevertheless, the National Assembly, which with this forming of a government was assuming that some fictitious nation state already existed, never succeeded in providing this centralised executive with power and authority. It had no civil service of its own and no army; a number of the German monarchs refused to swear the allegiance of their troops to the Imperial Administrator.

The most important and passionately discussed topic during parliamentary debates between June and September were the 'Basic Rights of the German People' which were not published until the 27th December 1848. The time taken over these debates proved costly as the old powers were able to strengthen their cause. It also showed the importance which the liberal forces attributed to social and legal reform in the nation state which they aimed to create. The Basic Rights were an expression of the attempt to abolish the class-based hierarchies of the old social order and in so doing to end the privilege of the aristocracy and the remaining feudal characteristics.

This was to be achieved by legally guaranteeing equality of opportunity and equal legal treatment for all citizens, by using

the same system that had been introduced following the revolutions in America and France.
Whilst the MPs were continuing discussions on the Imperial constitution, the National Assembly faced its most serious crisis in the late summer of 1848. The impotence of the central government became clear over the Schleswig-Holstein question. The German Confederation and the National Assembly came to the assistance of a German nationalist uprising in Schleswig, which was threatened with annexation by Denmark, by sending Prussian troops. However, under pressure from Russia and England the Prussians eventually halted their action and their troops were withdrawn following the signing of the armistice in Malmö. After having initially rejected the armistice the National Assembly eventually found itself with no alternative but to accept it since it was not a powerful enough body to pursue an independent policy. On the other hand, the radical democrats stepped up their actions: in Lorrach on 21st September Struve proclaimed the "German Social-Republic". This uprising was defeated in the same way that Hecker's had been in April 1848. In Frankfurt the National Assembly was directly threatened by a rebellion of the opponents of the cease-fire and the appeasement policies of the liberal majority which it represented. Indeed it was only saved with the help of Austrian and Prussian troops. This success and the crushing of other uprisings in Vienna in October and in Berlin in November 1848 strengthened the reactionary forces.
In September 1848 work on a German constitution was begun in the Paulskirche and here too the compromise policies of the Assembly were apparent: unitary and federal, democratic and monarchistic elements all joined forces. The main topic of discussion was the question of the territorial limits of the German nation state. At first the majority of MPs tended to favour a greater-German solution which would incorporate the Germanspeaking areas of Austria and thus separate these territories constitutionally from the remaining areas of the Habsburg Empire. This solution was thwarted by the Austrian Prime Minister Prince Felix Schwarzenberg, who introduced a centralised constitution for the entire Austrian Empire following the suppression of the non-German nationalist movements. This action ended the hopes for a greater-German solution and the Assembly decided to offer the hereditary title of Emperor of a "kleindeutsch" nation state to the Prussian King. However,

Frederick William IV, who supported romantic and legal nationalist ideas, refused this offer made by a people's assembly which had been established by revolutionary means. Moreover, he spoke out against the 28 governments which had already recognised the Imperial Constitution. In early 1849 there were fresh revolts whose aim was to implement the Imperial Constitution by exerting pressure from below. The uprisings were, however, put down in bloody fashion. Following the resignation of a large proportion of the liberals the National Assembly became dominated by the republican left and it was finally disbanded by the military forces of Württemberg in Stuttgart where the 'Rump Parliament' was still meeting. Thus the work of the Paulskirche had failed. The 'March Achievements' were repealed in all German states with the help of the reinstated German Confederation. The Basic Rights too were abolished again almost everywhere in 1851. The German Revolution of 1848/49, which had been an attempt to establish a constitutional state by liberal and democratic means, which corresponded to the political and social demands of the time, failed in its final stages mainly due to the problem of German unity. The national question became a pure powergame between the restrengthened forces of Prussia and Austria. Whilst the path to social reforms was blocked by reactionary forces – only the 'new Era' in Prussia offered some fresh hope – the question of a unified German state remained the focal point of Austro-Prussian dualism, which dominated the politics of the following decades. In the wake of increasing scepticism surrounding the ideals of the previous years support increased for a policy of realism which offered practical solutions within the existing conditions. One of the proponents of the Revolution, D. F. Strauss, wrote in 1852: "Compared to the unification question I approach with total indifference the pros and cons of despotism, or constitutionalism, a society dominated by aristocrats or a democracy." The national idea began to distance itself from social-reformist aspirations.

1. The March Revolution of 1848

In 1847/48 social and political tension increased, against the background of a European economic crisis, and led to uprisings, with the exception of Russia and England, in all European countries against the existing order: in France against the selfish policies of the upper middle class; in Italy and Germany against the territorial fragmentation, against the remaining features of the feudal system and the state constitutions parts of which were still absolutist; in Eastern Europe there were rebellions against foreign domination and social injustice. The initial conditions and the problems faced differed so greatly that there was no uniform revolutionary pattern in Europe.
In Germany the uprising was supported by a strong national movement which combined the demands for national unity with those for social and political reforms. These demands found expression in the desires of people from all classes for a national parliament and a constitution valid for the whole of Germany. In the first phase of the Revolution in March 1848 the revolutionary forces succeeded, first in Southern Germany and, after street fighting, also in Vienna and Berlin, in winning concessions from the governments: they granted constitutions where none existed, guaranteed the freedom of the press and appointed liberal ministers.

The Revolution in France

The Revolution in Paris gave the signal for the Revolution and for the overthrow of the old European political order. The economic crisis of 1846/47 caused a food shortage in France and as a consequence the new urban proletariat and the rural population became more radical. Petits bourgeois and workers – led by Louis Blanc – demanded public job-security in nationalised factories. Attempts at political reform by the democratic middle class failed. This led to the February Revolution. Workers, citizens and national guards fought side by side and forced the abdication of the King Louis Philippe, and the Republic was proclaimed *(cat. illustr. 62).* The conflict between the bourgeois majority and the radical socialists soon came to a head over the aims of the revolution: the bourgeoisie and the military formed an alliance. The workers' rebellion in June was put down in bloody fashion.

III/62 Storming of the Palais Royal on 24th February 1848.

III/63 The battle of Porta Tosa in Milan on 22nd March 1848.

III/64 Breaking of the Mariahilfer line in Vienna on 13th March 1848.

III/65 Cavalry attack on the people in front of the Castle in Berlin on 18th March 1848.

III/66 Food Riots in Stettin, 1847.

III/67 The Burning of the Waldenburg Castle on 5th April 1848.

III/68 Members of the working and middle classes fight together on barricades in March 1848.

III/69 Conflict between the Mannheim civic guard and protesting supporters of Hecker on 9th April 1848.

The March Revolution in Central Europe

Under the impact of the events that had occurred in February in Paris, a series of revolutions was triggered in the German states too. Popular assemblies, demonstrations and petitions that were often accompanied by social turmoil, particularly in the country, reflected the political unrest felt by the population. First, the so-called March demands were formulated in Southern Germany. Their aims were, above all, freedom of the press, courts sitting with professional and lay judges, arms for the people, constitutions in the individual states and the convening of a German parliament. Constitutions and the nation-state in particular symbolized a fundamentally new order; all the revolutionary forces shared these values but differed substantially over how to translate them into political reality. The governments mostly did not dare to quell the uprisings by force. In many cases power fell almost automatically into the hands of the liberal bourgeoisie.

The economic plight of the workers and peasants, the even more determined suppression of freedom of the press and of freedom of opinion as well as the outbreak of the revolution in Paris, which was enthusiastically acclaimed by the masses, furthered the social uprising in Austria too. While the Czechs, Hungarians and Italians rebelled at the same time, on 13th March, after a demonstration, a fight broke out in Vienna between the military on the one hand and workers and students on the other *(cat. illustr. 64)*. The chief minister, Chancellor of State Prince Metternich, was ousted and fled to England. The Imperial Government had to allow the civic guard to carry arms and promised to grant a constitution, which it did in April.

In Berlin the political unrest which had been noticeable since the beginning of March turned into open rebellion on 18th March. When, in front of the Castle, the cavalry sought to end a demonstration for a civic guard, freedom of the press and a Prussian parliament, barricades were erected and defended by members of the bourgeoisie, workers and students *(cat. illustr. IX and 65)*. Finally the King ordered the withdrawal of his troops and gave in to the revolutionaries. With the words "Prussia will merge with Germany" the King became reconciled on the 21st March to the demand for national unity. A liberal ministry was introduced, a Prussian National Assembly was convened in May and Prussia was to become a constitutional monarchy.

The Social Causes of the Revolution

In 1846 and 1847, in the wake of a number of poor harvests, Germany was hit by a serious agricultural crisis and by famine. As a result of rising food prices and falling real incomes, large sections of the population suffered extreme hardship *(cat. illustr. 66).* In addition, there occurred a global economic crisis, which, in 1847 and early 1848, adversely affected production and led to rising unemployment. The crisis in agriculture and trade did not last very long, however; in the course of 1848 the situation improved again. The revolution was supported above all by the rural population, particularly in Southern Germany and Silesia. The situation was reminiscent of the peasants' war, with radical groups marching to the castles and demanding that they be freed from their remaining feudal obligations *(cat. illustr. 67).*

However, the agricultural revolts did not really pose a threat to the existing order. When their demands were met and the "peasants' liberation" had largely been achieved, the rural population soon stopped supporting the revolution.

Moreover, the rapid success of the revolution was due not least to the large measure of support which it enjoyed among the urban population: members of the bourgeoisie and workers, master craftsmen and journeymen, members of the urban middle and lower classes fought together on the barricades *(cat. illustr. 68).* In the course of the revolution, however, the social differences between the various groups became ever more apparent *(cat. illustr. 69).* The majority of the bourgeoisie soon prevented the lower social classes from pursuing the revolution further. The controversy about their more radical political and social demands did not merely destroy the unity that had originally existed but also split the bourgeoisie itself.

2. The Emergence of the Political Nation

The Road to the Paulskirche

Meetings, demonstrations and street fighting had hitherto determined the course of the revolutionary events. In view of the success achieved, the bourgeois-Liberal majority and also many democrats wanted to take the road of reforms sanctioned

III/70 The entrance procession of the Pre-Parliament into the Paulskirche on 30th March 1848.

III/71 Election meeting of the Berlin Political Club on 20th April 1848.

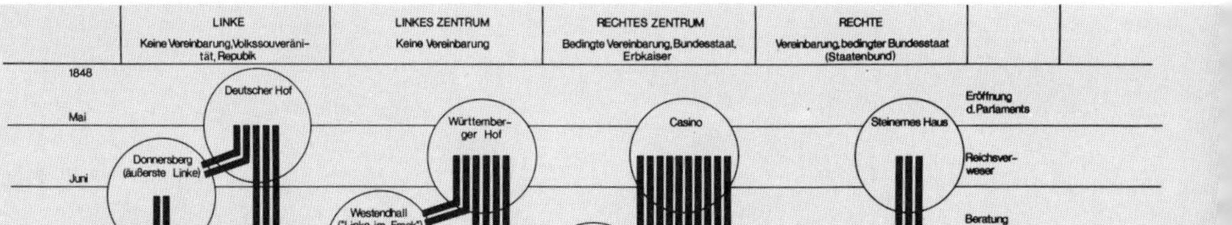

III/72 The various political groupings in the Frankfurt National Assembly 1848/49.

III/73 The Casino Party in the National Assembly.

III/74 The Left-wing in the National Assembly.

III/75 Meeting of democrats in Berlin, 1848.

by parliament. A national assembly was to draw up a pan-German constitution and set up a central authority capable of governing.
On the 5th March leading liberals and democrats from all over Southern and Western Germany met together and announced the convening of a National Assembly to be imperative. They directed their appeal to the existing governments but then nominated their own Committee of Seven whose task it would be to prepare for and elect a National Assembly. In this way the first revolutionary body was created. The Committee invited all "former or present leading personalities and those involved in the work of legislative bodies in all German states" and in addition a number of other leading public figures to participate in a Pre-Parliament in Frankfurt on the 30th March. They attracted over 500 men to the Paulskirche *(cat. illustr. 70).*
At this revolutionary meeting the individual German states were represented in different degrees of strength. Only the minority of left-wing democrats possessed a firm programme under the leadership of Gustav von Struve. This minority demanded the setting up of a federal republic and immediate acceptance by the Pre-Parliament of the revolutionary executive powers. The majority was a long way from holding this viewpoint; by contrast they wanted to establish a new political order by coming to an agreement with the sovereigns. Due to this stance, which was later shared by the majority of the National Assembly, the revolutionary position was for all intents and purposes abandoned and in its place the idea of compromise with the old authorities came to the fore. When the 'radicals' recognised this fact 40 members left the Assembly under the leadership of Hecker.
Hecker began his rebellion for the realisation of a social republic in Baden with bands of volunteers and he was also supported by a group of German exiles from Switzerland and France. However, he overestimated the public support for the republican idea and after only a few days he was defeated by regular troops from Baden and Hessen. Hecker fled to Switzerland and later emigrated to the U.S.A.
The Pre-Parliament had worked out the principles of an election and a future German constitution and convened a committee of fifty to prepare for elections. This revolutionary committee worked with the old Parliament and the state governments, which were eager to legitimise the election and the electoral

laws. All 'independent people' should have the right to vote, a clause interpreted in very different ways by the various states. In certain areas workers and domestic servants were to be excluded from the election and in only six states was a direct election to be permitted, with delegates doing the voting indirectly in all other states *(cat. illustr. 74).* Members of the Political Club in Berlin demanded in vain direct elections for Prussia at an election meeting 'in the tents' *(cat. illustr. 72).* There were as yet no political parties and local candidates were nominated either by the political clubs which existed all over Germany or by hastily organised election committees. Almost everywhere middle class liberals were elected.

The National Assembly

On the 18th May the National Assembly met in the Paulskirche *(cat. illustr. 76).* Enthusiasm and expectations were riding high. In the first speech after his election to the presidency of the National Assembly Heinrich von Gagern called for the granting of the 'sovereignty of the nation' and of their right to draw up a new constitution. At the same time he stressed the necessity for cooperation with the governments.

Including substitutes, 831 MPs were elected to the Paulskirche of whom initially 350 and later on average 400–500 were present. The majority of the parliamentarians came from the liberal, educated middle class. Civil servants and academics – above all lawyers – played a prominent role. Trade and industry were only represented by a few MPs; the same applied to the nobility and the petite bourgeoisie. Peasants and workers remained without direct representation in the National Assembly

On the basis of the experience gained in the Land assemblies in Southern Germany, more stable political groupings which endeavoured to organize parliamentary work effectively soon formed in the Frankfurt National Assembly too. Most MPs belonged to such groupings which met regularly in the inns of Frankfurt and took their names from their meeting places *(cat. illustr. 72).* The groupings elected executive committees, produced membership lists and drew up manifestos. They soon fulfilled the task of preliminary discussions for plenary sessions and were called 'parties' by many people.

III/76 Initiation of Arch-Duke Johann of Austria, Imperial Administrator of Germany, in the constituent Assembly on the 12th July 1848 in the Paulskirche.

Beschlüsse
des
Arbeiter-Kongresses.

Erster Theil.

Statut für die Organisation der Arbeiter.

I. Die Lokal-Komites für Arbeiter.

§. 1. Es bilden die verschiedenen Gewerke und Arbeitergemeinschaften im weitesten Sinne des Worts Vereinigungen und wählen, je nach dem Verhältniß ihrer Zahl, Vertreter zu einem Lokal-Komite für Arbeiter. Für Gewerke, welche vereinzelt dastehen, dürfte der Kreis Vereinigungen bieten.

§. 2. Diejenigen Arbeiter, welche noch keine Gemeinschaften bilden, haben sich ebenfalls zu vereinigen und Vertreter zu wählen, z. B. die Eisenbahnarbeiter 2c.

§. 3. Das Lokal-Komite hat die Verpflichtung, a) regelmäßige Versammlungen der Arbeiter zu veranlassen; b) die Bedürfnisse und Uebelstände der Arbeiter in ihren Orten oder Kreisen genau zu erforschen und auf Abhülfe derselben hinzuwirken; c) aus sich einen Ausschuß zu wählen, der die Geschäfte leitet, bestehend aus 1 Vorsitzenden, 1 Beisitzer, 2 Schreibern, 1 Kassirer und 2 Kassenaufsehern.

§. 4. Die Lokal-Komites verschiedener Orte stehen mit einander in Verbindnng und zwar a) indem sie sich in kleinere oder größere Bezirke ordnen und für alle ein Bezirks-Komite bilden; b) durch briefliche Mittheilungen, welche sie an das Bezirks-Komite zur Beförderung an die einzelnen Lokal-Komites und an das Central-Komite machen; c) durch Absendung von Abgeordneten zu den Bezirksversammlungen und der vom Central-Komite ausgeschriebenen Generalversammlung für ganz Deutschland.

II. Die Bezirks-Komites

§. 5 haben vorläufig ihren Sitz in folgenden Städten: Danzig, Königsberg, Stettin, Cöln, Bielefeld, Frankfurt, Hamburg, Stutt-

III/77 Decrees of the Berlin Workers' Congress from 23rd August – 3rd September 1848.

Decrees of the Workers' Congress

First Section

Statute for labour organisation

1. *The Local Workers' Committees*

1. Factory and Working Communities, in the widest sense of the word, should convene meetings and elect, in ratio to their numbers, representatives for a local workers' committee. For isolated factories the district level could offer a meeting point.

2. Those workers who still have not formed associations should meet and elect representatives: e. g. railway workers.

3. It is the duty of the local committee:

a) regularly to summon meetings of the workers,

b) to investigate carefully the requirements and complaints of the workers in their area or district and to provide solutions,

c) to elect an executive committee from amongst themselves which will direct their business, consisting of: chairmen, ordinary members, minute-takers, treasurers and fund-inspectors.

4. The local committees of various areas should be interlinked and should form one area-committee, whether they are grouped in small or large areas,

b) they should communicate by letters which they should send to the area committee for forwarding to the central committee,

c) they should send delegates to the area meetings and the general assemblies for the whole of Germany, which are convened by the central committee.

2. *The Area Committees*

5. Will meet temporarily in the following towns: Danzig, Königsberg, Stettin, Cologne, Bielefeld, Frankfurt, Hamburg, Stuttgart . . .

The democratic left, which was in a minority, organised itself the quickest *(cat. illustr. 74).* Under the leadership of Robert Blum they met in 'the Deutscher Hof'. However, the most committed republicans soon broke away to form their own group known as 'Donnersberg' and represented the far left in the Parliament. Despite their political differences the majority of the left formed an alliance with 'the Pariser Hof' of the right wing, on the national question, in favour of the pan-German solution in February 1849, after the little German-Prussian solution had been mooted. A liberal-conservative group provided the right wing of the Paulskirche. This group, which was mainly catholic and Austrian, met in 'the Steinernes Haus' and later, under the leadership of the Prussian Freiherr von Vincke, became based in the 'Café Milani'. In contrast to the left wing, this group wanted to restrict the duty of the National Assembly to the formulation of the constitution and to underline support for the document by reaching an agreement with the sovereigns.
The liberal centrists made up the majority of MPs but were divided into two wings: 'the Württemberger Hof' (left of centre) and the 'Casino-Party' (right of centre) *(cat. illustr. 73).* The 'Württemberger Hof' agreed with the left wing in rejecting the idea of reaching agreement with the sovereigns. The 'Casino-Party' was the strongest group, both numerically and intellectually and had most influence on the course of events in the Parliament and, in addition, provided the President, Heinrich von Gagern. Many professors belonged to the 'Casino', such as the historians Dahlmann, Droysen, Waitz and Giesebrecht. The majority of the group's members favoured constitutional monarchy with restricted electoral rights and later supported the little German solution.

The Emergence of Parties

Even though there had been a number of precursors, above all in the West and South of Germany, the revolution of 1848/49 marked the birth of political parties in the modern sense of the word. Once public censorship had been abolished and people were allowed to form associations and to assemble, large sections of the population engaged in political activities as early as March. In many towns and cities the socio-political

groups achieved such a high degree of organization that five groupings similar to parties could be distinguished: the Liberals and the Democrats, the Conservatives, political Catholicism, and an early form of the workers' movement. At the same time, all kinds of interests began to be articulated and in some instances those concerned also formed associations and groups. German society thus became politically organized to a far greater extent than ever before.
The bourgeois-Liberal centre was the strongest force in Parliament. While it advocated the extensive liberalization of the economy and society, it wanted to introduce political democracy on a step-by-step basis. The monarchy was perceived as a bulwark of the bourgeois order against the dangers of a social revolution. Outside Parliament, the Liberals were clearly not as well organized as the Democrats. It was mostly only in response to the activities of the latter that the Liberals too started to form associations and groups.
The bourgeois Democrats were the first to set up an organization of their own similar to a party. It consisted of an extensive network of groups and associations at regional level, with conferences and central associations at national level *(cat. illustr. 75).* On the basis of the principle of popular sovereignty, the Democrats mostly advocated a republican order. In their view, this presupposed social reform and an open society, in which the lower strata were to be included from the very start.
The conservative counter-revolutionary forces, which had initially adopted a hesitant and defensive approach, started to form groups too, particularly in Prussia. In Berlin they published the "New Prussian Newspaper", the so-called "Kreuz-Zeitung". At the same time, the Prussian landed gentry, the Junker, organized the defence of the monarchical system in patriotic clubs; they also set up associations in line with their economic interests and privileges. There soon existed a large number of such clubs and associations in Eastern Prussia.
In the spring of 1848 there emerged a broad-based Catholic movement which fought for the freedom of the Church. A large number of newspapers, assemblies and petitions, associations advocating religion freedom, such as the "Piusvereine für religiöse Freiheit", and finally the first Catholic Church Conference held in Mainz in 1848 were the instruments of a political movement which was hardly represented in parliament. This broad-based Catholic movement included supporters of Chris-

III/78 Entrance of the Imperial Administrator into Frankfurt am Main on 11th July 1848.

An das deutsche Volk.

Deutsche! Eure in Frankfurt versammelten Vertreter haben mich zum deutschen Reichsverweser erwählt.

Unter dem Zurufe des Vertrauens, unter den Grüßen voll Herzlichkeit, die mich überall empfingen, und die mich rührten, übernahm ich die Leitung der provisorischen Centralgewalt für unser Vaterland.

Deutsche! nach Jahren des Druckes wird Euch die Freiheit voll und unverkürzt. Ihr verdient sie, denn Ihr habt sie muthig und beharrlich erstrebt. Sie wird Euch nimmer entzogen, denn Ihr werdet wissen sie zu wahren.

Eure Vertreter werden das Verfassungswerk für Deutschland vollenden. Erwartet es mit Vertrauen. Der Bau will mit Ernst, mit Besonnenheit, mit ächter Vaterlandsliebe geführt werden. Dann aber wird er dauern, fest wie Eure Berge.

Deutsche! Unser Vaterland hat ernste Prüfungen zu bestehen. Sie werden überwunden werden. Eure Straßen, Eure Ströme werden sich wieder beleben, Euer Fleiß wird Arbeit finden, Euer Wohlstand wird sich heben, wenn Ihr vertrauet Euren Vertreten, wenn Ihr mir vertraut, den Ihr gewählt, um mit Euch Deutschland einig, frei und mächtig zu machen.

Aber vergeßt nicht, daß die Freiheit nur unter dem Schirme der Ordnung und Gesetzlichkeit wurzelt. Wirkt mit mir dahin, daß diese zurückkehren, wo sie gestört wurden. Dem verbrecherischen Treiben und der Zügellosigkeit werde ich mit dem vollen Gewichte der Gesetze entgegentreten. Der deutsche Bürger muß geschützt seyn gegen jede strafbare That.

Deutsche! Laßt mich hoffen, daß sich Deutschland eines ungestörten Friedens erfreuen werde. Ihn zu erhalten ist meine heiligste Pflicht.

Sollte aber die deutsche Ehre, das deutsche Recht gefährdet werden, dann wird das tapfere deutsche Heer für das Vaterland zu kämpfen und zu siegen wissen.

Frankfurt am Main, den 15. Juli 1848.

Der Reichsverweser

Erzherzog Johann.

Die Reichsminister

Schmerling. Peucker. Heckscher.

Druck von Benjamin Krebs

III/79 Proclamation of the Imperial Administrator after assuming power over the temporary central administration.

To The German People

Germans! Your representatives, assembled in Frankfurt, have elected me as the Imperial Administrator.
Amidst the declarations of trust, amidst the greetings of goodwill which I received everywhere and which moved me I accepted the leadership of the temporary central administration of our Fatherland.
Germans! After years of pressure total freedom will be granted you. It shall serve you since you have sought it hard and long. It will never more be withdrawn since you will know how to preserve it.
Your representatives will complete the German Constitution. Await it with trust. The construction will be built seriously, thoughtfully and with a deep love of the Fatherland. Then it will stand as firm and fast as your mountains.
Germans! Your Fatherland will have to withstand severe tests. These will be overcome. Your roads, your streams will survive, your diligence will find work, your prosperity will increase, if you allow your representatives and I whom you elected to make Germany free and powerful with your help.
However, do not forget that freedom goes hand in hand with order and lawfulness. Ensure that these are protected where they are threatened. I shall counteract criminal acts and licentiousness with the full weight of the law. The German citizen must be protected against all punishable acts.
Germans! Let me hope that Germany will live in undisturbed peace. My most sacred duty is to preserve it.
Should, however, German honour or German law be endangered then the brave German army will be in a position to fight and gain victory for the Fatherland.

Frankfurt am Main, 15th July 1848

The Imperial Administrator
Archduke Johann

The Imperial Ministers
Schmerling, Peucker, Heckscher

tian democracy, who supported many of the aims of the March Revolution, as well as the majority of the ultramontane, strictly conservative forces.
In 1848/49 the political organization of the workers as an independent movement was still very rudimentary *(cat. illustr. 77)*. Often the workers' associations could not yet be clearly distinguished from the democratic movement. Moreover, the existing social classification – journeymen, the proletariat in its early form, and the propertyless lower classes – frequently made it difficult to set up a uniform organization. Alongside groups which advocated a conservative social policy or social reforms, the "League of Communists" led by Marx and Engels strongly urged a social revolution.
Great progress was made in organizing all kinds of economic and social interests in the course of 1848. Most groups wanted to give expression to their wishes through addresses and petitions, assemblies and newly formed groups so as to make them known to the public at large and above all to the National Assembly. The Congress of German Crafts and Trades in particular could rely on the support of large sections of the population; the same is true of the movement which advocated protective tariffs and was to some extent linked to it.

3. The Work of the National Assembly and the Crisis of the Revolution

The Central Authority: a Head without a Body

The election of the Imperial Administrator marked the first major achievement of the National Assembly. It was based on a compromise between the ideas of the various groupings with regard to a provisional central authority. The left wing favoured the election of one man to assume executive powers, the right wing a collegiate body; the left wing favoured the election of an MP by the National Assembly who in his turn would be responsible to Parliament, the right wing favoured an appointee of the sovereigns who would have no parliamentary responsibility.
In order to force a decision despite the differences of opinion, the President Heinrich von Gagern played a 'bold stroke': he proposed to the National Assembly the election of an Imperial

Administrator. Arch-Duke Johann was chosen, "not because but although he was sovereign". He was not responsible to the National Assembly and was accepted, following his election, by the state sovereigns. Thus he became the 'legitimate' successor of the Assembly of the Confederation, which handed over its powers to the Imperial Administrator. This compromise agreement with the old powers created additional problems for the National Assembly. At its head there was now a member of the Austrian Royal House. Thus, the whole question of the membership of the multi-national Austrian state to the future German nation state became more difficult to resolve.
Initially, however, great hopes were placed on the Imperial Administrator *(cat. illustr. 78).* In a declaration to the 'German People' he promised, "after years of pressure ... total freedom" and the completion of a constitution for German *(cat. illustr. 79).* Democratic associations appealed to the Imperial Administrator to respect the sovereignty of the people and to ensure that a future head of state be responsible to the people.
Soon, however, the weaknesses of the central administration became apparent. After the formation of the Imperial Ministry under Leiningen, an aristocrat and relation of the British monarchy, it was abvious that the bargaining position of the central administration was severely hampered by a weak organisational structure and difficulties over the sharing of power with the individual states. Without an army, a police force and a civil service, the central administration was dependent upon the political leaders of the individual states for the implementation of their decisions and they held discussions with these leaders in Frankfurt. In these negotiations international representation proved to be a controversial point. The states refused in part to place their armies under the command of a centralised leadership.
On the 6th August an appeal was made to the armies of all states that they should swear allegiance to the Imperial Administrator. Prussia and Austria agreed to this with some reservation.

The Debate on Basic Rights

The Paulskirche Assembly directed their first major efforts towards the drafting of a compulsory catalogue of human and citizens' rights following the example of the American and

French Revolutions. On the 3rd July 1848, after the establishment of the temporary central administration, the National Assembly declared that they would make a start on "the establishment of general rights which the constitution would grant to the German people... The task of drawing up a constitution to be carried out now will provide a lasting foundation for the unity and freedom of Germany and the welfare of the people".

The liberal middle class debated hard and long over freedoms which had finally been won. The discussion centred on a new social order and the founding of a German nation state with a democratic constitution.

The whole of Germany followed closely the debates in the Paulskirche. Many Germans tried to exert an influence on the establishment of fundamental citizens' rights by issuing pamphlets, signing petitions and making suggestions for change.

The National Assembly's decision to begin by discussing basic rights and to leave until later the remaining constitutional problems was a direct result of the MPs' experiences with the pre-March police system. Above all they were keen to secure the rights of the individual vis à vis the state. "We want to end the situation which has been caused by the police-state of the previous centuries. We wish to establish a constitutional state for Germany... We must end the tutelage system which imposes a burden on Germany from above".

The Basic Rights *(cat. illustr. X)* guaranteed a citizen's constitutional state. For the first time in German history a uniform 'national bill of rights' was established (§ 2). Class privileges were to be abolished by a system of general equality before the law. "The aristocracy as a privileged class no longer exists... Germans are equal in the eyes of the law" (§ 7).

Equality before the law, uniform civic rights and equal treatment of citizens by the authorities constituted the main features of the Basic Rights. Above all the Paulskirche Assembly was concerned about guaranteeing the rights of the individual vis à vis the state. "The freedom of the individual is inviolable" (§ 8). Every citizen had freedom of thought and conscience: "Every German has the right to express his opinion, be it verbally, in writing, in print or in picture" (§ 13). The freedom of association and assembly was guaranteed (§ 29, § 30) and especially the freedoms of learning and teaching (§ 22, § 23). The question of the church's separation from the state was keenly debated.

III/80 Prussian troops march into Schleswig on 23rd April.

III/81 Stormy debate in the Frankfurt National Assembly on 5th September 1848.

III/82 Prussian troops attack barricades in Frankfurt/Main on 18th September 1848.

Finally, the Basic Rights guaranteed the full authority of the citizen over his property: "Property is inviolable" (§ 32). All aristocratic privileges which still existed were abolished. On the one hand all taxes and produce-payments which were still in force were declared redeemable and on the other hand the propertyless dependents were granted free authority over their own work: „All bondes of dependency and serfdom will be broken for ever" (§ 34).
The Basic Rights aimed to make possible the free development of the individual by protecting his property and thus aimed also to free all the forces of the individual and make them subject to legal rules which would be generally applicable to all people. On the other hand, all social reform measures concerning the constitution guarantees for the individual were not approved by the majority of the MPs. Although the 'social question' had attracted most people's attention, because of the miserable plight of large numbers of the population, there was nothing in the Basic Rights about a social obligation to protect property or about demands for social security. On this point the document was criticised by workers' and artisans' associations and by committed democrats. The conflicts of interest on the social question, which were to be a great stumbling block for the Paulskirche document, were already becoming clear.

The Schleswig-Holstein Question

A significant crisis, which was to influence the fate of the National Assembly, occurred during the discussion on the Basic Rights. The Dukes of Schleswig and Holstein had joined the German Revolution and had revolted against their ruler, the Danish King, because he wanted to annex Schleswig, which unlike Holstein did not belong to the German Confederation, into the Danish nation state. The temporary revolutionary government of the Dukes sought military assistance from the Bundestag and received this under a Prussion commander.
The German nationalist movement took up the cause of the Schleswig-Holstein struggle with unparalleled enthusiasm and it became a focal point of aspirations for German unification and a matter of prestige for the National Assembly. The German troops pursued a successful campaign under their Prussian commander *(cat. illustr. 80)*. However, due to pressure

from abroad, notably from England and Russia, Prussia was forced to accept the cease-fire treaty of Malmö, the content of which imposed severe burdens on the inhabitants of Schleswig-Holstein. During the cease-fire negotiations the temporary Frankfurt central administration, the constitutional seccessor of the Bundestag, in whose name the war had been fought, was ignored by Prussia. Thus Prussia neglected the nationalist idea in favour of its own interests as a European power.

This first foreign policy crisis showed the problems facing the National Assembly which the latter had partly created for itself. The election of the Imperial Administrator had, for a short time, created the impression that power actually did reside with the new central administration. However, during the course of the disputes over Schleswig-Holstein there was a confrontation between the real power blocs. The moderate and radical MPs in the Paulskirche reacted differently and the fundamental differences between the various political groups became clearer than ever before.

The National Assembly had to come to a decision about the unauthorised behaviour of Prussia because not only the fate of Schleswig-Holstein was at stake over the question of acceptance or rejection of the cease-fire by the National Assembly but also the fate of the whole of Germany. Its acceptance meant a victory for Prussia over the national movement, the victory of a monarch over the pan-German parliament. Refusal would mean that National Assembly was determined to stand against Prussia and the European Powers and in so doing to prevent any possibility of reaching agreement with the German sovereigns. On the 5th September the National Assembly rejected the cease-fire, after the most turbulent debate since its inception, by 238 votes to 221 *(cat. illustr. 81).* This marked the first victory for the left in the Paulskirche. Many liberals supported the decision including the leading spokesman of the Schleswig-Holstein delegation, Dahlmann, who in his speech, said that the Parliament would lose face completely if it bowed to foreign pressure and betrayed the cause of the unification of Schleswig-Holstein with Germany. The Leinigen Ministry resigned after the vote. However, Dahlmann did not succeed, either in forming a new ministry or in taking up the demand of the left up the fight against Prussia.

The National Assembly became entrenched in powerless passivity. On the 16th September it eventually accepted the cease-

III/83 Prince Lichnowsky and General von Auerswald are murdered in Frankfurt/Main on 18th September 1848.

III/84 Gustav von Struve proclaims the German Republic from the town hall in Lorrach.

III/85 The Austrian War Minister, Latour, is murdered on 6th October 1848.

fire by 257 votes to 236. Many liberals, like Dahlmann, who had previously spoken out strongly against it, now voted in its favour. In this way the National Assembly surrendered its authority by now accepting Prussian policy. The Paulskirche finally allowed itself to become dependent on the sovereigns. Cartoonists saw in this decision the funeral of the 'seven-month child' of German unity.
The inability of the National Assembly to move the Prussian Government intro rejecting the cease-fire treaty was characteristic of its powerlessness in the face of the ruling forces. For the republicans this proved the futility of the moderate-liberal idea of persuading the sovereigns, through discussion, to renounce their control voluntarily in favour of a German nation state and a parliamentary system.

Rebellions against the National Assembly

Republicans and democrats now gained increasing support from the Frankfurt population. The advocates of the cease-fire were depicted as traitors whereas the republicans were increasingly seen as the proponents of the revolutionary national movement. Large gatherings of Worker and Democrat associations, at which red flags were beginning to outnumber the black-red-gold, demanded an en bloc walk-out from the Paulskirche by the entire left wing or else the dissolution of the National Assembly. The temporary central administration requested at the same time the protection of the National Assembly by Prussian and Austrian troops. The situation became more serious.
Animosity was directed principally at the Prussian troops which were now being deployed on the streets against the revolutionaries. Whilst the freedom of education was being debated in the Paulskirche street battles raged outside *(cat. illustr. XI)*.
After the murder of two right wing MPs, Lichnowsky and Auerswald, *(cat. illustr. 83)* the town was placed under a state of siege. The rebellion was defeated *(cat. illustr. 82)*.
After this military victory the central administration felt in a stronger position. It became increasingly closer allied to the old ruling powers and began to introduce counter-revolutionary measures. It planned to impose punishment for infringements

III/86 Shooting of Robert Blum by firing squad in the Brigittenau near Vienna on 9th November 1848.

III/87 Burning of the Vienna Library after the capturing of the town by troops from Windischgrätz.

of the 'Press Laws' directed against officials and public authorities and requested the states to submit exact "statistics of democratic associations and their branches which existed in Germany". Nevertheless, in the end, the main beneficiaries of the victory were not the central authorities but the old forces.

The Republic is proclaimed

The unrest in Frankfurt spread to mid and South-west German states. Everywhere social revolutionary and republic demands were now made which went beyond the aims of the majority in the National Assembly.
In Baden, where new financial laws and legal proceedings against those involved in the Spring uprisings had led to great unrest amongst the lower classes, Gustav von Struve attempted a putsch. His leaflets, after the acceptance of the Malmö ceasefire by the National Assembly, reflected the mood: "Triumph: The Frankfurt Parliament is exposed! There is no longer a German Parliament – just an enraged population face to face with a handful of scoundrels . . . The whole of Germany is rebelling against their Sovereigns and is fighting for the freedom of the people". Under the slogan of "prosperity, education, freedom for all" he proclaimed the "German Social Republic" on 21st September from the Lorrach town hall *(cat. illustr. 84).* Money was collected from the population covered by I.O.U.s to finance it. The monarchists were to be arrested, the wealth of the state, the church and the monarchs to be impounded and distributed to the local authorities *(cat. illustr. 85).* The uprising quickly spread to the uplands of Baden but was defeated on 26th September by superior Baden troops near Stauffen.

Reactionary Victory in Vienna

A new wave of unrest also broke out in the non-German parts of the Habsburg Empire, particularly in Hungary and Italy. The Hungarian Civil Defence Committee under Lajos Kossuth planned an offensive to aid the cause of independence. When, on 5th October, German and Italian troops based in Vienna were to be linked to the Imperial battalion to fight against the Hunga-

rians, open rebellion broke out in the Austrian capital. Students of the 'Academic Legion' joined forces with the civil militia and the workers and prevented the troops from leaving. This ministers and the Emperor fled the city and Vienna was in the hands of the revolutionaries.
The temporary central administration in Frankfurt despatched the liberal MP Welcker and Colonel Mosle to Austria as 'Imperial Commissars', with the task of "meeting all requirements for the ending of the civil war and the restoration of law and order and peace". However, they dared not enter Vienna and returned from the Imperial Headquarters without having achieved anything. Robert Blum on the other hand, left wing MP in the Paulskirche, fought with the revolutionaries on the barricades.
Field Marshall Prince Windischgrätz, the commander of the imperial troops, imposed a state of siege over Vienna. After just five days the city had been recaptured. The rebels offered bitter but vain resistance. Several thousand deaths and terrible destruction *(cat. illustr. 87)* were the cost of the victory of the monarchist reactionaries over the city. Robert Blum was shot by order of a court martial, with no consideration given to his immunity as an MP *(cat. illustr. 86).* The National Assembly protested only weakly. Prince Schwarzenberg, a strong proponent of the absolute monarchy and the pan-Austrian state, was appointed prime minister, the Reichstag was dissolved and a constitution was imposed. The Revolution had failed in Austria.

Counter Revolution in Berlin

Berlin was another centre of the second revolutionary wave. The event which sparked it off was the naming of Lieutenant General Brandenburg, a relative of the Royal House and a reactionary member of the 'Kamarilla', as prime minister. His task was to introduce the 'Counter Revolution'. Riots broke out in the city. Even the liberals were not prepared to accept this insult and the Prussian National Assembly rejected the crown ministry almost unanimously on 2nd November. They sent a deputation to inform the King of their decision but he would not allow them to speak to him *(cat. illustr. 89).* Against its will the Prussian National Assembly was displaced from Berlin to Brandenburg. Democratic and centre-left MPs who refused to

III/88 Civil militia shoots on revolutionary workers on 16th October 1848 in Berlin.

III/89 The Berlin civic guard is disarmed on 11th November 1848.

„Das ist immer das Unglück der Könige gewesen, daß sie die Wahrheit nicht hören wollen!“

Der König hat die mit Ueberreichung der bereits bekannten Adresse von der National-Versammlung beauftragte Deputation empfangen. Nach Verlesung derselben faltete der König die Adresse zusammen und wandte sich mit kurzer Verbeugung zum Fortgehen. Als nun der Präsident Unruh das Wort zu ergreifen zauderte, trat der Abgeordnete Jacobi vor und sprach dem, der Deputation in der Adresse ausdrücklich ertheilten Auftrage zufolge, die Worte:

„Majestät! Wir sind nicht blos hierher gesandt, um eine Adresse
„zu überreichen, sondern auch, um Ew. Majestät mündlich über
„die wahre Lage des Landes Auskunft zu geben. Gestatten Ew.
„Majestät daher —

hier unterbrach der König mit dem Worte:

„Nein!!“

Jacobi entgegnete:

„Das ist immer das Unglück der „Könige gewesen, daß sie die Wahr„heit nicht hören wollen!“

Der König entfernte sich.

Der Abgeordnete Jacobi hat sich hierdurch den Dank des gesammten Vaterlandes verdient. Möge er und seine Freunde in diesem hochwichtigen Augenblicke nicht nachlassen, die in Wien wie in Berlin bedrohte Sache des Volkes und der Wahrheit zu vertreten, dann werden alle ihm mit Gut und Blut zur Seite stehen, um endlich eine von Fürstenlaune unabhängige Grundlage der Volksfreiheit und des Volksglückes zu erlangen!

Berlin, den 3. November 1848.

Der democratische Club.

Druck von Ferd. Reichardt u. Co., Neue Friedrichs-Straße 24.

III/90 Pamphlet of the Democratic Club in Berlin, November 1848.

"It has always been the misfortune of kings that they are deaf to the truth!"

The King received the appointed delegation which delivered the already published message from the National Assembly. After having read it he folded it up and turned to leave with a curt bow. As President Unruh hesitated about speaking, M. P. Jacobi intervened and spoke the following words, as the message had expressly ordered to delegation to do:

"Your Majesty! We have not simply been sent here to deliver a message but also, your Majesty, to inform you verbally about the true state of the country. With your permission your Majesty therefore –"

Here the King interrupted with the word:

"No!!"

Jacobi retorted:

"It has always been the misfortune of kings that they are deaf to the truth!"

The King left.

Jacobi in this way portrayed the thoughts of the entire Fatherland. May he and his friends not give up their work, at this highly important stage, of representing the threatened interests of the people in Vienna and Berlin and the truth. If this be the case all men will stand firmly with them in order finally to achieve a basis for freedom and happiness of the people!

Berlin, 3rd November 1848
The Democratic Club

printed by Ferd. Reichardt & Co.
Neue Friedrich-Straße 24

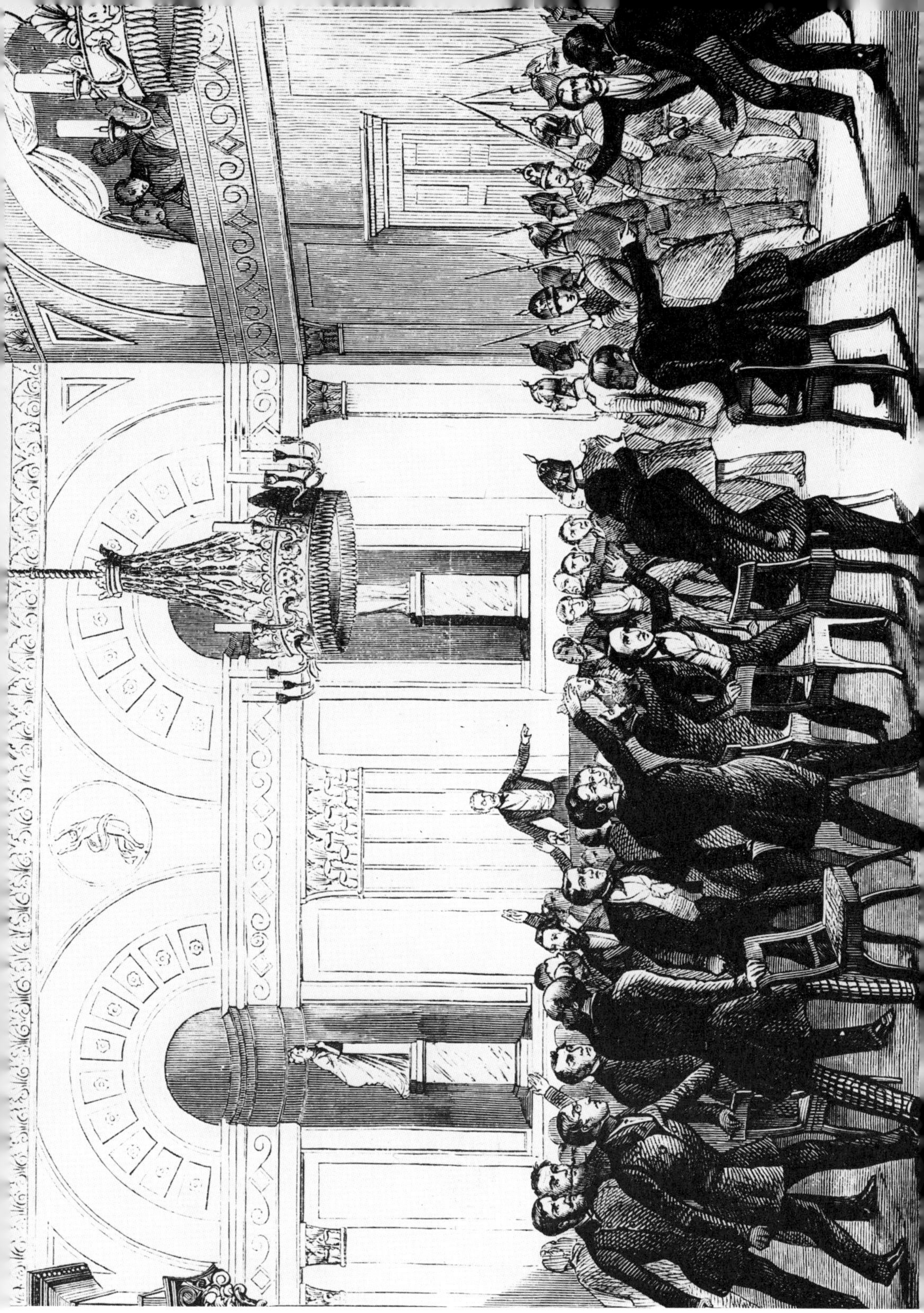

III/91 The dissolution of the Prussian National Assembly by force on 14th November 1848.

III/92 Medal commemorating the election of Frederick William IV of Prussia as 'German Emperor'.

III/93 Frederick William IV receives the 'Imperial deputation' of the National Assembly, 2nd April 1849.

acknowledge this displacement were banned from the inns where their groups met and finally they were dispersed by force of arms *(cat. illustr. 91).*
Although the 40,000 troops under General Wrangel, which marched into Berlin on 10th November, met no resistance, a state of siege was imposed on the city two days later on 12th November. It was not until this point that resistance grew amongst democratic groups in the city. The civil guard was called up to support the regulars. Thus the monarchy remained in control of the situation and eventually was in a position to be able to dissolve the National Assembly, which had been moved to Brandenburg, and to impose a constitution which appeased the liberal middle class by offering a series of concessions. However, even before this the breaking up of the revolutionary groups, which had been solidly united in March, had become apparent after the civil militia had fired on republican workers during the Spandau riots *(cat. illustr. 88).* In Berlin a brochure entitled 'Only soldiers help against democrats'. The majority of the liberal middle class acquisced and the monarchist counter revolution had also prevailed in Prussia.

4. The Failure of the Revolution

The Problem of National Unity

After the "second revolution" had been crushed, German unity became the object of a power game between Prussia, which had grown strong again, and Austria. Austria was concerned above all to extend its position as a great power. In line with Schwarzenberg's programme, the entire Habsburg monarchy was, together with all the German states, to form a Central European confederation of states, an empire with a population of seventy million. In contrast to this was the 'kleindeutsch' solution offered by the Prussians: a "kleindeutsch" confederation under Prussian leadership, which could later be extended to form a 'dual confederation' with Austria.
The majority of the National Assembly favoured the pan-German principle at the beginning of the debate in October 1848, which also formed the basis of the first draft constitution. The territory of the Empire should, according to the draft, include the areas of the German Confederation and, in addition, should

Mitbürger!

Der König und die Minister sind entflohen. Das Land ist ohne Regierung, sich selbst überlasse
worden. Die Reichsverfassung ist verleugnet.

Mitbürger! Das Vaterland ist in Gefahr! Es ist nothwendig geworden, eine provisorisch
Regierung zu bilden. Der Sicherheitsausschuß zu Dresden und die Abgeordneten des Volks habe
nun unterzeichnete Mitbürger zur provisorischen Regierung ernannt.

Die Stadt Dresden ist dem Vaterlande mit dem rühmlichsten Beispiele vorangegangen und ha
geschworen, mit der Reichsverfassung zu leben und zu sterben.

Wir stellen Sachsen unter den Schutz der Regierungen Deutschlands, welche die Reichsverfassun
anerkannt haben.

Zuzug von allen Ortschaften des Vaterlandes ist angeordnet und wird hiermit angeordnet.

Wir fordern den strengsten Gehorsam für die Befehle der provisorischen Regierung und des Ober
commandanten Oberstleutnant Heinze!

Wir werden Parlamentäre an die Truppen senden und sie auffordern, den Befehlen der proviso
rischen Regierung gleichfalls Gehorsam zu leisten. Auch sie bindet keine andere Pflicht, als die für di
bestehende Regierung, für die Einheit und Freiheit des deutschen Vaterlandes!

Mitbürger, die große Stunde der Entscheidung ist gekommen! Jetzt oder nie! Freiheit ode
Sklaverei! Wählt!

Wir stehen zu Euch, steht Ihr zu uns!

Dresden, den 4. Mai 1849.

Die provisorische Regierung.

Tzschirner. Heubner. Todt.

Fellow Citizens!

The King and his Ministers have fled The State is without government and left to its own devices.

Fellow citizens! The Fatherland is in danger! It has become necessary to form a temporary government. The security committee in Dresden and the peoples' representatives have named approved fellow citizens as members of the temporary government.

The town of Dresden has provided a glorious example for the Fatherland and has sworn to live or die by the Imperial Constitution.

We place Saxony under the protection of the governments of Germany, which have recognised the Imperial Constitution.

We hereby order the reinforcement of all districts of the Fatherland.

We demand the strictest obedience to the commands of the temporary government and of its supreme commander, lieutenant-colonel Heinze!

We shall send parliamentarians to the troops and order them also to swear obedience to the commands of the temporary government. They too are bound by no other duty than their allegiance to the existing government working for the unity and freedom of the German Fatherland!

Fellow citizens, the hour of decision has arrived! Now or never! Freedom or slavery! Make your choice!

We stand by you, stand by us!
Dresden, 4th May 1849
The temporary government
Tzschirner Heubner Todt

Ill/94 Proclamation of the temporary government of Saxony.

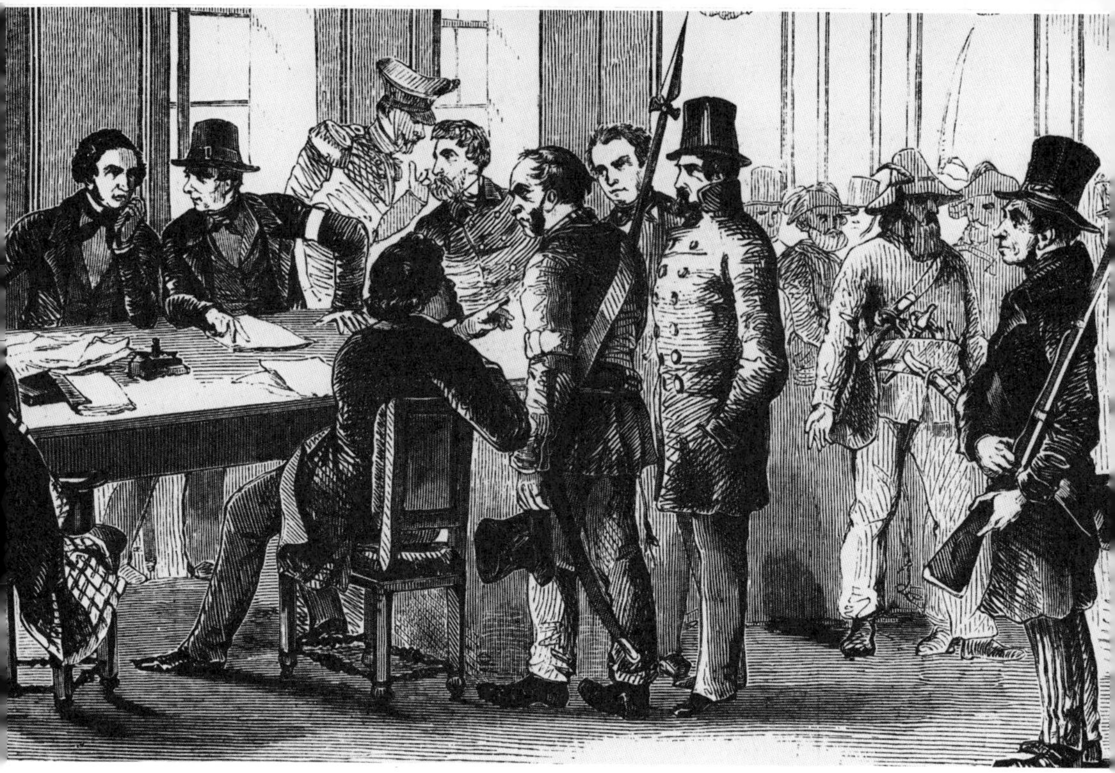

III/95 The temporary government of Saxony in the Dresden Town Hall, May 1849.

III/97 The outbreak of the Rastatt rebellion, 13th May 1849.

Die Landesversammlung in Offenburg

erklärt:

Deutschland befindet sich fortwährend im Zustand voller Revolution, aufs neue hervorgerufen durch die Angriffe der größeren deutschen Fürsten auf die von der deutschen Nationalversammlung endgültig beschlossenen Reichsverfassung und die Freiheit überhaupt. — Die deutschen Fürsten haben sich zur Unterdrückung der Freiheit verschworen und verbunden; der Hochverrath an Volk und Vaterland liegt offen zu Tage; es ist klar, daß sie sogar Rußlands sämmtliche Armeen zur Unterdrückung der Freiheit zu Hülfe rufen. — Die Deutschen befinden sich also im Stande der Nothwehr, sie müssen sich verbinden, um die Freiheit zu retten; sie müssen dem Angriff der fürstlichen Rebellen den bewaffneten Widerstand entgegensetzen.

Die deutschen Stämme haben die Verpflichtung, sich gegenseitig die Freiheit zu gewährleisten, um den Grundsatz der Volkssouveränität vollkommen durchzuführen; sie müssen daher unterstützen überall, wo sie angegriffen werden. —

Das badische Volk wird daher die Volksbewegung in der Pfalz mit allen ihm zu Gebote stehenden Mitteln unterstützen.

Die Landesversammlung des badischen Volkes in Offenburg hat nach vorhergegangener Berathung die gestellten Anträge in dem Landeskongresse der Volksvereine, nach ferner stattgefundener öffentlicher Berathung, wobei Abgeordnete aus allen Landestheilen vertreten waren, nach fernerer ausführlicher Diskussion in der Versammlung des Volkes

beschlossen:

1) Die Regierung muß die Reichsverfassung, wie sie nun nach der durch die Ereignisse beseitigten Oberhauptsfrage feststeht, unbedingt anerkennen und mit der ganzen bewaffneten Macht, deren Durchführung in andern deutschen Staaten zunächst in der baierischen Pfalz unterstützen.
2) Das gegenwärtige Ministerium ist sofort zu entlassen, und Bürger Brentano, Obergerichtsadvokat zu Mannheim, und Bürger Peter, Reichstagsabgeordneter von Konstanz mit der Bildung eines neuen Ministeriums zu beauftragen.
3) Es muß alsbald unter sofortiger Auflösung der jetzigen Ständekammern eine verfassungsgebende Landesversammlung berufen werden, welche in sich die gesammte Rechts- und Machtvollkommenheit des badischen Volkes vereinigt; — diese Landesversammlung soll gewählt werden von und aus den sämmtlichen volljährigen Staatsbürgern des Landes und zwar unter Beibehaltung der für die bisherige II. Kammer beanstandenen Wahlbezirke.
4) Es muß ohne allen Verzug die Volksbewaffnung auf Staatskosten in's Leben gerufen werden, und es sind alle ledigen Männer von 18—30 Jahren als erstes Aufgebot sofort mobil zu machen. — Alle diejenigen Gemeindebehörden, welche nicht alsbald die Bewaffnung ihrer Bürger anordnen, sind augenblicklich abzusetzen.
5) Die politischen Flüchtlinge sind sofort zurück zu rufen, die politischen Militär- und Civilgefangenen zu entlassen und alle politischen Prozesse nieder zu schlagen; — namentlich verlangen wir aber auch die Entlassung derjenigen Militärgefangenen, welche in Folge der politischen Bewegungen wegen sogenannter Disciplinar- und Insubordinationsvergehen bestraft wurden. —
6) Die Militärgerichtsbarkeit muß aufgehoben werden. —
7) Bei dem Heere soll eine freie Wahl der Offiziere stattfinden.
8) Wir verlangen alsbaldige Verschmelzung des stehenden Heeres mit der Volkswehr.
9) Es müssen sämmtliche Grundlasten unentgeldlich aufgehoben werden.
10) Es müssen die Gemeinden unbedingt selbständig erklärt werden, sowohl was die Verwaltung des Gemeindevermögens, als die Wahl der Gemeindevertreter betrifft; es müssen alsbald im ganzen Lande neue Wahlen für die Gemeindevertretung stattfinden.
11) Es werden sämmtliche von den s. g. Kammern in Karlsruhe seit dem 17. Januar d. J. gefaßten Beschlüsse für null und nichtig erklärt und darunter namentlich das s. g. Wahlgesetz vom 10. v. M., welches einen förmlichen Angriff auf die in den Reichsgesetzen gegebenen Bestimmungen enthält.
12) Die Geschwornengerichte sind augenblicklich einzuführen und kein einziger Criminal-Prozeß darf mehr von Staatsrichtern entschieden werden.
13) Die alte Verwaltungsbüreaukratie muß abgeschafft werden und an ihre Stelle die freie Verwaltung der Gemeinden oder andern Körperschaften treten.
14) Errichtung einer Nationalbank für Gewerbe, Handel und Ackerbau zum Schutze gegen das Uebergewicht der großen Kapitalisten.
15) Abschaffung des alten Steuerwesens, hierfür Einführung einer progressiven Einkommensteuer nebst Beibehaltung der Zölle.
16) Errichtung eines großen Landespensionsfonds, aus dem jeder arbeitsunfähig gewordene Bürger unterstützt werden kann. — Hierdurch fällt der besondere Pensionsfond für die Staatsdiener von selbst weg. Der Landesausschuß der Volksvereine besteht aus folgenden Mitgliedern:

L. Brentano von Mannheim.
J. Fickler von Konstanz.
A. Goeg von Mannheim.
Peter von Konstanz.
Werner von Oberkirch.
Rehmann von Offenburg.
Stay von Heidelberg.
Willmann von Pfohren.
K. Steinmetz von Durlach.
Wernwag von Kenzingen.
Richter von Achern.
Degen von Mannheim.
K. Ritter von Karsau, } Soldaten aus der Garnison
J. Stark von Lottstetten, } in Rastatt.

Als Ersatzmänner wurden gewählt:

H. Hoff von Mannheim.
Torrent von Freiburg.
K. Rotteck von Freiburg.
Happel von Mannheim.
Junghanns von Mosbach.
Kiefer von Emmendingen.

Ersatzmänner der Soldaten:

Aurelius Cordel aus Philippsburg.
Sebastian Bannwarth aus Bleichheim, Amts Kenzingen.

Derselbe wird beauftragt, die nöthigen Anordnungen zur Durchführung dieser Beschlüsse mit allen ihm zu Gebote stehenden Mittel zu treffen, und von dem Ergebniß der heutigen Volksversammlung dem Landesausschuß in Rheinbaiern, sowie den Landesausschüssen der übrigen Nachbarstaaten sofort Nachricht zu geben.

Offenburg, den 13. Mai 1849.

Im Namen der Landes-Volksversammlung.
Goegg.

* Der Landes-Ausschuß hat sich in zahlreicher Begleitung von Offenburg nach der Festung Rastatt begeben, wo er vorerst inmitten der Bürgerschaft und der braven 6000 Mann starken Besatzung in Permanenz berathet. Heute (14. Mai) Nacht 3 Uhr trafen die befreiten Bürger Struve, Blind, Bornstedt nebst den gleichfalls vom Volke aus den Bruchsaler Kerkern befreiten Soldaten in Rastatt ein.

The State Assembly in Offenburg

Declares:

Germany is in the throes of continual revolution which has been given fresh impetus by the attacks made by the larger German monarchs against the Imperial Constitution, which has been finally ratified by the German National Assembly, and against freedom itself. The German sovereigns have shown their determination to repress freedom and their betrayal of the people and the Fatherland is plain for all to see. It is clear that they are even prepared to request the assistance of Russia's various armies to aid them in their task – thus Germans find themselves with no alternative but to defend themselves, they must join together to save freedom. They must meet the monarchist rebels with armed resistance. It is the duty of German families to stand on the side of freedom in order to give complete reality to the principle of sovereignty of the people. They must assist one another whenever they are attacked.

Therefore the people of Baden will support the people's movement in the Palatinate with all availabove resources.

The State Assembly of the people of Baden in Offenburg has issued the following motion (to the State Congress of people's associations) after consultation with them and after further public consultation, when representatives from all areas of the state were present and after detailed discussion in the people's Assembly.

1. The Government must recognise the Imperial Constitution in the same way that it now stands by the outcome of the question of the head of state, which has been settled by events. The Government must offer all possible military support to ensure the constitution's acceptance in other German states and firstly in the Palatinate.

2. The present cabinet must be removed from office immediately and citizen Brentano, su-

III/96 Decrees of the Offenburg State Assembly.

preme court barrister in Mannheim and citizen Peter, Reichstag representative from Constance, are to be charged with the formation of a new cabinet.

3. Following the immediate dissolution of the class based Chamber a new constituent State Assembly will be set up as soon as possible, which will have full legal authority over the people of Baden. The State Assembly will be elected by and from the ranks of the adult state citizens under the same system of electoral districts which has hitherto operated for elections to the Second Chamber.

4. Without any delay the people must be armed at the state's expense and all single men between 18–30 must be conscripted and mobilised firstly. Any local authorities who do not order the arming of their citizens at the first opportunity are to be disbanded temporarily.

5. Political refugees are to be granted an immediate pardon. Political internees, both military and civilian, are to be released and all political trials are to be halted. We specifically demand the freeing of those military prisoners who were punished following the actions of the political movements, for disciplinary reasons or for insubordination.

6. The work of the military court must cease.

7. In the army there should be a free election of officers.

8. We demand the fusion of the standing army with the people's army at the earliest possible date.

9. Various property charges must be abolished gratuitously.

10. It must be explained to the local authorities what exactly both the administration of local affairs and the election of local representatives involves. Throughout the state there must be fresh elections for local representatives at the earliest possible moment.

11. Various decrees, which have been made by the so-called Chambers in Karlsruhe since the 17th January, are declared null and void, particularly the so-called electoral law of 10th May which is in direct violation of the outlines given in the Imperial laws.

12. For the meantime trial by jury is introduced and no criminal trial may be considered by state judges.

13. The old administrative bureaucracy must be abolished and in its place free local administration or some other appropriate system must be introduced.

14. A National Bank for business, trade and agriculture must be set up to counteract the predominant position of the large capitalists.

15. The old tax system will be abolished and replaced by a progressive income tax, the customs duties being retained.

16. A pension fund will be established from which all citizens incapable of working can be supported – in this way the special pension fund for state employees becomes irrelevant. The state committee of the People's Associations consists of the following members:

L. Brentano of Mannheim
J. Fickler of Constance
A. Goeg of Mannheim
Peter of Constance
Werner of Oberkirch
Rehmann of Offenburg
Stau of Heidelberg
Willman of Pfehren
K. Steinmetz of Durlach
Bernwag of Kenzingen
Richter of Archen
Degen of Mannheim
N. Ritter of Karsau } soldiers from the
J. Stark of Lottstetten } garrison of Rastatt

As substitutes the following were elected:

H. Hoff of Mannheim
Lorrent of Freiburg
N. Rotteck of Freiburg
Happel of Mannheim
Junghaus of Mosbach
Kiefer of Emmendingen

substitute soldiers:

Aurelius Cordel from Philippsburg
Sebastian Bannwarth from Bleichheim, stationed in Kenzingen.

The above committee are charged with the task of giving the necessary orders for the implementation of these decrees, using all means available to them and of informing the state committee in Rheinbaiern and the state committees of other neighbouring states immediately of the outcome of today's people's assembly.

Offenburg, 13th May 1849
In the name of the State-People's Assembly
Goegg

* The State Committee together with many others set off from Offenburg to the fortress at Rastatt, where it first of all addressed the citizens present and the brave 6,000 man strong garrison. Today (14th May) at 3 o'clock in the morning the freed citizens Struve, Blind, Bornstedt met with the soldiers, who had been likewise freed from the prison in Bruchsal by the people, in Rastatt.

incorporate the Duchy of Schleswig and the Prussian Eastern provinces, but not the non-German-speaking nationalities of the Habsburg monarchy. It became increasingly obvious that Austria was not willing to sacrifice her unity to a German nation-state. Therefore, Heinrich von Gagern, the new prime minister of the temporary central administration, eventually found a majority for his little-German programme.

In the debate on who should be the head of state in the Empire, the little-German party expressed its support for an hereditary Prussian Emperor. On the other hand contradictory plans were offered by pan-German side and its political groupings: they ranged from a dynastic imperial directorate to a united democratic republic.

The action taken by Austria, which, in March 1849, rejected the National Assembly and the adoption of a centralist constitution for the Habsburg Empire, destroyed once and for all any hopes of a "grossdeutsch" empire being established. Many advocates of the "grossdeutsch" solution joined the group led by Heinrich von Gagern which supported the "kleindeutsch" solution. The democratic Left was persuaded to support the "kleindeutsch" solution when general, equal and direct elections by secret ballot were introduced. On 28th March the National Assembly elected the Prussian King "Emperor of the Germans".

The Reich Constitution

In a phase of extreme tension, the National Assembly, whose freedom of manoeuvre had already been curtailed substantially, tackled the most delicate part of its work in October 1848: the institutional part of the constitution. The decisions taken on the size of the future empire and on the monarch at its head clearly reflected the influence of Austrian and Prussian power politics. Still, on 27th March 1849 the National Assembly succeeded, in what appeared to be a sovereign act, in adopting the Reich constitution.

To begin with, a constitutional committee comprising thirty members, among them those who had been the leading Liberals in the period prior to March 1848, was charged with drawing up a new constitution. The draft which it presented was fully in line with the ideas of the "Casino-Fraktion" and thus of the

IX Barricade in Neue Königsstrasse in Berlin, 19th March 1848.

X The Basic Rights of the German People, lithography by Adolf Schroedter, Mainz 1848.

Das merkwürdige Jahr 1848. — Eine neue Bilderzeitung. — 37stes Bild.

Wüthender Angriff der Republikaner
[a]uf das in der Paulskirche zu Frankfurt versammelte
deutsche National-Parlament, am 18. September 1848.

Was woget und brauset so dumpf heran,
Erfüllt mit Gebrülle die Straßen?
Es ist der Pöbel im tollen Wahn,
Er wüthet über die Maßen.

Warum wogt und braus't er so dumpf heran,
Erfüllt mit Morden die Straßen?
Er will sie morden Mann für Mann,
Die vom Recht sich nicht abbringen lassen.

Wer hat sie getrieben so toll heran,
Zu erfüllen mit Morden die Straßen?
Die Republikaner im irren Wahn,
Sie können die Ruhe nur hassen.

Die Abgeordneten Preußens für die deutsche National-Versammlung hatten sich ermannt, hatten für [Waf]fenstillstand mit Dänemark, für Ruhe und Frieden in ihrem Lande und in ganz Deutschland, für [un]d Ordnung gesprochen und der Fürst Lichnowsky und General v. Auerswald sich besonders [ausgezeich]net; und der größte Theil der Versammlung war auf ihre Seite getreten. Das hatte nun die Re[publikaner], deren Dichten und Trachten nur darauf geht, durch eine allgemeine Revolution alles von Unterst [zu Oberst] zu kehren, alles Bestehende zu vernichten und sich selbst zur Herrschaft zu bringen, aufs Höchste [erbittert]. Sie hetzten das Volk in großen Volksversammlungen auf, machten Verschwörungen und beschlossen [du]rch ihre angeworbenen Haufen die National-Versammlung in der Paulskirche aus einander zu jagen [und die], welche für die gute Sache gestimmt hatten, umzubringen. Sie setzten dies am 18. September in's [Werk. To]bende Haufen umlagerten die Paulskirche und wollten hineindringen, wurden aber durch das Militair vertrieben. Nun vertheilten sie sich in die Straßen, bauen Barrikaden und schießen aus den Fenstern der Häuser. Das Militair wird nun kommandirt, die Barrikaden zu nehmen, die Anführer zu vertreiben. Und sie rücken vor, die Oesterreicher treu, die Hessendarmstädter muthig und gewandt und die Preußen sicher, rasch und ohne Besinnen. Die Barrikaden werden überwältigt, das Feuer aus den Häusern gedämpft. Es war eine Freude, Offiziere und Mannschaft so vieler Stämme wie eine lebendige, muthvolle Mauer für die National-Versammlung des deutschen Reichs in den Tod gehen zu sehen. Das Gefecht entschied sich unaufhörlich zu Gunsten der Truppen. Aus der Umgegend waren schnell 6 — 7000 Mann versammelt. 12 Geschütze mit Kartätschen und Kavallerieangriffe bereiteten dem frevelhaften Aufruhr raschen Untergang. Abends 8 Uhr war der Sieg entschieden.

[...]u. Eigenthum No. 2108.

Neu-Ruppin, zu haben bei Gustav Kühn.

XI Street battles in front of the Paulskirche, 18th September 1848.

bourgeois-Liberal majority in the National Assembly. It was only in the winter of 1848/49, in the course of the struggle between the supporters of the "kleindeutsch" and the "grossdeutsch" solutions, that different parliamentary majorities emerged, which led to compromises being concluded also with the democratic Left.

All in all, the constitution represented a balanced compromise which has continued to inspire German constitutional developments. It was characterized above all by the ideas of the bourgeois-Liberal majority in the Frankfurt Parliament, providing for a federal state with a bicameral system and a hereditary monarch. As a result of concessions made to the Left, however, the monarch was granted only limited powers and universal, equal suffrage was introduced.

In March 1848 the Prussian King, Frederick William IV, had aroused liberal and national hopes with his slogan "Prussia will in future be an integral part of Germany". The party supporting the "kleindeutsch" solution believed that, with the constitution adopted by the Paulskirche, these hopes would now be fulfilled. On 28th March 1849 the National Assembly elected the Prussian King "Emperor of the Germans" *(cat. illustr. 91).* The delegation of the National Assembly headed by its President, Eduard von Simson, went to see the Prussian King to inform him of the result of the election *(cat. illustr. 92).* However, Frederick William IV insisted on the divine right of kings and categorically refused to be made Emperor by the people in a democratic election: German unity was not to be the result of a popularly elected, sovereign National Assembly, but was to be accomplished solely through "agreements" with the other princes. In a letter to Bunsen the King declared in December 1848: "A legitimate king by divine right and in this case even the King of Prussia, who may not be blessed with the oldest but with the noblest crown, which has not been stolen from anyone, is now expected to accept such an imaginary coronet made of mud and clay... Let me tell you bluntly: If the crown of the German nation, which is a thousand years old and has been suspended for 42 years, should ever be proffered again, this will be done by myself and by my peers; and woe betide anyone who arrogates to himself a right to which he is not entitled."

The fact that the Prussian King rejected the imperial crown meant that the constitution adopted by the Paulskirche had failed *(cat. illustr. 93).*

XII (illustr. left) Battle near Waghäusel, 22nd June 1849 between revolutionary and Prussian troops.

The Struggle for the Imperial Constitution

"The hour has come, since it will be decided whether Germany will be free and strong or subservient and scorned. The representatives of the German nation, elected by you and all citizens, have passed the Imperial Constitution for the whole of Germany and have proclaimed it as inviolable. The whole nation is completely resolved to implement the Imperial Constitution... The bigger sovereigns and their cabinets refuse to obey the principles of the Imperial Constitution. They are rebels acting against the will and the laws of the nation".
With these words the Congress of various March-associations called for the acceptance of the Imperial Constitution on 6th May 1849, which had been rejected by the larger states, notably Prussia, Saxony and Bavaria. Throughout Germany worker, people's and fatherland associations tried to exert pressure on their governments by organising petitions, press-campaigns and street meetings. They appealed to the 'holy right of the Revolution'. Everything that had been achieved by the middle class democratic revolution in Germany was now being questioned by this rejection by the monarchist governments. The resolutions being made stressed ever more clearly that the Constitution should be protected by force if necessary. Thus on 8th May Heidelberg citizens declared openly and solemnly that "at our own instigation and free will, we are prepared to protect and defend the German Imperial Constitution, together with the basic rigths and the electoral laws, which have been drawn up and proclaimed by the Constituent National Assembly in Frankfurt am Main, with our lives and property". In Saxony, in the Rhineland, in the Palatinate region and in Baden the unrest spilled over into open rebellion.
In Dresden the Committee of the 'Fatherland Associtation' called for an armed demonstration: "Hurry swiftly with weapons and ammunition! Now is the time!" During the afternoon of the 3rd May the people stormed the armoury. The King fled and a temporary government was installed *(cat. illustr. 93)*. For a short time sovereignty of the people became a reality.
In the old town barricades were erected against the Saxony forces and the approaching Prussian troops. However, the fight was restricted to Dresden and the proclaiming of the temporary government had no repercussions *(cat. illustr. 94)*. In the face of the opponents' superiority the revolutionary front in the

III/98 “Reprieved by powder and lead”.

III/99 The reactionary victory in Europe, 1849, sketch by F. Schroeder in the 'Düsseldorf Monthly'.

besieged town collapsed. The civil militia withdrew from the barricades and those who continued the fight – amongst them the Russian anarchist Michail Bakunin and Richard Wagner – surrendered after a six day struggle to the troops which had been brought in from Prussia.

Despite the defeat in Saxony revolts broke out in the Palatinate and Baden. The citizens of the Palatinate were, in addition, fighting for their independce from Bavaria. Democratic-republican ideas dominated this civil war. On 17th May the Palatinate broke away from Bavaria.

In Baden on 13th May a People's State Assembly in Offenburg, at which 35,000 people were present, declared: "The German monarchs have declared their determination to repress freedom and joined forces in pursuit of this end; their betrayal of the people and the Fatherland is plain for all to see... The people of Baden will therefore support the people's movement in the Palatinate with all available resources." Indeed the Baden government accepted the constitution but the Baden republicans wanted more; apart from the constitutional-monarchist solution they demanded the setting up of a republic and democratic and social reforms, the free election of officers, the gratuitous removal of various property taxes, protection against the predominant position of capitalists and state unemployment benefits *(cat. illustr. 96).*

Between 10th and 12th May, the Baden military forces mutinied in the most important fortresses of the state *(cat. illustr. 97).* The troops' rebellion against their officers incited the democratic people's movement to open revolt. Conditions were favourable for the revolution and the last hopes of all democrats in Germany resided here. Companies of gymnasts and riflemen, workers' batallions, Polish and Hungarian legions all moved into Baden to offer their support. The Prussion military and troops of the Imperial Administrator under the command of the Prince of Prussia, who was later to become Kaiser Wilhelm I, intervened. The uprising in Baden and the Palatinate was defeated after a battle lasting almost two months *(cat. illustr. XII).*

Stamina, tenacity and the courage of the people's army could not counteract their growing military disorganisation. The temporary government itself in Baden, under the leadership of the hesitant Lorenz Brentano, prevented a powerful advance. Firstly they failed to provide serious military support for the

III/100 Trial by Jury of Johann Jacoby, December 1850.

III/101 Emigrants' ship, 1850.

poorly armed Palatinate rebels and then they outlawed the radicaldemocratic opposition which was grouped together in the 'Club of resolute progress'. In particular, however, they were opposed to a spreading of the struggle to other German states.
Even the left wing in the Frankfurt Paulskirche were not able to assert their leadership over the movement after the liberal and conservative representatives had left the Assembly, leaving the implementation of the Imperial Constitution in the "hands of the nation itself".
Rastatt, the last remaining stronghold of the revolutionaries, and the place where the uprising had begun, fell on 23rd Juli 1849. The Prussian military courts sat in Baden until the end of October 1849; the outcome was court-material firing squads, prison sentences and terms of hard labour *(cat. illustr. 98).* 80,000 wanted people, about 6 per cent of the population of Baden, emigrated.
By Autumn 1849, the liberal and democratic movement in France, Italy, Hungary and Germany had been defeated.

The Reaction in the 1850s

The Revolution failed. It failed because of the opposition of the old ruling forces and the armies loyal to the monarchy and because of the opposition of the bureaucray. However, it also failed because of growing antagonisms in its own camp. The middle class liberals recoiled before the radical political demands of the republicans and the committed democrats. In addition, there was the conflict between property-owners and the propertyless which intensified continuously during the early days of the industrial revolution.
With the onest of reaction in all German states liberal ministries were replaced by conservative ones. Many parliaments were dissolved and the constitutions revised. The monarchs ruled once again without any real control being exercised by the people.
The Prussian government introduced the three class voting system. Under this system the voters were divided into three categories according to the amount of tax they paid: the minority category of high wage earners, which formed the first class (4% of the population) were able to elect just as many can-

didates and representatives as the largest category of low wage earners (80% of the population). Moreover, by making the election public the dependent voters could be controlled.
Freedoms of opinion and the press were restricted by censorship and police surveillance. In 1851 the German Confederation repealed the 'Basic Rights of the German People'. It had been reintroduced by Austria and Prussia, the major proponents of reaction, as an instrument of oppression *(cat. illustr. 99)*.
At the same time that the last national uprisings in multinational Austria were being squashed, reaction triumphed everywhere under the leadership of the German Confederation. Liberals, democrats and social revolutionaries were arrested and sentenced to long terms of imprisonment *(cat. illustr. 100)*. All 'suspicious' political associations were banned.
Mass emigrations to Switzerland, England and the United States occurred as a direct consequence of the oppression *(cat. illustr. 101)*. The attempt by the German people to set up a democratic Empire had failed.

The German Empire 1871 – 1918

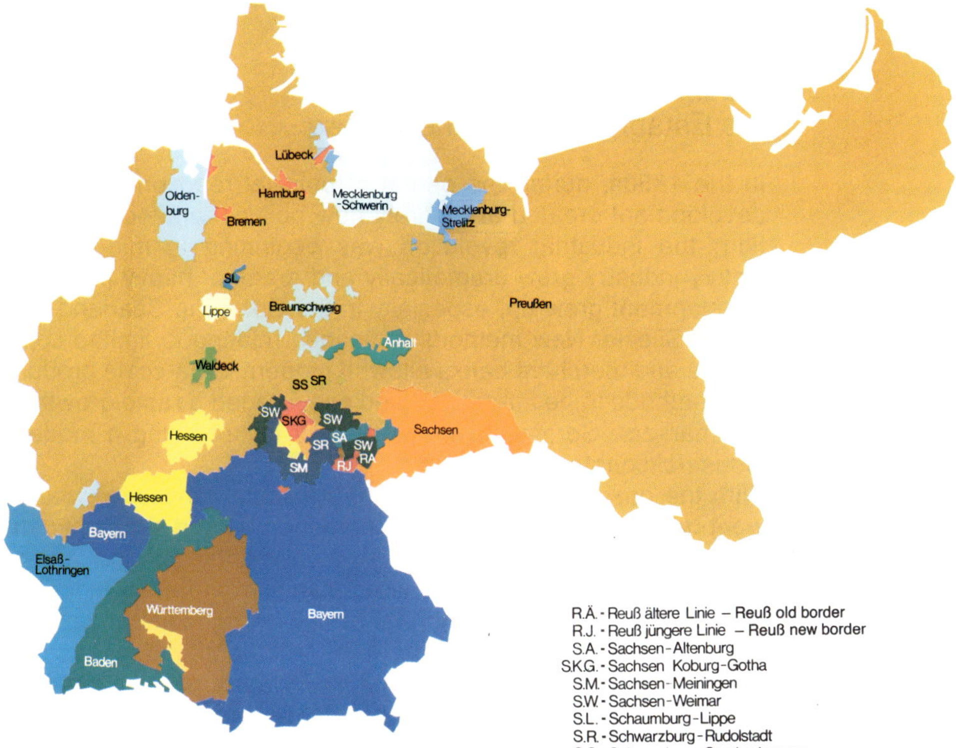

R.Ä. - Reuß ältere Linie – **Reuß old border**
R.J. - Reuß jüngere Linie – **Reuß new border**
S.A. - Sachsen-Altenburg
S.K.G. - Sachsen Koburg-Gotha
S.M. - Sachsen-Meiningen
S.W. - Sachsen-Weimar
S.L. - Schaumburg-Lippe
S.R. - Schwarzburg-Rudolstadt
S.S. - Schwarzburg-Sondershausen

Room IV

Industrial Revolution and the Establishment of the Empire – Imperial Germany

Industrial Revolution and the Establishment of the Empire

In the 1850s, during the period of political reaction, economic development created an entirely new political and social situation: the industrial revolution was beginning in mid-Europe. Heavy industry grew dramatically and areas of heavy industrial development grew up, especially in the Ruhr, the Saarland and Upper Silesia. New methods of finance relating to limited companies and merchant banks allowed modern large-scale production methods to be introduced and encouraged a rapid growth of the markets. Germany was on its way to becoming a modern industrial country.

With the onset of industrialisation, the social landscape underwent basic changes. Parallel to a prosperous and self-confident industrial middle class there arose a constantly growing industrial proletariat which was recruited mainly from former independent tradesmen and from the large flow of agricultural workers coming into the large towns. The latter's situation became increasingly serious because of a lowering of real wages. The workers often lived in appalling conditions and their wages were usually barely on the bread line. Self-help associations, like consumer organisations, health insurance schemes and mutual loan societies, tried to alleviate the worst problems. Charitable organisations, such as the Kolping associations, also operated with the same aim in mind. However, all these institutions did not question the existing economic and social order. In contrast, socialism sought radical solutions and called for the overthrow of the capitalist system by the workers. It found its leading theoretician in Karl Marx.

The heartland of industrial development was Prussia, which as the strongest power in the customs union, gained increasing economic influence within Germany. In this way its political position vis à vis Austria was also strengthened. Moreover, of great significance for further political development was the fact that, even in the years of reaction, the economic policy of Prussia benefitted large sections of the middle class.

After 1858 there also seemed to be a chance that the Prussian state would be sympathetic to the political aims of the liberal middle class.

Many people saw the accession to government of the Prince

Regent Wilhelm, who formed a liberal-conservative cabinet and in an inaugural speech to the state cabinet announced far-reaching reforms, as the beginning of a 'new era'. This accession was a great incentive to political liberalism throughout Germany. There was hope that the promised reforms would be carried out and additionally that the unification of the nation would be achieved under the leadership of liberal Prussia.

Encouraged by the developments in Prussia, and spurred on by Italian unification, liberals and democrats now formed the National Association. It readopted the little German idea, which had failed in 1849, of national unity with a parliamentary system under Prussian leadership. In 1861 the "Executive of the National Association" was established with the Progress Party: a party alliance of committed liberals and democrats whose leaders belonged to the National Association. The Progress Party had the same aims in Prussia as the National Association. Instead of cooperating with the liberals, as was the case in other German states, there were soon fundamental disputes between the executive and the Parliament on the question of army reforms, which developed into a constitutional conflict. The Progress Party saw this as a decisive test of power against the conservative-monarchist state and with the "junkerdom and their absolutist tendencies". However, this test of power could not be resolved. With Bismarck, who was appointed as Prussian prime minister in 1862, the great opponent of the liberal movement entered the political stage. By 1848 he had already become wellknown as an ultra-conservative Junker and now he steered a tough anti-parliamentary course and ruled unconstitutionally with a budget which had been passed without consulting the people's representation. In the end the Progress Party was powerless against him. The conservative attitude of the state population and the common interest of large sections of the porperty owning middle classes with the Prussian state forced the Progress Party to turn away from any revolutionary action. Therefore, they opposed against a background "where the property owning classes are still not against us".

This attitude was one of the reasons why the workers turned away from the Progress Party. With the establishment of the General Association of German Workers by Lassalle in 1863 the Progress Party only had the middle class to fall back on as a reservoir of electoral support, having originally seen itself as the focal point for all liberal and democratic support. Middle and

working class democratic ideas went their own ways from this time on.
Whilst the opposition front was crumbling Bismarck was continually winning new successes in his foreign policy. In the conflict over Schleswig-Holstein, in which all national forces, whether pan German or little German, were passionately involved, Prussia assumed the leadership role and forced Austria to fight on its side. After the victory over Denmark the Duchies were placed under the administration of the two leading powers in the war. Prussia, however, pressed for annexation of the Duchies and the conflict with Austria eventually escalated into a war. With Prussia's victory the fight for supremacy in Germany had finally swung in her favour. The German Confederation was dissolved and the way lay open towards the little German solution of the national question under the leadership of conservative Prussia.
Success in foreign policy also brought domestic successes for Bismarck. A section of the liberals now supported his power politics (Machtpolitik) because in this way – although it ran contrary to all liberal traditions – he gave them hope of achieving a German nation-states.
Whilst the left wing of the Progress Party stood firmly by their views on freedom and thus rejected the Prussian claims to national leadership, "as long as Prussia has not achieved internal freedom" (Waldeck), other liberals believed that conditions in Prussia could only be liberalised after German unification. "Without a reshaping of German conditions . . . there is absolutely no long term possibility of achieving a decent and free constitution in Prussia" (Forckenbeck).
The North German Confederation, the first stage of German unity, extended the Prussian sphere of influence as far as the Main. The representatives of the Reichstag were elected by a general, secret, equal and direct voting system but even so, the powers of the Parliament were limited. Bismarck as Chancellor was responsible solely to the King of Prussia as the head of state, but not to Parliament.
The Constitution of the North German Confederation made provisions for a possible unification with the South German states. In addition, the South German states were linked to the North German Confederation by military alliances. Another link was achieved by the founding of the Customs Parliament of the German customs union, to which representatives from all German states were elected. However, initially, Bismarck did not,

for foreign policy reasons, yield to the national liberals' pressure, which urged him to complete the process of political unification. Above all, he feared any intervention by France, the latter being concerned that the Prussian victory over Austria threatened her supremacy in Europe. The growing tension between Prussia and France, which was augmented by the complexities of the Hohenzollern succession-candidacy, eventually led to a French declaration of war. This sparked off a wave of national indignation. The military pacts between the German states were activated and were cemented during the war, following diplomatic negotiations, by the conclusion of something approaching international treaties between the German monarchs and governments. After the military defeat of France and the collapse of the French Empire on 18th January 1871 in the Hall of Mirrors in Versailles, the founding of the German Empire was completed from above by the conservative Prussian state and the monarchs in an imperial and military ceremony.

The Industrial Revolution – Social and Political Consequences (Board 1–40)

Board 1

At the start of the 1850s the real 'industrial revolution' began in Germany, linked with a general worldwide economic upturn. The first major areas of development were railway construction and heavy industry *(cat. illustr. XIII and 102).* The major development was in railway construction and the network increased rapidly: around 1845 it had 3,280 kms of track, in 1860 it was 11,633 kms and in 1870 19,575 kms. In the peak period of the 1860s the railway companies were paying out dividends of between 10 and 20%. At the same time the production of steam engines and machine tools was increasing *(cat. illustr. 103).* Cheap labour was recruited from the declining artisan sectors, especially from the eastern German agricultural proletariat and these people poured into the industrial centres. Limited companies and large banks provided the necessary capital. The 'Industrial Revolution' was accompanied by a new, self-confident, economically powerful and often unpolitical upper middle class.

In addition, the process of unification favoured the economic upturn. However, the boom of the 'early years' was soon followed by the great crisis of 1873 and a long period of economic uncertainty.

Board 2

A workforce on a scale previously unknown was required for railway construction, the expansion of the heavy industry sector and for the machine tool industry. This was largely provided by the influx from the agricultural areas of eastern Germany. From this source a kind of reserve industrial army was provided by the impoverished agricultural proletariat who were only seasonally employed, in the wake of the "peasants' liberation" and the capitalisation of rural economic relations. They migrated in large numbers during and after the 1860s from east to west into the Berlin area, into the undustrial towns and the new industrial heartland of the Ruhr.

Board 3

The second precondition of economic growth is the availability of capital. Limited companies and joint stock banks were formed with the sole function of financing industrial concerns *(cat. illustr. 104, 105).* Whereas between 1818 and 1849 only 18 limited companies were formed, 251 were established in the period between 1850 and 1859 alone.

Board 11

New business and economic methods also made for a rapid

IV/102 View of an iron-rolling factory in Hagen around 1860.

IV/103 Machine room of the Hartmann Machine Tool factory in Chemnitz.

IV/104 Great Room of the Berlin Stock Exchange.

IV/105 The Reichsbank building in Berlin.

IV/106 Steel making by the Bessemer Process.

IV/107 The giant Krupp canon at the Paris World Exhibition, 1867.

IV/109 Machinisation of agriculture: steam driven threshing machine.

IV/110 Weekly market on the Alexanderplatz around 1860.

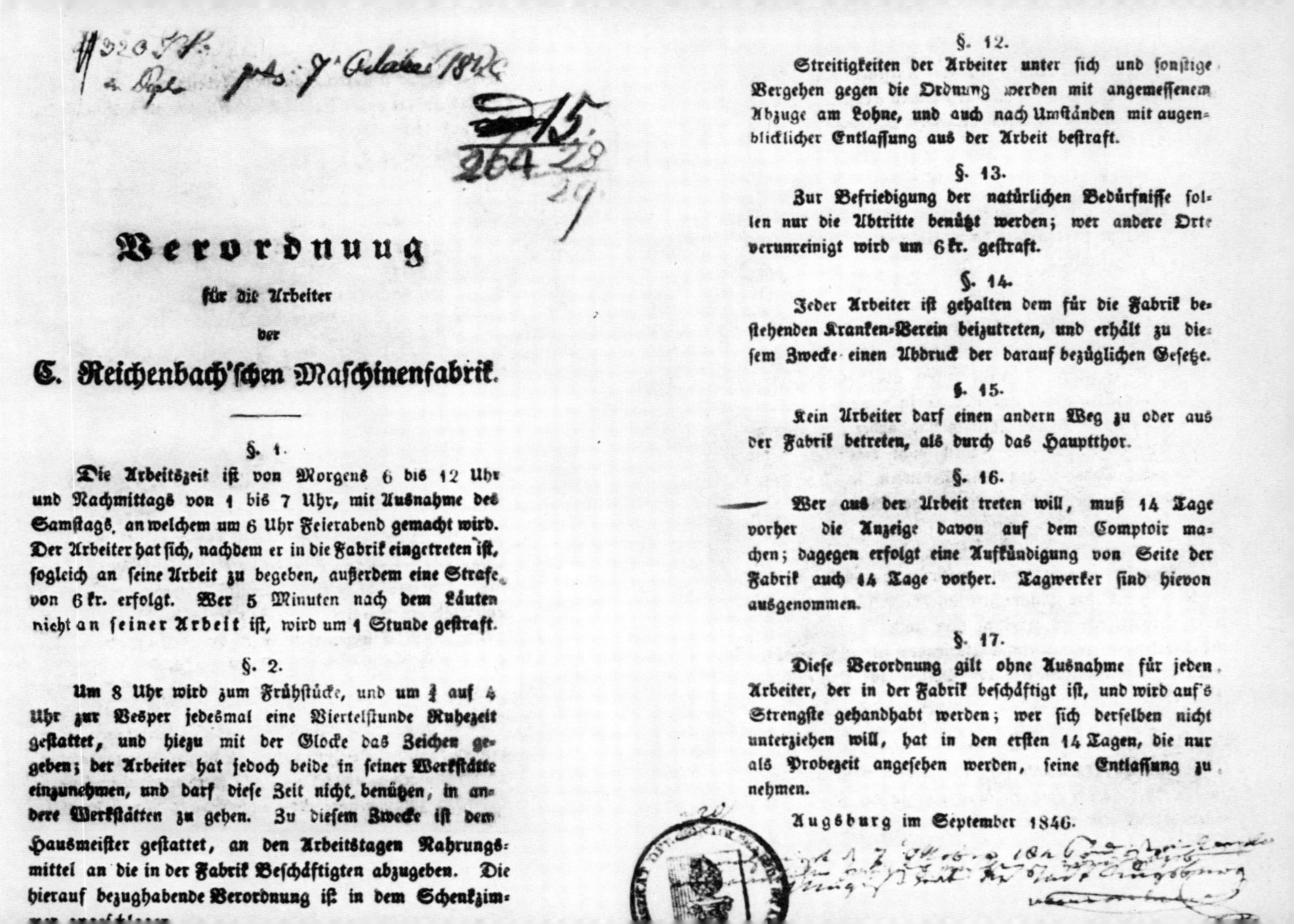

Verordnung

für die Arbeiter

der

C. Reichenbach'schen Maschinenfabrik.

---

§. 1.

Die Arbeitszeit ist von Morgens 6 bis 12 Uhr und Nachmittags von 1 bis 7 Uhr, mit Ausnahme des Samstags, an welchem um 6 Uhr Feierabend gemacht wird. Der Arbeiter hat sich, nachdem er in die Fabrik eingetreten ist, sogleich an seine Arbeit zu begeben, außerdem eine Strafe von 6 kr. erfolgt. Wer 5 Minuten nach dem Läuten nicht an seiner Arbeit ist, wird um 1 Stunde gestraft.

§. 2.

Um 8 Uhr wird zum Frühstücke, und um ¾ auf 4 Uhr zur Vesper jedesmal eine Viertelstunde Ruhezeit gestattet, und hiezu mit der Glocke das Zeichen gegeben; der Arbeiter hat jedoch beide in seiner Werkstätte einzunehmen, und darf diese Zeit nicht benützen, in andere Werkstätten zu gehen. Zu diesem Zwecke ist dem Hausmeister gestattet, an den Arbeitstagen Nahrungsmittel an die in der Fabrik Beschäftigten abzugeben. Die hierauf bezughabende Verordnung ist in dem Schenkzim-

§. 12.

Streitigkeiten der Arbeiter unter sich und sonstige Vergehen gegen die Ordnung werden mit angemessenem Abzuge am Lohne, und auch nach Umständen mit augenblicklicher Entlassung aus der Arbeit bestraft.

§. 13.

Zur Befriedigung der natürlichen Bedürfnisse sollen nur die Abtritte benützt werden; wer andere Orte verunreinigt wird um 6 kr. gestraft.

§. 14.

Jeder Arbeiter ist gehalten dem für die Fabrik bestehenden Kranken-Verein beizutreten, und erhält zu diesem Zwecke einen Abdruck der darauf bezüglichen Gesetze.

§. 15.

Kein Arbeiter darf einen andern Weg zu oder aus der Fabrik betreten, als durch das Hauptthor.

§. 16.

Wer aus der Arbeit treten will, muß 14 Tage vorher die Anzeige davon auf dem Comptoir machen; dagegen erfolgt eine Aufkündigung von Seite der Fabrik auch 14 Tage vorher. Tagwerker sind hievon ausgenommen.

§. 17.

Diese Verordnung gilt ohne Ausnahme für jeden Arbeiter, der in der Fabrik beschäftigt ist, und wird auf's Strengste gehandhabt werden; wer sich derselben nicht unterziehen will, hat in den ersten 14 Tagen, die nur als Probezeit angesehen werden, seine Entlassung zu nehmen.

Augsburg im September 1846.

IV/108 The first and last pages of a set of work regulations from the time of the Industrial Revolution.

Regulation

for the workers of the
G. Reichenback machine factory

§ 1

Working time is from 6 am to 12 o'clock midday and from 1 pm to 7 pm, with the exception of Saturdays when work will end at 6 pm. As soon as the worker enters the factory he must begin work otherwise he will be fined 6 Gr. Those who are not working 5 minutes after the specified time will lose an hour's pay.

§ 2

A breakfast break at 8 am and at 3.45 pm, a break for vespers are to be allowed, the bell signalling the appropriate times; however, the worker must spend both breaks in the workshop and may not use this time to go into other workshops. With this in mind the foreman is allowed to give food to those working in the factory on working days. The regulation hereto referred applies to the distribution room.

§ 12

Disputes between workers and other infringements of the regulations will be punished by appropriate reductions being made from wages and also, in certain circumstances, with immediate sacking.

§ 13

Only the facilities provided may be used for the satisfaction of natural requirements. Anyone dirtying other places will face a fine of 6 Gr.

§ 14

Every worker must join the factory sickness-association and receives a copy of the appropriate laws and regulations.

§ 15

No worker may enter or leave the factory by any other way than the main door.

§ 16

Anyone wishing to leave work must provide 14 days notice. The factory will also give 14 days notice of redundancy. Casual labour is not included in this provision.

§ 17

The Regulation applies, without exception, for every worker employed in the factory and will be most strictly adhered to. Anyone refusing to accept this regulation must hand in his notice during his initial fourteen day probationary period.

Augsburg, September 1846

development of new production techniques and thus made possible a sharp increase in productivity: a puddling oven needed 24 hours to 'refine' three tons of iron ore, only 20 minutes was needed by the Bessemer process to refine the same quantity *(cat. illustr. 106)*. However, the high phosphorous content of German ores prevented the large scale introduction of the Bessemer process in Germany. Ores with a low phosphorous content had to be imported and were therefore expensive. Only after the development of the Siemens-Martin oven and the Thomas convertor, a refined form of the Bessemer convertor, did the smelting of Lothringen ore become economically viable and make possible the mass production of steel in Germany. New industrial sectors, such as the chemical and electronics industry, were established. B.A.S.F. (Badische Anilin und Sodafabrik) was founded in 1863 and in 1866 Werner von Siemens developed the dynamo machine. World exhibitions became the showpieces of competing nations.

Self-confidently a German spoke about the Paris Exhibition of 1867 in the following terms: "Our cast steel was unbeatable, our glass and our paper ranked amongst the best, in chemical products we beat the English and French competition. Our mechanical weaving looms, machine tools and engines were at least as good as their English and American counterparts – and all this had been achieved in a relatively short space of time" *(cat. illustr. 107)*. During a period of great economic prosperity Germany developed into an industrial state within a few decades.

Board 14

Agricultural production was also greatly increased by new, more rational production methods because the large corn growing areas, especially on the farms east of the Elbe, made mechanisation a profitable proposition *(cat. illustr. 109)*. Mineral fertilisers, the pioneering discovery of Justus von Liebig, permitted a more extensive use of farm land. Agricultural associations sprung up in large numbers and pressed for new production methods and provided the required machinery.

Sales prospects for agricultural products had never been as favourable. The idea of free trade allied together at that time the large landowners, who were mainly conservative, with the liberal middle class. Not until the 1870s did the increasing threat from cheap Russian and American corn imports lead to a reverse of the situation.

The founding years

Board 18

The impetus provided by unification in 1871 and the thousands of millions of marks demanded from the French as reparation payments led to the boom of the 'founding years'. In an extremely frantic economic situation companies sprung up like mushrooms. This wave of setting up businesses often led to a haphazard economic growth which frequently had irreversible social consequences.

Boards 20/21

In 1873 the "epidemic of unleashed greed for money making" (S. v. Waltershausen) collapsed. The stock exchange collapse, which occurred in Vienna and then Berlin, led to a slump in prices on the share market which was caused by industrial overproduction. There were many bankruptcies. Companies, which had been formed without any solid basis but more with an 'eye to the future', could not survive this crisis. The answer was to form concerns and trusts, which would aim to dominate the market and also provide security in times of economic recession. The self confidence of the middle class was shattered by the reversal of 1873 and the absence of real economic growth. The lawyer Rudolf von Gneist summed up the general feeling of the time when he referred to the years after 1873 as "a period of general dissatisfaction" in which "the pessimistic outlook on life dominated the thoughts of the time".

Upheavals in Social Structure and Political Theories

Board 25

The years of rapid economic growth between 1850 and 1870 had as a further consequence the transformation of the Pre-1848 agricultural and artisan proletariat into an industrial proletariat. The process of urbanisation also began during this period. Artisans, who could no longer hope to find security of work, craftsmen, who suffered from the increase of competition, and former journeymen all sought work in the factories *(cat. illustr. 108)*. It is impossible to describe the wretched social misery of the workers. Charity organisations were formed with the aim of alleviating serious social need. New socialist theories also became more widespread, theories which considered the destruction of capitalism as the only possible method of liberating the working class.

Board 26

In the 1850s and 60s the growing industrial towns drew in the workforce mainly from the directly surrounding area. At the same time the great east-west migration flow began. To an ever increasing extent the agricultural workers from east of the Elbe became the labour reservoir of Rhineland-Westphalian industry. The population grew from 35 to 41 million between 1850 and 1870; of this number around 1860, 2.6 million lived in cities with a population of over 100,000. Factory buildings transformed the towns' appearances and the Ruhr area in particular, developed an industrial landscape. In 1873, however, two-thirds of the German population still lived on the land.

The plight of the industrial workers was in no way improved by the favourable economic climate. Above all, the housing conditions of the workers, who had recently poured into the towns, were appalling. On the outskirts of Berlin shanty towns grew up *(cat. illustr. 111).* In addition, tenement houses were built, where, in 1867, on average 6–7 people lived in one room. 18 hour working days, breadline wages and child labour completed the miserable situation of the industrial workforce.

Board 27

The social groups threatened by the industrial development joined self-help organisations. Raiffeisen founded rural loan societies, Schulze-Delitzsch credit associations for the small businesses; consumer associations and the first trade unions were formed. The catholic and protestant churches both ran charitable institutions for tradesmen and workers. Kolping and Ketteler, Wichern and Bodelschwingh tried to find in Christianity an answer to the social problems of the time. All these attempts to alleviate the social consequences of industrialisation and the capitalist economic structure for certain sections of the population were limited to suggestions for improvements to the existing order *(cat. illustr. 112).*

Boards 28/29

On the other hand, for Marx and Engels the members of the working class were not objects in need of assistance: they were not concerned with reformist improvements but insisted that the system of capitalist exploitation itself must be destroyed in an act of self liberation by the members of the working class, who were its victims. At the beginning of the 1848 Revolution Marx and Engels had written the "Manifesto of the Communist Party" in London *(cat. illustr. 113, 114).* Not until now did it take on any real significance. It ended with the words: "Workers have nothing to lose but their chains. They have a world to gain. Workers of the world unite". In the 1850s and 60s Marx began to research the motivating forces and trends of the capitalist sys-

IV/111 Shanty town outside Berlin around 1875.

IV/112 Berlin public kitchen.

Manifest

der

Kommunistischen Partei.

Ein Gespenst geht um in Europa—das Gespenst des Kommunismus. Alle Mächte des alten Europa haben sich zu einer heiligen Hetzjagd gegen dies Gespenst verbündet, der Papst und der Czar, Metternich nnd Guizot, französische Radikale und deutsche Polizisten.

Wo ist die Oppositionspartei, die nicht von ihren regierenden Gegnern als kommunistisch verschrieen worden wäre, wo die Oppositionspartei, die den fortgeschritteneren Oppositionsleuten sowohl, wie ihren reaktionären Gegnern den brandmarkenden Vorwurf des Kommunismus nicht zurückgeschleudert hätte?

Zweierlei geht aus dieser Thatsache hervor.

Der Kommunismus wird bereits von allen europäischen Mächten als eine Macht anerkannt.

Es ist hohe Zeit daß die Kommunisten ihre Anschauungsweise, ihre Zwecke, ihre Tendenzen vor der ganzen Welt offen darlegen, und den Mährchen vom Gespenst des Kommunismus ein Manifest der Partei selbst entgegenstellen.

Zu diesem Zweck haben sich Kommunisten der verschiedensten Nationalität in London versammelt und das folgende Manifest entworfen, das in englischer, französischer, deutscher, italienischer, flämmischer und dänischer Sprache veröffentlicht wird.

IV/113/114 Karl Marx and Friedrich Engels, the authors of the communist manifesto.

Manifesto of the Communist Party

A ghost is present in Europe – the ghost of communism. All the forces of the Old Europe have joined in a holy witch-hunt against this ghost, the Pope and the Czar, Metternich and Guizot, French radicals and German policemen.
Where is there an opposition party which would not have been decried as communist by its political opponents, where is the opposition party and those representatives of the more progressive opposition parties who would not have been reproached with the communist brandmark?
Two matters arise from this fact.
Communism will be recognised as a force to be reckoned with by all European powers.
It is high time that the communists openly presented their thoughts, their aims, their tendencies, to the whole world and set them against the myth of the communist ghost in a party manifesto.
To this end communists of many nationalities met in London and drew up the following manifesto which is published in English, French, German, Italian, Flemish and Danish.

Statut

des

Allgemeinen Deutschen Arbeitervereins.

§. 1.

Unter dem Namen

„Allgemeiner Deutscher Arbeiterverein"

begründen bie Unterzeichneten für die Deutschen Bundesstaaten einen Verein, welcher, von der Ueberzeugung ausgehend, daß nur durch das allgemeine gleiche und direkte Wahlrecht eine genügende Vertretung der sozialen Interessen des Deutschen Arbeiterstandes und eine wahrhafte Beseitigung der Klassengegensätze in der Gesellschaft herbeigeführt werden kann, den Zweck verfolgt,

auf friedlichem und legalem Wege, insbesondere durch das Gewinnen der öffentlichen Ueberzeugung, für die Herstellung des allgemeinen gleichen und direkten Wahlrechts zu wirken.

§. 2.

Jeder Deutsche Arbeiter wird durch einfache Beitrittserklärung Mitglied des Vereins mit vollem gleichen Stimmrecht und kann jeder Zeit austreten.

IV/115/116 Ferdinand Lassalle and the statute of the General German Workers' Association of 1863.

IV/117 Commemorative Scroll for the 'Unification Party's Congress', 1875.

tem in order to prove that the proletariat revolution was not merely a subjective goal but was an objective historical necessity. He published these thorough investigations in his uncompleted work "Das Kapital" the first volume of which appeared in 1867.

Parties and Associations (Boards 30–40)

The Industrial Revolution, in addition to transforming the social landscape also caused fundamental changes in the political system. The groupings which had hitherto been similar to political parties attempted to adapt to the new conditions and developed programmes, which offered varying solutions to the problems caused by the birth of the industrial society. In addition, entirely new parties were formed as an expression of the growing social, religious and national political tensions. These compete against the established political forces and over the next few decades influenced the development of the political structure. Despite all the mergers, rifts and name changes, above all in the liberal camp, the party system, which had evolved in the decade before the establishment of the Empire, remained largely intact until the end of the Kaiser's reign in 1918.

The origins of Social Democracy

Board 30 The industrial proletariat, whose numbers were continually increasing as industrialisation progressed, soon began to join forces in independent organisations and also became politically motivated.

The first workers' associations, which had been formed in the wake of the 1848 Revolution, were suppressed in the period of reaction which ensued. Nevertheless, the establishment of trade unions and parties continued. In 1863, Ferdinand Lassalle founded the "General German Workers' Association" *(cat. illustr. 115, 116).* He demanded equal and universal suffrage and state supported companies.

Boards 31/32 In 1869 a more strongly marxist oriented Workers' Party was formed in parallel to the "General German Workers' Association", led by August Bebel and Wilhelm Liebknecht. This party took the name "Social Democratic Workers' Party" (S. D. A. P.) and was formed in Eisenach. The two parties of "Lassalle" and "Eisenach" merged in Gotha in 1875 to form a unified German Workers' Party *(cat. illustr. 117).* At first glance it seemed as though the more radical "Marxists" had gained the upper hand in the party. However, the "Gotha Programme" revealed that a whole series of "Lassallean" ideas had remained untouched. Marx's response therefore was to offer a sharp "critique of the Gotha Programme".

The Conservatives

Boards 33/34 The conservatives fought against the social consequences of the Industrial Revolution from a different angle. They feared the crumbling of the foundations of the existing political and social order. Their aim was therefore to establish a political system which was both patriarchal and welfarist and which had a hier archical organisation of the social groupings.

Conservatism fought against the "supposed progress" and saw it as an attack against the natural order of human life, which had been ordained by God *(cat. illustr. 121).* Its fight against liberalism represented a struggle to preserve the old order against the rising power of the industrial middle classes. The men who supported this allegedly God-given order were the ones for whom it would guarantee political and economic privileges: aristrocratic big land owners and supporters of the crown fought against the removal of class barriers, against equal suffrage and for the restoration of the privileges of estate owners and the upper classes. The caricature shows the "Knights of the Kreuzzeitung": Ludwig von Gerlach, the leader of the party, as Don Quichote on a donkey flanked by the "Jesuit father" Friedrich Julius Stahl, the conservative theoretician, and Bismarck in protective shell of backwardness. *(Cat. illustr. 118)*

Liberalism

Board 35 Liberalism's political, economic and social demands – safeguarding of the constitutional state, parliamentary control of the executive, unrestricted economic liberalism and unrestricted freedom in social relations – aimed to achieve a society of free and independent citizens. Nevertheless the necessary social and economic conditions, which would make the realisation of such aims a possibility, scarcely existed. However, the need, which arose out of the absence of such conditions, for a state social policy in support of their own aims, was recognised by only a few liberals.

Board 36 The replacement of the mentally ill Friedrich Wilhelm IV by Prince Wilhelm, the future Kaiser Wilhelm I, led to a 'new era' in Prussia: the reactionary cabinet was discharged and the House of Representatives dissolved. In the elections, which were this time not controlled by the government, the liberals gained an overwhelming majority. Prince Wilhelm appointed a liberal-conservative cabinet and aroused great expectations amongst liberals not only in Prussia but throughout Germany when he formed his government.

The National Association

Board 37 Little-German liberals and democrats founded the National Association in 1859 *(cat. illustr. 126).* This organised rerpresentative of the citizens' wishes was to help bring about the unification of Germany under Prussian leadership. The National Association reasserted the ideas of 1848. It demanded a central government and the formation of a national assembly. It was prepared to cooperate with the German princes. However, only a few of them, for example the Grand Duke of Baden, accepted this proposal.

The Reform Association

Board 38 As a reaction to the disappointment expressed by many people at the anti-parliamentary course steered by the Prussian government in the army conflict, conservatives, pan-German liberals and democrats formed the Reform Association in Frankfurt in 1862. Its aim was the national unification of German through a reform of the German Confederation under Austrian leadership. Austria attempted to exploit the anti-Prussian feeling expressed by the movement but her attempts to push through a reform of the Confederation failed: Prussia refused even to take part at the meeting of princes in Frankfurt in 1863 *(cat. illustr. 122).*

IV/118/121 Leading representatives of the Conservatives in Prussia: Friedrich Julius Stahl, Leopold von Gerlach, Otto von Bismarck and the Rules for Prussian subjects.

IV/122 The Frankfurt meeting of princes of 1863.

Left wing liberalism in Prussia: the German Progress Party

Board 39 In Prussia there was increasing conflict between the crown and parliament over the question of the army reform. Opposition left wing liberals and democrats formed the German Progress Party *(cat. illustr. 123–125).* It advocated a determined struggle for a parliamentary constitutional state and a new social order. For the first time a Prussian party included a call for national unity in its manifesto. The left wing trend in the Prussian middle class was demonstrated in the parliamentary elections of 1861: whilst the conservative group gained only 14 seats the Progress Party won 109 seats.

Board 40 The refusal of this liberal majority to pass the necessary bills for the reorganisation of the army in the Lower House escalated the army conflict into a constitutional conflict because both the government and the monarch refused to compromise: the latter wanted to make the army an instrument of the crown by abolishing the militia, which had been created by the army reforms of the Prussian war minister von Boyen, the civil militia, which was extremely popular with the liberals and by introducing a written law requiring three years' military service with a concurrent four to five year period of service in the reserve. Thus the army's constitution would be transfored to fit the absolutist state tradition. Bismarck's hour arrived during this conflict: he was appointed as Prussian prime minister and opposed the Progress Party as the political defender of the monarchist government. He declared to the Lower House: "The Prussian Kingdom has not yet completed its mission, it is not yet ready to make a purely ornamental decoration out of its state building, not yet ready to be incorporated into the mechanisms of the parliamentary system as a useless piece of machinery".

The Establishment of the Empire (Boards 41–52)

Board 41 Bismarck, dubbed as the 'Conflict Minister' in domestic politics and apparently hopelessly isolated, gained a whole series of impressive successes in foreign policy by virtue of his enormous diplomatic skill. They led, since they were interpreted as steps along the road to solving the national question, to a gradual swing in public opinion. In the Schleswig-Holstein conflict, in which all the national forces whether pan-German or little-

German were deeply involved, Prussia assumed the leadership role and forced Austria onto its side. After the victory over Denmark the Duchies were placed under the administration of the two powers. Eventually, however, Prussia pressed for the annexation of the Duchies and thus caused a conflict with Austria, which ended with war. Following the Prussian victory the struggle for dominance in Germany was finally resolved in their favour. The German Confederation was dissolved and the way was clear for the little-German solution of the national question under the leadership of conservative Prussia.
The newly established North German Confederation, to which all states north of the Main belonged, was obviously only a transitional solution. Its constitution had provisions for the possible annexation of the South German states. Napoleon III's France felt threatened by the expansionist power politics (Machtpolitik) of Prussia. The continuous increase in tension eventually led to a military conflict following the confusion over the Hohenzollern throne candidacy. In this war the South German states immediately sided with Prussia.
In defeated France on 18th January 1871 Wilhelm I was proclaimed as German Emperor and head of state of the new German Empire.

The German-Danish War

Board 42

In 1864 the Prussian prime minister succeeded in playing a master stroke in Germany and in Europe: Prussia assumed the leadership in the fight against Denmark. She forced Austria to side with her and thus separated her from her former allies in Germany, the small and medium sizes states.
After the victory over Denmark, Schleswig was initially placed under the administration of Prussia and Holstein under Austrian administration by the Treaty of Gastein. Austria's weakened position made it possible, however, for Prussia eventually to demand openly the annexation of the Duchies. At the same time Prussia finally foiled Austrian plans for a mid-European economic customs union.

V/123/124/125 Leading representatives of the German Progress Party: Virchow, Schulze-Delitzsch, Mommsen.

IV/126 "... unfortunately we often give offence above", caricature of the difficulties of the National Association.

IV/127 Battlefield of Sadowa (Königgratz), 3rd July 1866.

IV/128 Ceremonial reception of the victorious Prussian army on 21st September 1866 in Berlin.

The Year of Decision: 1866

Board 43 The Austro-Prussian conflict in the fight for the political and economic dominance of Germany culminated in the 1866 war *(cat. illustr. 127, 128)*. With the Prussian victory at Königgrätz Bismarck's concept of "national unification from above" triumphed by means of diplomacy and war.

Board 44 Bismarck also used the victory for domestic political ends. He now requested the Prussian Lower House to sanction his unconstitutional act on the question of army reforms (indemnity proposal). Under pressure from Bismarck's successes the majority of Parliament yielded. The events of 1866 split the liberals: the majority ended their previous opposition to Bismarck's power politics. They placed their hopes on the realisation of their national political aims on the "Revolution from above". In so doing they gave priority to their national aims over their liberal views. "Freedom through unity" was one of the slogans they used to set their minds at rest. In the Autumn of 1866 the national liberal group was formed and Bismarck was able to rely upon them to support his policies for a decade.

The North German Confederation

Boards 45/46 With the annexation of Schleswig-Holstein, Kurhessen, Nassau and Frankfurt the Prussian military and authoritarian state dominated the territory as far south as the Main *(cat. illustr. 130)*. Austria, separated from this "little Germany" was spared in the Prague peace treaty of 1866 but had to pay for this by agreeing to the Prussian annexations. Moreover, the Austrians had to abandon their hopes for the restoration of the German Confederation and had to agree to the setting up of the North German Confederation *(cat. illustr. 129)*.

The constitution of the North German Confederation, which was founded on 16th April 1867, was largely Bismarck's personal work. It guaranteed a dominant position and formed the basis for the Reich Constitution of 1871. The King of Prussia became the hereditary head of state of the Confederation and the Chancellor was only responsible to the King and was not dependent on the elected Reichstag. Prussia also had a dominant position in the Bundesrat. In this constitutional-monarchy constitution the introduction of universal, equal, direct and secret voting was of little significance because the Reichstag still had only limited powers and could exert practically no influence over the government formation *(cat. illustr. 131).* The national liberal middle class, which supported the Confederation, was the major beneficiary of the unitary North German economic territory. The opponents of the Confederation were the left wing liberals, socialists, old guard conservatives and political section of the catholic church. Many citizens in the annexed German states were still anti-Prussian, especially in Hannover and the old Free City of Frankfurt. The South German states rejected the Confederation and formed defensive alliances.

The Hohenzollern Throne Candidacy in Spain and the Franco-Prussian War

Boards 47/48 Since the Prussian victory over Austria France had feared that its dominant position in Europe was being threatened. The issue of the succession to the Spanish Throne by a Hohenzollern prince eventually led to a war between the two countries, since neither France nor Prussia was willing to accept a diplomatic defeat *(cat. illustr. 132–134).*

Boards 49–52 The whole of Germany was gripped by a sense of nationalist indignation following the French declaration of war. Even the South German states rushed to aid of Prussia and placed their troops under Prussian command. The march to the French border was completed with unexpected speed thanks to the new railway network. At the Battle of Sedan the decisive victory over the French was won and Napoleon III was amongst the prisoners taken *(cat. illustr. 135, 136).* The victory at Sedan was celebrated in great style in Germany. The comradeship displayed at Sedan opened a new chapter in German history: in a great over-estimation of their achievements the victory over the French was seen as a fateful sign of the calling of the Germans to greatness and unity *(cat. illustr. 137).* The war now entered a new phase; the setting up of the republic was declared in Paris and Léon Cambetta organised the civil war.

Although an acceptable peace treaty was not excluded from possibility the military success gave German war policy new impetus and it was no longer based on defence but looked for financial and territorial gains.

IV/129 Constituent session of the North German Reichstag on 24th February 1867.

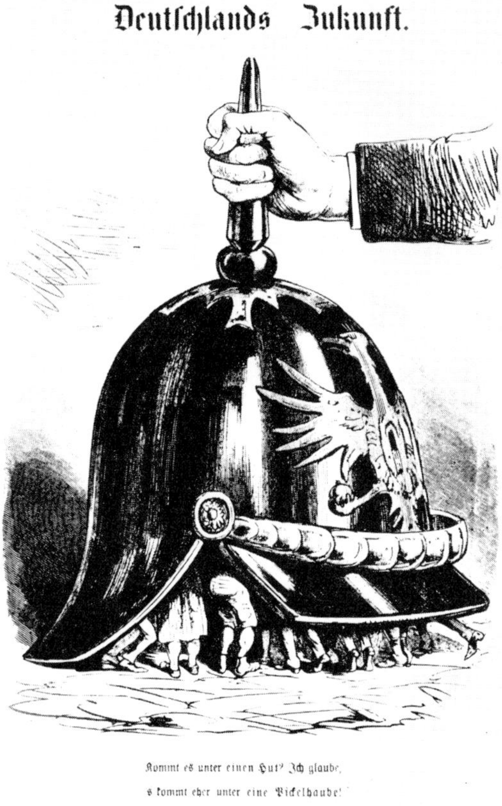

IV/130 Caricature of Prussian dominance in Germany.

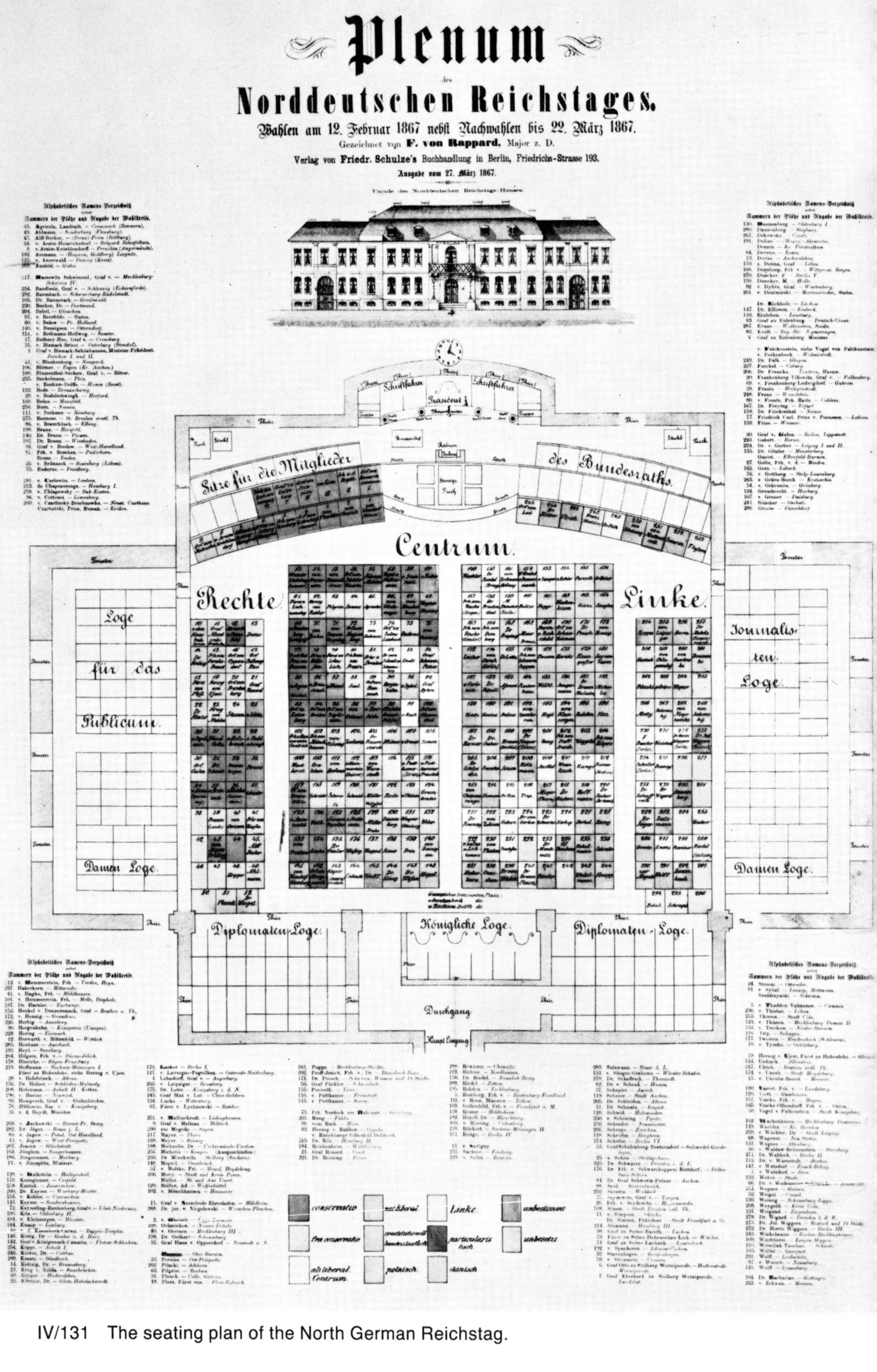

IV/131 The seating plan of the North German Reichstag.

IV/133 Wilhelm I and the French envoy Benedetti in Bad Ems.

IV/134 War fever in Paris on 19th July 1870.

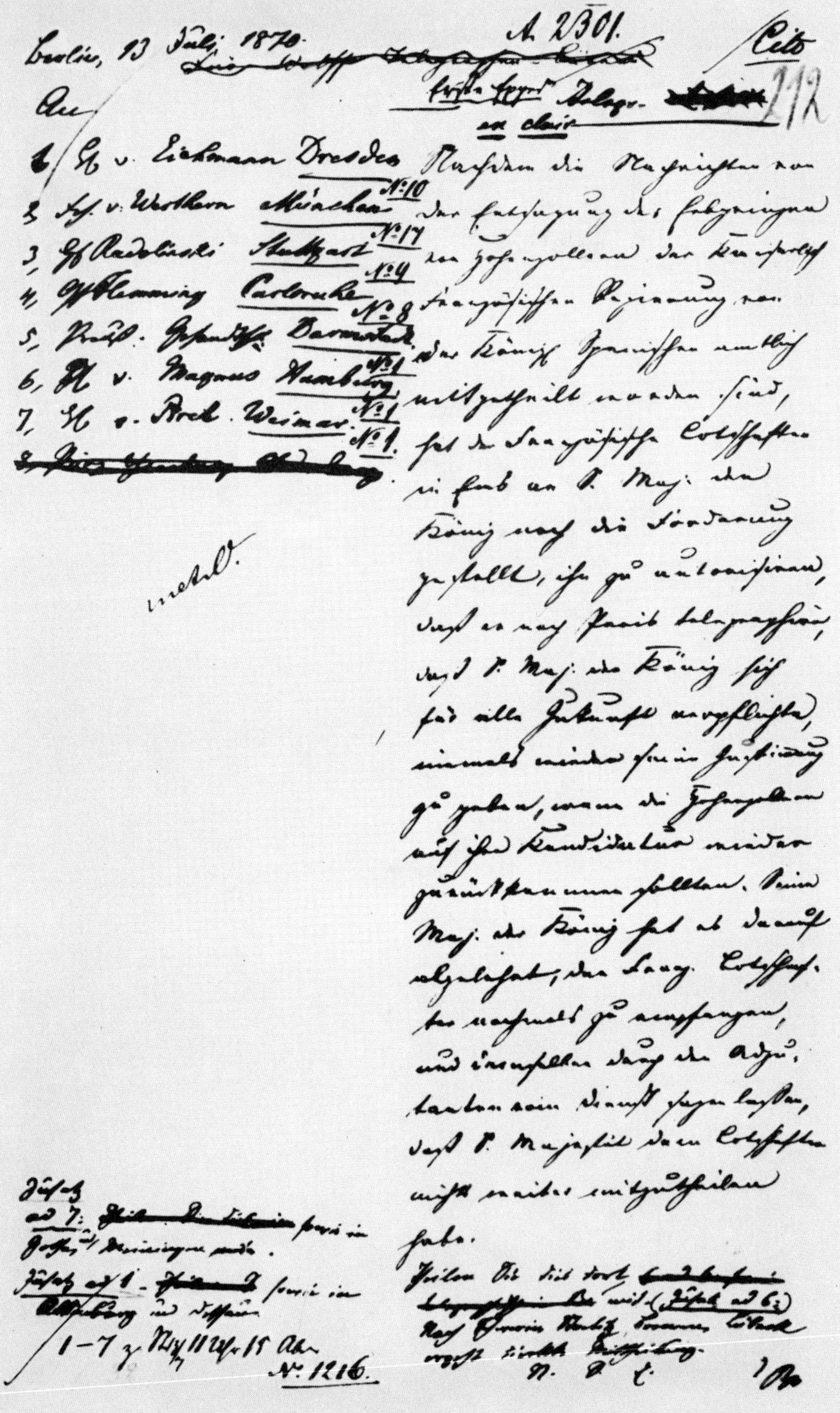

Berlin, 13 Juli 1870.

A. 2301.

Cito

Nachdem die Nachrichten von der Entsagung des Erbprinzen von Hohenzollern der Kaiserlich französischen Regierung von der Königlich Spanischen amtlich mitgetheilt worden sind, hat der französische Botschafter in Ems an S. Maj. den König noch die Forderung gestellt, ihn zu autorisiren, daß er nach Paris telegraphire, daß S. Maj. der König sich für alle Zukunft verpflichte, niemals wieder seine Zustimmung zu geben, wenn die Hohenzollern auf ihre Kandidatur wieder zurückkommen sollten. Seine Maj. der König hat es darauf abgelehnt, den franz. Botschafter nochmals zu empfangen, und demselben durch den Adjutanten vom Dienst sagen lassen, daß S. Majestät dem Botschafter nichts weiter mitzutheilen habe.

Nº 1216.

IV/132 Bismarck's draft of the "Ems Telegramme".

Berlin, 13th July 1870.

urgent

Copy to be sent to:
1
2
3
4
5
6
7

(Prussian Emissaries in the German States
– in South Germany, Dresden, Hamburg and Weimar.)

For open publication

When the Imperial French Government was officially informed by the Royal Spanish Government that the Hohenzollern Crown Prince had renounced his claim to the throne, the French Ambassador demanded, moreover from His Majesty the King, in Ems, that he be authorised to telegraph Paris with the message that His Majesty the King undertook to swear that never again would a Hohenzollern put himself forward as a candidate for the throne of Spain. Thereupon, His Majesty the King refused to see the Ambassador of France and instructed his private secretary to inform him that His Majesty had no further communication for the Ambassador.

39ste Depesche

vom

Kriegs-Schauplatz.

Der Königin Augusta in Berlin.

Vor Sedan, den 2. September, ½2 Uhr Nachm.

Die Capitulation, wodurch die ganze Armee in Sedan kriegsgefangen, ist soeben mit dem General Wimpfen geschlossen, der an Stelle des verwundeten Marschalls Mac-Mahon das Commando führte. Der Kaiser hat nur sich selbst Mir ergeben, da er das Commando nicht führt und Alles der Regentschaft in Paris überläßt. Seinen Aufenthaltsort werde Ich bestimmen, nachdem Ich ihn gesprochen habe in einem Rendezvous, das sofort stattfindet.

Welch' eine Wendung durch Gottes Führung!

Wilhelm.

Berlin, den 3. September 1870.

Königliches Polizei-Präsidium.
von Wurmb.

Druck v. Ernst Litfaß, Königlichem Hofbuchdrucker. Adlerstr. 6.

IV/135 The victory note from Sedan.

39th Dispatch from the battlefront

To Queen Augusta in Berlin

The surrender of the totally captured army has just been accepted from General Wimpfen, who was acting on behalf of the wounded Marshall MacMahon. The Emperor has only surrendered himself personally to me since he is not assuming command and is leaving everything to the regency in Paris. I shall decide upon a place for him to stay after I have spoken to him at a meeting which is to take place immediately.

What a turn of events has occurred through God's guidance.

Wilhelm

Berlin, 3rd September 1870

Royal Police Presidium
von Wurmb

IV/136 Wilhelm I on the battlefield at Sedan, 2nd September 1870.

IV/137 This picture is taken from a postcard printed to celebrate the victory at Sedan in Berlin on 1st October 1895. Sedan "What a turn of events has occurred through God's guidance".

Most political groups in Germany vociferously demanded the annexation of Alsace-Lorraine to the Reich following the great victory in August and Bismarck, too, spoke in favour of this move since it was in line with his views on Machtpolitik. The voices which referred to the fact that Alsace-Lorraine did not want to join the German state were few in number; they rejected the idea of annexation, the liberal democratic "Frankfurter Zeitung" expressing such a viewpoint as did many representatives of the labour movement: they considered the separation of Alsace-Lorraine from France to be a flagrant violation of the oft cited sovereign right to belong to one's own nation. "The military camarilla, the professors, citizens and bar-room gossip asserts that this (the annexation) is the way to provide permanent protection for Germany against war with France . . . (. . .) It is the best possible way of changing the coming peace into a mere ceasefire until such time that France has recovered and is once again in a position to demand back her lost territory. It is the best possible way to ruin both France and Germany by causing them to mutually destroy one another" (Manifesto of the Social Democratic Workers' Party, 5th September 1870).

Indeed relations with France in the coming decades were poisoned by the annexation with the consequence that Germans had placed a millstone around their neck as far as foreign policy was concerned.

After the military successes of the early months, the collapse of the French Empire and the siege of Paris, the way was now open for the completion of German unity by annexing the South German states to the North German Confederation. Diplomatic negotiations and the military power of Prussia made possible the founding of the Empire "from above". The German Empire was not established by decree of the German National Assembly but by a series of what resembled international treaties between the various monarchs and governments, which were later ratified by the North German Reichstag and the South German Landtage.

The act of establishing the Empire was completed on 18th January 1871: the Emperor's proclamation before the German princes in the Hall of Mirrors of Versailles was a Prussian military show-piece, the portrayal of a sovereign state *(cat. illustr. 138).*

The nationalist enthusiasm of the people for the newly won Empire could only superficially conceal the deep internal rifts in the alliance between Bismarck and the liberal and national movement.

Imperial Germany

The German Empire of 1871, founded on an unequal alliance between the national and liberal movement and the conservative Prussian state-leadership, had been established after a large number of compromises had been agreed and was immediately open to the criticism of being incomplete. However, the great majority of people warmly greeted the achievement of national unity. Nevertheless, when this achievement was measured against the great aims of the 1848/49 Revolution to create unity through freedom and to build the state on new political, economic and social foundations, the founding of the Empire signified a defeat for middle class liberalism. The problem of being internally and externally incomplete proved to be the heaviest burden which the Empire had to bear and from the outset hindered its further development.

Left wing liberal critics dismissed the Empire as an incomplete constitutional state. The liberals claimed that it should be governed on a wider parliamentary basis. In reality it was ruled by one man who was responsible only to the Emperor. The extremely complicated constitutional system depended solely on the personality of Bismarck, who dominated the government and administration by holding the key positions of Chancellor and Prussian prime minister: these included the imperial authorities at whose head were subservient state secretaries and not responsible ministers, the Bundesrat which was dominated by the Prussians, the Prussian state cabinet of which Bismarck was chairman. The only area where the Reichstag had any real influence was that of legislation. No firm parliamentary principle was established, i.e. a government responsible to a strong and sovereign parliament – rather the situation was one of "government of the parties", a system which was dubbed "Chancellor Dictatorship". Whereas a democratic, constitutional nation-state under the principle of sovereignty of the people was aimed for in 1848, the Empire of 1871 was a nationalist authoritarian monarchy.

The Empire was also incomplete with regard to the social-political demands of the middle class emancipation movement. Their claims that the new state should adapt itself to the new industrial society were not met and nor was their demand that the nation should, as the sum of the social forces, have an active role to play in the political process. The Empire did not aim to

make changes but rather to preserve the old Prussian social order which had been reinforced by the dominant position of the Junkers. The opposition parties were denounced as enemies of the Reich: the left wing liberal Progress Party, the Social Democrats and the Catholic Centre Party. The first decade of the Reich was filled with high social and party political tensions.
There was also a bitter cultural struggle in which the autonomy of the state and politics from the catholic interests of the Centre Party was strongly defended. Because of its connection with the papacy the Centre Party was seen as a papist party and internationalist in outlook. Bismarck feared a coalition between the catholics and the other opposition groups in the Reich, especially the catholic Polish national minority in the eastern provinces of Prussia. In an "internal private war" after 1871 Bismarck strove to master these forces. At the same time the ideological disputes between liberalism and catholicism sharpened the party political differences. The Special and Prohibition Laws of the cultural struggle destroyed the belief that the national community would eventually smooth over its differences and become a tolerant society. By agreeing to the prohibition and expulsion of the Jesuit order the National Liberal Party abandoned its own constitutional principles.
The battle against social democracy shook the internal structure of the Reich even more fiercely. The Anti-Socialist Law (Sozialistengesetz) forbade the integration of the labour force within the national state. Only one party was allowed under a special law to follow its convictions – a flagrant violation of liberal principles. Nevertheless, Bismarck won the support of the middle classes who had for a long time feared "red anarchy". Two assassination attempts on Kaiser Wilhelm I in the spring of 1878 provided the opportunity for the Reichstag to be dissolved and for new elections to be called although no link could be proved between the assassination attempts and the social democrats. In the new elections Bismarck won a comfortable parliamentary majority – the National Liberal Party also agreed to the anti-socialist law, having taken account of the public outrage and the fear of revolution amongst its voters. However, only after great efforts had been made was a split by the left wing of the party avoided. Critics asserted that Bismarck had used the Socialist laws as a tool against the National Liberals in order to cause internal rifts in the party. In the years that followed the liberals could find no solution to the social question.

Bismarck's state social policy – the positive counterpart to the anti-socialist laws – was rejected by the liberals. This social policy did not aim to reconcile the workers with existing state and social order by providing them with increased material wealth. This policy was only a limited success, although, in the Wilhelminian era, the system of social insurance was extended. The workers' organisations and the big industrial and agricultural associations which had been formed during the economic crisis after 1873 were even more at loggerheads now than they had previously been. The national state became increasingly class-divided.

The foreign policy problems of the new Reich were no less serious. Since the new little-German Empire incorporated only a portion of all Germans within its boundaries, fears were expressed in many quarters that the Reich would now pursue a policy which sought to gain new territory. In addition, there was the problem of national minorities within the Reich, which were never really integrated before 1918 and also posed a serious domestic policy problem. Only by means of an extremely complicated system of alliances and repeated declarations that Germany was 'saturated' did Bismarck succeed in gaining a place for the Reich in the traditional continental European power structure. The Berlin Congress of 1878 represented a peak in this diplomatic struggle. The international crises of the 1880s proved however that it was not enough to avert the danger of a war on two fronts. The new alliances – the Triple Alliance between Germany, Austria-Hungary and Italy and the Reinsurance Treaty with Russia – only provisionally restored a state of equilibrium to the European power system, the German Reich in particular deviated from this course by turning to a colonial policy, on the grounds of "territorial saturation", a policy which placed them on a head-on collision course with England. Thus, the Reich remained as "an incomplete national state", was threatened internally and externally. In order to control all these problems, Bismarck relied repeatedly on the same method: the stabilisation of the conservative state and the cementing of the status quo. In addition, the alliance with the National Liberals also broke up, an alliance which had only been made because of Bismarck's foreign policy successes in 1864 and 1866 and which from the outset had been based on a domestic political compromise: the ending of the constitutional conflict by the Indemnity Bill, which was later sanctioned by Bismarck's anti-parliamentarian policies. The turning point in domestic politics in 1878/79 was the equivalent of the founding of a second conservative Reich which prevented the liberals from having any further influence on developments. The change in economic policy from liberal free trade to protectionism, which favoured heavy industry and large scale farmers, led to a split in the National Liberal Party. The new tariff barriers and the increase in indirect taxes penalised the economically weak classes and favoured the "productive classes" and gave political impetus to the social democrats. The liberal middle class forces were swallowed up in the struggle between agriculture and industry on the one hand and the workers on the other. At the same time the alliance between industrialists and large scale farmers cemented the influence of the old Prussian ruling classes, who supported the conservative policies of the government. The ideological methods used to implement the protective economic policy and the simultaneous propaganda campaign in favour of the Socialist laws encouraged extremist words from conservative farmers such as: "The constitutional state has had its day. We shall have to return to the patrimonial and patriarchal state system". The liberal era came to an end in 1878/79: the officials in government and administration were largely replaced by supporters of the conservative policy and the liberal ministers in Prussia resigned. The newly organised institutions of the Reich and the financial reforms introduced strengthened the powers of the Empire and thus that of the Chancellor. The later years of the Bismarck era were characterised by the furtherance of the common interests of the Junker-dominated agricultural areas east of the Elbe, heavy industry and the conservative government.

After Bismarck's dismissal in 1890 the Reich was faced with a governmental crisis. The young Kaiser Wilhelm II wanted to be "his own chancellor". However, the attempt to set up a "personal system of government", an autocracy, which demanded of its ministers only the obedient implementation of the Kaiser's wishes, failed. The Kaiser lacked the knowledge and ability to pass binding directives in domestic and foreign policy affairs and he was unable to ignore the institutions of the Reich – ministers of the Empire, the Bundesrat, Prussian State Cabinet, Reichstag, Prussian Landtag – or to play them off against each other. Nevertheless, a "new course" was advocated, the Socialist laws were repealed and in the February Decrees of 1890 a

IV/138 The Kaiser's Proclamation in Versailles, 18th January 1871, engraving by Anton von Werner.

IV/139 Reichstag session, 1908.

IV/140 Ludwig Windthorst.

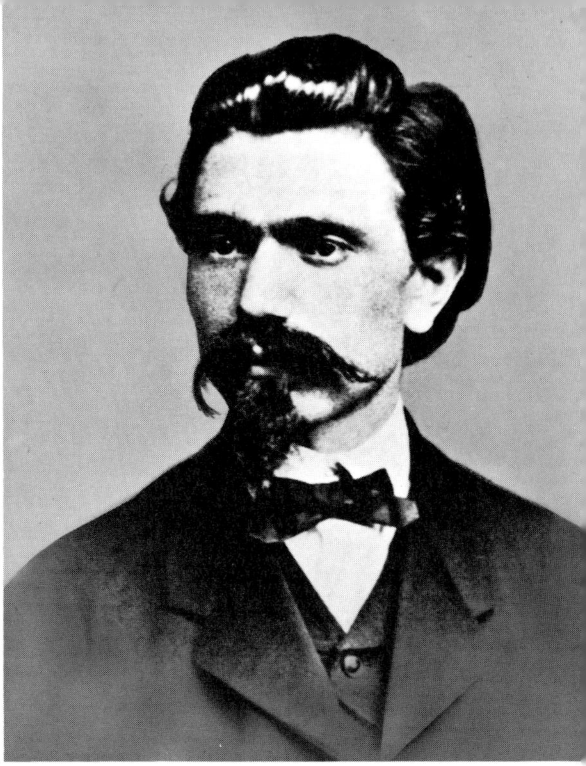

IV/141 August Bebel.

IV/142 Eugen Richter.

IV/143 Eduard Lasker.

comprehensive system of labour protection was announced. However, this did not succeed in reconciling the labour force to the "Social Empire". The Social Democrats were able to increase their share of the vote from 763,000 in 1887 to 1.4 million in 1890.

The new policy of imperialism represented the final attempt to conceal internal tensions by foreign policy successes. However, the hopes of liberal imperialists, such as Max Weber and Friedrich Naumann, who expected both dynamic foreign and domestic policies, remained unfulfilled. The new "Weltpolitik" strengthened the nationalist claims of the conservatives, who, especially in their propaganda-campaigns for a strong German navy, were able to gain widespread support. Kaiser Wilhelm's claim that Germany had become a "World Power" was enthusiastically received. In reality, his successes were small and the price paid for his prestige policy was the self-inflicted isolation of Germany and the forming of an alliance by her rivals, England, France and Russia. The mishandling of world politics eventually led to a blind push forwards into the catastrophe of the First World War.

The cessation of party strife – even the social democrats agreed to the war credits – and the general enthusiasm for the war in 1914 were not, however, long lasting. The war increased internal political conflicts which became embroiled in foreign policy aims – some advocated a negotiated peace, others a victorious peace with annexations. The radicalisation of the left and right was demonstrated in 1917 by the founding of the "Deutsche Vaterlandspartei" on the one hand and the Spartakus League on the other.

Nevertheless, the political and military collapse of the Empire provided the chance for a new beginning and for a reconsideration of the liberal and democratic ideals which had been extolled by the nationalist thinking in the early 19th century.

XIII (illustr. right) Inside view of an iron foundry in Königshütte (Upper Silesia), painting by Adolf Menzel.

XIV (illustr. left)
Prince Otto von Bismarck, portrait by Franz von Lenbach.

XV (illustr. right)
Reichstag session, 1905, painting by Georg Waltenberger.

The Little-German Nation State: Institutions, Parties, Problems (Boards 53–87)

Board 53

The Kaiser's Empire of 1871 realised the long sought aim of national unity, even if it was only "unity from above". Sovereignty lay not with the people but-with the 22 princes and three free cities which had joined together to form a federal state. The predominance of Prussia was overwhelming and many of the goals of the liberal and democratic movements remained unachieved. The Chancellor of the Reich was not responsible to Parliament but to the Kaiser. The rights of the Reichstag, which had been previously democratically elected, were more or less restricted to participation in the passing of legislation. The struggle to extend the Reichstag's role and to create a parliamentary system in the Reich was a fundamental internal problem.
The incomplete constitutional state was also, however, an incomplete nation state since there were large German-speaking groups outside its borders. On the other hand, national minorities presented a major integration problem for the Reich.

The Reichstag

Board 54

The Reichstag was convened by universal, equal, direct and secret elections *(cat. illustr. 139)*. Next to the Kaiser, it was the second most important institution. However, its political influence was limited to the area of legislation. It exerted only a very small influence over the formation of governments and government policy. Characteristic of the Reich was the "government over the parties" and the restriction of the peoples' representation to a position in which it was only able to express a non-binding opinion on important political questions. The system was described at the time as a "chancellor dictatorship".

XVI (illustr. left) Krupp Steel Factory, 1912 (extract).

The Chancellor

Board 55

The Constitution of 1871, influenced largely by Prince Otto von Bismarck *(cat. illustr. XIV)* guaranteed the Chancellor a position of power, which was unrestricted by either Parliament or the political parties. The Chancellor was politically responsible not to Parliament but to the Kaiser. Mutual loyalty and trust were therefore prerequisites of this post. The Chancellor decided upon policy outlines and he proposed the appointments and dismissals of state secretaries who were in turn responsible for the administration of the ministries of the Reich. He chaired the sessions of the Bundesrat, which was formally the highest government institution of the Empire and was traditionally the leader of the Prussian state cabinet, at least for the greatest part of the imperial era.

Boards 56/57

The Special Position of the Military

The generals were responsible for all matters concerning "military command" in the same way that the Chancellor was responsible for directing the civilian policies of the Reich. The Kaiser was the commanding officer of the armed forces. The constitution did not, however, provide any political check on the armed forces and thus, later, in the First World War, generals and admirals were able to exert what turned out to be a disastrous influence on policies.

Federalism

Board 58

The German Reich was a federal state, which was overwhelmingly dominated by Prussia. More than half of the total population lived within the Prussian borders and almost two-thirds of the Reich's territory was Prussian. In the Bundesrat, the legislative organ of the federal states, Prussia had a blocking minority. The decisive question of German federalism was, however, the financial dependence of the Reich on the financial contributions of the federal states (Matrikularbeiträge). Thus, the financial reform of the Reich developed into a fundamental constitutional problem for the Empire.

Nationality Problems

Board 59

There were sizeable minority groups incorporated in the Reich of 1871. Instead of giving these minorities political status attempts were made to integrate them by bureaucratic means.

In 1872/73 German was made the only language used in schools in the Polish-speaking areas and in 1876 the only business language. From 1878 onwards German was the only language permitted in schools in Northern Schleswig.
However, even the people of Alsace-Lorraine became a problem, where the majority were German speaking. They recognised the advantages of the French constitution and were not prepared to be treated by an imperial administration as second-class Germans.

Internal Development of the Reich

Board 60

The founding of the Reich created a unified economic and customs area and this led to a period of rapid economic growth, advantage being taken of the existing technical opportunities for industrial production. Progress was also made in unifying the areas of transport, the postal system, currency, weights and measures and in achieving a uniform legal system: in 1872 a uniform penal code (St. GB) was introduced and in 1900 a code of civil law (B. G. B.). Both of these codes are still in force today, having been only partly amended or extended.

The Parties of the Reichstag

Boards 61/62, 65, 68, 71/72

As a consequence of universal suffrage the loose groupings and electoral associations which had previously existed were replaced by well-organised mass parties with wide support-bases and distinct programmes.
The 1871 constitution of the Reich, however, only gave parties the opportunity to be either governmental, thus supporters of the Chancellor, or to join the opposition *(cat. illustr. 140–143).* It provided for no real party participation in the governing of the Reich. Thus a difficult distinction must be made between pure party interests and the superior interests of state, which were ostensibly only dealt with by the government.

The National Liberals

Board 63

The main supporters of the National Liberal Party were recruited from the educated protestant middle classes and the industrial upper middle classes. The party's aims were for a powerful nation-state and a liberal constitutional state. In practice, however, the consolidation of the powerful position of the nation-state became of paramount importance and until 1878 the National Liberal Party was Bismarck's staunchest parliamentary ally.

Left wing Liberalism

Board 64

The aims of left wing liberalism were for a further refinement of the constitutional state and parliamentary monarchy. The bulk of their support came from craftsmen and the self-employed. Until 1910 left wing liberals were divided between the German Progress Party and the German People's Party and not until they were united as the Progressive People's Party was a common organisational base achieved.

The influence of Leopold Sonnemann led South German liberalism to adopt the idea of a state social policy. In the long term this provided the opportunity for cooperation with the social democrats. Friedrich Naumann and Theodor Barth were the pioneers of cooperation with the left.

The Conservatives

Board 66

Historic tradition and legalistic thoughts bound the conservatives to the old individual state dynasties. They remained sceptical about the unification of the Reich and about a "German Policy". Not until 1876 did the majority of the Prussian Conservative Party assent to the founding of the Reich. "Old conservative" opponents of Bismarck and "new conservatives" joined forces to set up the "German Conservative Party". The majority of their members came from the big land-owners of agriculture and the farming population of Eastern Germany provided their electoral support.

The Reichspartei

Board 67

Conservative industrialists and land-owners, who agreed with Bismarck's policy, found their political home as "Free Conservatives" in the Reichspartei. They accepted Bismarck's constitution and its unifying elements but rejected any step in the direction of the creation of a parliamentary system in the Reich.

The Centre

Board 69

Political catholicism considered itself threatened by the founding of the Reich. The predominance of protestants in the little-German nation-state and the influence of liberal ideas forced the catholics into opposition. In the cultural struggle Bismarck declared them as enemies of the Reich ("Reichsfeinde").
Southern German and Rhineland political catholicism was, however, more than simply a confessional representation of interests. Strong social reform forces made it into a focal point of the non-socialist lower classes.

Social Democracy

Board 70

In 1875 in Gotha, the "Lassallean" General German Worker's Association" of 1863 and the Social Democratic Workers' Party of 1869, which was strongly influenced by Karl Marx, joined forces to form the Socialist Workers' Party of Germany (SAPD). From 1891 onwards (after the Erfurt Programme) the party bore the name of "Social Democratic Party of Germany".
Labour production societies, radical-democratic aims and union demands were the central points of the Gotha Programme of the SAPD, which aimed for changes in the German nation-state in the form of internal reforms. Karl Marx criticised the Gotha Programme and its reformist tendencies sharply. He himself advocated radical changes for the German nation-state in the form of a revolutionary upheaval.

The Reich under Bismarck (Boards 73–91)

Boards 73/74 Serious crises, which were not just caused by the consequences of unrestricted economic growth after 1871, plauged the internal development of the Reich in the first decade following its establishment. The turning point in domestic policy, the change from free trade to protective policies in 1878/79, marked the end of the liberal era, even if the latter policies had never been fully carried through.

In 1878/79, on the basis of a temporary alliance of interests between heavy industry and the big land-owners, social and political positions were reinforced and ensured which blocked any further development of the Reich constitution along liberal and parliamentary-cemocratic lines. Quite justifiably, therefore, critics spoke of a Reich which was incomplete, not just as a constitutional state but also with regard to the social policy demands of the middle class emancipation movements. Their demands that the new state should adapt to the new industrial society and that the nation should be given an active role in the political process since it was the sum of the social forces, were ignored. The Reich was not founded on a desire for change but rather on the preservation of the old Prussian structure of society, in which the Junkers had a dominant position.

Boards 75/76 The social and party political arguments reached a peak with the conflict between the "enemies of the Reich", the Centre and the Social Democrats. This "private internal war" began with the conflict with the Catholic Church and the Catholic Movement over the inspection of schools and civil marriages *(cat. illustr. 144).*

The paragraph on sermons (Kanzelparagraph), which forbade the clergy to meddle in state matters "in a manner which might endanger peace", the May Laws of 1873 and the banning of the Jesuit Order, placed the church and clergy under state supervision. This led to the beginning of special legislation against "enemies of the Reich". The latter were suspected of "international connections" and of conspiracies with the national minorities.

The special and prohibition laws of the cultural struggle destroyed the belief that the national community would peacefully iron out problems caused by conflicting interests and would lead to mutual tolerance. Even after the special laws were repealed political catholicism remained mistrustful of the Reich.

IV/144 “a real mix up” – caricature of the cultural struggle from 1875.

IV/145 Hödel's assassination attempt on Kaiser Wilhelm I in Berlin, 11th May 1878.

IV/147 Police disband a workers' meeting.

IV/148 House-search of a political suspect.

Reichs-Gesetzblatt.

№ 34.

Inhalt: Gesetz gegen die gemeingefährlichen Bestrebungen der Sozialdemokratie. S. 351.

(Nr. 1271.) Gesetz gegen die gemeingefährlichen Bestrebungen der Sozialdemokratie. Vom 21. Oktober 1878.

Wir Wilhelm, von Gottes Gnaden Deutscher Kaiser, König von Preußen &c.

verordnen im Namen des Reichs, nach erfolgter Zustimmung des Bundesraths und des Reichstags, was folgt:

§. 1.

Vereine, welche durch sozialdemokratische, sozialistische oder kommunistische Bestrebungen den Umsturz der bestehenden Staats- oder Gesellschaftsordnung bezwecken, sind zu verbieten.

Dasselbe gilt von Vereinen, in welchen sozialdemokratische, sozialistische oder kommunistische auf den Umsturz der bestehenden Staats- oder Gesellschaftsordnung gerichtete Bestrebungen in einer den öffentlichen Frieden, insbesondere die Eintracht der Bevölkerungsklassen gefährdenden Weise zu Tage treten.

Den Vereinen stehen gleich Verbindungen jeder Art.

§. 2.

Auf eingetragene Genossenschaften findet im Falle des §. 1 Abs. 2 der §. 35 des Gesetzes vom 4. Juli 1868, betreffend die privatrechtliche Stellung der Erwerbs- und Wirthschaftsgenossenschaften, (Bundes-Gesetzbl. S. 415 ff.) Anwendung.

Auf eingeschriebene Hülfskassen findet im gleichen Falle der §. 29 des Gesetzes über die eingeschriebenen Hülfskassen vom 7. April 1876 (Reichs-Gesetzbl. S. 125 ff.) Anwendung.

§. 3.

Selbständige Kassenvereine (nicht eingeschriebene), welche nach ihren Statuten die gegenseitige Unterstützung ihrer Mitglieder bezwecken, sind im Falle des

Ausgegeben zu Berlin den 22. Oktober 1878.

IV/146 The “law against the aims of social democracy which are a danger to the people”, passed in 1878 by the Reichstag.

Law-Gazette of the Reich

No. 34

Content Law against the aims of social democracy of danger to the public.
(Nr. 1271) Law against the aims of social democracy of danger to the public. 21st October 1878
We, William, German Emperor and King of Prussia by the grace of God
decree in the name of the Reich, with the consent of the Bundesrat and Reichstag, as follows:

§ 1

Associations, which further social democratic, socialist or communist aims and thus threaten to overthrow the existing state – and social – structure, are banned.
The same applies to associations in which social democratic, socialist or communist aims are directed at the overthrow of the existing state – and social – structure in a manner which threatens peace and harmony amongst the population.
The same law on associations applies to alliances of any kind.

§ 2

In the case of registered societies, § 1 sect. 2 of § 35 of the law of 4th July 1868 concerning the status in private law of registered cooperative and business societies, applies (Federal Law Gazette pp 415 ff).
In the case of registered relief funds § 29 of the law on registered relief funds of 7th April 1876 applies (Reich's Law Gazette, pp 125 ff).

§ 3

Independent financial associations (unregistered) which according to their statutes mutually support their members, are subject to . . .

Law-gazette of the Reich 1878
Published in Berlin, 22nd October 1878

Board 77

At the peak of the quarrel with the Centre, Bismarck gave the Reichstag a taste of his political power. In 1874, he tabled a motion, concerning the law on the armed forces of the Reich, according to which the strength of the German army during peacetime would be constantly set at 402,000. This proposal would have deprived the Reichstag of four fifths of its prerogative powers over the state budget. "The seven year solution" was the compromise agreed: in view of the heavy French rearmament the Reichstag agreed to the military budget being set each seven years. In this way only every second Reichstag enjoyed full budgetary rights, its strongest weapon against the Chancellor and the government.

Boards 78/79

The foundations of the Reich were shaken even more strongly by Bismarck's battle against social democracy, which he began in spring 1878 out of fear of a social and political revolution and "red anarchy", when be blamed social democrats for two isolated attempts on the Kaiser's life *(cat. illustr. 145)*. The Reichstag was dissolved. The Anti-Socialist Law ensured a comfortable parliamentary majority *(cat. illustr. 146)*. Even the majority of National Liberals betrayed the constitutional state. All socialist and communist associations were disbanded, their publications were outlawed and socialist "agitators" were deported by the police authorities *(cat. illustr. 147/148)*. However, the workers stood by their political leaders. The failure of the repressive policies was not recognised until 1890. The Anti-Socialist Law was not renewed but the social democrats were still dubbed as enemies of the Reich.

Board 80

The counterpart to the Anti-Socialist Law was the state social policy *(cat. illustr. 149)*. With the assistance of the latter policy, i.e. through a social insurance scheme, the workers' support for the authoritarian state was to be gained. The "State socialism" of the insurance legislation (sickness, disability and old-age schemes) – without question a great, exemplary and effective achievement in the direction of social progress – was not however conceived by the chancellor as a social reform measure in the sense that it would provide protection for the workers and help to humanise the industrial environment. Rather, it was expressly aimed at winning over the "great mass of propertyless people" to the conservative way of thinking which accompanies the age of retirement. "Whoever has a pension for his old age", Bismarck once commented on his "taming policy", "he is much more content and easier to handle than the person who has no prospects". However, his attempt to alienate the labour force from social democracy failed.

Board 81 In the period of economic crisis after 1873 the worker-movement became more radical. In addition, the first big industrial and agriculatural associations grew up. They demanded the end of liberal free trade and favoured the erection of protective barriers. The deflection of cheap imports would make it possible to maintain excessively high domestic prices, which for their part would make it possible to export at predetermined low price levels. In 1876, the central organisation for industrial associations, the "Central Association of German Industrialists" (c.v.d. I) was formed.

Board 82 The agricultural crises of the 1870s also led the large land-owners of Eastern Germany to turn away from free trade principles. "The union of tax and economic reformers" (founded in 1876) became their representative which advocated the erection of protective barriers. The German Conservative Party, which was formed in the same year, took on the economic policy demands of the large agricultural land-owners. Thus heavy industry and agriculture had found common ground in that they both demanded protective barriers. Their struggle was significant for the economic policy ideas of liberalism.

Board 83 Bismarck's plans, however, went far beyond a simple change in direction with regard to customs policy. A clear rift with the liberals, his former allies during the cultural struggle, made a political alliance with the conservative parties more easy to attain. According to Bismarck, the "Junkers" had "the advantage of being a patient, loyal, conservatively minded people". They gave "the state a wealth of taxes", they were experienced as a "reliable source on which the state must rely" in all internal and external crises.

A tax and finance reform was aimed at strengthening the Reich. The increased income from customs and indirect taxes (tobacco, brandy, coffee) would have made the Reich financially self-supporting without taking account of the budgetary contributions of the federal states. However, this plan failed mainly because of resistance from the federalist Centre Party.

Boards 84–87 The National Liberal grouping collapsed over the issues surrounding the protective barrier proposal with only a minority remaining in Bismarck's camp. In this way the conservative leaders of the Reich had achieved a major success. The hopes for the establishment of a true parliamentary system, namely an

IV/149 Portrayal of Bismarck's social legislation "The German Social Insurance Scheme stands as an unrivalled model before the whole world".

IV/151 “Dropping the Pilot”, cartoon by Sir John Teniel from ‘Punch’, March 1890.

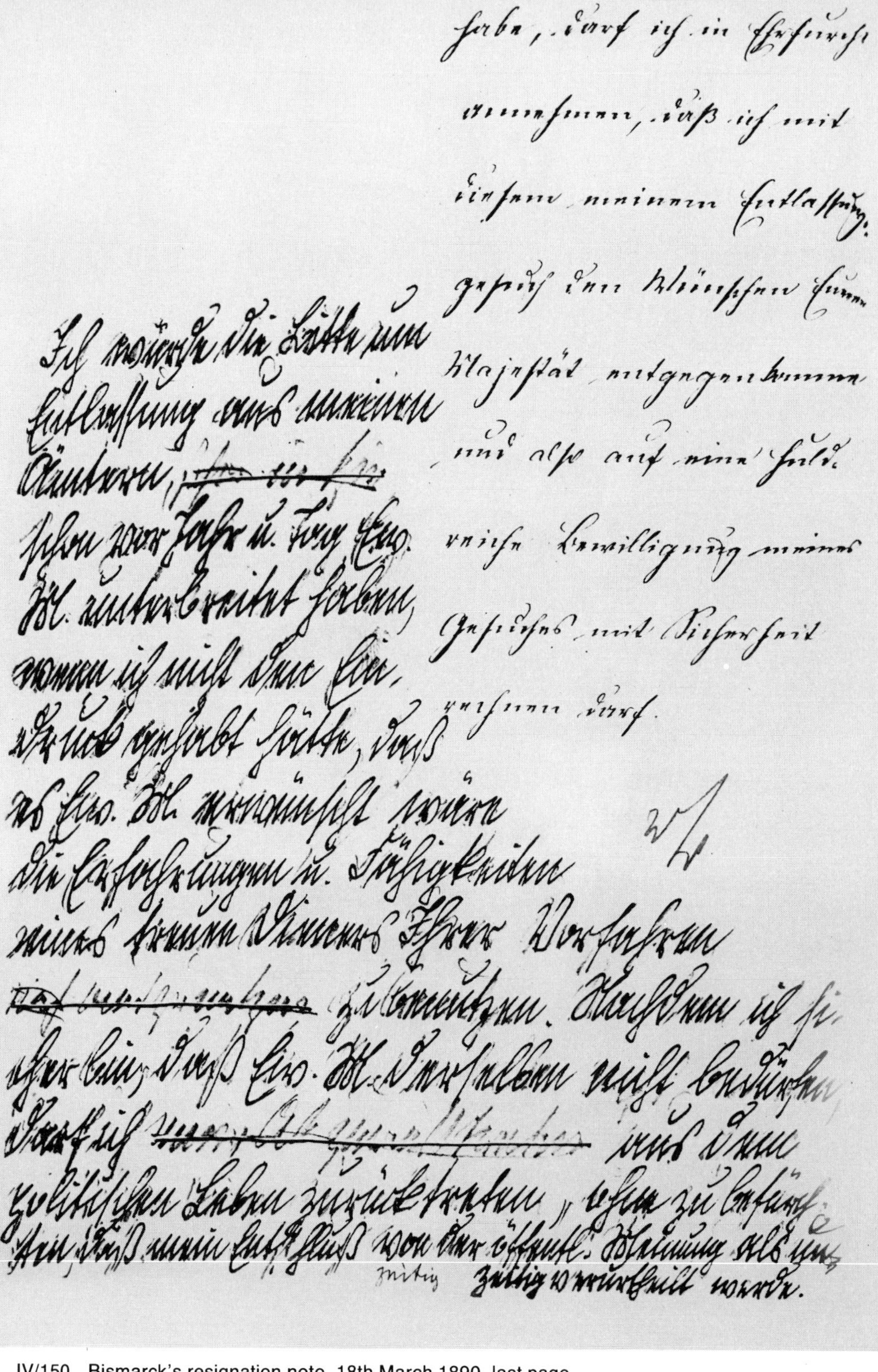
habe, darf ich in Ehrfurcht
annehmen, daß ich mit
diesem meinem Entlassungs-
gesuch den Wünschen Eurer
Majestät entgegenkomme
und also auf eine huld-
reiche Bewilligung meines
Gesuches mit Sicherheit
rechnen darf.

v B

Ich würde die Bitte um
Entlassung aus meinen
Ämtern, ~~[illegible]~~
schon vor Jahr u. Tag Ew.
M. unterbreitet haben,
wenn ich nicht den Ein-
druck gehabt hätte, daß
es Ew. M. erwünscht wäre
die Erfahrungen u. Fähigkeiten
eines treuen Dieners Ihrer Vorfahren
~~[illegible]~~ zu benutzen. Nachdem ich si-
cher bin, daß Ew. M. derselben nicht bedürfen
darf ich ~~[illegible]~~ aus dem
politischen Leben zurücktreten, ohne zu befürch-
ten, daß mein Entschluß von der öffentl. Meinung als un-
zeitig
zeitig verurtheilt werde.

IV/150 Bismarck's resignation note, 18th March 1890, last page.

I hereby request that I be relieved of my offices acknowledging that the experience and ability of a faithful servant are no longer required. Attached as I am to the service of the Royal House and of Your Majesty, and accustomed for many years to conditions which I have hitherto regarded as permanent, it is very painful for me to sever my wonted relations with your majesty and to break off my connection with the entire policy of the Reich and of Prussia.

IV/152 Wilhelm II, portrait by Max Koner, 1890.

effective controlling function for the Reichstag over the executive, were dashed. The Reich assumed, in many respects, the character of a class-based state. This turning point in domestic policy in 1878/79 was quite justifiably referred to as the establishment of a "second Reich".

Wilhelminian Germany (Boards 92–112)

Boards 92/93 The major domestic political issues of the 'Wilhelminian Era' were the fight against social democracy, the tough policy pursued against national minorities, the Prussian three class voting system and the failures along the road towards establishing a system where the government would be responsible to Parliament. Only the dynamic growth of Germany into the greatest European industrial state prevented the eruption of smouldering tensions. The bureaucratisation and militarisation of public life and an imperialist foreign policy which stirred people's emotions at home bound nationalism and militarism with the monarchist authoritarian state.

Bismarck's dismissal

Board 94 Kaiser Wilhelm II wished to reduce Bismarck's political influence. He was aiming to set up a 'personal regime'. A 'new course' was to be steered: at home there was to be a reconciliation with the social democrats and his foreign policy aim was to win for Germany world power status. These aims provoked a conflict between Wilhelm and the Chancellor. Bismarck considered his policy of keeping socialism and nationalism in check to be threatened, in addition to his plans for maintaining peace. In 1890 Bismarck was dismissed *(cat. illustr. 150, 151).*

Bismarck's successors

Boards 95/96 Caprivi's and later Hohenlohe's concepts of a 'government above the parties' were just as unsuccessful as the efforts made by Bülow to prop up the government by creating a 'block' of middle class and conservative groupings. The careful attempt made by Bethmann Hollweg to free the Reich from its rigid

IV/153 Car from 1897.

IV/154 Landing of the first 'Parseval' airship in Munich, 14th October 1909.

Abonnements.

[Abonnements w]erden beim Verlag und dessen [b]ekannten Agenten entgegengenommen, und zwar zum
voraus zahlbaren
Vierteljahrspreis von:
Mk. 4,40 für Deutschland (direkt per Brief-Couvert)
fl. 2,75 für Oesterreich (direkt per Brief-Couvert)
Schill. 2,— für alle übrigen Länder des Weltpostvereins (Kreuzband)

Inserate
die dreigespaltene Petitzeile
3 Pence = 25 Pfg. = 30 Cts.

Der Sozialdemokrat

Organ der Sozialdemokratie deutscher Zunge.

Erscheint
wöchentlich einmal
in
London.

Verlag
der
German Cooperative Publishing Co.
E. Bernstein & Co., London N. W.
114 Kentish Town Road.

Postsendungen
franko gegen franko.
Gewöhnliche Briefe
nach England kosten Doppelporto.

№. 10.

Briefe an die Redaktion und Expedition des in Deutschland und Oesterreich verbotenen „Sozialdemokrat" wolle man unter Beobachtung äußerster Vorsicht abgehen lassen. In der Regel schicke man nur die Briefe nicht direkt, sondern an die bekannten Deckadressen. In zweifelhaften Fällen eingeschrieben.

8. März 1890.

20 Mandate im ersten Wahlgang, 16 in der Stichwahl.
1,341,587 sozialdemokratische Wähler — 567,405 Zuwachs

Im ersten Wahlgang gewählt:

Glauchau-Meerane:
J. Auer, Sattler (Schriftsteller) in München.
Hamburg I.:
A. Bebel, Drechslermeister (Schriftsteller) in Dresden.
Hamburg II.:
J. H. W. Dietz, Buchdrucker in Stuttgart.
Greiz:
E. Förster, Zigarrenarbeiter in Hamburg.
Altona:
Karl Frohme, Schlosser (Schriftsteller) in Hannover.
Leipzig-Land:
F. Geyer, Zigarrenarbeiter in Großenhain.
Nürnberg:
K. Grillenberger, Schlosser (Korrektor) in Nürnberg.
Barmen-Elberfeld:
F. Harm, Weber (Gastwirth) in Barmen.
Mülhausen i./Elsaß:
F. Hickel, Schreiner in Mühlhausen.
Berlin VI.:
W. Liebknecht, Schriftsteller in Borsdorf.
Hamburg III.:
Wilhelm Metzger, Spengler (Journalist) in Hamburg.
Chemnitz:
Max Schippel, Schriftsteller in Berlin.
Mittweida-Limbach:
A. Schmidt, Buchdrucker in Berlin.
Solingen:
Gg. Schuhmacher, Gerber in Solingen.
Schneeberg-Stollberg:
J. Seifert, Schuhmacher in Zwickau.
Berlin IV.:
P. Singer, Kaufmann in Dresden.
Zwickau-Crimmitschau:
W. Stolle, Gärtner (Gastwirth) in Gesau.
München II und Magdeburg:
G. Vollmar, Schriftsteller in München.
Gera:
E. Wurm, Schriftsteller in Dresden.

In der Stichwahl wurden gewählt:

München I:
J. Birk, Gastwirth in München.
Braunschweig:
W. Blos, Schriftsteller in Stuttgart.
Bremen:
J. Bruhns, Zigarrenarbeiter in Bremen.
Mannheim:
A. Dreesbach, Tischler (Kaufm.) Mannheim.
Calbe-Aschersleben:
Aug. Heine, Hutfabrikant in Halberstadt.
Mainz:
Franz Jöst, Tischler in Mainz.
Halle a. Saale:
Fritz Kunert, Lehrer (Redakteur) in Breslau.
Hannover:
H. Meister, Zigarren-Arbeiter in Hannover.
Ottensen-Pinneberg:
H. Molkenbuhr, Zig.-Arbeiter in Kellinghusen.
Frankfurt a./M.:
Wilh. Schmidt, Lithograph in Frankfurt.
Sonneberg:
P. Reißhaus, Schneider in Erfurt.
Königsberg i. Pr.:
Carl Schultze, Zigarrenarbeiter in Königsberg
Lübeck:
Th. Schwartz, Koch (Gastwirth) in Lübeck.
Nieder-Barnim:
Arth. Stadthagen, Rechtsanwalt in Berlin.
Breslau-Ost:
Franz Tutzauer, Tischler in Berlin.
Offenbach-Dieburg:
Carl Ulrich, Schlosser (Redakteur) in Offenbach.

Siegreiche Stichwahlen:

	1890	1887	Stichwahl
München I	7,570	4,563	10,433
Braunschweig	13,621	10,656	15,000
Bremen	14,843	7,743	16,404
Mannheim	8,701	5,128	12,601
Calbe-Aschersleben	12,514	4,827	16,373
Mainz	8,000	5,526	10,900
Halle a./S	12,618	6,550	14,500
Hannover	16,570	12,210	19,900
Ottensen	10,820	6,520	13,010
Königsberg	12,327	7,987	13,138
Frankfurt a. M.	12,654	8640	18,090
Lübeck	6,[illegible]	4,254	7,316
Nieder-Barnim	13,628	5,680	15,400
Breslau-Ost	9,996	7,781	12,337
Offenbach	10,334	8,024	13,000
Sonneberg	7,215	4,659	10,000

IV/155 The mouthpiece of the German social democrats, which appeared in London, announces the electoral successes in the Reichstag elections of 1890.

political system by cooperating with the left wing liberal Progressive People's Party and with the social democrats also failed. The conservative forces in the civil service and amongst the officer ranks were able to exert a crucial influence upon the course of German domestic policy.

The Period of Economic Prosperity

Board 97 1895 heralded the start of a new period of economic prosperity and rapid technical development for German industry *(cat. illustr. 153, 154)*. The expansion of the chemical and electronics industries in particular led to a second wave of industrialisation. Powerful concerns such as Krupp, Siemens, and the dyers Meister Lucins and Brüning dominated the market *(cat. illustr. XVI)*. However, whilst Germany was becoming the greatest industrial nation in Europe, domestic political conflicts were beginning to escalate again.

The Fight against Social Democracy

Board 98 The repealing of the anti-socialist law and the passing of social legislation in 1890/91 were aimed at reconciling the social democrats with the Reich. Nevertheless, the social democrats under August Bebel stuck to their opposition stance. Disappointed, the Kaiser dropped the 'treacherous comrades' but Chancellor Caprivi refused to renew the policy of suppression of this party whose support was growing steadily *(cat. illustr. 155)*. His successor, Prince Hohenlohe-Schillingfürst, however, tried to implement this policy again; he proposed a tightening up of the political laws and that coalitions which were forced by strikes should be avenged by prison sentences. However, his 'subversion' proposal (1894) and 'prison' proposal (1899) were rejected by the Reichstag.

'Revisionists' and 'Orthodox supporters' in the SPD

Board 99 The question: revolution or reform? was much disputed by social democrats. Full employment and rising real incomes cast doubt on Marx's theories of impoverishment and revolution.

Georg von Vollmar and Eduard Bernstein were the leading spokesmen of the reformists, who were opposed by the marxist 'Centre Party' led by Karl Kautsky. The reformists received their strongest support from the trade unions.

The Trade Unions

Board 100

Trade unions had been established as early as the 1860s as representatives of the economic and social interests of the workers. However, they were unable to develop into mass organisations until the anti-socialist laws had been repealed. The Free Socialist Unions, organised into industrial federations, had 50,000 members in 1890, 680,000 in 1900 and more than 2.5 million in 1913. The top tier of their organisation, the 'General Commission', became the largest labour organisation in Europe under Carl Legien's leadership. The liberal Hirsch-Dunker labour association and the Christian unions remained in existence but were of less importance.

Industrial and Agricultural Interest Groups

Board 101

The employers also formed large and influential organisations. As a response to the great textile workers' strike in Crimmitschau (1904) the employers' associations amalgamated to form two confederations: the 'Headquarters of German Employers' Associations' and the 'Association of German Employers'. Both of these confederations were closely linked to the 'Central Association of German Industrialists'. The 'Federation of Industrialists' Bd I split from the conservative 'Central Association of German Industrialists' cvd I who supported protective tariff barriers. The breakaway 'Federation of Industrialists' represented mainly the growing chemical and middle class export-oriented industries and supported the policies of the National Liberals. The 'Federation of Farmers' had been fighting against the reduction in corn tariffs since 1893. One of its 'weapons' was agitation of a strongly anti-semitic nature.

The 'Grouping of middle class forces'

Board 102

The liberal middle class, which was in danger of being crushed and destroyed between agriculture and industry on the one hand and the workers on the other, was summoned by Johann Miquel, the new leader of the National Liberals, to form a 'collective movement' which would aim to prevent any further strengthening of the social democrats' position. On the defensive in domestic political affairs, the middle class forces pursued a line of aggressive, imperialistic, power politics. The 'Pan German Association', the 'Flottenverein' and the colonial associations spread nationalist and anti-semitic ideas. Interest and pressure groups not only dominated parliamentary lobbies; in view of the impotence of the Reichstag they gained a dangerously strong influence over German politics as a whole.

The idea of the 'Social Empire': Friedrich Naumann

Board 103

Leading left wing liberals such as Max Weber and Friedrich Naumann saw in the pursuit of a dynamic foreign policy the promise of a break-up of the rigid domestic political structures. An Empire which carried out social reforms should be able to reconcile the workers with the state. However, Naumann's plans were foiled, along with his National Social Association which he had founded in 1896, by powerful conservative interests opposing them.

In other areas attempts to make reforms were blocked from the outset: they were faced with the growing demands for power made by the Kaiser and the armed forces, the fragmentation of political parties, which, in addition, because of the electoral laws in Prussia and the Reich, only reflected the true relative political positions in the country to a limited degree, and the overwhelming influence of the interest groups.

The 'Daily Telegraph' Affair

Board 104

In October 1908 an interview given by the Kaiser to the 'Daily Telegraph' was published which did a good deal of harm to German external relations. All parties were sorely angered by the Kaiser's despotic action. Chancellor von Bülow refused to accept responsibility for this before Parliament. Wilhelm II backed down in the face of such harsh criticism and he explained publicly that he would in future observe only his 'constitutional responsibility'. The Reichstag gained considerable ground through this affair but the chance to secure a parliamentary regime was missed. Only the social democrats, the Centre and left wing liberals demanded a change in the constitution.

The Three Class Voting System in Prussia and the Constituency Policy in the Reich

Board 105

The social democrats and liberals fought in vain for a change in the three class voting system in Prussia which divided the enfranchised citizens into three classes on the basis of the amount of tax they paid. However, there were not only injustices in Prussian Landtag elections; these also occurred in Reichstag elections. In 1871 the constituencies in the Reich were divided up so that one MP represented approximately 100,000 inhabitants. However, the urbanisation of the main industrialised areas created many distortions which, in the main, worked against the workers' party. Nevertheless, the SPD succeeded in becoming the largest party in the Reichstag in 1912.

The Policy on National Minorities

Board 106

In the East the expropriation law passed in 1908 made it possible to confiscate Polish property as part of the Prussian policy of Germanisation. Germans were then housed on this property. The Ostmarkenverein pursued a public propaganda campaign against the 'Poles'. In Alsace-Lorraine the conflicts reached a peak with the Zabern incident of 1913. Prussian troops broke up a public meeting there and arrested 28 demonstrators. The commander responsible for the troops, in ordering his troops to make the arrests, had taken the law into his own hands. However, a military court pronounced him to be innocent of all charges. The Reichstag tried in vain to intervene.

Boards 108–112

It became clear during these crises and the ensuing parliamentary debates before the war that the Reichstag was in no position to challenge the authority of the traditional powers in the Kaiser's court, in agriculture, industry, the bureaucracy and the armed forces.

German Foreign Policy 1871–1914 (Boards 113–127)

Board 113 When the Empire was founded in 1871 an economic and military sphere of influence was established in middle Europe which the other great powers conceived as a political threat to the balance of power in Europe. The annexing of Alsace-Lorraine made an enemy of France for the Reich. Bismarck only succeeded in incorporating Germany into the traditional European balance of power system and by so doing ensuring her security, by forming a complex series of alliances and by making repeated statements promising that Germany had enough territory and no more expansionist aims. Wilhelm II steered a different course. His 'Weltpolitik' was to secure for Germany a 'place in the sun'. The foreign policy of the Reich thus reached incalculable heights. Following the break with Russia, the building up of the fleet and the continual boasting about Germany's strength caused a worsening of relations with Great Britain. The final outcome of all these developments was the self-inflicted isolation of the Reich.

Board 114 Bismarck laid down the outlines of his foreign policy in the 'Kissingen Statement' *(cat. illustr. IV/156)*. Henceforth, Germany should profit from its 'free middle position' by seeking to regulate the conflicts between the great powers in their colonial policies and by diverting tension away from the middle of Europe to the periphery. He mapped out 'the ideal overall political situation, in which all the powers, exept for France, will need us and will be prevented, as far as is possible, from forming alliances against us because of their relations to one another'. The Reich should become the 'lead surround of the European kelly doll'.

Boards 115/116 The driving force behind this concept was the nightmare that the other European powers might form powerful alliances directed against Germany ('cauchemar des coalitions'). This fear was sparked off by the diplomatic intervention of Great Britain and Russia in favour of France in 1875 when the German press and the general military staff discussed private war plans in view of the reorganisation of the French army. "Is war in sight?" asked

IV/157 Bismarck at the Berlin Congress of 1878, woodcarving of a painting by Anton von Werner.

Wenn ich arbeitsfähig wäre, könnte ich das Bild vervollständigen und feiner ausarbeiten, welches mir vorschwebt: nicht das irgend eines Ländererwerbs, sondern das einer politischen Gesammtsituation, in welcher alle Mächte außer Frankreich unserer bedürfen, und von Koalitionen gegen uns durch ihre Beziehungen zu einander nach Möglichkeit abgehalten werden.

IV/156 Extract from the 'Kissingen Statement' of 16th June 1877 in the handwriting of Herbert von Bismarck.

"... If I were fit for work then I should be able to complete and refine the plan which I have conceived: that an overall political situation is created, in which not just one country but all the powers, with the exception of France, depend on us, and through their relations to one another are prevented, as far as is possible, from forming alliances against us".

the free conservative newspaper 'Die Post' on the 8th April 1875. However, Bismarck denied this.

Board 117 The foreign policy idea of a voluntary limitation of German leadership claims within the European balance of powers was transformed into a practical policy at the Berlin Congress of 1878. Bismarck offered that the Germans would act as intermediaries in the search for a solution to the quarrel between England, Austria-Hungary and Russia over the sharing of territory in the Balkans. He became the 'honest broker' of European interests *(cat. illustr. 157)*. The Reich became the power which guaranteed stability in Europe.

Boards 118–120 Colonial policy was less important in Bismarck's opinion than the task of pushing European conflicts to the 'periphery'. Only hesitantly and then because of consideration for the European equilibrium, did he give in to the pressure of the Colonial Association and the Society for German Colonisation (Carl Peters). In 1884/85 parts of South West Africa, the Cameroons, Togoland, several South Sea islands and an area in East Africa were colonised by Germany.

Board 121 After Bismarck's dismissal Wilhelm II steered a 'new course': his motto was "'Weltpolitik' as a task, to become a world power as an aim and the fleet as an instrument" (cat. illustr. 152, 158). The building up of the fleet was a matter of prestige for him and his advisers, in which account was taken of the collision course that this meant with Great Britain. Bismarck's 'line to Petersberg' was also severed: the 'Reinsurance Treaty' of 1887 was not renewed in 1890. The consequence of this policy was a Franco-Russian rapprochement. The Reich overestimated its strength.

Boards 122/123 In the imperialist states' race to divide up the world between themselves Wilhelm II demanded a 'place in the sun' for Germany. However, attempts to expand the German Colonial Empire did not have any great success: between 1897 and 1899 Tsingtau, the Caroline-Marianne-Palau islands and parts of the Samoa islands were colonised.

The Kaiser's aggressive speeches and the brutality shown by the 'Expeditionscorps' and the 'Schutztruppen' (colonial troops) in putting down uprisings in the colonies damaged German standing in the world.

Board 124 Moreover, the Reich did not take advantage of the opportunity for a rapprochement with Great Britain when Anglo-French rivalry reached a peak over the Sudan in the Faschoda conflict of 1898. In addition, the building up of a battle fleet and the construction of the Baghdad railway damaged British interests. In 1904 Britain and France finally settled their differences over colonial policy and signed the Entente Cordiale. German attempts to take control of Morocco failed because of the joint opposition of Britain and France. Finally, in 1907 an Anglo-Russian agreement was reached on their respective spheres of interest in Asia and the Reich began to feel 'encircled'.

Board 125 The attempt made by the Balkan people to become united in nation states, by dividing up the European territories of Turkey, who had been defeated in 1912, and by taking some Austro-Hungarian territory, conflicted with the economic and political interests of the great powers. This complicated political and military situation threatened to become the fuse on the 'Powder-barrel of Europe' *(cat. illustr. 159)*.

Boards 126/127 On 28th June 1914, the Austrian heir to the throne, Archduke Franz Ferdinand, and his wife were murdered by a Serbian nationalist in Sarajewo. As a result, Vienna wanted to solve the Serbian question in its own way. In order to do so Austria needed German support. German diplomacy was geared, in contrast to the armed forces, towards avoiding a great war, if at all possible. England also wanted to negotiate. On the other hand, France was bound to support the Russians in any Balkan conflicts by the Poincaré Agreement of 1912. Therefore, she supported a policy of firm rejection of all Austrian annexation plans. When the Russians ordered a general mobilisation on 31st July 1914 the dice were cast in Berlin in favour of a military solution. The automatic mobilisation of the various powers destroyed any hope of solving the problem through political means *(cat. illustr. 160)*.

The First World War (Boards 144–155)

Board 144 The Franco-German arms race and the naval rivalry with England were just as important causes of the First World War as Russia's aggressive Balkan's policy and the close links forged between the German Reich and the uncertain fate of the multinational Austrian state. Finally, a blind trust in German military superiority led to a policy of offensives being adopted. In 1917 the USA entered the war. In the same year the Bolschevik Revolution succeeded in Russia. These two events marked the

Die Marine-Tabellen Seiner Majestät des Kaisers Wilhelm.

Verkleinerte Facsimile-Nachbildung der Kaiserlichen Originale.

Deutschland's Neubauten

in und seit 1893 bewilligt

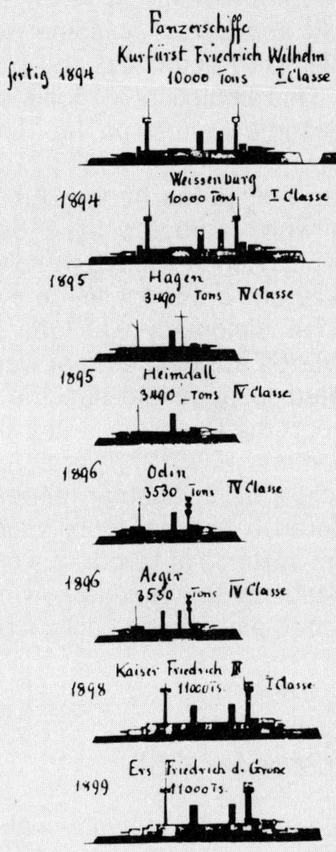

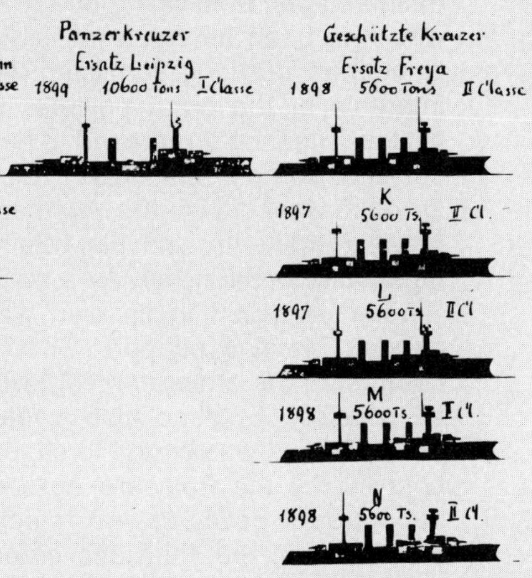

1893 — 1897 inclusive.

Anmerkungen

In derselben Zeitperiode hat Frankreich gebaut: oder im Bau:
10 Panzerschiffe I Classe 4 Panzerschiffe II Classe 8 Panzerkreuzer I Classe
19 Panzerdeckskreuzer I–III Classe: Summe: 41 Schiffe = 10 Divisionen à 4 Schiffe
In derselben Zeitperiode hat Russland gebaut oder im Bau (nur in der Ostsee)
7 Panzerschiffe I Classe 2 Panzerschiffe III Classe 4 Panzerkreuzer I Classe,
3 Panzerdeckskreuzer II Classe = 10 Schiffe = 4 Divisionen à 4 Schiffe
Mithin werden Frankreich und Russland Ende 1899 an neuen Schiffen im Dienst haben:
Summe: 17 Panzschiffe I Classe, 6 Panzer II Classe, 12 Panzerkreuzer I Cl, 22 Panzerdeckskreuzer II Cl
im Ganzen 57 neue Schiffe = 14 Divisionen à 4 Schiffe
Deutschland: 4 Panzerschiffe I Classe, 4 Panzerschiffe II Classe, 1 Panzerkreuzer I Cl, 5 Panzerdeckskreuzer II Cl
Summe 14 Schiffe = 3 Divisionen à 4 Schiffe
Mithin 43 Schiffe Uebermacht über Deutschland im Neubau begriffen
= 13 Divisionen à 4 Schiffe

W. I. R 7/II 97

IV/158 A naval chart drawn by Wilhelm II.

IV/159 "The Boiling Kettle", 'Punch' cartoon from 1908 on the Balkan Crisis.

Ich bestimme hiermit: Das Deutsche Heer und die Kaiserliche Marine sind nach Maßgabe des Mobilmachungsplans für das Deutsche Heer und die Kaiserliche Marine kriegsbereit aufzustellen.

Der 2. August 1914 wird als erster Mobilmachungstag festgesetzt. – Berlin, den 1. August 1914

Wilhelm

I. R.

v. Bethmann Hollweg

An den Reichskanzler (Reichs-Marineamt) und den Kriegsminister.

IV/160 Mobilisation order of 1st August 1914.

"... I hereby announce: the German Army and the Imperial Navy are ordered to take the necessary measures to implement the mobilisation plan and to prepare themselves for war.
The 2nd August is laid down as the first day of mobilisation – Berlin, 1st August 1914".

Wilhelm

Bethmann Hollweg

To the Reich Chancellor (Naval Office) and the War Minister.

IV/161 General war fever, beginning of August 1914.

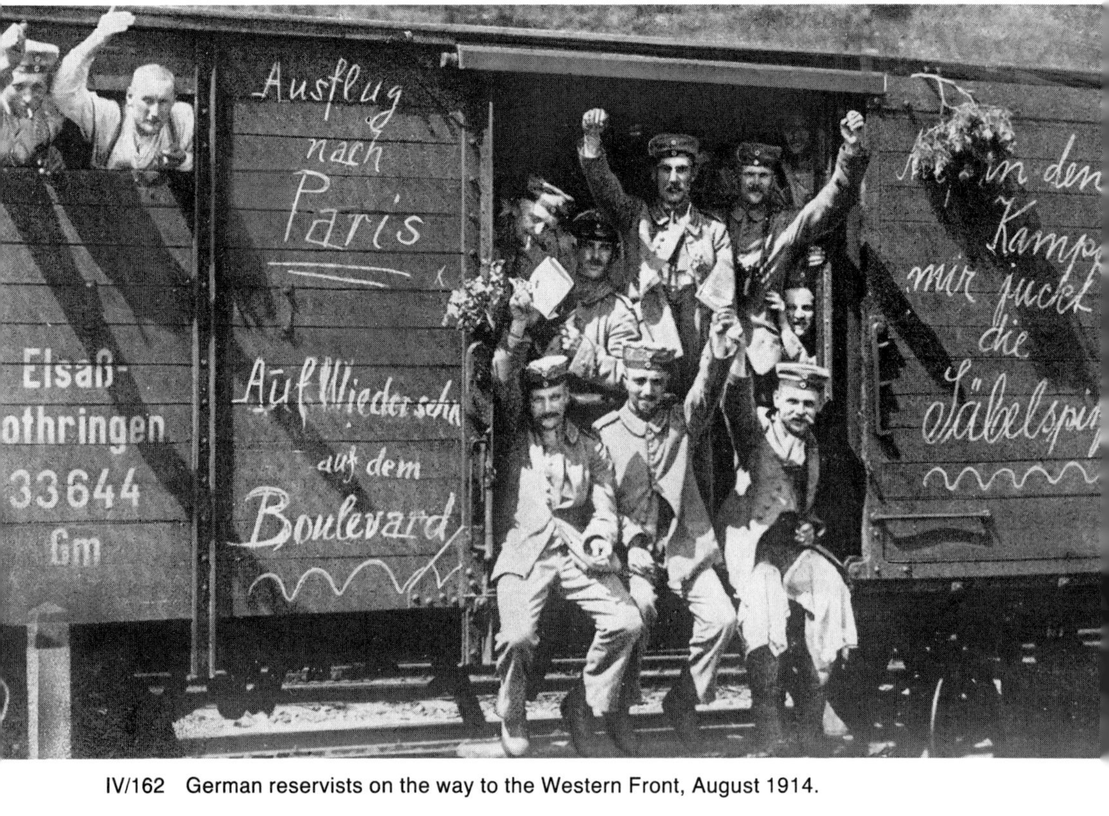

IV/162 German reservists on the way to the Western Front, August 1914.

end of an era of middle class self-confidence and of European world dominance. The defeat of the German Reich also meant the defeat of its conservative leaders. The struggle to restructure Germany and to establish a social democracy began, faced with the burden of the Versailles Peace Treaty.

Boards 145/146 The declaration of war aroused initially much enthusiasm *(cat. illustr. 161, 162)*. Only a minority warned of the dangers. The political parties agreed to a 'truce'. The nation was apparently united behind the banner of a fully justified war of self defence. Even the social democrats voted in favour of the war credits.

Board 147 With invasion of Belgium in the West the mobile warfare began. However, the German advance was halted in the Autumn at the Battle of the Marne.

The year-long battle waged near Verdun in northern France and in Flanders claimed the lives of millions of soldiers. The 8th August 1918 came to be known as the 'black day' of the German army: allied tanks broke through the front near Amiens. The withdrawal to the defensive position of the 'Siegfried line' began. The hope of a victory in the West had long since been abandoned in the face of the danger of a total collapse of the front.

Board 148 In the East, the Reich had initially to adopt a defensive position. In August 1914 Eastern Prussia was threatened by the 'Russian steamroller'. This danger was, however, averted by General von Hindenburg by his pincer movements at Tannenberg and the Masurian Lakes. After early successes the Russian offensive also failed in the Carpathian Mountains where they suffered heavy losses. Austro-German counter-offensives under General von Mackensen brought Russia to the brink of collapse. The agitation of the revolutionaries found fertile ground in the Russian army. In 1917 the supreme German army command permitted Lenin, the Bolshevik leader, to travel through Germany by rail.

Board 149 In March 1918 the Bolsheviks, who had succeeded with their October Revolution, had to accept the Peace Treaty of Brest-Litowsk. Russia lost her western provinces; the Ukraine was granted independence. Reparations were exacted by the German 'rail-advance' although troops were urgently required in the West. Under the command of Hindenburg and Ludendorff the army had, with their 'great eastern solution', won a questionable victory over the political leaders.

Board 150 In December 1916, the Reich made a first attempt to begin peace negotiations but these were turned down by the Allies. The Germans reacted to this refusal by becoming determined to win victory at all costs and resolved at home to guard against any democratic 'softness'. The Chancellor, Bethmann Hollweg, was dismissed. His successor, Michaelis, was completely under the influence of the supreme army command. Hindenburg and Ludendorff now enjoyed not only military leadership but also de facto political control.

Board 152

In 1917 the 'Inter Group Committee' was formed by the SPD, the Centre and the Progressive People's Party. Its aim was: the establishment of a parliamentary monarchy and a negotiated peace without victors or losers. This programme formed the basis of the Reichstag's peace resolution of July 1917.

Boards 153–155

For a section of SPD representatives the ideas of the inter group committee did not go far enough. As committed pacifists they refused to agree to further war credits and broke away from the SPD to form the 'Independent Social Democratic Party' (USPD). The USPD formally joined the 'International Group' which, under the leadership of Karl Liebknecht and Rosa Luxemburg, had been actively opposed to the war policies of the Reichstag majority since 1915 under the banner of 'Down with the war'. As the 'Spartakus Group' the 'International Group' formed the germ cell of the future German Communist Party (KPD).

The military and political tensions of 1917 caused Wilhelm II to think about a possible reform of the three class voting system in Prussia. However, the leadership of the Reich, under the influence of the Supreme Army Command, only agreed to any real political concessions after the military situation had become hopeless: the October Reforms of 1918, introduced by the Chancellor, Prince Max von Baden, represented the first real step towards a parliamentary system of government – too late, as was already apparent.

The German Empire after 1918

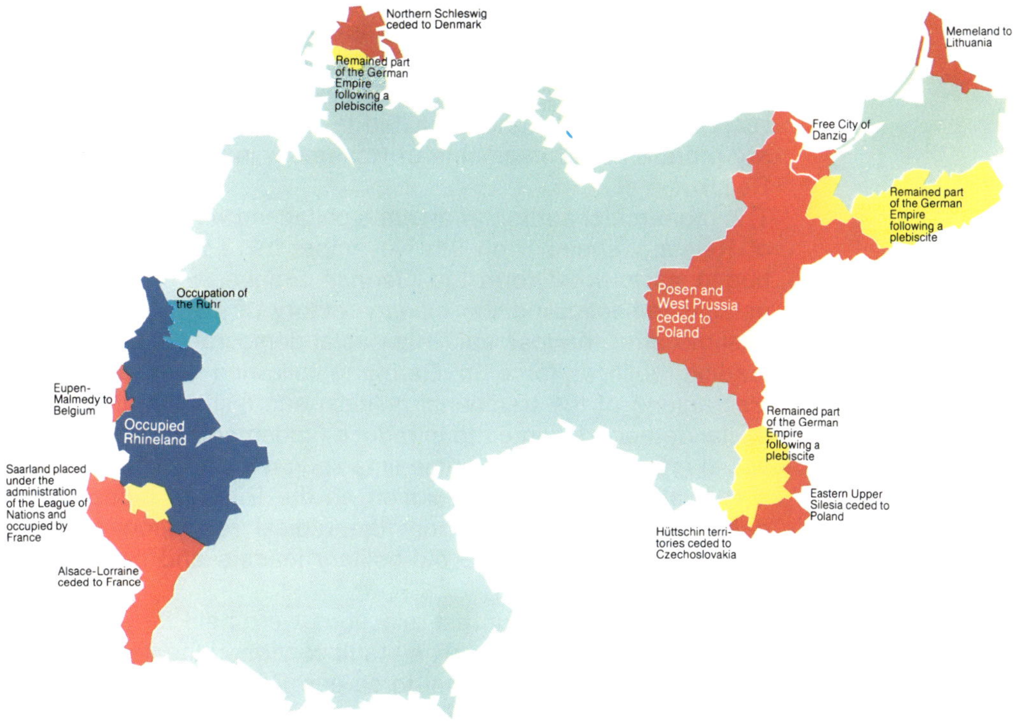

Room V

The Weimar Republic

In the autumn of 1918 after four years of war the national fervour, which had united Germans of all persuasions as one, in August 1914, had turned into complete disillusionment and exhaustion. The imminent military defeat caused old conflicts to reappear and eventually resulted in a spontaneous revolutionary protest at the beginning of November in many areas of the Reich.

The monarchist authoritarian state collapsed with the abdication of Kaiser Wilhelm II on 9th November 1918. Arguments then began as to what form the German Empire, which had been established following the military victory of 1871, should now assume after the lost war. The social democrats were now the leading political force in Germany following the widespread discrediting of the traditional political and military leaders. The social democrats aimed to introduce fundamental economic and social reforms but at the same time sought to prevent at all costs a radicalisation of the revolution on the Russian model. As a defence against attacks from the radical revolutionary camp they cooperated with the old military leaders and the imperial administration.

Amidst revolutionary unrest, elections were held for a constitutional National Assembly. The result confirmed the social democrats as the leading political force and Friedrich Ebert became the first President of the Reich. The constitution of 11th August 1919 ended the transition period of almost one year since Wilhelm II's abdication. It fulfilled the old liberal call for a parliamentary democracy and also guaranteed for the population a direct influence on the political decision-making process. Before the introducation of the constitution, however, significant decisions were taken which had a lasting effect on future developments in Germany and which were to affect adversely the political atmosphere. The victors dictated, in the Treaty of Versailles, that Germany should cede certain territories and this weakened considerably the economic power of the Reich. Demands for reparations were a financial burden, which weighed all the more heavily since the German currency had lost much of its value due to the war debts. The warguilt article of the Treaty of Versailles was, however, the main reason why it was unanimously rejected in Germany. Nevertheless, the leading politicians had no other choice but to sign the Treaty. The nationalist right wingers, who had found the defeat and the revolution impossible to accept, now spread the 'stab in the back' legend and accused the parties, which had accepted a negotiated peace in 1917 and which were now jointly governing the country, of betraying an army which was 'undefeated in the field'. The right wing radical agitation escalated into a series of putsches and political assassinations and provoked a counter-reaction from left wing radicals. The Reichstag elections of 1920 reflected the anti-republican feeling, which was further strengthened by economic developments. The Reich shifted the costs of the lost war onto those, who had financed the war through loans, and in so doing it lost the support of large sections of the middle class, whose standard of living was threatened by a depreciations of their savings. Inflation reached a peak in 1923 which was caused mainly by reparations and the occupation of the Ruhr. Before the 'Rentenmark' restored some stability to the economy, a redistribution of national income had taken place which severely shook the social structure of the Reich.

The Allies recognised that the necessary economic conditions for reparations' payments to be completed did not exist in Germany. Therefore a series of conferences and plans sought to find a solution to the problem of reparations which dominated German domestic and foreign policy for years. Even though the burden of the rearranged reparations was heavy, German factories were modernised thanks to foreign investment and this led to the recovery of the German economy, which considerably influenced social and political developments after 1924. Real wages, production and export figures reached and exceeded their pre-war levels around 1926. This relative prosperity produced a sense of recovery and even gave some limited hope for the future; people clearly had a deceptive picture in their minds of the 'golden twenties'.

Foreign policy successes of the Weimar Republic, to which Gustav Stresemann's six years in office gave a unique continuity, strengthened the position of the Reich, alleviated the consequences of the lost war and ended Germany's postwar isolation. International treaties, the withdrawal from occupied areas, further reductions in reparations' demands and progress towards Germany gaining equality of status were all stages along the way to a revision of the Versailles Treaty. In domestic politics, the arguments between the Reich and the princes, the conduct of the law courts and the conflicts with the army and navy were all striking reminders that the continuity of the authoritarian forces had not been broken. Symbolic of these mainly antirepublican forces was the fact that General Field Marshall von Hindenburg, who remained loyal to the Kaiser, was elected second President of the Reich by the majority of the Reichstag after Friedrich Ebert's death in 1925 – a post which had been endowed with considerable power by the republican constitution.

The world economic crisis which began in 1929 brought basic changes to the German political scene. It brought to an end the consolidation phase and led to a radicalisation and polarisation in politics, which gradually crippled the democratic institutions. Foreign capital, which had mainly been offered in the form of short term loans, was withdrawn. Industry sought to hold down wages in an attempt to remain competitive. With unemployment increasing the traditional union weapon, the strike, became ineffective. The radical parties of the left and right, which had consistently rejected the parliamentary structure, suddenly found themselves able to prevent the formation of stable democratic majorities since the middle class democratic parties were fragmented and were continually losing support. The party crisis became a parliamentary crisis and thus a national crisis. From March 1930 onwards there was no longer a republican parliamentary majority. The Chancellor governed by virtue of a series of emergency decrees, which made him independent from Parliament. In this situation the President of the Reich became an increasingly important political figure. The carrying out of his constitutional duties gave him a dominant position vis à vis the parliament where majority decisions could no longer be reached. Political decisions were being taken not by the people's representative but by the President. In view of Parliament's weakness and the fact that the Chancellor only had to rely on the President's support, the Weimar system resembled the prerepublican system of government of the Kaiser's reign. The democratic achievements of the 1918/19 Revolution had, with the demise of Parliament, lost their political basis. However, democratic elections were still held but their results strengthened the undemocratic parties and further undermined the parliamentary system. Disappointed, large and crucial sections of the population turned their backs on the parliamentary system and looked to an authoritarian solution to political and social conflicts. Whilst the communists and social democrats were waging a bitter battle and the Republic faced additional, increased pressure from the extreme left, the right wing formed an alliance which aimed to persuade the president to 'form a truly national government'. The re-election of Hindenburg as president in spring 1932 paved the way for the solution to the crisis, which had in the meantime gained the support of the majority of the German people. Two years' experience of the anti-parliamentary presidential cabinet system did not lead to a return to a constitutional form of government. By contrast, it made the president prepared, after two further failed attempts with presidential cabinets, to 'place his trust' in the man, who had for years been the most radical anti-republican and anti-parliamentarian and who, moreover, had mass support: Adolf Hitler, the leader of the National Socialist German Workers' Party (NSDAP).

The 1918/19 Revolution (Boards 1–13)

The revolution of 1918/19 failed to achieve a fundamental political and social change in Germany. Nevertheless, the old system of a constitutional monarchy with strongly authoritarian features was replaced by a parliamentary democracy. However, aspirations for a more thoroughgoing democratic restructuring of the state, the economy and society had only a limited success. The historian Friedrich Meinecke summed up the situation: "there has been no complete revolution of the state and social structure here".

Board 1 Hopes for a victory, which were pinned on the German offensive of March 1918, were destroyed by the allied counter offensive. In September 1918 the German leaders had to admit that the war, which was to have made Germany the masters of Europe, was lost. The German nation was exhausted and there were increasing food shortages. Strikes spread.

In order to save the monarchy and to shift the responsibility for the lost war, the exponents of the old order introduced a parliamentary system at the beginning of October 1918. From the parties which had joined forces in 1917 to establish the Intergroup Committee, a government was formed under Prince Max von Baden which included the majority socialists (Mehrheitssozialisten MSPD). Electoral and constitutional reforms were agreed upon. Germany was on its way from being an 'authoritarian state' to becoming a 'republic'. However, the reforms came too late and the parliamentary monarchy was unable to hold on to power. Naval revolts spread to the Reich *(cat. illustr. 163, 164).* Workers' and soldiers' councils were spontaneously formed during the revolution and they took control of the political and military forces in Germany. The councils wanted an end to the war and also wanted rid of the old political and military ruling classes.

Board 2/3 On 17th September 1918 Josef Hofmiller the co-editor of the respected 'Süddeutsche Monatshefte' stated: "Everyone is physically exhausted. 1. The workers are exhausted, 2. the farmers, 3. (actually I should have placed them first) the armed forces, 4. the women, 5. all employees, 6. all officials, 7. the press. Demobilisation has already begun in spirit. That is bad, very bad. The mood of the country is overtaking events. There are no inhibitions, no restraints, the mood of the country is dreadful. Who still believes in a successful outcome?"

V/163 Mutiny of the Fleet in Wilhelmshaven, beginning of November 1918.

V/164 Demonstration in Berlin, 9th November 1918.

2. Extraausgabe Sonnabend, den 9. November 1918.

Vorwärts

Berliner Volksblatt.

Zentralorgan der sozialdemokratischen Partei Deutschlands.

Der Kaiser hat abgedankt!

Der Reichskanzler hat **folgenden** Erlaß herausgegeben:

Seine Majestät **der Kaiser** und **König** haben sich entschlossen, dem Throne zu entsagen.

Der Reichskanzler bleibt noch so lange im Amte, bis die mit der Abdankung Seiner Majestät, dem Thronverzichte Seiner Kaiserlichen und Königlichen Hoheit des Kronprinzen des Deutschen Reichs und von Preußen und der Einsetzung der Regentschaft verbundenen Fragen geregelt sind. Er beabsichtigt, dem Regenten die Ernennung des Abgeordneten Ebert zum Reichskanzler und die Vorlage eines Gesetzentwurfs wegen der Ausschreibung allgemeiner Wahlen für eine verfassungsgebende deutsche Nationalversammlung vorzuschlagen, der es obliegen würde, die künftige Staatsform des deutschen Volk, einschließlich der Volksteile, die ihren Eintritt in die Reichsgrenzen wünschen sollten, endgültig festzustellen.

Berlin, den 9. November 1918. **Der Reichskanzler.**

Prinz Max von Baden.

Es wird nicht geschossen!

Der Reichskanzler hat angeordnet, daß seitens des Militärs von der Waffe kein Gebrauch gemacht werde.

Parteigenossen! Arbeiter! Soldaten!

Soeben sind das Alexanderregiment und die vierten Jäger geschlossen zum Volke übergegangen. Der sozialdemokratische Reichstagsabgeordnete Wels u. a. haben zu den Truppen gesprochen. Offiziere haben sich den Soldaten angeschlossen.

Der sozialdemokratische Arbeiter- und Soldatenrat.

V/165 Front page of the Social Democratic paper ‘Vorwärts’, 9th November 1918

Extra Edition **Saturday, 9th November 1918**

Vorwärts

Berlin Newspaper

Mouthpiece of the German Social Democratic Party

The Kaiser has abdicated!

The Chancellor has issued the following decree:

His majesty the Kaiser and the King has decided to renounce his throne.

The Chancellor remains in office until all matters have been settled concerning the abdication of his majesty, the renunciation of his royal highness the crown prince of the German Reich and Prussia of his succession claims, and the establishment of a regency. He intends to propose to the regent that Ebert should become Chancellor and the drafting of a legislative proposal ordering a general election for a constitutional German National Assembly whose role it would be to decide upon the future system of government in Germany, which will include all areas which so desire.

Berlin, 9th November 1918 **Reich Chancellor**
Prince Max von Baden

No shots will be fired!

The Chancellor has ordered the armed forces not to use their weapons.

Party members! Workers! Soldiers!

The Alexander Regiment and the Fourth Jäger Regiment have just joined forces with the people. The Social Democratic representative Wels inter alia has addressed the troops. Officers have joined the soldiers.

The Social Democratic Workers' and Soldiers' Council

Boards 4/5 On 9th November 1918 Wilhelm II saw no other alternative but to abdicate *(cat. illustr. 165).* From the Reichstag, Philipp Scheidemann announced "the German Republic". Shortly afterwards in front of the castle the leader of the Spartakus League, Karl Liebknecht, proclaimed the "free socialist republic". Thus, arguments began as to the structure of the new republic.

Board 6 The social democrats considered it their most urgent task to save the "German people from civil war and starvation" (Ebert). Economic and social reforms were to be constitutionally passed by a National Assembly. They considered that the crisis situation ought not to be made worse by reforms. The majority of the social democrats (MSDP) wanted to avoid at all costs a radicalisation of the revolution based on the Russian model. Opposed to them was the left wing of the SPD, which had split with the majority during the war and had formed their own grouping, the Independent Social Democratic Party (USPD). The latter had joined the government with the aim of 'reinforcing the revolutionary socialist achievements'. Not until this aim had been achieved could one think about National Assembly elections *(cat. illustr. 172).* One group in the USPD, based around Rosa Luxemburg and Karl Liebknecht, the Spartakus League, went even further and demanded, not a parliamentary democracy but a soviet system. The League's second major aim was the nationalisation of heavy industry and the property of the large landowners.

Board 7 Friedrich Ebert attempted to keep the government machinery working. He kept the civil service of the deposed Kaiser's Reich in office and believed that it would only be possible to ensure the restoration of the army and to feed the population with the help of the imperial armed forces. Both groups performed their duties in the new state but had no feeling of loyalty towards it. The MSPD saw the state's existence threatened not by counter-revolutionary trends but by radical revolutionary groups. The MSPD considered the political control of the conservative forces by workers' and soldiers' councils to be sufficient. The government did indeed, under the MSPD, manage to prevent a civil war but at the same time the position of the authoritarian forces in the administration, judiciary, army and industry was strengthened.

Board 8 The Berlin Workers' and Soldiers' councils handed the functions of government to the "Council of People's Delegates" which was made up of MSPD and independent USPD members *(cat. illustr.*

166, 167). The Social democrats accepted this 'revolutionary mandate' in order to secure their position as the leading political force in Germany.

Board 9 An important decision on future worker-management relations in Germany was taken by the Stinnes-Legien Agreement of 15th November 1918: industry recognised trade unions as partners in negotiations on wages and working conditions. In return the unions dropped their demands for nationalisations. In reality this social partnership only meant a formal equality of status.

The Decision Against the Soviet System

Board 10 At the Reich's Congress of Workers' and Soldiers' Councils (16th–21st December 1918) the representatives of the MSPD were in the majority. The Congress decided in favour of a constituent National Assembly *(cat. illustr. 171).* Thus it decided in favour of parliamentary democracy and against the Soviet (council) system. However, at the same time far-reaching reforms were demanded. In the months which followed workers' and soldiers' councils became less and less influential.

At the end of December Ebert called for the help of the troops from the old army against mutinying sailors in Berlin. As a protest against this the three independent social democrats (USPD) resigned from the Council of People's Delegates. Two majority socialists replaced them.

Board 11 The conflict between the SPD leadership and their critics on the left led in the first half of January 1919 to the Spartakus uprising in Berlin *(cat. illustr. 1970).* The government engaged the help of Freikorps (volunteer corps) who put down the revolt after much bloodshed *(cat. illustr. 169).* However, the troops who were protecting the parliamentary republic were themselves undemocratic. On 15th January 1919 Rosa Luxemburg and Karl Liebknecht were murdered by Freikorps soldiers.

The National Assembly Elections. The Weimar Coalition

Board 12 The SPD emerged as the strongest party in the National Assembly elections of 19th January 1919, in which women were allowed, for the first time, to participate *(cat. illustr. 173, 174).* However, the SPD did not gain an absolute majority in the constituent assembly, which was convened in Weimar because of unrest in Berlin in February 1919 and was thus forced into what came to be known as the 'Weimar coalition' with the Centre party and German Democratic Party (DDP), the former Progressive People's Party. This coalition had won 76% of the votes cast and represented the same political forces which had formed a reformist alliance in the form of the "Intergroup Committee". Friedrich Ebert became the first president of the new republic.

The Constitution *(see appendix for flow diagram of the constitution)*

Board 13

The constitution of the Weimar Republic upheld most of the liberal and democratic traditions of 1848. The Reichstag was now the central political institution and the Chancellor and his ministers were responsible before it. However, the President also enjoyed considerable powers and above all his post as supreme commander of the armed forces and his right to dissolve the Reichstag. In addition, Article 48 provided him with the ability to declare a state of emergency and assume full authority "If public security and order in Germany are seriously disturbed or threatened". The system of pure proportional representation caused a fragmentation of the parties, which were still not obliged to have democratic constitutions. The Federal Constitution and the strong position enjoyed by Prussia remained intact. However, the Reich's power increased, notably as a result of the Erzberger financial reform. German unity in the form achieved in 1871 was questioned again after the defeat of what had not been a decisive majority of the German people.
The constitution of the Weimar Republic pointed the way towards a democratic social order. Social welfare aims put forward by the social democrats were also present. Nevertheless, the contradictions between the democratic constitution and a social reality, which remained far behind the aims set by the constitution, were a serious problem for the young republic.

V/166 The First Council of People's Delegates.

V/167 Revolutionary soldiers at the Brandenburg Gate, November 1918.

V/168 Government troops in operation, December 1918.

V/169 Sentinels of the government troops during the Spartakus Uprising, January 1919.

V/170 Fighting spartakus supporters in the newspaper district.

V/171 Election banner for the National Assembly elections, 19th January 1919.

V/172 Demonstration against the National Assembly election.

V/173 Opening speech by Friedrich Ebert in the National Assembly in Weimar, February 1919.

V/174 The first female representative.

The Development of the Weimar Republic (Boards 14–37)

The passing of the Weimar Constitution heralded a decade of German politics in which the Republic was firstly able to ward off the attacks of its opponents and then, having overcome its initial crises, was able to gain a more stable base. At the end of this decade the political and social structure of the Republic was shaken by the consequences of a world economic crisis. The hopes and expectations, which the changes of 1918/19 had aroused, were shattered by increasing political extremism. Large sections of the population lost confidence in the parliamentary system, which at the beginning of the Weimar Republic seemed to have solid foundations thanks to the new electoral laws, more solid majorities and a liberal constitution.

The Parties

Boards 14/15 In contrast to the majority voting system of the Kaiser's time the system of pure proportional representation introduced after 1918 led to significant changes in voting patterns, in the party structures and also in the structure of party groupings. However, a more significant change was the different role now played by the parties: the constitution of 1871 banned them from the 'corridors or power'; by contrast, the 1919 constitution made parliament full political decisionmaking powers, i.e. the parties now carried the full weight of responsibility. All the parties drew up new manifestos in view of the new situation. These reflected in detail the full breadth of public opinion and different interests and also differences within the parties.

Board 16 On major points of principle the parties took up clearly diverging stances. Thus the German Social Democratic Party (SPD, also M.S.P.D. as distinct from its breakaway left wing) demanded, in addition to the democratisation of the administration and the restructuring of relations between church and state, basic reforms in structures of the armed forces and the economy, "which corresponded to the demands and possibilities of the time". The MSPD joined forces with the Independent Social Democrats "in support of democracy" and opposed all ideas of dictatorship and putsches (June 1919).

The demands of the Independent Social Democratic Party went much further however: they wanted the "disclosure of all military, civil and police information", the "establishment of a revolutionary guard" and the immediate nationalisation of capitalist concerns (banking and insurance companies, mining companies, energy, iron and steel production, transport and communications). In addition, they demanded the nationalisation of large landowners' property and the transfer of private land and property "in towns and predominantly industrial areas" to public ownership. Moreover, plans for the nationalisation of state education and training institutions and the total separation of church and state were major points in their manifesto. Although the U. S. D. P. favoured a political leadership organised on the council system it also saw parliament as a possible instrument for the implementation of its aims (December 1919).

Board 17 The demands made by the German Communist Party (K. P. D.), which had grown out of the Spartakus League, were even more radical. They saw parliament as a "weapon of the ruling classes for the exercise and preservation of their political power" and thus considered it completely impossible to achieve revolutionary aims by parliamentary decrees and so totally rejected a parliamentary system. The capitalist market economy should be replaced by a socialist planned economy and, of the "counter revolutionary trades' union burearcracy" it was said that the "political power of the bourgeoisie" should be broken and replaced by the "dictatorship of the proletariat" (October 1919).

The anti-republic party on the right was the German National People's Party (DNVP). This party was the direct successor of the two conservative parties in the Kaiser's Reich and was the only strong advocate of the "renewal of the Hohenzollern Kaiser's Empire". Its demand for the protection of private property was backed by its rejection of "the ideas of the marxist class struggle" since it considered them to be "the destroyers of all culture". In the battle for electoral support in the countryside the DNVP adhered to the anti-semitic views of the conservative parties of the Kaiser's Reich and of the "League of Farmers": "We expressly oppose the increasingly dominant position in government and public life which the Jews have acquired since the Revolution" (1920).

Board 18 The demands of the Centre Party were identical to those of the Bavarian People's Party (BVP). They aimed above all for the guarantee of "civil liberties based on Christian principles" and

V/175 The German delegation before setting off for Versailles, 1919.

V/176 Demonstration against the Versailles Treaty in Berlin.

for the "preservation of the private economy based on personal property which adhered to the principle of solidarity and served the common good". Both parties supported a federal structure for the Reich and the BVP stressed the independence of Bavaria: "the considerable governmental, economic and fiscal dependence of Bavaria on the predominant north must, as a matter of priority, cease. Bavaria for the Bavarians", (December 1918).

Board 19 The religiously independent liberal parties took particular account of the interests of the middle class in their programmes. The German Democratic Party (DDP) demanded a democratic "state with social rights" in which the private economy was maintained with a limit placed on "monopolistic dominance". As far as land and property were concerned the DDP favoured "prevention of land speculation, a real distribution of landed property in order to create economically independent rural family concerns and to allow farm labourers to be housed". Tradesmen and small businessmen should be protected and the participation of employees in the running of a firm should be ensured ("industrial citizens") and in this way a "responsible workers' and people's community" would be created (December 1919).

The German People's Party (DVP), which was formed on 18th December 1918, supported mainly by members of the former National Liberal Party, gave priority to the demands of a large artisan and rural middle class. Private property and the dominant position of the entrepreneur should be protected. The DVP represented "the deepening and reconciliation of liberal and social ideas on the basis of ideas on national government". (October 1919).

The Treaty of Versailles and its Domestic Political Consequences

The opportunities available for transforming political declarations into practical policies depended less on the wishes of the parties represented in the National Assembly than on the conditions which prevailed as a result of the lost war and which dominated the economic life of the Republic and soured the domestic political atmosphere.

Boards 20–22 In the Treaty of Versailles the victorious Allies dictated that

Germany should cede some of her territories and engage in large scale disarmament *(cat. illustr. 175).* Demands for reparation payments were justified on the grounds that Germany alone had been guilty for the war, a justification which was strongly contested by the German delegation. The unity of Germany was not, however, to be affected. Nevertheless, Germans in Austria were deprived of the right of self-determination by the Annexation Ban (Anschlußverbot) which was passed for security reasons. The Treaty of Versailles was unanimously rejected in Germany *(cat. illustr. 176).* The "War Guilt Clause" in particular provoked an active campaign against those republican politicians who had reluctantly signed the Treaty, having no other alternative in view of the circumstances. Thus, the fight against the Treaty of Versailles developed into a fight against the Weimar Republic. The representatives of the Republic were branded and defamed as "puppet politicians" and "November criminals".

Board 24

The murders of Matthias Erzberger and Walter Rathenau occurred at the height of the campaign. The "Republikschutzgesetz" was passed with the aim of blocking further acts of political violence. However, a politically biased, or at the very least not often neutral, judiciary considerably weakened the effects of the law by the way in which they applied it to political offenders. In addition, the army (Reichswehr), which had been reduced to 100,000 by the Treaty of Versailles, also behaved in a biased way in situations which were of critical importance for the Republic. Many officers, who remained loyal to the Kaiser and who were unable to come to terms with the defeat of 1918 conceived the Reichswehr as a "state within a state" (v. Seeckt). For many this rejection turned into a political pipedream and into open attacks on the Republic.

Board 28

On 13th March 1920 right wing radicals staged the Kapp-Putsch in Berlin. The rioters wanted to abolish parliamentary democracy and sought the restoration of the old pre-1914 political order *(cat. illustr. 177).* The Reichswehr did not perform its duty, which was to put down the uprising. They left the Republic in the lurch. The SPD and the trade unions called for a general strike *(cat. illustr. 178),* whereupon the Putsch quickly collapsed.

In response to the right wing putsch, left wing radicals staged uprisings in the Rhineland and in Saxony-Thüringen *(cat. illustr. 179).* This time the Reichswehr did not hesitate and intervened immediately *(cat. illustr. 180).* The increase of political extrem-

V/177 Kapp-soldiers with the Kaiser's imperial flag in Berlin, March 1920.

V/178 Potsdamer Platz during the General Strike, March 1920.

V/179 Members of the “Red Ruhr Army”, 1920.

V/180 Occupation by Government troops to quell communist unrest in Saxony, 1920.

V/181–184 Inflation 1922/23. V/181 Sale of butter under police supervision.

V/182 Bread shortage.

V/183 Searching for coal.

V/184 Official destruction of inflation-money.

V/185 Occupation of the Ruhr, January 1923.

V/186 Passive resistance: Friedrich Ebert in the Ruhr Industrial Area.

ism and the hopeless foreign policy situation were reflected in the Reichstag elections of June 1920: the Weimar coalition lost almost 40% of its seats and with them their majority. The Republic survived but large sections of the population opposed the new political order.

Boards 29/30

This rejection turned to hostility as inflation, which had begun shortly after the war, rapidly grew worse in 1922/23 and caused social hardship for the majority of the population *(cat. illustr. 183)*. In particular, the middle classes blamed their economic and social demise on the "Weimar system". The inflationary situation hit them especially hard: they lost their savings and loans which had financed the lost war. On the other hand the state was freed of practically all its obligations. However, the workers were also victims of inflation. Their wages ran through their fingers like water, there was too much money chasing too few goods and this forced up the prices *(cat. illustr. 181, 182, 184)*.

Industry was paying low wages and increased exports. It received generous credits for capital investment, which were only a small financial burden and which were partly repaid in worthless banknotes during the period of inflation. Skilful speculators were able to make huge profits in these and such people did not want the inflation to end, rather they wished to exploit the situation.

Board 31

The uncertain financial situation in the Reich made it almost impossible to fulfil reparation repayment requirements. The Allies reacted by threatening to impose sanctions (London Ultimatum). Chancellor Wirth resigned. His successor Cuno and his "right of centre" government were dependent upon the support of the SPD. Because of allegedly outstanding reparation payments, French and Belgian troops occupied the Ruhr in January 1923 *(cat. illustr. 185)*. The reaction of the German government was to offer "passive resistance" *(cat. illustr. 186)*. However, this policy crippled politics and the economy and wasted even more of the Reich's finances. In order to end the stagnation, a new government under Stresemann, a large coalition of the SPD, DDP, Centre Party and DVP, proclaimed an end to the passive resistance on 26th September 1923: "the courage to accept the responsibility for passive resistance is perhaps more national than the phrases expressed in opposition to it. I was aware that, at the time that I did so, as leader of my party which had a totally different viewpoint, I was placing in

V/187 The funeral of Reich President Friedrich Ebert: the Laying in State of the coffin at Potsdam Station in Berlin, 1925.

V/188 The New Reich President, von Hindenburg, Defence Minister Gessler (half hidden) and General von Seeckt inspecting a company receiving military honours.

V/189 SPD poster on the controversy surrounding the expropriation by the princes, 1926 (ach, the princes are so *badly* off!).

V/190 Reichswehr manoeuvres 1927: amongst the observers a Soviet officer (far left).

V/191 Workers' children demonstrate against confessional schools.

V/192 Model housing project: the horseshoe-shaped suburban estate in Berlin-Britz – by Bruno Taut and Martin Wagner, 1925–1931.

jeopardy not only my own political position in the party but my status in life in general. But what are we the German race lacking? We are lacking the courage to accept responsibility" (Stresemann).
The policy of realism was accepted by the SPD. Nevertheless the biased action of the Reichswehr against the SPD-KPD government coalition in Saxony-Thüringen, whilst radical anti-republican riots in Bavaria were treated leniently, caused the SPD to defeat the Stresemann government through a vote of no-confidence. Reich President Ebert condemned the SPD's action: "What caused you to defeat the Chancellor will have been forgotten in six weeks but you will suffer the consequences of your stupidity for ten years!".

1924–1928: Years of Stabilisation

Board 32 A new ruling on reparation repayments was accompanied by a stabilising of the Mark. The Dawes Plan of 1924 started from the basis that payments could only be made by a stable economy and therefore the former enemies of Germany must have a vested interest in supporting her economy. Foreign loans poured into the country. The economy was "stimulated" by these investments. Factories were modernised and production increased. At the same time, however, foreign capital gained a significant influence on German economic developments. The political situation also became more stable as a result of the economic upturn. The December elections of 1924 brought losses for the radicals and gains for the middle of the road republican parties. The German National People's Party (DVP) joined the new centre right government as the largest party.

Board 33 Although stabilisation prevented any further growth of the anti-republican movement, the republican forces still suffered a considerable defeat in 1925. After Ebert's death General Field Marshall von Hindenburg, who remained loyal to the Kaiser, was elected as the new President of the Reich *(cat. illustr. 187, 188).* The choice characterised the continuation of the authoritarian forces.

Board 34 In the ranks of the bureaucracy, the universities, above all in the army and in the judiciary, there were many who were opposed to the Republic. In 1926 monarchist judges decided mainly in favour of the princes in their legal battle with the Reich about their wealth which had not been confiscated in 1918/19 but rather commandeered *(cat. illustr. 189).* The domestic policy of the Reich was troubled by arguments with the Reichswehr: on his own initiative Senior General von Seeckt, the head of the armed forces, invited the crown prince to Reichswehr manoeuvres. As a result Seeckt was dismissed. The disclosing of secret cooperation between the Reichswehr and the Red Army led to the downfall of the Marx government *(cat. illustr. 190).*

Board 35

Despite these setbacks there were internal reforms, notably in the area of social policy, where, helped by the relatively stable economic prosperity, the social welfare state was extended *(cat. illustr. 192).* In July 1927 a law was passed concerning "job supply" and "unemployment benefits". Whereas the old support regulations had demanded a means test, basically each unemployed person now had the right to support. The contribution clauses allowed for 800,000 unemployed people to be supported if average wages were taken as an indicator. Thus the old union demand was met and a legal provision for social security was created. However, because of its social policy the government faced increasing opposition from industry.

Board 36

The common ground shared by the parties participating in the government remained small. In 1928 the fifteenth government of the Republic collapsed over the question of a law concerning schools in the Reich. The Reichstag elections of May 1928 produced once again a favourable result for the Republic. Despite internal conflicts over the building of the "Battleship A" the SPD joined the government: Grand Coalition was formed unter Chancellor Hermann Müller (SPD). However, there were fundamental differences of opinion between the coalition parties on defence policy and basic economic policy questions. Nevertheless the government was able to settle the stormy labour conflict in the iron industry in the Rhineland and Westphalia in the Autumn of 1928 but the social partners became increasingly polarised: industry demanded tax changes which would be to their advantage and unemployment grew.

The efforts to attain a new settlement of the reparation question contributed considerably to the increasing conflicts since the parties of the right continued to reject fundamentally any obligation to pay reparations *(cat. illustr. 193).* The Young Plan of 1929 was drawn up to replace the Dawes Plan of 1924. The Dawes Plan had abandoned the 1921 policy of ultimatums and sanctions. Since it aimed to develop German economic oppor-

V/193 Supplying reparations to France.

V/194 Invitation to a protest meeting against the Young Plan, 1929.

tunities it had led to a depoliticisation of the reparation problem but the Plan impinged on German sovereignty, a policy which the Young Plan had dropped. The regulations for reparation payments based on the Young Plan contained a payment mechanism which was, from the outset, made impossible by the economic crisis. Once more a strong anti-republican campaign was launched, which reached a peak with the "Plebiscite against the Young Plan", supported largely by the German nationalists *(cat. illustr. 194).*

Foreign Policy

Board 37

The foreign policy of the Weimar Republic was mainly influenced by Gustav Stresemann (DVP) in the 1920s. During his six years of office between 1923 and 1929 he witnessed eight government reshuffles. He acted as the mediator and "compromise minister" between the social democrats, the liberals, the Centre Party and the conservatives. His foreign policy aim was to regain a dominant position for Germany in mid-Europe under the new conditions which had been created by the war. In order to achieve his aim he sought a reconciliation with the Western powers, above all with France, and at the same time tried to gain a revision of the Eastern territorial agreements of the Treaty of Versailles.

The Treaty of Versailles and the problem of reparations formed a limiting framework within which the foreign policy of the Weimar Republic was pursued. In 1921 the Allies demanded that Germany acknowledge a debt of 13.2 billion Marks. The acceptance of this demand led to the right wing witch hunt against the Republic being stepped up.

In the Treaty of Rapallo of 1922 Germany and Russia agreed mutually to cancel all financial claims from the war and they agreed also to closer economic cooperation. Great Britain and France were angered by this German-Russian 'solo' which was the origin of the "Rapallo Complex".

In the Treaty of Locarno of October 1925 Stresemann recognised the new territorial boundaries which had been drawn up in the West; however, he made no firm commitment to the eastern border *(cat. illustr. 195).* In the same year Germany applied to join the League of Nations. After the withdrawal from the Ruhr in July 1925 French troops also left the Cologne area. The Soviet

V/195 The concluding conference in Locarno, October 1925.

Nr. 195 ◆ 43. Jahrg.

Ausgabe A Nr. 99

Bezugspreis:

Wöchentlich 70 Pfennig, monatlich 3.– Reichsmark voraus zahlbar. Unter Kreuzband für Deutschland, Danzig, Saar- und Memelgebiet, Oesterreich, Litauen, Luxemburg 4.50 Reichsmark, für das übrige Ausland 5.50 Reichsmark pro Monat.

Der „Vorwärts" mit der Sonntagsbeilage „Volk und Zeit" mit „Siedlung und Kleingarten" sowie der Beilage „Unterhaltung und Wissen" und Frauenbeilage „Frauenstimme" erscheint wochentäglich zweimal, Sonntags und Montags einmal.

Telegramm-Adresse: „Sozialdemokrat Berlin"

Morgenausgabe

Vorwärts

Berliner Volksblatt

Zentralorgan der Sozialdemokratischen Partei Deutschlands

10 Pfennig

Anzeigenpreise

Die einspaltige Nonpareillezeile 80 Pfennig. Reklamezeile 5.– Reichsmark. „Kleine Anzeigen" das fettgedruckte Wort 25 Pfennig (zulässig zwei fettgedruckte Worte), jedes weitere Wort 12 Pfennig. Stellengesuche das erste Wort 15 Pfennig, jedes weitere Wort 10 Pfennig. Worte über 15 Buchstaben zählen für zwei Worte. Arbeitsmarkt Zeile 60 Pfennig. Familienanzeigen für Abonnenten Zeile 40 Pfennig.

Anzeigen für die nächste Nummer müssen bis 4½ Uhr nachmittags im Hauptgeschäft, Berlin SW 68, Lindenstraße 3, abgegeben werden. Geöffnet von 8½ Uhr früh bis 5 Uhr nachm.

Redaktion und Verlag: Berlin SW. 68, Lindenstraße 3
Fernsprecher: Dönhoff 292–297.

Dienstag, den 27. April 1926

Vorwärts-Verlag G.m.b.H., Berlin SW. 68, Lindenstr. 3
Postscheckkonto: Berlin 37 536 – Bankkonto: Bank der Arbeiter, Angestellten und Beamten, Wallstr. 65; Diskonto-Gesellschaft, Depositenkasse Lindenstr. 3.

Der Freundschaftsvertrag mit Rußland.

Einmütige Billigung im Auswärtigen Ausschuß.

Der am 24. April in Berlin unterzeichnete Vertrag zwischen Deutschland und Rußland, der sogenannte „Berliner Vertrag" ist gestern abend der Presse zur Veröffentlichung übergeben worden. Er hat folgenden Wortlaut:

Die Deutsche Regierung und die Regierung der Union der Sozialistischen Sowjet-Republiken, von dem Wunsche geleitet, alles zu tun, was zur Aufrechterhaltung des allgemeinen Friedens beitragen kann, und in der Ueberzeugung, daß das Interesse des deutschen Volkes und der Völker der Union der Sozialistischen Sowjet-Republiken eine stetige vertrauensvolle Zusammenarbeit erfordert, sind übereingekommen, die zwischen ihnen bestehenden freundschaftlichen Beziehungen durch einen besonderen Vertrag zu bekräftigen und haben zu diesem Zwecke zu Bevollmächtigten ernannt:

Die Deutsche Regierung: den Reichsminister des Auswärtigen Herrn Dr. Gustav Stresemann,

die Regierung der Union der Sozialistischen Sowjet-Republiken: den außerordentlichen und bevollmächtigten Botschafter der Union der Sozialistischen Sowjet-Republiken, Herrn Nikolai Nikolajewitsch Krestinski,

der Notwendigkeit der Erhaltung des allgemeinen Friedens leiten lassen.

2. In diesem Sinne haben die beiden Regierungen auch die grundsätzlichen Fragen erörtert, die mit dem Eintritt Deutschlands in den Völkerbund zusammenhängen. Die deutsche Regierung ist überzeugt, daß

die Zugehörigkeit Deutschlands zum Völkerbund

kein Hindernis für die freundschaftliche Entwicklung der Beziehungen zwischen Deutschland und der Union der Sozialistischen Sowjetrepubliken bilden kann. Der Völkerbund ist seiner grundlegenden Idee nach zur friedlichen und gerechten Ausgleichung internationaler Gegensätze bestimmt. Die deutsche Regierung ist entschlossen, an der Verwirklichung dieser Idee nach Kräften mitzuarbeiten. Sollten dagegen, was die deutsche Regierung nicht annimmt, im Rahmen des Völkerbundes irgendwann etwa Bestrebungen hervortreten, die, im Widerspruch mit jener grundlegenden Friedensidee, einseitig gegen die Union der Sozialistischen Sowjetrepubliken gerichtet wären, so würde Deutschland derartigen Bestrebungen mit allem Nachdruck entgegenwirken.

und daß somit eine in dieser Hinsicht etwa von anderen Mächten gegen die Union der Sozialistischen Sowjetrepubliken erhobene, nach deutscher Ansicht nicht berechtigte Beschuldigung Deutschland nicht zwingen würde, an irgendwelchen auf Grund des Artikel 16 eingeleiteten Maßnahmen teilzunehmen. Wegen der Frage, ob und in welchem Maße Deutschland im konkreten Falle überhaupt imstande sein würde, an einem Sanktionsverfahren teilzunehmen, verweist die deutsche Regierung auf die bei Gelegenheit der Unterzeichnung des Vertragswerkes von Locarno an die deutsche Delegation gerichtete Note vom 1. Dezember 1925 über die Auslegung des Artikels 16.

4. Um für die reibungslose Erledigung aller zwischen ihnen auftauchenden Fragen eine sichere Grundlage zu schaffen, halten die beiden Regierungen es für zweckmäßig, alsbald in Erörterungen über den Abschluß eines allgemeinen Vertrags zur friedlichen Lösung der zwischen den beiden Teilen etwa entstehenden Konflikte einzutreten, wobei insbesondere die Möglichkeiten des schiedsgerichtlichen Verfahrens und des Vergleichsverfahrens berücksichtigt werden sollen.

Genehmigen Sie, usw. (gez.) Stresemann.

V/196 Report of the newspaper 'Vorwärts' on the 'Treaty of Berlin', April 1926.

V/197 The Foreign Ministers of France and Germany: Aristide Briand and Gustav Stresemann.

V/198 Stresemann addressing the League of Nations in Ghent.

V/199 Potsdamer Platz in the heart of Berlin (May 1933).

V/200 Dole queue in Berlin during the world economic crisis.

Union's worries about a unilateral concentration of German foreign policy on the West were dispelled by the Treaty of Berlin of April 1926 *(cat. illustr. 196)*; this built on the foundations of the Treaty of Rapallo of 1922.
On the 9th September 1926 Germany was accepted as a member of the League of Nations *(cat. illustr. 198).* In their speeches Stresemann and Briand reinforced the desire for a further reconciliation. However, progress towards a rapprochement between Paris and Berlin was made more difficult by public opinion in both countries. The efforts of foreign ministers Stresemann and Briand to secure peace in Europe were rewarded in 1926 when they were both awarded the Nobel Peace Prize *(cat. illustr. 197).*
The death of Stresemann in October 1929 was a severe loss for the Republic.

The Collapse of the Republic (Boards 38–49)

Board 38

The onset of the world economic crisis in 1929 destroyed all the foundations which had been laid for further stabilisation. As a direct consequence economic, social and political conflicts were increased in Germany. The radical parties on the left and right, which rejected the parliamentary order, increasingly blocked the formation of stable democratic majorities. The middle class democratic parties became fragmented and continually lost support. Thus, for many the only way out of the crisis appeared to be an authoritarian government which would be above individual and party interests.
The Brüning government (Centre Party), which had no parliamentary majority but was rather supported by the President alone as a "government above the parties", was unable to come to grips with either the economic crisis or the internal conflicts in Germany. The obvious lack of governmental success led to the "Weimar System" becoming increasingly discredited, a development which was to the advantage of the radicals on both sides of the political spectrum, the KPD and, in particular, the National Socialist German Workers' Party (NSDAP). Above all the permanent application of Article 48 of the Weimar Constitution made a nonsense of the parliamentary system of government.

V/201 Insolvent bank, 1931.

V/202 Consequences of the depression, shops closing down.

V/203 Heinrich Brüning, Chancellor 1930–1932.

Whilst it was hoped that the increasing gravity of the depression and the problems of mass unemployment and political extremism would be alleviated following foreign policy successes, the Republic was in fact fighting a losing battle against the party which had become its most serious opponent: the NSDAP under Adolf Hitler.

Board 39 The collapse of the New York stock exchange led to an international financial crisis. In order to remain solvent themselves the foreign investors withdrew their short term credit investments from Germany. The consequences were declining investment, factory closures and mass unemployment *(cat. illustr. 200, 201, 202).*

The Move Towards a Presidential System

Board 40 The economic and financial crises developed into a crisis for the parliamentary system when the last parliamentary government to be formed, the Grand Coalition under Hermann Müller, collapsed. The "Frankfurter Zeitung" commented after the breakdown of the Grand Coalition: "the future government, whatever shade of opinion it might represent, must consist of men who firmly support the constitution and who are backed by parties and groups which are also loyal to it. Parliamentary democracy yesterday suffered a blow – being already threatened with tax reforms under Article 48 – We cannot afford to go further down the slippery slope". The number of unemployed aready far exceeded 800,000, which was the number for which unemployment benefit funds could provide. A rift developed in the Reichstag over the discussions on the necessary legal amendments concerning unemployment benefits: the SPD left the government and Heinrich Brüning (Centre Party) was named as Chancellor by the President on 30th March 1930 although he had no parliamentary majority *(cat. illustr. 203).*

Board 41 The Reichstag rejected Brüning's radical austerity programme, whereupon, on Brüning's suggestion, the President dissolved the parliament *(cat. illustr. 204).* Brüning hoped to gain a wider support-base from new elections.

However, just the opposite occurred. The elections produced a landslide: the communists almost doubled their number of seats compared to the previous Reichstag elections of 1928

Verordnung

des Reichspräsidenten über die Auflösung des Reichstags

vom 18. Juli 1930.

Nachdem der Reichstag heute beschlossen hat, zu verlangen, dass meine auf Grund des Artikel 48 der Reichsverfassung erlassene Verordnungen vom 16.Juli ~~über Deckungsmaßnahmen für den Reichshaushalt 1930~~ ausser Kraft gesetzt werden, löse ich auf Grund Artikel 25 der Reichsverfassung den Reichstag auf.

Berlin, den 18.Juli 1930.

Der Reichspräsident

von Hindenburg.

Der Reichskanzler

Brüning

V/204 The Dissolution of the Reichstag, 18th July 1930.

Decree

of the President of the Reich concerning the dissolution of the Reichstag
of 18th July 1930

After the Reichstag has today decided to demand that my decree of 16th July under Article 48 of the constitution of the Reich ~~concerning budgetary matters for 1930~~ be annulled, I hereby dissolve the Reichstag, in accordance with Article 25 of the Constitution of the Reich.

Berlin, 18th July 1930

Reichspräsident
von Hindenburg

Reichskanzler
H. Brüning

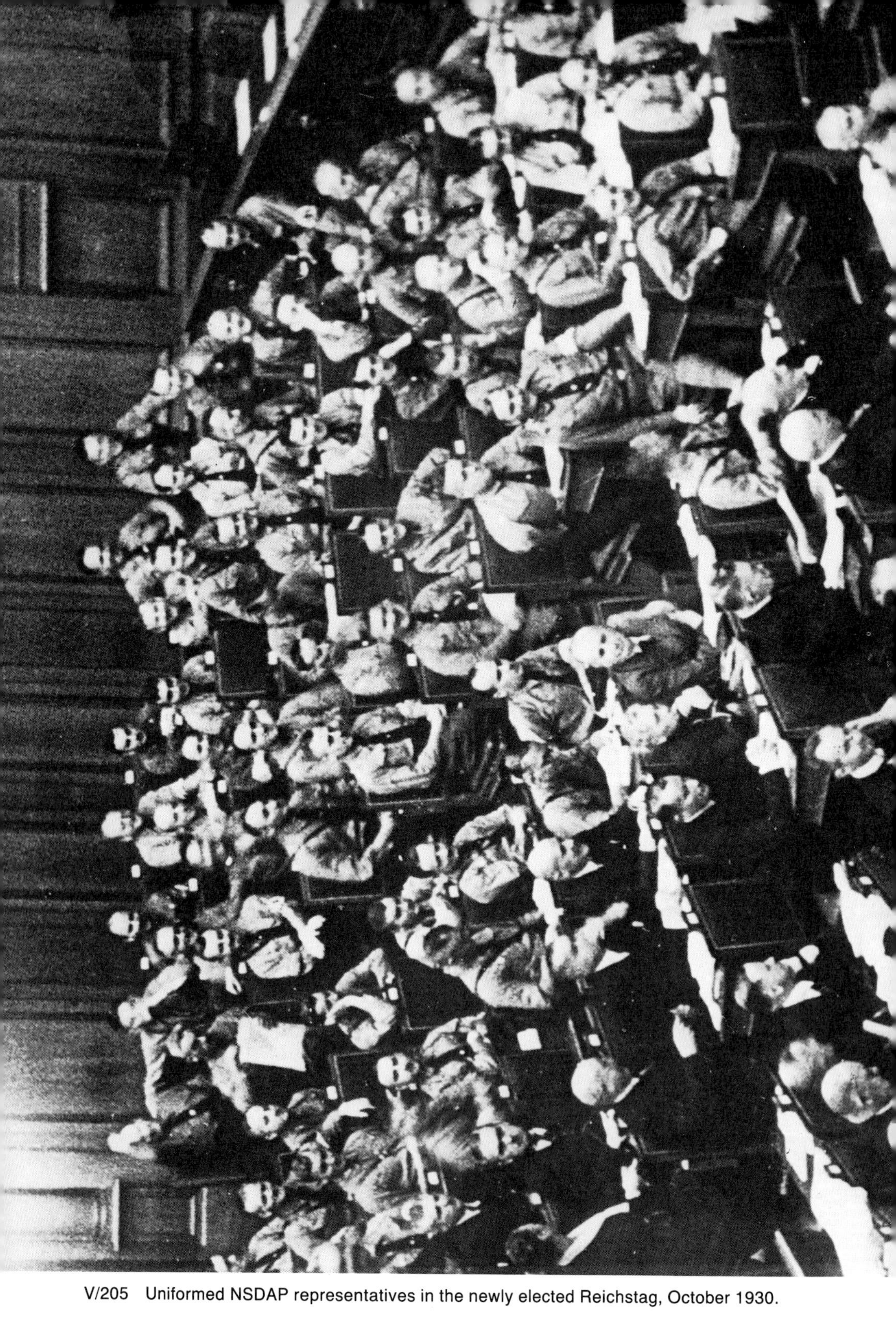

V/205 Uniformed NSDAP representatives in the newly elected Reichstag, October 1930.

V/206 Meeting of the right-wing opposition in Bad Harzburg: Hugenberg at the rostrum.

V/207 March past Hitler in Bad Harzburg, October 1931.

V/208 March displaying the "Reich's Banner Black-Red-Gold".

V/209 Propaganda march by the Communist league of ex-servicemen in Berlin 1927 (led by Ernst Thälmann on the left).

V/210 Meeting of the Poetry section of the Academy of Arts in Berlin 1929 (from the left: Alfred Döblin, Thomas Mann, Ricarda Huch, Bernhard Kellermann, Hermann Stehr, Alfred Mombert, Eduard Stucken).

V/211 Cheering people in front of the "Führer's" Mercedes on the day of the seizure of power.

V/212 Hitler with his cabinet members on 30th January 1933.

and the National Socialists won 107 seats instead of their previously held twelve *(cat. illustr. 205)*.

Board 42 The growing polarisation in the Reichstag and the consequent increase in extremism expressed in parliamentary conflicts prevented any majority decisions. Thus parliament became totally ineffective as a legislative body and was no longer able to fulfil its constitutional duty. Increasing use was made of legislation "from above", i.e. the practise of emergency decrees under Article 48.

Board 43 Abroad, there was a nervous reaction to the September elections. The share levels of German companies fell on the stock market. Further credit facilities were withdrawn. The banks became insolvent. The number of unemployed grew.

Board 44 The NSDAP, the German National People's Party (DNVP), nationalist combat groups (e.g. Stahlhelm) and representatives of right wing economic and financial circles joined forces in October 1931 to form the "Harzburg Front" *(cat. illustr. 206, 207)*. They demanded Brüning's resignation. In spite of assuming quasi-dictatorial power and despite the fact that the SPD tolerated such a practice, Brüning was unable to stabilise relations. Even President von Hindenburg, on whose support Brüning depended, pleaded for a "further opening to the right".

Boards 45 and 48 By skilfully manipulating the other groupings Hitler increasingly succeeded in becoming the key figure. Sections of industry and the financial world and the traditional right wing believed that they could make use of the "drummer" who laid out his political programme in Spring 1932: "I have set myself a goal: to sweep the thirty parties out of Germany!".

Board 46 Brüning's failure in domestic policy and disappointment and anger at the contents of important speeches made by the President caused the latter to sack the Chancellor, although Brüning had recently strongly supported Hindenburg's re-election and although further successes were beginning to be achieved in foreign policy in May 1932. Brüning's successor was Franz von Papen with his so-called "cabinet of barons".

Board 47 The vocal points of Papen's "state reform plans" were the withdrawal of parliament's powers and a change in the electoral laws. Whereas the Kapp-Putsch of 1920 had failed because of the general strike, Papen succeeded in taking power in Prussia on 20th July 1932 without any violence: the SPD government was replaced and the heartland of the Reich was no longer a republican bastion.

Board 49

Defence Minister von Schleicher opposed Papen's intention to implement his "state reform plans" by force. Papen was dismissed. As his successor Hindenburg appointed General von Schleicher.

Schleicher's surprising attempt to group all republican forces together against the NSDAP failed. The President who was irritated by this "volte-face policy" dismissed Schleicher and appointed a "national government", Hitler's government *(cat. illustr. 212).*

The German Empire 1939

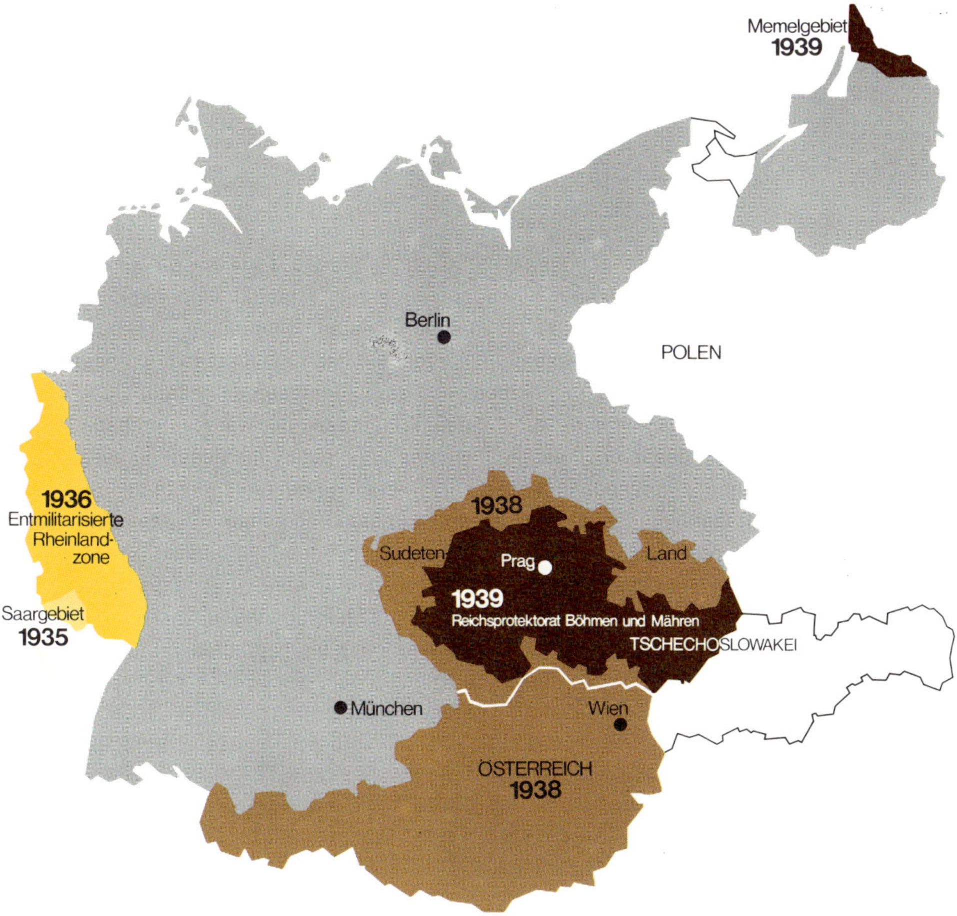

Room VI

The Third Reich

The 30th January 1933 was to a certain extent the result of a series of attempts to overcome the economic, political and social crises which had confronted the Weimar Republic after 1929 by authoritarian means. In addition, however, it also marked the starting point of a development which immediately pushed aside such attempts to find a solution and which within a short space of time abolished the parliamentary democratic system in radical fashion. Initially the National Socialists were able to take advantage of the idea, supported by many right-wingers and members of the middle class, of a renewal of state and society by means of a strong national government with a wide support-base. Support for the idea also led to Hindenburg's opposition to the appointment of Hitler as Chancellor being ignored. Who was using whom in pursuit of his own aims quickly became all too clear. Although the National Socialists were initially in the minority, with Adolf Hitler as Chancellor, in the government of "national unity" the illusion that Hitler could be influenced, as the charismatic "drummer" and eventually pushed aside, was dispelled within a few weeks.

The National Socialists still did not win a majority of the votes cast on 5th March 1933 in the last elections which could to a certain extent be said to be free. However, together with the German Nationals the National Socialists had a majority in Parliament. Through his Enabling Law Hitler freed himself of all constitutional obligations and of parliamentary control. After the elimination of the KPD only the SPD opposed the Law in the Reichstag. The Centre Party and middle class parties voted in favour of it. The next step was the banning or voluntary dissolution of political parties. The NSDAP became the state party of the Third Reich. The Reichstag became merely an institution which acclaimed Hitler and his decisions. The idea of a parliamentary democracy was conclusively destroyed. Henceforth, the NSDAP and its organisations supervised and determined all aspects of political, economic and cultural life in the state. The police were placed under national socialist control. The police force, the S.A. (Sturmabteilung) and S.S. (Schutzstaffel) were the instruments with which the Party extended the totalitarian system and secured its dominant position. In February 1933 the first concentration camps for political internees were opened. When the S.A. demanded widespread powers of control in line with those of the Party, it was stripped of power by Hitler at the end of June 1934. The S.S. became the most powerful state organisation. They saw themselves as the élite. In the war the S.S. was the organisation which carried out the extermination of European Jews.

Federal representatives (Reichsstatthalter) were appointed in the German Länder and the state parliaments were dissolved. The independence of the Länder and the local authorities' right of self administration were abolished. The federal state structure, which had existed since the founding of Bismarck's Empire, was transformed into a unitary state.

After the death of Hindenburg Hitler took control of the now combined functions of President and Chancellor. As the "Führer of the German Reich and people" all officials and soldiers had to swear an oath of allegiance to him. In this way he bound the officers and officials, who were mainly sworn in on a traditional oath of allegiance, even closer to him.

With the help of its various organisations the NSDAP controlled political life and society itself. All political, economic and cultural organisations were "brought into line". This began with the state organisation of the economy. Trade unions were abolished. The workers were deprived of their right to form trade unions, which had been fought for in the nineteenth century to enable them to have their interests represented. Workers and management were joined together in a unitary state organisation, the "German labour front". The fixing of wages by the state replaced the notion of social partnership. Restrictions were imposed on the right to choose one's place of work and the position of the employer was strengthened by the adoption of the Führer – subservient followers' attitude in factories. The principle of a capitalist private economy was not affected by the Party but production was largely controlled by the state. During the World War concentration camps and eventually the whole of occupied Europe became recruitment areas for the German armaments industry.

National socialism aimed to harness together the contradictory ideas of "nationalism" and "socialism" in the "national community" ("Volksgemeinschaft"). In reality, it broke away from German nationalist ideas and preached a racist ideology. An example of the principle of the personal and ideological grip on the whole nation was to be found in the youth organisation. All previous youth associations were disbanded and replaced by the state association, the Hitler Youth movement (H.J.). This was an instrument of national socialist education and pre-military training.

The upturn in the world economy after 1933 contributed to the recovery of the German economy. A job creation programme launched by the National Socialists included primarily public work schemes. This did little to assist industrial production but did take the unemployed off the streets and offered them low wages. The rearmament programme, which was initially disguised, and the building up of the Wehrmacht with two year's compulsory service also contributed to the reduction in unemployment. This success was one of the reasons why the national socialist regime had hardly any opponents in the whole German nation.
The job creation programme and build-up of arms were financed by foreign exchange, Reich loans and finally by the printing of banknotes. The Reich had debts on a scale which was hitherto unknown. The national socialist economic policy after 1933 primarily served Hitler's plan, which was kept a secret from the public: the war of conquest in the East which was to provide "a final solution for the future . . . by extending the 'Lebensraum' and the supplies of raw materials and food for our nation". Hitler gave the Wehrmacht and the economy the following tasks: "I. The German army must be ready for active duty within four years; II. The German economy must be equipped for war within four years".
Foreign policy, which at first seemed to continue the revisionist policies of the Weimar Republic, actually served this prime national socialist aim. For fear of a war the Western powers reacted cautiously and in so doing allowed Hitler to continue his aggressive and expansionist foreign policy. Not until German troops had occupied Czechoslovakia in the spring of 1939 did France and England adopt a firmer stance and jointly offer Poland a guarantee of military assistance. It now became clear that Hitler's next step risked causing a world war.
Anti-semitism, whose roots went back as far as the nineteenth century, had already been widespread in the Weimar Republic. For Hitler the racist ideology was the central idea of his philosophy. The NSDAP succeeded in transforming the feeling of being at the mercy of anonymous social forces – which had been experienced by the masses in the uncertain life of the world economic depression – into aggression against the "world conspiracy of Jews and Bolsheviks". Following the acquisition of power by the National Socialists Hitler's ideas about the "Volksfeinde" were consistently turned into reality. This began with

acts of violence against Jewish citizens and their property. Step by step life was made impossible for German Jews. Finally, the extermination of the "Jewish-Bolshevik ruling class" and of the Jews in Eastern Europe became, along with the winning of "Lebensraum" for the "German master race", a fundamental war aim.

The chances of the opposing forces offering any effective opposition to the N.S. regime were small from the outset. The political left, sections of the middle class conservative camp, churchmen and some military officers were united in their opposition to Hitler but were unable to form a common front against him because of their diverging political views and above all because of the perfect surveillance system operated by the state apparatus. Not until the 20th July 1944, with the threatening consequences of a military defeat staring them in the face, was there any attempt to overthrow Hitler. However, this did not succeed in ousting Hitler and in ending the war, at least in the West but rather led to the physical extermination of all German opposition. The war, which was continued and accompanied by increased internal terror campaigns, claimed more victims between the 20th July 1944 and the end of the war than in the previous four years.

The Path to the 30th January 1933

The Seizure of Power

Tower 1 (Exterior)

The start of the world economic depression in autumn 1929, which hit Germany particularly hard, increased social and political tension in the Weimar Republic. Influenced by mass unemployment and economic depression large sections of the population turned to extremism. The economically threatened middle classes in particular, the traditional supporters of the liberal parties, turned their backs on the Republic and moved towards the right. The right wing opposition, which was grouped around the NSDAP, grew into a mass movement and helped Adolf Hitler to power, with the support of sections of heavy industry and of the financial world *(cat. illustr. 213).*
Hitler's government was initially no different from its predecessors: it depended as a "presidential cabinet" not on a parliamentary majority but alone on the support of the President of the Reich. The majority of the conservatives and the nationalist middle class, large sections of the unemployed especially first time voters amongst them approved Hitler's seizure of power. They saw in it the promise of an end to the "confusion of the Republic". The rejection of the Weimar Republic, however, did not lead to the hoped-for "conservative renewal". The result was rather the totalitarian "Führer state".

The NSDAP before 1930

Tower 1 (Interior)

In the form of Adolf Hitler the leader of a party came to power which had, after the First World War, come onto the political scene as just one of many nationalist splinter groups. The driving forces behind the party's programme were confused anticapitalism, antiparliamentarianism, antimarxism, antisemitism and, in a time of growing political and social conflict, an obviously attractive ideology of a national community *(cat. illustr. 214).* National socialist propaganda condensed all these elements into a philosophy ("Weltanschauung") which, against the background of the social crisis, offered a solution for an antidemocratic mass.
Hitler began attempts to make political reality of his programme at an early stage. In similar fashion to Kapp in 1920 he believed

XVII (illustr. right): "Bauhaus staircase", painting by Oskar Schlemmer, 1932.

XVIII Friedrich Ebert, portrait by Lovis Corinth, 1924.

XIX "Session of the Reichstag 1930: Breitscheid making a speech", painting by Annot.

XX Sketch by A. Paul Weber to E. Niekisch, Hitler – German destiny.

VI/213 "The meaning of the Hitler salute": poster by John Heartfield: "Millions stand behind me".

Grundsätzliches Programm
der nationalsozialistischen
Deutschen Arbeiter-Partei.

Das Programm der Deutschen Arbeiter-Partei ist ein Zeit-Programm. Die Führer lehnen es ab, nach Erreichung der im Programm aufgestellten Ziele neue aufzustellen, nur zu dem Zweck, um durch künstlich gesteigerte Unzufriedenheit der Massen das Fortbestehen der Partei zu ermöglichen.

1. Wir fordern den Zusammenschluß aller Deutschen auf Grund des Selbstbestimmungsrechtes der Völker zu einem Groß-Deutschland.
2. Wir fordern die Gleichberechtigung des deutschen Volkes gegenüber den anderen Nationen, Aufhebung der Friedensverträge in Versailles und St. Germain.
3. Wir fordern Land u. Boden (Kolonien) zur Ernährung unseres Volkes u. Ansiedelung unseres Bevölkerungs-Ueberschusses.
4. Staatsbürger kann nur sein, wer Volksgenosse ist. Volksgenosse kann nur sein, wer deutschen Blutes ist, ohne Rücksichtnahme auf Konfession. **Kein Jude kann daher Volksgenosse sein.**
5. Wer nicht Staatsbürger ist, soll nur als Gast in Deutschland leben können u. muß unter Fremdengesetzgebung stehen.
6. Das Recht, über Führung u. Gesetze des Staates zu bestimmen, darf nur dem Staatsbürger zustehen. Daher fordern wir, daß jedes öffentlich Amt, gleichgiltig welcher Art, gleich ob im Reich, Land oder Gemeinde nur durch Staatsbürger bekleidet werden darf. — Wir bekämpfen die korrumpierende Parlamentswirtschaft einer Stellenbesetzung nur nach Parteigesichtspunkten ohne Rücksichten auf Charakter und Fähigkeiten.
7. Wir fordern, daß sich der Staat verpflichtet, in erster Linie für die Erwerbs- u. Lebensmöglichkeit der Staatsbürger zu sorgen. Wenn es nicht möglich ist, die Gesamtbevölkerung des Staates zu ernähren, so sind die Angehörigen fremder Nationen (Nicht-Staatsbürger) aus dem Reiche auszuweisen.
8. Jede weitere Einwanderung Nicht-Deutscher ist zu verhindern. Wir fordern, daß alle Nicht-Deutschen, die seit 2. August 1914 in Deutschland eingewandert sind, sofort zum Verlassen des Reiches gezwungen werden.
9. Alle Staatsbürger müssen gleiche Rechte u. Pflichten besitzen.
10. Erste Pflicht jedes Staatsbürgers muß sein, geistig oder körperlich zu schaffen. Die Tätigkeit des Einzelnen darf nicht gegen die Interessen der Allgemeinheit verstoßen, sondern muß im Rahmen des Gesamten u. zum Nutzen Aller erfolgen.

Daher fordern wir:

11. Abschaffung des arbeits- und mühelosen Einkommens,

Brechung der Zinsknechtschaft.

12. Im Hinblick auf die ungeheuren Opfer an Gut und Blut, die jeder Krieg vom Volke fordert, muß die persönliche Bereicherung durch den Krieg als Verbrechen am Volke bezeichnet werden. Wir fordern daher **restlose Einziehung aller Kriegsgewinne.**
13. Wir fordern die Verstaatlichung aller bisher bereits vergesellschafteten (Trust's) Betriebe.
14. Wir fordern Gewinnbeteiligung an Großbetrieben.
15. Wir fordern einen großzügigen Ausbau der Alters-Versorgung.
16. Wir fordern die Schaffung eines gesunden Mittelstandes und seine Erhaltung. Sofortige **Kommunalisierung der Groß-Warenhäuser** und ihre Vermietung zu billigen Preisen an kleine Gewerbetreibende, schärfste Berücksichtigung aller kleinen Gewerbetreibenden bei Lieferung an den Staat, die Länder oder Gemeinden.
17. Wir fordern eine unseren nationalen Bedürfnissen angepaßte Bodenrefom, Schaffung eines Gesetzes zur unentgeltlichen Enteignung von Boden für gemeinnützige Zwecke. Abschaffung des Bodenzinses und Verhinderung jeder Bodenspekulation.
18. Wir fordern den rücksichtslosen Kampf gegen diejenigen, die durch ihre Tätigkeit das Gemein-Interesse schädigen. Gemeine Volksverbrecher, **Wucherer, Schieber** usw. sind **mit dem Tode zu bestrafen,** ohne Rücksichtnahme auf Konfession und Rasse.
19. Wir fordern Ersatz für das der materialistischen Weltordnung dienende römische Recht durch ein Deutsches Gemein-Recht.
20. Um jedem fähigen und fleissigen Deutschen das Erreichen höherer Bildung und damit das Einrücken in führende Stellungen zu ermöglichen, hat der Staat für einen gründlichen Ausbau unseres gesamten Volksbildungswesens Sorge zu tragen. Die Lehrpläne aller Bildungsanstalten sind den Erfordernissen des praktischen Lebens anzupassen. Das Erfassen des Staatsgedankens muß bereits mit Beginn des Verständnisses durch die Schule (Staatsbürgerkunde) erzielt werden. Wir fordern die Ausbildung geistig besonders veranlagter Kinder armer Eltern ohne Rücksicht auf deren Stand oder Beruf auf Staatskosten.
21. Der Staat hat für die Hebung der Volksgesundheit zu sorgen durch den Schutz der Mutter und des Kindes, durch Verbot der Jugendarbeit, durch Herbeiführung der körperlichen Ertüchtigung mittels gesetzlicher Festlegung einer Turn- und Sportpflicht, durch größte Unterstützung aller sich mit körperlicher Jugend-Ausbildung beschäftigenden Vereine.
22. Wir fordern die Abschaffung der Sölnertruppen und die Bildung eines Volksheeres.
23. Wir fordern den gesetzlichen **Kampf** gegen die **bewußte politische Lüge** und ihre Verbreitung durch die Presse. Um die Schaffung einer deutschen Presse zu ermöglichen, fordern wir, daß:
    a) Sämtliche Schriftleiter u. Mitarbeiter von Zeitungen, die in Deutscher Sprache erscheinen, Volksgenossen sein müssen.
    b) Nichtdeutsche Zeitungen zu ihrem Erscheinen der ausdrücklichen Genehmigung des Staates bedürfen. Sie dürfen nicht in deutscher Sprache gedruckt werden.
    c) Jede finanzielle Beteiligung an Deutschen Zeitungen oder deren Beeinflussung durch Nichtdeutsche gesetzlich verboten wird, u. fordern als Strafe für Uebertretungen die Schließung einer solchen Zeitung, sowie die sofortige Ausweisung der daran beteiligten Nichtdeutschen aus dem Reich.
    Zeitungen, die gegen das Gemeinwohl verstoßen, sind zu verbieten. Wir fordern den gesetzlichen Kampf gegen eine Kunst- u. Literatur-Richtung, die einen zersetzenden Einfluß auf unser Volksleben ausübt u. die Schließung von Veranstaltungen, die gegen vorstehende Forderung verstoßen.
24. Wir fordern die Freiheit aller religiösen Bekenntnisse im Staat, soweit sie nicht dessen Bestand gefährden oder gegen das Sittlichkeits- u. Moralgefühl der germanischen Rasse verstoßen. Die Partei als solche vertritt den Standpunkt eines positiven Christentums, ohne sich konfessionell an ein bestimmtes Bekenntnis zu binden. Sie bekämpft den jüdisch-materialistischen Geist **in** und **außer** uns und ist überzeugt, daß eine dauernde Genesung unseres Volkes nur erfolgen kann von **innen** heraus auf der Grundlage:

Gemeinnutz vor Eigennutz.

25. Zur Durchführung alles dessen fordern wir die Schaffung einer starken Zentralgewalt des Reiches. Unbedingte Autorität des politischen Zentralparlaments über das gesamte Reich u. seine Organisationen im allgemeinen. Die Bildung von Stände- und Berufskammern zur Durchführung der vom Reich erlassenen Rahmengesetze in den einzelnen Bundesstaaten.

Die Führer der Partei versprechen, wenn nötig unter Einsatz des eigenen Lebens, für die Durchführung der vorstehenden Punkte rücksichtlos einzutreten.

München, den 24. Februar 1920.

Für den **Partei-Ausschuß:** Anton Drexler

Spenden und Beiträge sind zu richten an die Geschäftsstelle München: Corneliusstr. 12 (Tel. 23620)

Geschäftsstunden 9—12 Uhr vorm., 2—6 Uhr nachm.

Münchener Plakatdruckerei, Schreiber & Nertl
Geschäftsstellen: Rosenthal 6 und Ledererstraße 3

P 00088 a

VI/214 The NSDAP programme of 1920.

Basic Programme of the National Socialist

German Workers' Party

The programme of the German Workers' Party is a static programme. The leaders reject the idea of setting new goals after the initial aims laid down in the programme have been achieved simply in order to ensure the continued existence of the party by artificially increasing unrest amongst the masses.

1. We demand the uniting together of all Germans, on the basis of the people's right of self-determination, in a greater Germany.
2. We demand equal status for Germany vis à vis other nations and the annulling of the Peace treaties drawn up in Versailles and St. Germain.
3. We demand land and property (colonies) to provide food for our nations and settlement areas for our population surplus.
4. Only a fellow German can have right of citizenship. A fellow German can only be so if he is of German parentage, irrespective of religion. **Therefore no Jew can be considered to be a fellow German.**
5. Those people who have no right of citizenship should only be guests in Germany and must be subject to laws concerning foreigners.
6. Only citizens should have the right to decide the leadership and laws of the state. Therefore, we demand that only those with rights of citizenship should have access to employment in any public office, whether it be at national, Länder or local level – we oppose the corrupt parliamentary system in which people are employed only on the basis of which party they belong to and not according to their character or ability.
7. We demand that the first priority of the state should be to ensure that its citizens have a job and a decent life. If it should prove impossible to feed the whole population of the state, foreign nationals (with no right of citizenship) should be repatriated.
8. Any further immigration of non-Germans must be prevented. We demand that all non-Germans who have entered the Reich since 2nd August 1914 be forced to leave immediately.
9. All citizens must have equal rights and obligations.
10. The first duty of all fellow citizens must be to work, either physically or mentally. The actions of an individual must not run contrary to the general interest and must have consideration for the common good.

Therefore, we demand:

11. Abolition of income for unemployed people or for those making no effort.

The breaking of the dominance of invested capital.

12. With regard to the huge physical and personal sacrifice which all wars demand of the people, personal enrichment by means of war must be seen as a crime against the nation. Therefore, we demand **the collection of all wartime profits.**
13. We demand the nationalisation of all publicly owned companies (Trusts).
14. We demand profit-sharing by large companies.
15. We demand that generous improvements be made in the old age pension system.
16. We demand the establishment and maintenance of a healthy middle class. The large department stores should be immediately placed under the control of the local authority and should be rented out to small businesses at low prices. All small businesses should have the keenest regard for their deliveries to the state, the Länder or the local authorities.
17. We demand a property reform, which is in line with our requirements, and the creation of a law, which would allow the confiscation of property without compensation if this were in the general interest of the nation. We demand the abolition of all ground rents and the banning of all property speculation.
18. We demand an all-out battle against those who damage the common interest by their actions – criminals against the nation, profiteers, racketeers etc. should be punished by death, without regard for religion or race.
19. We demand the replacement of the system of Roman law, which serves the materialistic world order, by a system of German common law.
20. In order to make it possible for all capable and diligent Germans to receive a good education, thus enabling them to take up leading positions of employment, the state must carry the burden of a thorough overhaul of the national education system. The curricula of all institutions of education must adapt to the practical requirements of life. We must aim to instil national ideas from the earliest age in school (lessons in citizenship). We demand that the brightest children of poor parents should be supported by the state irrespective of their class or job.
21. The state must ensure the general good health of its citizens, by providing for mothers and children, by banning child labour, by ensuring the development of physical fitness, by making it a legal obligation to participate in sport or gymnastics and by providing all possible support for associations involved in instructing the youth in physical fitness.
22. We demand the abolition of the Söldnerheer and its replacement by a people's army (Volksheer).
23. We demand a legal battle against **open political slander** and its publication in the press. In order to make possible the establishment of a German press, we demand that:
    a) Newspaper editors and employees whose work appears in German must have German citizenship rights.
    b) Non German newspapers must have the express permission of the state before they can appear in Germany. They must not be printed in German.
    c) Any financial contributions to German newspapers or any influence at all by non-Germans should be banned by law. Furthermore, we demand that any contraventions of the above should lead to the closing down of the newspaper in question and to the immediate expulsion from the Reich of those non-Germans involved.
    Newspapers which are deemed to be against the common good should be banned. We demand a legal battle against any art and literature which exerts a harmful influence on public life and we demand that all institutions which contravene the afore-mentioned standards be closed down.
24. We demand the freedom of religion in the Reich so long as they do not endanger the position of the state or adversely affect the moral standards of the German race. As such the Party represents a positively Christian position without binding itself to one particular faith. The Party opposes the materialistic Jewish spirit within and beyond us and is convinced that a lasting recovery of our people can only be achieved on the basis of:

Common Good before Personal Gain

25. In order to achieve all of the aforegoing we demand the setting up of a strong central administration for the Reich.
    We demand unrestricted authority for the central parliament over the whole Reich and its organizations. We demand the establishment of professional and industrial chambers to assist the implementation of the laws of the Reich in the Länder.

The leaders of the party promise to commit themselves fully to the achievement of the above aims, and to sacrifice their lives if need be.

Munich, 24th February 1920

For the **Party Committee:** Anton Drexler

Contributions should be sent to the Head Office: **Corneliusstraße 12** (Tel. 23620)
Business Hours 9–12 (am), 2–6 (pm)

Proklamation

an das deutsche Volk!

Die Regierung der Novemberverbrecher in Berlin ist heute für abgesetzt erklärt worden.

Eine provisorische deutsche National-Regierung ist gebildet worden.

Diese besteht aus

General Ludendorff, Adolf Hitler

General von Lossow, Oberst von Seisser

VI/215 Hitler Putsch, 9th November 1923.

Proclamation to the German People!

We declare that today the government of the November traitors has been removed from office.

A temporary German national government has been formed.

This consists of:

General Ludendorff, Adolf Hitler, General von Lossow, Colonel von Seisser.

V/216 Mass meeting of the NSDAP in a sports stadium before 1933.

V/217 S.A. premises in Berlin, 1932.

that it would be possible to stage a successful putsch against the "November Republic" during the crisis year of 1923 *(cat. illustr. 215)*. With the failure of the Putsch the danger of a national socialist take-over was avoided for the time being. Hitler was tried on a charge of high treason. During his period of imprisonment he set down his political aims in his book "Mein Kampf": his foreign policy plans, which were in many respects based on extreme war aims of the First World War, revolved around the central aim of exterminating the Jewish "mortal enemy" of the "aryan race". During the first stage, following the "seizure of power", the "cancerous democracy" was to be abolished and Jews, Bolsheviks and Marxists were to be banished from the national community. Following the internal consolidation of the Reich the German position in central Europe was to be secured stage by stage and then strengthened and finally Germany, as the "Great Germanic Reich of the German Nation", would achieve a position of world dominance.
Following his early release Hitler adopted a new tactic: power was to be won slowly and legally. In the ensuing peaceful years of the Republic he systematically built up the Party *(cat. illustr. 216)*.

The Consolidation of N. S. – Dominance

The Elimination of Political Opponents (Gleichschaltung)

Tower 2
(Exterior)

The "seizure of power" on 30th January 1933 marked not just the end of the Weimar Republic but also the abolition of the federal structure which had existed since 1871 in the German Reich. The same was also true of the existing institutions of political and social life. The "Gleichschaltung" of the German Länder, the administration and the judiciary *(cat. illustr. 227)*, the press, the arts and sciences, meant the path was cleared for a centralist unitary state. The banning of political parties and the aggressive elimination of political opponents, including those amongst their own ranks, were further steps along the road to the establishment of a dictatorship. With the death of Hindenburg in August 1934 the concentration of internal political power was secured: Hitler was the leader of the state party, head of government and head of state. As the "Führer of the

German Reich and nation" he forced officials and soldiers to swear an oath of allegiance to him.
The N. S. government used the Reichstag fire on 27th February 1933 *(cat. illustr. 218)* as an opportunity for replacing the constitutional laws of the Weimar Republic on the following day by passing an emergency decree "to protect the people and the state" *(cat. illustr. 219).* This marked the beginning of the hounding and arresting of political opponents, especially those of the left *(cat. illustr. 220).*
Fresh elections of 5th March followed the dissolution of the Reichstag. However, although the NSDAP declared it "the day of the awakening nation" and although left wing party newspapers had been banned since the Reichstag fire and communists and social democrats had been pursued or suppressed, the NSDAP only won 43.9% of the votes cast and thus had no parliamentary majority.
At the opening of the newly elected Reichstag on 21st March Hitler testified to the "spirit of Potsdam" *(cat. illustr. 221).* In so doing he adopted Prussian traditions for himself and his party, which, in place of the "spirit of Weimar", were to support the "awakening of the nation".
By means of the "Enabling Act" of 23rd March Hitler freed himself from all constitutional and parliamentary control *(cat. illustr. 222).* The Centre and middle class parties voted in favour of the Law. After the banning of the KPD the social democrats were the only party to vote against it after a courageous speech by their chairman Otto Wels. The Law made the Reichstag a superfluous institution. The legislature and the executive were coordinated. Only the government could now pass laws.
On 31st March the independence of the Länder and the local authorities' powers of self administration were abolished. The Länder parliaments were reformed in accordance with the result of the March Reichstag elections. Federal representatives (Reichsstatthalter) ensured that the "policy guidelines set out by the Chancellor of the Reich" were adhered to *(cat. illustr. 224).* Officials who did not support the national socialists could be dismissed in accordance with the "law on the recreation of the professional and service" of 7th April and Jewish officials could be dismissed on the grounds of a special "Aryan paragraph". Opponents of the regime in the Länder and their civil services were also eliminated.
The 1st May, the traditional celebration day of the labour move-

V/218 The Reichstag Fire of 27th February 1933 (Press culting).

Reichsgesetzblatt

1933	Ausgegeben zu Berlin, den 28. Februar 1933	Nr. 17

Inhalt: Verordnung des Reichspräsidenten zum Schutz von Volk und Staat. Vom 28. Februar 1933....... S. 83

Verordnung des Reichspräsidenten zum Schutz von Volk und Staat. Vom 28. Februar 1933.

Auf Grund des Artikels 48 Abs. 2 der Reichsverfassung wird zur Abwehr kommunistischer staatsgefährdender Gewaltakte folgendes verordnet:

§ 1

Die Artikel 114, 115, 117, 118, 123, 124 und 153 der Verfassung des Deutschen Reichs werden bis auf weiteres außer Kraft gesetzt. Es sind daher Beschränkungen der persönlichen Freiheit, des Rechts der freien Meinungsäußerung, einschließlich der Pressefreiheit, des Vereins- und Versammlungsrechts, Eingriffe in das Brief-, Post-, Telegraphen- und Fernsprechgeheimnis, Anordnungen von Haussuchungen und von Beschlagnahmen sowie Beschränkungen des Eigentums auch außerhalb der sonst hierfür bestimmten gesetzlichen Grenzen zulässig.

§ 2

Werden in einem Lande die zur Wiederherstellung der öffentlichen Sicherheit und Ordnung nötigen Maßnahmen nicht getroffen, so kann die Reichsregierung insoweit die Befugnisse der obersten Landesbehörde vorübergehend wahrnehmen.

§ 3

Die Behörden der Länder und Gemeinden (Gemeindeverbände) haben den auf Grund des § 2 erlassenen Anordnungen der Reichsregierung im Rahmen ihrer Zuständigkeit Folge zu leisten.

. . . .

§ 6

Diese Verordnung tritt mit dem Tage der Verkündung in Kraft.

Berlin, den 28. Februar 1933.

Der Reichspräsident
von Hindenburg

Der Reichskanzler
Adolf Hitler

Der Reichsminister des Innern
Frick

Der Reichsminister der Justiz
Dr. Gürtner

VI/219 Extract from the Emergency Decree of 28th February 1933.

Reich Law Gazette

1933 Published in Berlin, 28th February 1933 Nr. 17

Decree of the Reich President on the protection of the people and the state. 28th February 1933.

On the basis of Article 48, para 2 of the constitution of the Reich the following is decreed as a protection against communist acts of violence endangering the state:

§ 1

Articles 114, 115, 117, 118, 123, 124 and 153 of the constitution of the German Reich are cancelled until further notice. This allows certain restrictions to be imposed on personal freedom, on the right to express a free opinion, the freedom of the press, of association and the right to hold meetings, it allows restrictions on the secrecy of the mail, post and telecommunications systems, the ordering of house searches and confiscation of property and restrictions on property rights.

§ 2

Should the necessary steps to restore public security and order not be taken in the Länder, the government of the Reich is empowered to enforce such measures in its capacity as the highest government authority.

§ 3

The authorities of the Länder and the local level must perform the following duties, in accordance with decrees of the government of the Reich set out in § 2.

. . . .

§ 6

This decree applies from the day of publication.

Berlin, 28th February 1933.

Reich President
von Hindenburg

Reich Chancellor
Adolf Hitler

Interior Minister of the Reich
Frick

Justice Minister of the Reich
Dr. Gürtner

Reich Law Gazette

1933 Published in Berlin, 24th March 1933, Nr. 25

Law concerning the solving of the emergency of the people and the Reich, 24th March 1933.

The Reichstag has issued the following decree, which is hereby announced with the agreement of the Reich Council, after having ensured that the necessary legal constitutional amendments have been made:

Article 1

Laws of the Reich can be passed by the government, in addition to the procedure laid down in the constitution of the Reich. This also applies to laws covered by Articles 85, para 2, and 87 of the Reich constitution.

Article 2

The laws passed by the Reich government do not have to adhere to the constitution provided that the institutions of the Reichstag and Reichsrat have no objection. The rights of the President of the Reich remain unaffected.

Article 3

The laws passed by the government of the Reich will be drafted by the Chancellor and announced in the Law Gazette. They will apply, provided that no other provision is made, from the day following their publication. Articles 68–77 of the constitution do not apply to the laws passed by the government of the Reich.

Article 4

Treaties agreed by the Reich with foreign states, which concern the constitutional affairs of the Reich, do not require the consent of the legislative institutions. The government of the Reich will issue the necessary instructions for the implementation of these treaties.

Article 5

This law applies from the day of its publication. It will expire on the 1st April 1937; it will also be annulled if the present government of the Reich is replaced by another.

VI/221 The Potsdam State Act.

Reichsgesetzblatt

1933	Ausgegeben zu Berlin, den 24. März 1933	Nr. 25

Inhalt: Gesetz zur Behebung der Not von Volk und Reich. Vom 24. März 1933 .... S. 141

**Gesetz zur Behebung der Not von Volk und Reich.
Vom 24. März 1933.**

Der Reichstag hat das folgende Gesetz beschlossen, das mit Zustimmung des Reichsrats hiermit verkündet wird, nachdem festgestellt ist, daß die Erfordernisse verfassungändernder Gesetzgebung erfüllt sind:

Artikel 1

Reichsgesetze können außer in dem in der Reichsverfassung vorgesehenen Verfahren auch durch die Reichsregierung beschlossen werden. Dies gilt auch für die in den Artikeln 85 Abs. 2 und 87 der Reichsverfassung bezeichneten Gesetze.

Artikel 2

Die von der Reichsregierung beschlossenen Reichsgesetze können von der Reichsverfassung abweichen, soweit sie nicht die Einrichtung des Reichstags und des Reichsrats als solche zum Gegenstand haben. Die Rechte des Reichspräsidenten bleiben unberührt.

Artikel 3

Die von der Reichsregierung beschlossenen Reichsgesetze werden vom Reichskanzler ausgefertigt und im Reichsgesetzblatt verkündet. Sie treten, soweit sie nichts anderes bestimmen, mit dem auf die Verkündung folgenden Tage in Kraft. Die Artikel 68 bis 77 der Reichsverfassung finden auf die von der Reichsregierung beschlossenen Gesetze keine Anwendung.

Artikel 4

Verträge des Reichs mit fremden Staaten, die sich auf Gegenstände der Reichsgesetzgebung beziehen, bedürfen nicht der Zustimmung der an der Gesetzgebung beteiligten Körperschaften. Die Reichsregierung erläßt die zur Durchführung dieser Verträge erforderlichen Vorschriften.

Artikel 5

Dieses Gesetz tritt mit dem Tage seiner Verkündung in Kraft. Es tritt mit dem 1. April 1937 außer Kraft; es tritt ferner außer Kraft, wenn die gegenwärtige Reichsregierung durch eine andere abgelöst wird.

VI/222 The “Enabling Act” of 24th March 1933.

Morgen-Ausgabe
Nr. 59 A 30 50. Jahrg.

Redaktion und Verlag:
Berlin SW 68, Lindenstr. 8

Vorwärts

BERLINER VOLKSBLATT

GRATIS!

SONNABEND
4. Februar 1933

Zentralorgan der Sozialdemokratischen Partei Deutschlands

Der Polizeipräsident
Tgb.-Nr. I³ 41⁰¹ Pr. 33

Berlin, den 3. Februar 1933

Verbot

Auf Grund des § 6 der Verordnung des Reichspräsidenten zur Erhaltung des inneren Friedens vom 19. Dezember 1932 (RGB. I 548) in Verbindung mit den §§ 81 bis 86, StGB. verbiete ich die in Berlin erscheinende Tageszeitung

„Vorwärts"

einschließlich der Kopfblätter mit sofortiger Wirkung bis zum 6. Februar 1933 einschließlich.

Das Verbot umfaßt auch jede angeblich neue Druckschrift, die sich sachlich als die alte darstellt oder als ihr Ersatz anzusehen ist.

Gegen das Verbot ist binnen zwei Wochen — vom Tage der Zustellung ab — die Beschwerde zulässig, sie hat keine aufschiebende Wirkung. Die Beschwerde ist bei mir einzureichen.

Sollte von dem Beschwerderecht Gebrauch gemacht werden, so empfiehlt es sich zur Beschleunigung der Angelegenheit, die Beschwerdeschrift in vierfacher Ausfertigung vorzulegen.

Gründe:

In der Morgenausgabe Nr. 57, A. 29, 50. Jahrgang, befinden sich in dem Aufruf auf der Titelseite unter der Ueberschrift: „Deutsches Volk, Frauen und Männer" u. a. folgende Sätze:

> „Gegen solche Pläne rufen wir euch zum Kampf! Wehrt euch. Schützt euer Selbstbestimmungsrecht als Staatsbürger. Erhebt euch gegen eure Bedränger, gegen die feinen Leute, die hauchdünne Oberschicht des Großkapitals! Zerbrecht ihre politische und wirtschaftliche Macht!
> Kämpft darum mit uns für die Enteignung des Großgrundbesitzes und die Aufteilung des Landes an Bauern und Landarbeiter! Kämpft mit uns für die Enteignung der Schwerindustrie, für den Aufbau einer sozialistischen Plan- und Bedarfswirtschaft!"

Durch diese Ausführungen wird im Zusammenhang mit dem Inhalt der Ausführungen des gesamten Aufrufs der Tatbestand des § 85 R.St.G.B. in Verbindung des § 81 Ziff. 2 R.St.G.B. erfüllt.

gez. Dr. Melcher.
Für die richtige Abschrift:
(Stempel) Böhm
Kanzleiinspektor.

Verantwortlicher Redakteur: Rudolf Brendemühl, Berlin. Verlag: Vorwärts-Verlag G. m. b. H. — Druck: Vorwärts-Buchdruckerei und Verlagsanstalt, Berlin SW 68, Lindenstraße 3.

VI/220 The last publication of 'Vorwärts', 4th February 1933.

Vorwärts

Central organ of the Social Democratic Party of Germany

Berlin, 3rd February 1933

Ban

On the basis of § 6 of the decree of the Reich President on the preservation of internal peace of 19th December 1932 (R.G.B. I 548) in connection with § 81–86, St.G.B., I ban the Berlin daily newspaper,

'Vorwärts'

including all its leader articles, with immediate effect from the 6th February 1933.

The ban includes all attempts to produce a new paper which might represent the opinions of the old one or replace it.

An appeal against the ban is permitted provided that it is lodged within two weeks of issue. It has no delaying effect. The appeal should be made to me.

Should use be made of the right of appeal, it is recommended that four copies of the appeal document be forwarded in order to speed up procedures.

Reasons

In the morning edition Nr. 57, A. 29, 59, in the appeal on the front page, beneath the headline: "German People, Women and Men" it is stated, inter alia . . .

"We call you to fight against such plans! Arm yourselves. Protect your right of self determination as a citizen. Rise up against your oppressors, against the well off people, the wafer-thin upper class of large capitalists! Break their political and economic powers!

Join our fight for the dispossessing of the large land owners and for the distribution of land to farmers and farm workers! Join our fight for the expropriation of heavy industry and for the establishment of a socialist planned economy to meet our requirements!"

Through this statement, together with the content of the whole appeal, the evidence required for § 85 R.St.G.B., in connection with § 81 Ziff. 2 R.St.G.B., is complete.

Dr. Melcher

VI/223 The aligned Reichstag.

VI/224 The appointment of the Federal Representatives (Reichsstatthalter).

VI/225 Occupation of the Trade Union Headquarters, 2nd May 1933.

VI/226 Swearing an oath of allegiance to Hitler, 2nd August 1934.

VI/227 The aligned Judiciary.

VI/228 After the arrest of political opponents, 1933.

ment, was declared a "day of national labour" by the government of the Reich. Hundreds of thousands supported the regime's appeal. The trade union leaders accepted the decision in the hope of at least saving their organisation. However, on the following day, the 2nd May, the leading union officials were arrested and sent to concentration camps *(cat. illustr. 225).* The union organisation was "aligned" and the "working Germans of brow and fist" were united in the "German Labour Front".

By voting in favour of the Enabling Act most political parties had renounced in March any hope of a decisive role in political affairs, for which they had been struggling and had eventually won in 1918 after several vain attempts. Under increasing pressure from the NSDAP they either disbanded during 1933 or were banned. A law passed on 14th July "against the establishment of new parties" completed the process and cemented the NSDAP's role as the sole party in the unitary state.

After Hindenburg's death the concentration of internal political power was complete. A symbol of this concentration of power was the oath of allegiance which Hitler made the Reichswehr swear on 2nd August 1934: "I swear to God this holy oath that I shall offer total obedience to the Führer of the German Reich and Nation, Adolf Hitler, the supreme commander of the Wehrmacht, and that I shall be prepared, as a brave soldier, to lay down my life at any time" *(cat. illustr. 226).*

The Liquidation of Political Opponents

Tower 2 (Interior)

Parallel to the political alignment process a policy of elimination of political opponents, of "enemies of the state" was pursued *(cat. illustr. 228).* According to the statutes of the security police the following categories were sought out: "communists, marxists, Jews, politically-active churches, freemasons, politically dissatisfied people (grumblers), members of the national opposition, reactionaries, members of the Black Front, economic saboteurs, common criminals, abortionists and homosexuals, traitors and those guilty of high treason".

The June murders of 1934 claimed both men from the opposition within the Party and conservative and religious opponents of the regime as victims *(cat. illustr. 229).* As a measure to ensure law and order, aimed at rebel forces in the S.A., the actions of the party leadership and the S.S. were accepted by the President of the Reich and by the Reichswehr. Moreover, the "Röhm Affair" ended the aspirations of the social revolutionary forces in the national socialist leadership, who had previously blocked an agreement between Hitler and the Reichswehr and industry.

The N. S. State

Tower 3 (Exterior)

By the middle of 1934 the N.S. position of dominance had been largely secured. The NSDAP, which before 1933 had been primarily a party struggling against the Weimar Republic, had achieved its task of taking power. However, the Party did not then become superfluous. "The NSDAP remains, in order that the people remain national socialists", announced propaganda minister Dr. Joseph Goebbels. The institutions of the state should, by means of education and propaganda and with the support of the judiciary and the police, create a situation in which "national socialism is the only air which we breathe" (Goebbels). The real aim remained a secret: the preparation of state, economy and society for an expansionist war.
National socialism aimed to bring together the contradictory forces of "nationalism" and "socialism" in a "people's community" *(cat. illustr. 234).* An example of the personal and ideological grip held on the entire nation was the youth organisation. All previous youth associations were disbanded and replaced by the state association of the "Hitler Youth" (H.J.). This was an instrument of national socialist education and pre-military training from which Hitler wanted to create a youth which was "as tough as leather, as hard as Krupp steel, as quick as greyhounds". The state education institutions held a grip on citizens from childhood and taught them "to think nothing but German, to feel German and to behave German".
The "publicity work" of the regime also served this aim. Various pieces of information in the press, on the radio and on film could be traced back to the same source and were all vetted by the same organisation: the Ministry for Propaganda under Joseph Goebbels. His precise instructions about the way to deal with political, economic or even artistic themes ensured, together with the pressure placed on journalists, a uniform and,

Einzelnummer 10 Pfg.

Extra-Blatt

Oberbayer. Gebirgsbote, Holzkirchen • Miesbacher Anz., Miesbach • Tegernseer Ztg., Tegernsee, Aiblinger Ztg., Bad Aibling • Rosenheimer Tagbl., Rosenheim • Kolbermoorer Volksblatt, Kolbermoor • Chiemgau-Ztg., Prien • Tölzer Ztg., Bad Tölz • Wolfratshauser Tagbl., Wolfratshausen, Wasserburger Anzeiger, Wasserburg a. I. • Grafinger Zeitung, Grafing.

Samstag, 30. Juni 34

Röhm verhaftet und abgesetzt

Röhm aus Partei und S.A. ausgeschlossen

München, 30. Juni

Die Reichspressestelle der N.S.D.A.P. teilt folgende Verfügung des Führers mit:

Ich habe mit dem heutigen Tage den Stabschef Röhm seiner Stellung enthoben und aus Partei und S.A. ausgestoßen. Ich ernenne zum Chef des Stabes Obergruppenführer Lutze.

S.A.-Führer und S.A.-Männer, die seinen Befehlen nicht nachkommen oder zuwiderhandeln, werden aus S.A. und Partei entfernt bzw. verhaftet und abgeurteilt.

gez. **Adolf Hitler**

Oberster Partei- und S.A.-Führer

Aufruf des neuen Stabschefs

Der Führer hat mich an seine Seite als Chef des Stabes berufen. Das mir dadurch bewiesene Vertrauen muß und werde ich rechtfertigen durch unverbrüchliche Treue zum Führer und restlosen Einsatz für den Nationalsozialismus und dadurch für unser Volk.

Als ich vor etwa 12 Jahren zum erstenmal Führer einer kleinen S.A. war, habe ich drei Tugenden an die Spitze meines Handelns gestellt und sie von der S.A. gefordert. Diese drei Tugenden haben die S.A. groß gemacht und heute, wo ich in schicksalsschwerer Stunde meinem Führer an hervorragender Stelle dienen darf, sollen sie erst recht Richtschnur für die ganze S.A. sein:

Unbedingte Treue!

Schärfste Disziplin!

Hingebender Opfermut!

So wollen wir, die wir Nationalsozialisten sind, gemeinsam marschieren.

Ich bin überzeugt, dann kann es nur ein Marsch zur Freiheit werden.

Es lebe der Führer! Es lebe unser Volk!

Der Chef des Stabes:

gez. Lutze.

Der Führer an den neuen Stabschef

München, 30. Juni

Der Führer hat folgendes Schreiben an den Obergruppenführer der S.A. Lutze gerichtet:

An Obergruppenführer Lutze.

Mein lieber S.A.-Führer Lutze!

Schwerste Verfehlungen meines bisherigen Stabschefs zwangen mich, ihn seiner Stellung zu entheben. Sie, mein lieber Obergruppenführer Lutze, sind seit vielen Jahren **in guten und schlechten Tagen ein immer gleich treuer und vorbildlicher S.A.-Führer gewesen.** Wenn ich Sie mit dem heutigen Tage zum Chef des Stabes ernenne, dann geschieht dies in der festen Ueberzeugung, daß es Ihrer treuen und gehorsamen Arbeit gelingen wird, **aus meiner S.A. das Instrument zu schaffen, das die Nation braucht und ich mir vorstelle.**

Es ist mein Wunsch, daß die S.A. **zu einem treuen und starken Glied der Nationalsozialistischen Bewegung** ausgestaltet wird. Erfüllt von **Gehorsam** und **blinder Disziplin,** muß sie mithelfen, den neuen deutschen Menschen zu bilden und zu formen.

gez. **Adolf Hitler**

Befehl des Obersten S.A.-Führers Adolf Hitler

Adolf Hitler hat an den Chef des Stabes, Lutze, folgenden Befehl gegeben:

Wenn ich Sie heute zum Chef des Stabes der S.A. ernenne, dann erwarte ich, daß Sie sich hier eine Reihe von Aufgaben angelegen sein lassen, die ich Ihnen hiermit stelle:

1. Ich verlange vom S.A.-Führer genau so wie er vom S.A.-Mann blinden Gehorsam und unbedingte Disziplin.

2. Ich verlange, daß jeder S.A.-Führer wie jeder politische Führer sich dessen bewußt ist, daß sein Benehmen und seine Aufführung vorbildlich zu sein haben für seinen Verband, ja für unsere gesamte Gefolgschaft.

3. Ich verlange, daß S.A.-Führer — genau so wie politische Leiter —, die sich in ihrem Benehmen in der Oeffentlichkeit etwas zuschulden kommen lassen, unnachsichtlich aus der Partei und der S.A. entfernt werden.

4. Ich verlange insbesondere vom S.A.-Führer, daß er ein Vorbild in der Einfachheit und nicht im Aufwand ist. Ich wünsche nicht, daß der S.A.-Führer kostbare Diners gibt oder an solchen teilnimmt. Man hat uns früher hierzu nicht eingeladen, wir haben auch jetzt dort nichts zu suchen. Millionen unserer Volksgenossen fehlt auch heute noch das Notwendigste zum Leben, sie sind nicht neidig dem, den das Glück mehr gesegnet hat, aber es ist eines Nationalsozialisten unwürdig, den Abstand, der zwischen Not und Glück ohnehin ungeheuer groß ist, noch besonders zu vergrößern. Ich verbiete insbesondere, daß Mittel der Partei, der S.A. oder überhaupt der Oeffentlichkeit für Festgelage und dergleichen Verwendung finden. Es ist unverantwortlich, von Geldern, die zum Teil sich aus den Groschen unserer ärmsten Mitbürger ergeben, Schlemmereien abzuhalten. Das luxuriöse Stabs-Quartier in Berlin, in dem, wie nunmehr festgestellt wurde, monatlich bis zu 30 000 Mark für Festessen usw. ausgegeben wurden, ist sofort aufzulösen.

Ich untersage daher für alle Parteiinstanzen die Veranstaltung sogenannter Festessen und Diners aus irgendwelchen öffentlichen Mitteln. Und ich verbiete allen Partei- und S.A.-Führern die Teilnahme an solchen. Ausgenommen davon ist nur die Erfüllung der von Staats we-

Folgende sieben Verräter wurden bereits erschossen:

Im Zusammenhang mit dem aufgedeckten Komplott wurden folgende Meuterer erschossen:

Obergruppenführer A. Schneidhuber;
Obergruppenführer Edmund Heines;
Gruppenführer Ernst, Berlin;
Gruppenführer Schmidt, München;
Gruppenführer Hans Heym;
Gruppenführer Heydebreck;
Standartenführer Graf Spreti, München.

Druck: Münchner Buchgewerbehaus M. Müller & Sohn, G.m.b.H. München. Verantwortlich: Hauptschriftleiter W. Kittich.

VI/229 **Special Issue – Röhm Arrested and Dismissed –** The 30th June 1934 in the aligned press.

VI/230 Press conference with propaganda minister Goebbels.

VI/231 “My honour is my faithfulness”, inspection of S. S. recruits by Heinrich Himmler.

VI/232 The People’s Court (Volksgerichtshof).

VI/233 National Labour service in action.

VI/234 Winter relief work: appeal for national solidarity: The money goes to the armaments industry. "Berlin is eating its hot pot today".

moreover, perfect control of public opinion *(cat. illustr. 230).* The Propaganda Ministry controlled the public image of the party regime. Even the "spontaneous" character of mass actions were regulated: from "plebiscites" to the "Reichskristallnacht" of 1939.

The public, whose attitude varied from those who agreed with the regime to those who feared reprisals, was subjected to a perfect system of surveillance: the police, secret agents, the S.A. and the S.S. were the instruments used by the Party to extend their totalitarian system and to secure their dominant position. In February 1933 the first concentration camps were set up for political internees. From the "Black Shirts" ("Schutzstaffel"), Hitler's bodyguard, the S.S., under Heinrich Himmler, became a "state within a state" *(cat. illustr. 231).* S.S. members considered themselves to be the new ruling élite of the nation. They swore total obedience to Hitler and pledged themselves to the fight, as an end in itself "and also to remain at their post when all is lost: there can be no such word as 'impossible' and there never will be amongst our ranks. It is not what we are fighting for which is all important but how we fight".

By 1939 the S.S., together with the "Geheime Staatspolizei" (Gestapo), was occupied with the task of surveying and persecuting opponents of the regime. During the war, having by then been expanded to form the "Waffen-S.S.", they were assigned to various "special duties" in occupied territories. The extermination of the Warsaw Ghetto in 1943 was one of these "special missions" *(cat. illustr. 241).*

Despite its position of unrestricted and unchecked power the totalitarian state set up a judiciary, which sanctioned what was happening and by its total subservience to the "will of the Führer" renounced its classical function as an independent third force in the state. Now the "basis for the interpretation of all laws is the national socialist philosophy, as expressed in the party programme and in the speeches of our Führer. The judge had no right to question the decisions of the Führer, which were disguised as laws or decrees" (legal expert of the Reich, Hans Frank). There was "no legal means of appeal" against decisions of the "people's court" (Volksgerichtshof), which had been set up in 1934 to deal with cases of high treason and treachery *(cat. illustr. 232).* In this way the constitutional state was delivered into the hands of the "healthy feelings of the nation".

The control exerted over all areas of life and the establishment of a state and society based on the principle of the "Führer and his followers" also included economic affairs. Laws were passed to replace the independent bargaining process between the social partners and "determined" the working conditions in a new and authoritarian manner. The right to choose one's place of work was restricted. The dismantling of workers' rights showed just how far the NSDAP was removed from its "socialist" beginnings. The position of the employers was even strengthened. The principle of a private capitalist economy was unaffected by the Party. The National Socialist Job Creation Programme provided new jobs for many people *(cat. illustr. 233)*. On the other hand, the workers lost the right to have their views represented by an organised body, the coalition right. In its place a mock sense of harmony was created amongst workers. This succeeded in winning over a high proportion of the labour force to the Third Reich and thus in extending the social base of national socialist dominance and in creating the necessary conditions for gearing the economy towards the production of armaments.

The Job Creation Programme and the build up of armaments was financed by foreign exchange, loans and finally by printing money. The Reich fell into debt on a previously unknown scale. By employing intensive agricultural techniques and by acquiring industrial raw materials the dependence of the Reich on the world market was to be lessened. The economic policy of the national socialists served one major purpose after 1933: the pursuit of Hitler's plan, which was concealed from the public, to prepare for the "conquest of new Lebensraum in the East and for the germanification of these areas" *(cat. illustr. 236)*. Hitler set the Wehrmacht and the economy the following task in 1936 in his Four Year Plan:

"1. The German army must be ready for active duty in four years.

2. The German economy must be equipped for war in four years" *(cat. illustr. 235)*.

Göring promised in December 1936: "Victory or ruin. If we are victorious the economy will be amply rewarded. The cost must not be calculated. We are playing here for the highest stakes. What would be more profitable than orders for armaments?" Industrial circles were concerned simply about the speed of the arms build-up and not interested in the Programme. "We Krupp people only wanted a system which worked. Politics is not our game" said Alfred Krupp von Bohlen and Halbach in 1945.

VI/235 Armaments Industry.

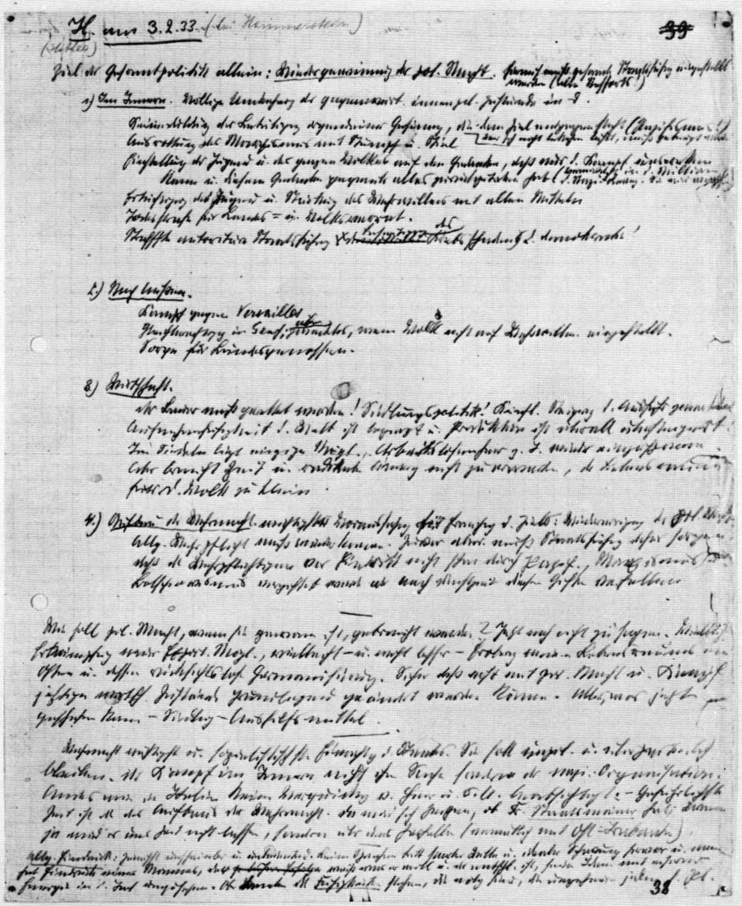

VI/236 Extract from notes by Lieutenant-General Liebmann, 3rd February 1933.

The aim of overall policy: regaining of political power. The entire state leadership must be engaged in this task (at all costs!).

1. In domestic policy. Complete reversal of the present domestic political situation in Germany. No putting up with any activity which stands in the way of this aim (pacifism!). Those who don't agree must be broken. Elimination of Marxism lock, stock and barrel. Winning over of the youth and the whole nation to the viewpoint that this fight alone can save us and all thoughts must be based on this idea (made reality by the millions who have joined the Nazi movement. It will continue to grow.). Training of the youth and strengthening of the military preparedness by all possible means. The death penalty for high treason and treachery. Strongest authoritarian state leadership. Abolition of the cancerous democracy!

2. Foreign policy. Fight against Versailles. Equality of rights in Geneva; this is useless though if the nation is not prepared to accept military action. Care for fellow citizens.

3. Economy! The farmer must be saved! Housing policy! Future increases in exports useless. Capacity of the world to absorb these is limited and production is too high everywhere. In housing policy, only one possibility; to reharness the workforce. But time and a radical change needed, as Lebensraum for the German nation is too small.

4. Rebuilding of the Wehrmacht. Most important precondition of achieving our aim. Regaining of political power. General conscription must be reintroduced. Beforehand, however, the state leadership must ensure that the conscripts do not become poisoned by pacifist, marxist or Bolshevik ideas and that this does not happen after their period of service.

How should political power be used, once it has been won? Can't yet say. Perhaps new export markets will be won – and even better – conquest of new Lebensraum in the East and their Germanification. Certain that present economic situation can only be changed after political power has been won. All that can happen in the meantime – housing – assistance.

Wehrmacht – most important and most socialist state institution. It should remain unpolitical and have no party allegiance. Internal struggle not Wehrmacht's concern – Nazi organisation's c.f. Italy, no amalgamation of the Army and the Wehrmacht intended – most danger period is during the Wehrmacht build-up. Then it will become apparent if France has real statesmen. If it has that will not leave us enough time, they will attack us (with the East probably following suit).

The Persecution and Elimination of the Jews

Tower 3 (Interior)

Antisemitism, the origins of which can be traced back to the nineteenth century, was also widespread in the Weimar Republic. For Hitler the racist ideology was the central point in his philosophy. It was included in the Party Programme of 1920 which laid down the aggressive policy of the NSDAP towards the Jews. "A fellow citizen can only be someone who is a fellow German. A fellow German can only be someone who is of German blood, regardless of his religion. Thus no Jew can be a fellow German". The NSDAP succeeded in transforming the feeling of being at the mercy of anonymous social forces – which had been experienced by the masses in the uncertain life of the world economic depression – into aggression against the "world conspiracy of Jews and Bolsheviks". Once Hitler had seized power reality was made of his ideas on the "national enemies". Acts of violence against Jews and their property on 1st April 1933 marked the beginning of the persecution of the Jews *(cat. illustr. 237).* The dismissal of Jewish judges and civil servants heralded the systematic elimination of Jews from all aspects of life. Increasing use was made of the legal basis for this action, the "Aryan paragraph": against doctors, dentists, chemists, lawyers, solicitors, artists and journalists. Universities and state run schools were now open to an increasingly smaller number of Jews. They were also barred from holding honorary positions, from tax benefits and many social benefits, from military service and from all clubs and associations. Jewish works were removed from galleries, libraries, concert halls, theatres and cinemas, streets named after Jews were renamed and Jewish names were erased from the rolls of honour on war memorials. It was also possible to forbid Jews to enter bars and to ban them from using public baths and park benches *(cat. illustr. 239).* The main driving force behind this campaign was the "law to protect German blood and German honour" of September 1935: "passed in the knowledge that the purity of German blood is necessary for the continuation of the German nation . . ., the Reichstag has unanimously accepted the following law, which is hereby announced:

§ 1 1. Marriages between Jews and citizens of German or some related blood are forbidden. Such marriages which take place despite the law are invalid, even if the ceremony has taken place abroad to avoid the law.

§ 5 1. Anyone who disregards § 1 is liable to a term of imprisonment."
In November 1938 the regime used the assassination attempt by a seventeen year old Jew on a German diplomat in Paris as an excuse for a massive persecution campaign throughout the Reich. On the "Reichskristallnacht" Jewish shops were destroyed by the police and SA forces, almost all synagogues burned down, Jewish property looted and wealthy Jews were arrested and sent to concentration camps. Three month later Hitler announced to the people, on the radio and in the press: "If the international Jewish financiers within Europe and beyond should succeed in leading the nations into another World War, the result will be not the conversion of the world to Bolshevism and the Jewish victory that would accompany this, but the extermination of the Jewish race in Europe!". The complete social outlawing of the Jews as a preliminary to Hitler's concealed aim became perfectly clear in 1941 with the "police decree concerning the marking of Jews" *(cat. illustr. 240).*
"§ 1 1. It is forbidden for Jews, who have reached the age of seven, to appear in public without the mark of a Jewish star.
2. The Jewish star consists of a hexagonal star the size of the palm of the hand, drawn in black on a yellow background with the inscription "Jew" in black. It must be worn on the left hand side of the chest in a clearly visible position."
The extermination of the "Jewish-Bolshevik ruling élite in the Reich" and of the Jews in Eastern Europe became, along with the need to acquire "Lebensraum" for the "German master race", an expressed war aim. The decision on this matter was taken at the "Wannsee Conference" in January 1942 on the "final solution of the European Jewish question". The minutes of the conference leave no doubt in one's mind as to the nature of the procedure: "Under appropriate leadership, in pursuit of the final solution, the Jews should be suitably employed in the East as forced labour. The Jews, who are capable of working, will be transported to these areas in large work-teams, with men and women to be kept separate, to be employed in road building operations. Doubtless, a large percentage will die and cause a natural reduction in numbers. The eventual survivors, since they will doubtless represent the most resistant section, will have to be treated accordingly because, representing a selection of the strongest, they would act as the germ-cell for the building up of a new Jewish race (look at historical experience). During the

VI/237 1st April 1933, Boycott of Jewish shops: "Germans beware! Don't buy from Jews".

VI/238 Burning of Books, 10th May 1933: "German students are marching against the un-German spirit".

VI/239 – 240 Public discrimination against Jews.

VI/241 Persecution of the Jews in Poland: Razzia in a ghetto.

course of the implementation of the final solution, the whole of Europe, from East to West, will be scoured". Thus, the title "final solution" was given to the systematic extermination of the Jewish population in Europe. The concentration camps, which were set up in Poland, such as Auschwitz, Belzek, Chelmno, Majdanek, Sobibor and Treblinka, became extermination camps in which Jews were murdered, frequently directly upon their arrival from transportation from the Reich and the occupied territories. These murders were partly carried out by means of poisonous gas in special gas chambers. If one adds to these victims the number of those who died in concentration camps in Germany and abroad as a result of forced labour and malnutrition or as a result of mass shootings by special firing squads (Einsatzgruppen) in the occupied territories, the total number of murdered Jews reaches between five and six million.

Power Politics and Resistance in the Reich

The National Socialist Foreign Policy

Tower 4 (Exterior)

From the outset, the aim of NS foreign policy went beyond the revision of the Treaty of Versailles demanded by all the other parties and entailed the acquisition of new "Lebensraum" and the establishment of a "Great German Reich of the German Nation". In the first years, however, this policy followed the same lines as the previously pursued revisionist policy. Initial successes encouraged Hitler to step up the tempo *(cat. illustr. 242).* Hitler finally embarked upon an imperialist expansionist policy when he occupied "the remnants of Czechoslovakia" in spring 1939.

The foreign office, which remained unaffected by the seizure of power by Hitler, seemed to be continuing with its revisionist policy that it had adopted during the Weimar Republic. The "Reich Concordat", agreed with the Vatican in July 1933, aimed to settle all previous differences between the Catholic Church and National Socialism. The nonaggression pact with Poland of January 1934 eased the tension existing in German-Polish relations. The increase in Hitler's international standing aroused hopes and also weakened internal opposition to him in Germany.

VI/242 Poster in April 1938: plebiscite about the Anschluß with Austria and elections to a great German Empire.

Step by step Adolf Hitler is tearing apart the dictated Treaty of Versailles!

1933 Germany leaves the League of Nations of Versailles.
1934 Reconstruction of the Wehrmacht, the navy and the Luftwaffe begun!
1935 Saarland brought back home! Armed power of the Reich regained!
1936 Rhineland completely liberated!
1937 The myth of war guilt ceremoniously extinguished!
1938 Germany and Austria united in the Reich! Greater Germany achieved!

Therefore the whole of Germany will acknowledge their liberator on 10th April.

Adolf Hitler. All say **YES!**

VI/243 Reoccupation of the demilitarised Rhineland, March 1936.

VI/244 Mussolini's state visit to Germany, September 1937.

VI/245 Banner in Vienna about the plebiscite on the Anschluß with Austria. "Common Blood belongs in a United Reich!"

VI/246 Before the conclusion of the Munich Agreement, September 1938: Göring, Chamberlain, Mussolini, Hitler.

VI/247 Hitler's entry into Karlsbad, October 1938.

VI/248 Non-violent protest by the population of Prague against the occupation by German troops in March 1939.

VI/249 Following the signing of the Hitler-Stalin, German-Soviet Non-Aggression Pact, Moscow, 23rd August 1939.

VI/250 Outbreak of war, 1st September 1939: inhabitants of Munich listening to the broadcast of Hitler's speech.

VI/251 Hitler with the head of the supreme command of the Wehrmacht, Colonel-General Keitel.

VI/252 Stalingrad, December 1942.

The reoccupation of the Saar in January 1935 was seen as a further success in NS foreign policy. This policy had still not contravened the Treaty of Versailles. By contrast, however, the reintroduction of conscription in March 1935 and the reconstruction of the Luftwaffe, which was no longer kept a secret, were open violations of the Treaty. However, the League of Nations, which Germany had left in 1933, and which was entrusted with the task of supervising international treaties, only managed a "condemnation" of the actions. The European powers could not succeed in forming a united front against this policy.
Instead of imposing sanctions the foreign powers effectively sanctioned such violations of the Treaty. The Anglo-German Naval Agreement of June 1935 averted the threat of German isolation and encouraged Hitler to violate the Treaty yet again by ordering his troops to march into the demilitarised Rhineland in March 1936 *(cat. illustr. 243).* A few months later the regime presented to the world, during the Olympic Games in Berlin, the picture of a peace-loving Germany, both at home and abroad. However, this was pure deception: in the Spanish civil war, which broke out in July 1936, the German "Condor Legion" supported the antirepublican Falangists of General Franco. The weapons, which had been developed as a result of the German policy on rearmament, were put to the test for the first time in Spain. Nevertheless, Hitler saw Mussolini rather than Franco as a potential ally of his own military plans and the two reached an agreement on the demarcation of their respective policies of expansionism in October 1936 *(cat. illustr. 244).* This Rome–Berlin axis was a prelude to the future war-time alliance.
The German-Italian agreement also paved the way for the realisation of a plan, which had failed in 1934, not least because of Mussolini's opposition to it; the Austrian national socialists' plan to unite their own country with the German Reich. In March 1938 German troops marched into Austria to be met by jubilant crowds and the country was annexed to the Reich as "Ostmark" *(cat. illustr. 245).* Thus the Greater German Reich was established by a policy of surprises and blackmail. The Gestapo accompanied the German troops in Austria and by December 1938 had taken over 20.000 people into "custody". After the "Anschluß" with Austria, which like the reoccupation of the demilitarised Rhineland, was a violation of the Treaty of Versailles, Hitler further incited the "Come Home to the Reich" movement. Nevertheless, England and France continued to follow

their policy of appeasement: in September 1938 they agreed to the ceding of the German Sudetenland in Czechoslovakia because they did not yet feel ready for a military conflict with the Reich *(cat. illustr. 246, 247).* Hitler was not yet satisfied, however: his next aim was the "wiping out of the remaining areas of Czechoslovakia". The alleged persecution of the German minority by the Czechs served as a pretext. The press were given orders to dramatise their reports of "horror, murder and mistreatment in order to demonstrate what a barbaric nation the Czechs are". Finally Hitler used the conflict between the Czechs and the Slovaks as an excuse for ordering his German troops to march into Prague in March 1939 *(cat. illustr. 248).* The Czech area of the country became the "protectorate of Böhmen and Mähren", Slovakia became an autonomous state under the "protection of the German Reich". As a reaction to this open aggression Great Britain and France issued a joint declaration guaranteeing protection for Poland.
The Anglo-German Naval Agreement was revoked by Hitler in April 1939. The "Steel pact" of May firmly committed Italy to Germany's aggressive policy. The German-Soviet Non-Aggression Pact of August 1939 *(cat. illustr. 249)* finally won over the "doves" in Germany to the idea of war; an additional secret clause dealt with the distribution of the spoils following the imminent German attack on Poland.

The Opposition

Tower 4 (Interior)

The seizure of power by Hitler in 1933 sparked off immediate opposition. In addition to the many thousands who saw emigration as the only solution, many people shunned the alignment policy at home and formed secret groups. In the first years of the regime it was above all the socialdemocratic and communist cells and churchmen who opposed the totalitarian system and the recognisable war aims of Hitler. Even during the period of foreign policy successes and before the outbreak of war opposition to Hitler was raising its head in middle class, conservative circles and in the form of individuals and certain groups in the state apparatus itself and amongst military officers. They became convinced that making a stand against Hitler's criminal policy in no way represented a betrayal of Germany. During the war these circles attempted to join forces with the labour move-

VI/253–254 After the assassination attempt of 20th July 1944: the Führer's headquarters.

VI/255 Trial at the People's Court.

ment. Hitler and the NSDAP were to be overthrown by a coup d'état even if this would still not prevent a German military defeat. However, diverging motives and different political aspirations along with uncoordinated action prevented the setting up of an effective front against Hitler. Moreover, the regime succeeded, with the help of a well-structured and efficient secret police system, in continually eliminating the opposition forces. Thus, the opposition was restricted to a "rebellion of conscience", which was witnessed with mistrust from abroad. The assassination attempt of 20th July 1944 represented an effort, by overthrowing Hitler, to create more favourable conditions for the end of the war and to prevent the further destruction of Germany *(cat. illustr. 253/254).* Even in the event of failure the conspirators expected to have an effect abroad: "the assassination attempt must take place . . . Even if it does not succeed negotiations must be held in Berlin because it is no longer a matter of being practical but that the German opposition movement, in the full view of the world and of history has dared to take a decisive step. Next to this everything else is immaterial" (General v. Tresckow).

The Second World War

Wall

Hitler had formulated his plan to expand German "Lebensraum" at all costs in his book "Mein Kampf" and had repeatedly reiterated it in his propaganda speeches. Just four days after his seizure of power he developed his political and military plans during secret discussions with the top officers of the Reichswehr *(cat. illustr. 236).* In November 1937 he saw "the way of force" as the only "solution to the German question", which can "never be without its risks" and he related his ideas on the appropriate time for an attack to the military leaders. On 1st September 1939 he announced the beginning of the war to the Reichstag and the nation *(cat. illustr. 250).* The attacks on Poland, Denmark, Norway, France and Yugoslavia represented Hitler's concept of lightning warfare (Blitzkrieg) *(cat. illustr. 251).* They led initially to quickly-won victories. The war took on new dimensions following the attack on the Soviet Union and the entry of the USA into the war after the Japanese attack on Pearl Harbour in 1941: it finally became a World War. National Socialist propaganda

attempted to meet the increasing difficulties, which Germany was facing from fighting a war on several fronts, with appeals to stick to the task and with promises for the "time after the victory". The "march on the East" signalled the beginning, not just of attempts to impose a military defeat on the Red Army but also of a systematic extermination of East European Jews.
In January 1943 the Allies demanded the unconditional surrender of Germany. Shortly after this the German defeat at Stalingrad marked the turning point of the war *(cat. illustr. 252).* The Western powers responded to Propaganda Minister Joseph Goebbel's call for "total war" in 1943 by stepping up their air attacks, including those against the civilian population. The war entered its final phase in June 1944 with the invasion by the Western Allies *(cat. illustr. 256, 257).* Simultaneously, the Soviet forces pushed the German troops in the East back as far as the German border. The end came in May 1945 with the total collapse and the unconditional surrender of Germany *(cat. illustr. 258, 259).*

VI/256 The day of the people's uprising (Volkssturm) – 12th November 1944.

VI/257 Final resistance: construction of anti-tank blockades in Berlin, 1945.

VI/258 Surrender of the German Wehrmacht in Berlin-Karlshorst, 8th May 1945.

VI/259 German city in 1945.

Germany 1945

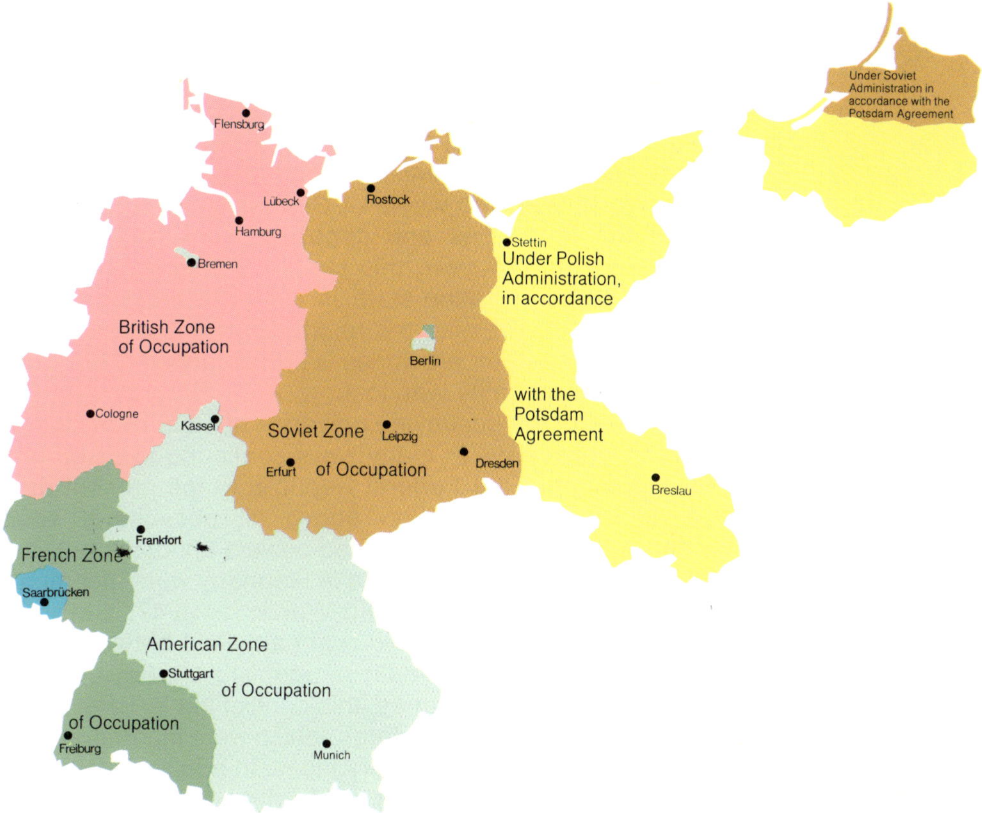

Room VII

Establishment and Development of the Federal Republic of Germany

The unconditional surrender of the German armed forces, which brought the war in Europe to an end on 8 May 1945, marked a greater political catastrophe for the German people than they had ever experienced in their history. In contrast to the First World War, the whole of Germany was occupied by forces of the four Allies and deprived of all governmental power. Above all, however, this second defeat signalled the end of the German nation-state in the form established by Bismarck in 1871. Prussia, the heartland of this empire, was dissolved, the eastern provinces were detached from Germany, and national unity was lost.

Under the rule of the occupying powers a number of decisions were taken which have in many ways continued to determine the development of the Federal Republic to the present day. These decisions were taken above all because it soon appeared that the ideas of the Allied powers about the political and social order to be established in Germany were incompatible. From the onset of the Cold War in 1946/47, Germany became the political and ideological battlefield between East and West, between the two main antagonists, the Soviet Union and the USA. In various stages, this conflict led in 1949 to the division of Germany into two states, which were incorporated in two opposing political and military blocs. In addition, however, this conflict determined which political forces would assert themselves and which political and social systems would be established on either side of the intra-German border.

In the Soviet sphere of influence, following a phase in which all the antifascist and democratic parties co-operated, a political system was established which came to be increasingly dominated by the communists alone; the economy was restructured along the lines of a socialist planned economy, which entailed the collectivization of land and the nationalization of banks and key industries. By contrast, the Western Allies encouraged the establishment in their zones of a liberal parliamentary democracy based on the rule of law and organized as a federal state. This process was completed on 23 May 1949, when the Basic Law for the Federal Republic of Germany was promulgated. Parallel to this, and following fierce controversies between the German parties, in which the occupying powers intervened on several occasions, the proponents of a market economy that would be largely free from state intervention and based on private ownership, but committed to the principle of social justice, asserted themselves in the face of the plans for nationalization, which had been actively advocated in the early postwar years.

This political decision greatly assisted the recovery of the West German economy, as did the USA's economic aid programme for Europe, the Marshall Plan, and the currency reform of June 1948. Boosted by the enormous reconstruction requirements of a country ravaged by war, and aided by a long period of global economic prosperity, this economic upturn continued unbroken until the 1960s. Its fruits soon benefited all sections of the population in the form of steadily increasing material wealth and prosperity. The "economic miracle" also made it possible rapidly to solve the immense social problems which National Socialism and the war had bequeathed to the new republic: pensions had to be provided for the war victims, restitution had to be made to the victims of National Socialism, the refugees had to be integrated, and the housing problem had to be solved. The booming economy also provided the financial basis for building an ever more comprehensive system of social security. Last but not least, continuing economic prosperity and the absence of serious social tensions in the postwar democracy produced the political stability which had been so grievously lacking in the Weimar Republic.

After a brief period in which the party landscape appeared to be rather fragmented, the large measure of public support which the political and social order of the Federal Republic enjoyed was also reflected in the fact that the electorate increasingly voted for the parties which supported this order. The CDU/CSU, led by Chancellor Konrad Adenauer, was the most popular party; it governed the country from 1949 onwards, initially together with the Free Democratic Party, the FDP. Konrad Adenauer's dominant position throughout that era, on which he left his stamp, was founded above all on this successful foreign policy. In the face of bitter opposition from the Social Democrats, who were more concerned to achieve national unity, Adenauer consistently pursued a policy of integrating the Federal Republic into the Western community of states and succeeded in gradually extending its freedom of action until it regained full sovereignty; finally, he ensured equal membership of the Western Alliance for the Federal Republic. The main elements of Adenauer's policy were the close alliance with the United States, reconciliation with France, and active participa-

tion in the incipient process of European integration. As a result of this policy, however, the division of Germany deepened; reunification became an ever more distant goal.
In the last years of the Adenauer era, a gradual change could be perceived in the specific postwar situation, to which the Federal Republic owed its foundation and which had decisively influenced its development.
On the international scene there was a thaw in the Cold War following increased efforts by the USA and the Soviet Union to improve their relations. As a result, the Federal Republic found itself increasingly on the defensive in the foreign policy field. In the economic sphere, the exceptional reconstruction boom was coming to an end in the mid-1960s. The first sharp economic downturn and the resultant crisis in the CDU/CSU/FDP government of Chancellor Erhard in the autumn of 1966 were considered so serious that the CDU/CSU and the SPD agreed to form a coalition for a limited period of time in order to overcome the difficulties. In particular, however, there was an increasing willingness to adapt the political and social order that had been built during the postwar years of reconstruction to the changed conditions. On the one hand, this desire was expressed, partly in radical form, by the protest movement of the late 1960s, which was supported above all by students. On the other hand, the majority of the electorate expressed a desire to chart a new course in the domestic and foreign policy field by voting for a change of government in 1969. For the first time after twenty years of CDU/CSU-led governments, a Social Democrat assumed the office of Federal Chancellor.
In the foreign policy field, the new Social-Liberal government sought above all to establish good-neighbourly relations with the Federal Republic's Eastern European neighbours too. The treaties concluded with the Soviet Union, Poland, Czechoslovakia and the German Democratic Republic provided for the renunciation of force, and the Federal Republic recognized the realities resulting from the Second World War. In addition, the Four-Power Agreement on Berlin and several agreements concluded with the GDR brought practical improvements for the people in both parts of Germany. However, the new Ostpolitik, which represented a radical departure from earlier positions, provoked sharp criticism from the CDU/CSU opposition and led to bitter domestic controversies. They culminated in the abortive attempt to oust Chancellor Brandt by means of a construc-

tive vote of no-confidence and only subsided after the clear victory of the Social-Liberal coalition at the polls in 1972.
By contrast, implementing the comprehensive domestic reform programme, which had brought the SPD/FDP government to power in 1969, turned out to be a much longer process. Despite considerable successes in the fields of legal policy, education policy, social policy and co-determination, the initial expectations proved to have been far too high in many respects. Apart from domestic opposition to these reforms, which came mainly from the CDU/CSU, it was above all the changed economic environment in the wake of the oil crisis of autumn 1973 which placed limits on the related endeavours. The change of leadership in the SPD/FDP coalition from Willy Brandt and Walter Scheel to Helmut Schmidt and Hans-Dietrich Genscher in May 1974 also marked the fundamental change in economic and political conditions that was affecting all advanced industrial countries at the time.
The threat of terrorism which the Federal Republic faced on various occasions, the dangers associated with increasing environmental pollution, renewed tensions between East and West, and above all the world economic crisis led to a period of general political reorientation. The reformist zeal of the early 1970s was replaced by an increasingly pessimistic outlook; crisis management became the focal point of political efforts. Against the background of persistent political and economic problems, the course to be followed and the question of how, and in what changed form, the essence of the political and social order of the Federal Republic can be preserved are the subject of the current political debate.

I 1945–49: The years of fundamental decisions

1. The Germany of the victors

Starting in September 1944, the entire German Reich was gradually occupied by Allied troops. On 8 May 1945 the military chiefs of Hitler's Germany had to sign the unconditional surrender. On 5 June 1945 the USA, Great Britain, France and the USSR announced that they were assuming supreme authority in defeated Germany. Hitler's attempt to establish hegemony on the European continent by means of brutal force had ended in total defeat. Germany was a mere pawn on the chessboard of the victorious powers.

At several conferences held during the war itself, the last of which took place in Yalta in the Crimea, the anti-Hitler alliance had agreed on the outlines of a European postwar order and on a series of measures for dealing with Germany. Large areas of the Reich to the east of the Rivers Oder and Neisse were to be detached from the country and placed under Polish or Soviet administration; the remaining area was to be divided up into four occupation zones and the capital of the old Reich, Berlin, was to be treated as a separate entity and governed jointly by the Four Powers. Responsibility for governing the whole of Germany was assigned to an Allied Control Council composed of the commanders-in-chief of the Four Powers.

For the rest, however, the unity of the Allies was limited to their resolve to prevent Germany from ever again causing another war and to eradicate completely the National Socialist regime. Even the agreements reached at the Potsdam Conference held between 17 July and 2 August 1945, including the pledge to treat Germany as a single economic unit and to rebuild a democratic system, were in many respects deliberately vague and reflected widely divergent aims and conflicting interests.

The Allied Control Council therefore soon proved incapable of reaching decisions on most questions and its responsibilities were increasingly transferred to the commanders-in-chief and the military governments in the individual occupation zones. The plan for a German central administration was vetoed by the French, who were determined to block any attempt at reuniting Germany. Economic unity fell victim to the disputes over reparations, which were demanded mainly by the Soviet

VII/260 Occupation of the Rhineland by American troops, March 1945

VII/261 Liberation of concentration camp inmates in Dachau, 29 April 1945

VII/262 Trek of refugees in Eastern Germany, 1945

VII/263 Plenary session of the Potsdam Conference, July/August 1945

Union. As for democratization, each occupying power increasingly sought to establish its own political system, since common solutions were proving ever more difficult to reach. In this way the four zones began to go their separate ways, which greatly facilitated the later division of Germany.

The period between liberation and occupation

The reaction of the German population to the advance of the Allied troops varied according to which of the four powers was occupying the area and according to the political opinions of those concerned. The hour of defeat and of the greatest humiliation that Germany had ever suffered in its history was also the hour of liberation and deliverance from a dictatorship which had been singularly inhuman. However, the dual concept of liberation and occupation also marked the dilemma that was to face Allied and German leaders in the years to come: while the victors were determined to impose their will, they also wanted to establish a democratic structure, and while the German side sought to represent German interests, it was also prepared to co-operate loyally with the occupying powers.

The policies of the occupying powers

The policies pursued by the victorious powers reflected their varying interests and aims: the requirement of security and their demand for reparations, the desire of the Allies to incorporate all or part of Germany into their own spheres of influence, and their widely divergent views on the establishment of a new democratic order in Germany. Against the background of their disputes over global issues, this led to tensions which made it possible to reach compromise solutions only for a short transitional period, which lasted until about the end of 1946. Even the occupation regime which had been agreed during the war – i.e. the division of Germany into four zones, the requirement of unanimity for decisions taken by the Allied Control Council, and the relationship between the Four-Power administration and the commanders-in-chief of the zones, which had never been properly clarified – failed to produce a common occupation policy.

Denazification

Punishment for the crimes committed under National Socialist rule and the removal of all active Nazis from their posts were among the foremost aims of the victorious powers. However, the Allies managed to adopt a common line only as regards the treatment of the major war criminals. On 1 October 1946 the International Military Tribunal in Nuremberg sentenced twelve of them to death, seven were given prison sentences, and three were acquitted. The actual denazification programme was approached differently in each zone. The Soviet Union considered it to be primarily part of the Communist restructuring process. By contrast, denazification in the Western zones, especially in the American zone, was treated as a question of individual guilt and as a re-education programme. In the course of the reconstruction process and with the onset of the Cold War, these policies, which had initially been pursued rigorously, became ever less severe and, as a result of German pressure, they were finally abandoned in 1948. Thus, the denazification process fell short of the high expectations that had been placed in it.

2. The establishment of democracy

1945 did not mark a completely new beginning. Even as regards the main task of setting up a democratic order after the Hitler dictatorship, personalities and political ideas played a role that were in many respects closely linked to the Weimar Republic or even older traditions. Moreover, the process of democratization was decisively influenced by the occupying powers.

The strongly federalist concept of the Americans provided for the gradual establishment of a democracy from below; in addition, all institutions were to be legitimized as soon as possible in democratic elections. By contrast, the British policy, although in many respects similar to that of the United States, placed greater emphasis on the model of a decentralized unitary state, and the British were reluctant to transfer decision-making powers to the Germans. The French were the most restrictive; in particular, they forbade almost all contacts

VII/264 The accused at the Nuremberg Trials, 1945/46

VII/265 Denazification committee in Berlin, 1946

VII/266 Meeting in Schumacher's office in Hanover, 1946

VII/267 Meeting of the CDU/CSU working group in Frankfurt/Main, April 1948

between German politicians across regional and zonal boundaries.

As in the Western zones, a democratic structure was set up in the Soviet zone too and, to begin with, it did not merely exist on paper. However, when the parties were incorporated in the "antifascist democratic bloc", when the SPD and the Communist Party (KPD) were forced to merge and form the Socialist Unity Party (SED) in April 1946, and when mass organizations dominated by the SED were formed, such as the FDGB and the FDJ, the foundations had been laid for the Communist seizure of power.

On the West German side, the newly established political parties soon played a key role. Alongside the Communist Party, the Social Democrats were the first successfully to reorganize themselves and to develop a coherent party programme. Under the leadership of Kurt Schumacher, they fought for a "parliamentary democracy" based on a socialist economy, which involved in particular the nationalization of basic industries and worker participation in the management of companies. Moreover, they emphasized the priority of national unity and followed a strictly anti-Communist line. By contrast, the CDU and the CSU, which had been newly founded by forces from the Catholic, liberal and conservative camps, were only later able to agree on a uniform programme and policy. Under Konrad Adenauer, the supporters of a policy of integrating the Federal Republic into the Western community of states and of a social market economy prevailed between 1948 and 1949. The two wings of Liberalism, which had been represented by different parties since 1866/67, joined forces to found the Free Democratic Party, the FDP. For a long time, however, there were heated discussions among its members about what should have priority: representing citizens' interests on the basis of economic liberalism, or defending and extending individual rights.

In the Western zones the process of democratization culminated in the drafting of a new constitution by the Parliamentary Council. In the light of the experiences of the Weimar Republic, its members rejected any kind of dictatorship and sought to return to the liberal democratic traditions of the 19th century. The Basic Law therefore contains a firm commitment to the rule of law, parliamentary democracy, federalism and the principle of social justice.

The new beginning

Even while the Allies were entering Germany, antifascist groups, building on the resistance to the Nazi regime, were being formed in many places. They wanted to help overcome acute shortages, take denazification into their own hands and in general ensure a new democratic beginning. However, the occupying powers prevented all political activity. As a first step, they installed mayors and chief administrative officers so as to rebuild the administration. It was only gradually and under close Allied supervision that German newspapers were allowed to appear and that new broadcasting stations were set up.

The founding of parties and trade unions

On 10 June 1945 – partly with the aim of influencing political developments throughout Germany – the USSR became the first occupying power to sanction political parties and trade unions. Moving more slowly, the Americans and the British followed suit in the late summer, and so did the French towards the end of the year. Following short-lived attempts to form coalitions on the left and right, the establishment of four parties was permitted in all zones, with few regional exceptions: the SPD and KPD were newly founded, the Liberals regrouped themselves under various names (FDP, LDP, DVP), and two new parties were formed by Catholic and Protestant Christian Democrats, the CDU and its Bavarian sister party, the CSU. At the same time, ideologically neutral trade unions, which were not attached to specific parties, were formed.

The re-establishment of the Laender

In all zones, the boundaries of the Laender, or federal states, were redrawn in 1945/46, not least because of the break-up of Prussia. The boundaries laid down by the occupying powers still apply today, with the exception of the southwest. The Laender played a particularly important role in American policy. The military government transferred almost all powers previously held by the Reich to the minister-presidents appointed in

VII/268 Meeting of the executive committee of the Liberal Party in Frankfurt/Main, 3 November 1947

VII/269 Representatives of the trade unions in the Bizone in Frankfurt/Main, January 1948

VII/270 Opening of the Constituent Assembly in Württemberg-Baden, July 1946

VII/271 Final vote of the Parliamentary Council on the Basic Law, 8 May 1949

1945 and to the Laenderrat, or Council of States, which they formed. Moreover, the Americans insisted upon the rapid realization of constitutional parliamentary democracy in the Laender. Even before the end of 1946 constitutions which had been drawn up by constituent assemblies and approved in referenda entered into force in Bavaria, Hesse and Württemberg-Baden. The fact that at Land level this happened a few years earlier than at federal level is one of the reasons why the Laender and their representatives play such a prominent role in the Federal Republic's system of government.

The Parliamentary Council and the Basic Law

On 1 July 1948 the three Western military governors handed over three documents to the minister-presidents of the Laender in Frankfurt: inter alia, they invited the minister-presidents to convene an assembly to draw up a constitution for the area covered by the three Western zones, which, after approval by the occupying powers, was to be ratified in a referendum. The military governors reserved the right to "resume their exercise of their full powers in an emergency threatening security, and if necessary to secure compliance with the constitutions or the occupation statute".

A week later the minister-presidents expressed their opinion on the "Frankfurt documents" in a resolution adopted at the "Rittersturz", a hotel near Koblenz. They wanted to postpone "the convening of a German national assembly and the preparation of a German constitution, until a solution for all of Germany is possible and until German sovereignty has been sufficiently restored". The military governors rejected this approach. After further negotiations near Rüdesheim the minister-presidents finally declared their readiness to pay the price demanded for an independent parliamentary democracy, provided, however, that the West German partial state would be founded only on a "Basic Law" which, according to the preamble, was to "give a new order to political life for a transitional period", until such time as the entire German people could freely vote on a constitution.

In August 1948 a committee of experts summoned to Herrenchiemsee by the minister-presidents drafted a constitution with various alternative proposals to serve as a basis for the deliberations of the Parliamentary Council. This document provoked an intense public debate, and the parties clashed over the constitutional rules governing public finances and the rights and responsibilities of the Laender. On 1 September the Parliamentary Council assembled in Bonn. Of its 65 members, 27 belonged to the CDU/CSU, 27 to the SPD, 5 to the FDP, and two each to the DP (German Party), the KPD and the Centre Party. Berlin was represented by 5 deputies who were not entitled to vote, however. A serious crisis which resulted from a dispute with the military governors over the distribution of competencies between the Federation and the Laender and jeopardized the success of the Parliamentary Council's work was finally settled by a compromise with the Western powers at the end of April 1949.

On 8 May 1949, the Parliamentary Council approved the "Basic Law for the Federal Republic of Germany" by 53 votes to 12, with the dissentient votes coming from the CSU, the DP, the KPD and the Centre. After the military governors had given their consent on 12 May and following ratification by the Land parliaments – only the Bavarian Parliament rejected the Basic Law because its CSU majority considered that the new constitution was too centralist – the members of the Parliamentary Council, the minister-presidents of the Laender, the presidents of the Land parliaments, the representatives of the military governments and of the Frankfurt Economic Council assembled in Bonn on 23 May 1949 in order to proclaim the Basic Law in a solemn ceremony.

Although the Basic Law was drawn up on the orders of the occupying powers, it represents an authentic German achievement. It reflects the determination to return to liberal democratic traditions and to take account of the experiences of the Weimar Republic. In the almost forty years that it has been in force, the Basic Law has proved to be a sound basis for the development of a stable democracy in the Federal Republic. Its basic principles are summed up in Article 20. In line with the **constitutional** principle, the rule of law, all state action must be based on the law; in line with the **democratic** principle, the use of state authority has to be legitimized by the people in elections; in line with the **social** principle, the state is committed to equal opportunities and social justice; in line with the **federalist** principle, power is shared between the Federation and the Laender, or federal states. Article 79 expressly states that these four central principles may not be amended. The same is true of the basic rights enumerated in Articles 1 to 20, which place the state under an obligation, in exercising its authority, to respect human dignity and human rights. This catalogue of rights reflects the liberal tradition of the Paulskirche and is more or less identical with the corresponding sections of the Reich constitution of 1849.

The Basic Law makes the freedoms and inviolable rights guaranteed in Articles 1–17 binding on the legislature, the executive and the judiciary as directly enforceable law. Although it is possible to restrict basic rights, this may only be done in accordance with certain constitutional principles or, in other words, by a law which expressly amends or supplements the provisions in question. The separation of powers, i.e. the separation of legislature, executive and judiciary, strengthens the principle of constitutionalism, makes it difficult to abuse state authority and prevents arbitrary government. A Federal Constitutional Court has been set up to ensure that all laws passed conform to the principles enshrined in the constitution. At the request of the Federal Government, a Land government, or one third of the Members of the Bundestag, cases where there are differences of opinion or doubts about the formal and material compatibility of federal law or Land law with the Basic Law are referred to it.

By means of a system of complex, interconnected rules and regulations, the Basic Law seeks to protect the constitutional state against attacks by individuals or groups. To this end, certain rights may be restricted which, as such, may well form part of the catalogue of basic rights. The exercise of a basic right may be restricted if this right is used to eliminate or call into question another basic right. Thus, for example, a political party which seeks to abolish the constitutional order laid down in the Basic Law can be banned.

The fact that the executive and the judiciary are under all circumstances bound by the law highlights the role played by the only institution which may pass laws – the legislature. Parliament is elected by the people by secret ballot in direct elections based on universal suffrage. Parliament embodies the principle of popular sovereignty.

Thus the German Bundestag is the most important political decision-making body. Although the people may also express their political will directly, this is normally done through democratic parties which, as the Basic Law expressly stipulates, participate in the forming of the political will of the people, and through their elected representatives. Being the constitution of a representative democracy, the Basic Law provides for referenda only in connection with a territorial reorganization of the Federal Republic.

According to Article 20, the Federal Republic is not only a democratic but also a social state. The Basic Law requires the state to further the aim of social justice and, to this end, allows it to restrict certain basic rights. This applies in particular to the right to own property, the use of which, as the Basic Law states, should also serve the common weal. In this connection, Article 15 of the Basic Law does not rule out the possibility of land, natural resources and the means of production being transferred to public ownership or other forms of social economy.

Finally, another major constitutional tenet is the federalist principle, according to which the federal territory is divided into autonomous Laender, or federal states. The Laender have their own constitutions; in line with the principle of constitutional homogeneity, they must, however, conform to the principles of republican democratic and social government based on the rule of law, as laid down in the Basic Law. The question of how to distribute competencies between the Federation and the Laender was the most difficult problem of constitutional law that had to be solved. Since it was recognized that the growing problems concerning societal policy and the infrastructure could only be solved by co-operation between the Federal Government, the Land governments and the local authorities, various compromises were worked out, which, although they do not encroach upon the autonomous rights of the Laender, emphasize the Federal Government's right to provide a legislative framework in certain fields. However, the federalist principle and the guarantee of autonomous local government restrict any moves to develop this "co-operative federalism" into a centralized system of government.

In seeking to place the rule of law on a secure basis through an appropriate distribution of competencies and a system of checks and balances, the founding fathers of the Federal Republic were guided by the experiences of the past, especially the final years of the Weimar Republic and the National Socialist period. They thus deliberately abandoned the plebiscitary elements of the Weimar Constitution and endeavoured to strengthen representative democracy. As a result, the head of state is no longer directly elected as in the Weimar Republic, where this procedure had led to the emergence of two rival power centres; instead, the Federal President is elected indirectly by a Federal Convention. At the same time, his powers have been substantially reduced: he can only stand for re-election once; he is not the supreme commander of the armed forces; he cannot declare a state of emergency on his own initiative; he cannot appoint or dismiss the Chancellor but can only propose a candidate; and he cannot dissolve Parliament at will. The general policy guidelines are determined by the Federal Chancellor, whose position is much stronger than that of his counterpart in the Weimar Republic. Being dependent on the support of the Bundestag, he cannot be ousted by a simple vote of no-confidence. Rather, in what is called a constructive vote of no-confidence, the Bundestag must at the same time elect a successor with the majority of its members. Thus, blocking majorities or, in other words, negative majorities which are united merely in their rejection of the government, can no longer perform the political function which, in the Weimar Republic, helped to make possible the transition from a parliamentary to an authoritarian system of government headed by the Reich President. Whereas the Weimar parliamentary system was paralysed by a multitude of feuding and often anti-parliamentary parties, the requirement that the parties represented in the Bundestag adhere to democratic principles, and the stabilizing effect of the five-per-cent clause (a party must poll at least five per cent of the popular vote to be represented in Parliament) have created favourable conditions for the further development of the Federal Republic as a state based on the rule of law and social justice.

3. Economic reconstruction

Considering the picture of devastation which Germany presented in 1945, there seemed to be little cause for optimism as far as either the future development of the economy or the standard of living of the population was concerned. Industrial production had sunk to less than one third of prewar levels. At the same time, the population had been swelled by almost ten million expellees and refugees, most of whom had ended up in the American and British zones. There were extremely severe housing problems, but the food shortage was even worse. In spite of Allied supplies, daily rations had to be reduced on several occasions – in the particularly hard winter of 1946/47 in some cases to about 1000 calories.

The economic policy of the occupying powers was initially dominated by the aim of eliminating Germany's war potential and obtaining compensation for their own wartime losses. The spectre of the Morgenthau Plan, which provided for the transformation of Germany into a purely agricultural country, hung over the economy. In addition to banning entire branches of industry, the industrial plan adopted by the Allied Control Council in March 1946 aimed to restrict German industrial production to between 70 and 75% of the 1936 level. It was never carried out, however, since in May 1946 arguments over the question of reparations put an end to the idea of treating Germany as a single economic unit.

The United States and Britain, concerned about the serious food situation and increasing tension with the USSR, resolved to give priority to the economic recovery of their zones. On 1 January 1947 the two areas were economically united. In the gradually developing institutions of the so-called Bizone, especially in the Economic Council which was elected by the Land parliaments, the Germans were increasingly able to assume control of economic policy.

In June 1947 a programme of economic aid for the whole of Europe was announced by American Secretary of State George C. Marshall. US assistance – starting in autumn 1948, the Western zones received, in addition to other aid, deliveries worth 1.56 billion dollars – did not merely contribute towards the recovery of the economy. The Marshall Plan also speeded up the division of Europe and Germany because, as was to be expected, the Eastern bloc refused any US aid. Moreover, it led to an early decision on the future economic system, since – as the American military government too made clear – socialization programmes were hardly compatible with the integration of the Western zones into the Western economic system. Thus, the basic decisions that were to determine the Federal Republic's development in the years ahead had been taken in the economic field too.

VII/272 Destroyed railway installations in Karlsruhe, 1945

VII/273 Dismantling of equipment at the Ruhrchemie company in Oberhausen, 1949

VII/274 Hunger demonstration by Munich students, summer 1947

Reconstruction against the background of shortages and the dismantling of industrial equipment

There were several barriers to be overcome before reconstruction could commence in postwar Germany. War damage was considerable, although it had initially been overestimated with regard to the industrial sector, and the problem was compounded by the dismantling of industrial equipment by the Allies. Moreover, the lack of raw materials and transport problems soon proved to be just as serious and restrictive as the grave food shortage. In addition, the economy was adversely affected by the collapse of the Reichsmark currency and the lack of all kinds of goods. Rationing and the black market determined people's lives. Nevertheless, the years preceding the currency reform were not simply a time of economic stagnation. As early as 1946 the urgent need for reconstruction triggered an economic upswing which, however, was halted by the particularly severe winter of 1946/47 and did not regain momentum until the late summer of 1947.

From discussions on socialization to the social market economy

Not only Communists and Social Democrats considered that reconstruction along socialist lines was the only possible solution. Even members of the CDU favoured socialization programmes for coal mining and other key industries, a redistribution of agricultural land, a far-reaching extension of employee participation, and state intervention in the economy, as the Ahlen party programme of February 1947 shows. In Hesse, a large majority voted for the socialization clause in the state constitution, and in the North Rhine-Westphalian Parliament a large majority voted in favour of nationalizing the coal mining industry. The mood only changed after the announcement of the Marshall Plan and the currency reform. In the Frankfurt Economic Council a coalition made up of the CDU/CSU, the FDP and the German Party supported the policy of a social market economy put into effect by Ludwig Erhard.

The dawn of the "economic miracle"

The chances of economic recovery in West Germany improved greatly with the economic fusion of the British and US occupation zones and the announcement of the Marshall Plan. Even so, the Western powers carried out the long-planned currency reform only after it had been decided to set up a West German state. On 20 June 1948 the practically worthless Reichsmark was devalued at a ratio of 1:10; every West German received an initial sum of 40 Deutsche Mark, to which another 20 Deutsche Mark were added later. Moreover, in the Economic Council Erhard gained acceptance for a series of deregulation measures, which gave a major boost to the industrial upswing which had already been set in motion. By the end of 1949, prewar production levels had almost been reached. However, it was only later that large sections of the population benefited from these developments. Although the shop windows filled up again "overnight", prices rose steeply in the first few months – against the background of a continuing wage freeze – and unemployment figures soared.

4. From the Reich to the Federal Republic

In 1945 the German Reich ceased de facto to exist. From the outset, the victorious powers were unable to agree on a common occupation policy and in this way to preserve the economic and political unity of Germany. The division of Germany was provisionally sealed by the Cold War, the origins and causes of which extended far beyond Germany and its specific problems.
The Soviet Union considered the Western protests against its conduct in Eastern Europe and the American refusal to meet its demand for reparations amounting to 10 billion dollars to be evidence that the capitalist countries were pursuing a policy of encirclement and it subsequently sought quite openly to secure its own sphere of influence. In response to these policies, which were perceived as expansionist, the United States abandoned its earlier policy of spheres of interest and of partial cooperation. On 12 March 1947, the American President announced the Truman Doctrine, which marked the beginning

VII/275 Ruhr coal miners demonstrating in favour of nationalization, 1947

VII/276 Reconstruction with Marshall Plan aid in the Western zones

VII/277 Distribution of new DM banknotes, 20 June 1948

VII/278 Filled shop windows after the currency reform

of a policy aimed at containing Communism. This new course was most clearly reflected in the Marshall Plan for the economic reconstruction of Western Europe, which also aimed to end France's special role in respect of policy on Germany. After the failure of the London Conference of the Foreign Ministers of the Four Powers in December 1947, which confirmed that the gulf between the former Allies had become unbridgeable, the steps necessary to establish a West German state were rapidly taken. The Soviet Union responded by taking corresponding measures in its zone and by attempting to exert pressure on the West. Following a six-power conference (the United States, Britain, France and the Benelux countries) held in London at the beginning of June 1948, at which the foundations of the future West German state were laid, the Federal Republic of Germany was, following the currency reform and the adoption of a constitution by the Parliamentary Council, officially proclaimed on 23 May 1949. Even though they found it difficult to accept the temporary division of Germany, most West German politicians and parties agreed with the measures taken by the Allies. In their view, this was the only way of mastering the dire economic problems facing the Western zones and of ensuring that, at least in one part of Germany, it would again be possible to assume responsibility for political affairs. Moreover, they still hoped that in this roundabout way it would be possible to restore German unity in the foreseeable future.

The Cold War

The global confrontation of two ideologically opposed power blocs, the first signs of which had already become apparent towards the end of the war, increasingly affected Europe in 1946. An "Iron Curtain", as Churchill put it, fell at the border of the territories dominated by the Soviet Union. Germany now increasingly became a focal point of the Cold War. Against the background of the East-West divide, the differences between the Allies over how to treat Germany became insurmountable. After the failure of the Moscow Conference of the Foreign Ministers in April 1947, the United States took the initiative: with the support of Britain and later also France, the Western zones were gradually integrated into the Western system. All attempts by the German side – for example at the Munich Conference of Minister-Presidents, the only meeting of all the heads of government of the German Laender – to prevent the division of Germany failed because of the strict conditions imposed by the occupying powers and because, on the German side too, the differences between the representatives of the Soviet occupation zone and those of the Western zones had become too great.

The division of Berlin

The East-West confrontation reached its climax in the controversies over Berlin, which was divided into four sectors. The Soviets reacted to the currency reform in the Western zones by closing all the approaches to Berlin by rail, land and water on 24 June 1948. The Western powers responded to this move – not least at the insistence of General Clay – by the Airlift. For eleven months – until the blockade was lifted on 12 May 1949 – the city, with a population of two million, was supplied exclusively from the air. It was also during this time that the political split was sealed. The Soviet representatives had already left the Allied Kommandantura on 16 June 1948. Following disruptions of their meetings by Communist demonstrators, the majority of the Magistrat and City Council moved to the Western sectors in September. At the end of 1948 separate municipal administrations were in place in the Western and Eastern sectors of the city; the spheres of power had thus been clearly delimited. Still, the attempt to integrate West Berlin into the Soviet zone had failed.

The establishment of two German states

Under the leadership of the United States, the Western powers were the first to draw the consequences from these postwar developments. When they handed over the Frankfurt Documents on 1 July 1948, they invited the minister-presidents of their zones to call a constituent assembly to draw up a constitution for a West German state. Against the background of the Berlin blockade and in the light of the arguments advanced by the Lord Mayor of Berlin, Ernst Reuter, the minister-presidents

VII/279 The “Airlift” during the Berlin blockade, 1948/49

VII/280 Demonstrators storming the new city hall in Berlin, 6 September 1948

VII/281 The military governors after handing over the Frankfurt Documents, 1 July 1948

VII/282 Signing of the Basic Law in the Parliamentary Council, 23 May 1949

reluctantly agreed, provided, however, that the arrangements made would only be "provisional". On 23 May 1949, the Basic Law was promulgated and the Federal Republic of Germany officially established. The Soviet Union followed suit on 7 October 1949 by founding the German Democratic Republic. For the time being, the division of Germany was complete.

II 1949–63: The Adenauer era

The establishment of parliamentary democracy

The elections to the first German Bundestag

After a fiercely fought election campaign, in which the question of the Federal Republic's future economic course was the central issue, the elections to the first German Bundestag took place on 14 August 1949. With 31.0% of the vote, the CDU and CSU emerged as the strongest parliamentary group, closely followed by the Social Democrats with 29.2%. Polling 11.9% of the vote, the FDP established itself as a third force; moreover, 8 other parties succeeded in winning seats in Parliament. Thus, a clear majority of the voters endorsed the parties which supported Erhard's social market policy. It was not yet clear, however, whether these parties would be able to form a coalition government.

The formation of the Adenauer Government

The CDU/CSU in particular was initially divided about whether the momentous decisions which now had to be taken required a broad parliamentary majority and thus a Grand Coalition between the CDU/CSU and the SPD, or whether, primarily for reasons of economic policy, a coalition of the centre parties should be formed with the FDP and the DP, the German Party. With great tactical skill, Konrad Adenauer succeeded in gaining acceptance in his own party and among his coalition partners for the second solution. On 12 September 1949, the Chairman of the FDP, Theodor Heuss, was elected Federal President, and three days later Adenauer himself – with a majority of only one vote – was elected Federal Chancellor. In his cabinet, the CDU held five ministerial posts, the CSU and the FDP three each, and the DP two.

VII/283 The first Federal Government after being sworn in, 20 September 1949

VII/284 First visit by Chancellor Adenauer to the High Commissioners, 21 September 1949

VII/285 Signing of the Treaty establishing the European Defence Community on 27 May 1952 in Paris

VII/286 Signing of the Bonn Conventions on 26 May 1952 in Bonn

1. Rearmament and integration into the Western community of states

The newly founded Federal Republic was initially not a sovereign state. The three High Commissioners resided on the Petersberg near Bonn as representatives of the occupying powers. Adenauer, who from the outset assumed control of foreign policy himself, was therefore concerned gradually to extend the Federal Republic's freedom of action.

In these endeavours, he was guided by the aim of integrating the Federal Republic into the Western community of states. The main elements of his policy were a close alliance with the USA, reconciliation with France, and the establishment of increasingly close economic and political ties with the Federal Republic's Western European neighbours. In his view, this could best be achieved by offering to rearm West Germany, in which the Western powers had a strong interest in view of the escalating East-West conflict. Under the leadership of Kurt Schumacher and later of Erich Ollenhauer, this course was rejected above all by the Social Democrats, even though most of them were not opposed in principle to either co-operation with the Western powers or rearmament; they criticized the often high-handed conduct of Konrad Adenauer and attached greater importance to the aim of a reunited Germany.

However, the Adenauer Government which, in the elections to the second German Bundestag in the autumn of 1953, had been returned with a large majority, was able to implement its policies. After the project of a European Defence Community had failed, the Federal Republic became a member of NATO in 1955, the occupation regime was ended, and the Federal Armed Forces were established. In 1957 the Saar, which the French had separated from the rest of their zone, was returned, and the European Economic Community was established. In 1963, Adenauer and de Gaulle put the seal on Franco-German reconciliation by signing a treaty of friendship, the so-called Elysée Treaty. From 1960 onwards, the integration of the Federal Republic in the Western community of states was fully accepted by the SPD, also in the military field.

However, Adenauer's hopes of being able, on the basis of the strength of the Western Alliance, to induce the Soviet Union to agree to reunification remained unfulfilled. Indeed, the division of Germany was deepened by the Cold War and the policy of

Western integration. It was cemented, in the literal sense of the word, by the erection of the Berlin Wall on 13 August 1961.

The initial situation

Adenauer's efforts gradually to bring the occupation regime to an end by making various concessions and offers were, among other things, rewarded by the Petersberg Agreements concluded on 22 November 1949: in return for Adenauer's pledge to co-operate with them on the International Authority for the Ruhr, the Western Allies agreed to curtail the dismantling of industrial plant and equipment. The Chancellor hoped to win full equality of status for Germany through Western European integration, which was supported and indeed enthusiastically acclaimed by large sections of the population in most Western European countries. This process of gaining full equality for the Federal Republic was accelerated when, following the outbreak of the Korean War in June 1950, increasing efforts were made to induce the Germans to make a contribution to Western defence.

The European Defence Community

The first step towards European co-operation was taken when France, Italy, the Benelux countries and the Federal Republic of Germany established the European Coal and Steel Community in April 1951. German rearmament, too, was to be carried out within a European framework by these six countries pooling their armed forces. In return, the three Western powers granted sovereignty to the Federal Republic in the Bonn Conventions signed in Bonn on 26 May 1952, one day before the Treaty establishing the European Defence Community was signed. Moreover, the three Western powers pledged to continue to make political efforts to bring about the reunification of Germany. Earlier on, the Soviet Union had tried to prevent the signing of these treaties by offering reunification if Germany remained neutral and if its eastern provinces were ceded.

VII/287 17 June 1953 in East Berlin

VII/288 Chancellor Adenauer's first visit to the Federal Armed Forces on 20 January 1956 in Anderna

VII/289 Herbert Wehner delivering a speech in the Bundestag, 30 June 1960

The domestic debate about the Federal Republic's political orientation

In 1949 and in the subsequent years a passionate debate about the orientation of the Federal Republic in the foreign policy field was conducted. In view of the short time which had elapsed since the war, the offer of West German rearmament provoked vehement protests. In fact, the argument centred on the question of whether the security of the Federal Republic could be guaranteed and reunification eventually achieved only by integrating the Federal Republic into the West, or whether absolute priority should be given to the aim of reunification and any steps which deepened the division should be avoided. These debates reached a climax in the discussion on whether Stalin's proposals, as set forth in the Soviet Notes to the three Western Powers of March and April 1952, were meant seriously.

Accession to NATO and sovereignty

After the death of Stalin in March 1953 the international situation eased. However, all hopes of a Soviet change of course with regard to Germany were shattered when the uprising in East Berlin and in the GDR on 17 June 1953 was quelled with the help of Soviet tanks. On 30 August 1954 the Treaty establishing the European Defence Community was rejected by the French National Assembly. Within a few weeks, new treaties were negotiated and signed in Paris on 23 October 1954. The Federal Republic of Germany was accepted as a member of NATO, the Western defence alliance. As a result, the 1952 Bonn Conventions could enter into force in a revised form. On 5 May 1955, the Federal Republic of Germany became a sovereign country. The Allies retained special rights only as far as matters concerning Germany as a whole and Berlin were concerned.

Domestic consequences

After the Federal Republic's accession to NATO, the West German armed forces were built up rapidly. As early as

November 1955 the first volunteers arrived at their barracks. The legislation governing the armed forces, under which compulsory military service was introduced in 1956, was supported to some extent even by the Social Democratic opposition, especially after it had ensured stronger political control and changes in the command structure. However, the controversy resurfaced in 1957 when plans for arming the Federal Armed Forces with atomic weapons became known. The influential associations of expellees in particular found it difficult to accept the fact that the idea of regaining the territories east of the Rivers Oder and Neisse was increasingly becoming an illusion. But it was not until the 1960s that any of the large parties dared to broach this subject.

The process of European integration

The incorporation of the Saarland in the Federal Republic on 1 January 1957, after the population of the region had, in a referendum, rejected the original agreement to "Europeanize" the Saarland, solved a problem which had placed a strain on Franco-German relations. When the European Economic Community was founded in March 1957, the ambitious but unrealistic plans for political union were abandoned in favour of more practical, concrete progress, particularly in the field of trade relations. The main pillar of Germany's policy towards the West – in addition to its close alliance with the USA – was intensive co-operation with France, especially after General de Gaulle assumed office in 1958.

Relations with the Eastern bloc

The Soviet Union responded to the entry into force of the Paris Treaties in May 1955 by setting up the Warsaw Pact, of which the GDR became a member. Soviet policy was now based on the premise that there existed two German states. This was also expressed in the invitation extended to Konrad Adenauer to visit Moscow. In return for the promise to release the remaining German prisoners of war, Adenauer agreed to establish diplomatic relations with the Soviet Union. Thus, for the first time there were two German ambassadors in one

VII/290 Reintegration of the Saarland, 1 January 1957

VII/291 Adenauer and de Gaulle on 22 January 1963 after signing the Franco-German Friendship Treaty

VII/292 Chancellor Adenauer being officially welcomed at Moscow Airport, 8 September 1955

VII/293 Building of the Berlin Wall, 13 August 1961

capital. In order to prevent worldwide recognition of the GDR, the Federal Republic proclaimed the Hallstein Doctrine, according to which the Federal Republic would not maintain diplomatic relations with any country that recognized the GDR. In view of its responsibility for the whole of Germany, the Soviet Union was to be the only exception. In the following years it was not only reunification, however, which became an ever more distant goal. The Federal Republic was increasingly forced on to the defensive also with regard to its policy towards the Eastern European countries, since the West was becoming increasingly interested in defusing the East-West conflict.

2. The "economic miracle"

The cornerstone of political and social stability in the Adenauer era was the sustained economic upswing, which lasted more than fifteen years. Thanks to annual growth rates of around 10% in real terms, the Federal Republic, which only shortly before had been a country ravaged by war, rapidly became the third strongest industrial country in the world. Even in the early 1950s, the catch phrase "economic miracle" was being used abroad to describe this development.

The sustained postwar boom was not only based on people's willingness to roll up their sleeves, but also on the immense need for reconstruction and on pent-up demand as well as on the large reservoir of skilled labour, which increased steadily throughout the 1950s as a result of the influx of expellees and refugees. The parallel world economic upturn was another fact of great significance because, as the Federal Republic became increasingly integrated into the West, it also became more involved in international trade. The willingness of management and labour to co-operate and, not least, the government's economic policy played a major role as well.

Under the leadership of Economics Minister Ludwig Erhard, that policy was based on the concept of a social market economy founded on private property which allowed competition and market forces to develop freely. The state was restricted to creating the environment in which the market could function, preventing distortions of competition resulting

from excessive concentration of economic power and, above all, balancing out any social inequalities.
The 1950s were not just a period of rapid economic growth and reconstruction, however. They also marked the beginning of fundamental structural change, the full extent and far-reaching social consequences of which only became apparent in the following decade. In trade and industry small and medium-sized firms faced increasing competition from large companies. In addition, new industrial centres grew up alongside the traditional industrial areas. Improvements in the transport network changed the landscape and not least the character of towns. All these developments gradually led to a thorough modernization of all spheres of life, which in retrospect makes the 1950s appear to be rather an idyllic period.

The economic development and its causes

After problematical early years when, despite high growth rates, major unemployment and balance-of-payment problems had to be overcome, the West German economy began to show a steady upward trend in mid-1951, which was helped by the economic boom triggered by the Korean War. Between 1950 and 1960 gross national product tripled. In 1961 unemployment was less than 1%, and inflation was less than 3% throughout the entire period. These achievements were rounded off by the growing successes of German industry in the field of exports, which substantially increased the gold and currency reserves held by the Bundesbank and thus made it possible to lift the remaining currency restrictions in 1958.

Economic policy

The social market economy faced its first major test in the early years of the Federal Republic. Erhard's conservative financial policy and export-oriented economic policy were designed above all to encourage investment while, at least initially, holding down domestic consumption. Erhard was thus prepared to accept temporary social imbalances. This difficult phase was mastered only because of the restraint shown by the trade unions. In later years the main problem tended to be

VII/294 Assembly-line production of Volkswagen cars, 1949

VII/295 2nd European Machine Tool Exhibition in Hanover, September 1952

VII/296 Refugee camp in Schleswig-Holstein, 1945

VII/297 Completion of the millionth publicly financed flat, December 1955

preventing the economy from overheating. Moreover, strict government controls were maintained in a number of vital sectors: primary commodities, food, public transport and housing.

The dawn of the affluent society

From 1952/53 onwards, broad sections of the population benefited from the economic boom in the form of significant increases in real incomes. The gradual improvement in the standard of living was reflected in "spending sprees" which were determined by the priorities of the population at a given time: the "food", "clothing" and "housing waves" were followed, in the late 1950s, by the travel and holiday boom.
At the same time the car was gradually becoming the most important status symbol. Increasingly widespread prosperity had a profound effect on the basic attitude of the vast majority of the population: a preoccupation with material improvements, with family and home life, and a pride in what had been achieved meant that, in these early years, little interest was shown in politics or social change.

3. The social state

Under the constitution, the Federal Republic is a social state and this principle is to guide all state action. As a result of the war and National Socialist policies, the newly established Federal Republic faced immense social problems. Not least as a result of the extraordinary boom of the 1950s, the conditions were created for rapidly solving these problems, mostly with the support of a broad parliamentary majority.
The immediate material needs of the population had largely been met by 1949. The main task then consisted in providing for the war victims, overcoming the housing shortage and ensuring the integration of refugees and expellees. To this end, a multitude of laws provided for substantial benefits that were financed from public funds and imposed a heavy burden in the form of taxes and social security contributions on the gainfully employed too. In addition to publicly assisted housing pro-

grammes, equalization-of-burden schemes played a major role, which consisted in a partial redistribution of the remaining wealth in favour of the refugees in particular, but also of those who had suffered special hardship as a result of the war and the currency reform.
From the mid-1950s onwards, sustained economic growth made it possible not only to tackle the problems inherited from the past but also to embark on a programme of social reforms. These reforms were introduced partly through collective agreements concluded with the trade unions, which provided, for example, for the introduction of the five-day week and the gradual transition to a forty-hour week. However, they were also the result of legislation, such as the major pension reform of 1957.
The revised pension laws, which were passed with the votes of the CDU/CSU, the SPD and the BHE, adapted the insurance system, which had remained basically unchanged since the Bismarck era, to the changed economic and social environment. The most important change was the new principle of index-linked pensions, which ensured that pensions would increase annually in line with general increases in income. As a result, the recipients of old-age pensions, who had until then benefited very little from the "economic miracle", not only received considerably higher pensions but were also guaranteed a fair share in any future increases in the general standard of living.

Overcoming the consequences of the war

The greatest social problem consisted in integrating the approximately 10 million expellees and refugees, a task which was made all the more difficult by the fact that they were distributed very unevenly among the Laender. However, after problematical early years, when they often spent long periods in camps and had no jobs, most expellees eventually succeeded, with the help of government programmes, in establishing themselves in the Federal Republic. That these efforts were successful is also borne out by the fact that the expellees' party, the BHE, failed to clear the 5-per-cent hurdle in the 1957 elections to the Bundestag and was thus no longer represented in Parliament. Restitution for the crimes committed by the

1/298 German Trades Union Congress poster in favour of the five-day week, 1958

VII/299 Chancellor Adenauer during the 1957 election campaign

VII/300 Federal Party Conference of the SPD in Bad Godesberg, November 1959

National Socialists, particularly in respect of the Jewish population, constituted a particularly serious problem. The Federal Republic did not only compensate individuals but also made payments amounting to DM 3.45 billion to the State of Israel.

Social reforms

In addition to shorter hours and the extension of the social security system, the third major reform consisted in the introduction of employee participation, for which the trade unions had fought particularly hard.
In the 1951 Co-determination Law, which provided for equal representation of labour and management on supervisory boards in the coal, iron and steel industries, the trade unions were largely able to assert themselves. They were helped by the fact that, once co-determination had been granted, the coal, iron and steel industries were able to prevent Allied conditions for decartelization of the companies concerned from being enforced. By contrast, the 1952 Law on Labour Relations at the Workplace, which gave employees in the other companies only one third of the seats on supervisory boards, fell short of trade union expectations.

4. The "Chancellor democracy"

Domestic developments in the Federal Republic during the Adenauer era appeared to be a model of stability, particularly compared to the Weimar Republic, which had been much criticized even at the time. Assisted by the rapid economic recovery and the continuing economic boom, the party system became a stabilizing factor. The CDU/CSU and, following its successful example, later also the SPD, developed into broad-based people's parties in whose policies ideology increasingly gave way to pragmatism and whose supporters transcended the traditional political boundaries. Only the FDP, which considered itself to be both a liberal corrective element of the CDU/CSU and an independent third force, has proved able to withstand the magnetic effect of the two major political camps. The personality of the first Federal Chancellor was another

major stabilizing factor. He succeeded in performing the functions of the head of government, who plays a particularly important role under the constitution, in such a way that the term "Chancellor democracy" was coined. This was primarily due to his acitivities in the foreign policy field and to his ability to hold together a coalition made up of extremely heterogeneous forces and use it to his advantage. In addition, Adenauer provided a vital link for many members of the middle-aged and older generations between the authoritarian past and the pluralistic, democratic present.
However, after the dynamic early years the political system, which was completely dominated by the successful Chancellor, began to appear increasingly rigid. The CDU's election slogan in 1957 – "No experiments" – showed that the party was concerned above all to preserve the status quo. The authoritarian ways and the dominating personality of the Chancellor, who was over 80 years old, were increasingly felt to be a paralysing element. Moreover, many other features of the domestic policy pursued in those years – the fierce anti-Communism and the tendency to refer to the past as little as possible – appeared to many critics to be an obstacle to further constructive developments.

The conflict with political extremism

In the early years of the Federal Republic the dangers of political extremism had not yet been contained. When the Federal Constitutional Court banned the KPD in 1956, this merely confirmed the Communist Party's decline, which had already been apparent for a long time. However, on the right the dissolution of the Socialist Reich Party in 1952 halted a dangerous movement which was gaining increasing support, especially in Northern Germany, and was seriously damaging the Federal Republic's reputation abroad. Overcoming the underlying problem of the National Socialist past proved a more difficult task. Throughout the Adenauer era controversies arose about the fact that people who had been involved in National Socialism were appointed to high political office in the young democracy.

Stability and change of the party system

Over and above the problem of extremism, the parties that had been licensed in 1945/46 came under increasing pressure from newly formed refugee and regional movements when Allied control ended. However, the five-per-cent clause effectively halted a tendency towards party fragmentation and indeed helped to set in motion a massive trend towards a three-party system. The governing CDU/CSU in particular showed itself to be capable of integrating a broad political spectrum. The SPD, too, became a people's party in 1959 following the adoption of the Godesberg Programme. The FDP, which had formed a coalition with the CDU/CSU since 1949, managed to survive the government crisis triggered by Adenauer's plans for electoral reform and the split in the party in 1956 – all four FDP ministers and a further 12 Members of the Bundestag left the party when a Social-Liberal government was formed in North Rhine-Westphalia – and asserted itself as an independent political force when in opposition.

The end of the Adenauer era

After the Bundestag elections of 1957, in which, with 50.2% of the vote, the CDU/CSU obtained an absolute majority, the Federal Chancellor's prestige was gradually undermined in a series of crises at home and abroad – Khrushchev's Berlin ultimatum of 1958, Adenauer's candidature for the office of Federal President in 1959, and the building of the Berlin Wall. In particular the "Spiegel Affair" in October 1962 made many critics feel that the action taken against the Hamburg magazine "Der Spiegel" and its editor, Rudolf Augstein, because treason was allegedly involved, posed a threat to the freedom of the press and to liberal democracy. The resultant government crisis led to increased pressure from the FDP and also from many CDU/CSU politicians for a change in leadership. At the age of 87 and after 14 years in office, Konrad Adenauer announced his resignation on 11 October 1963.

III 1963–69: The years of transition

1. Old and new problems

On 16 October 1963 Ludwig Erhard, previously Economics Minister and Vice-Chancellor, was elected Federal Chancellor by the German Bundestag. His government too was based on a coalition made up of the CDU/CSU and the FDP. Initially Erhard seemed to succeed Adenauer in an unchanged environment, and this impression was confirmed by his clear victory at the polls in the autumn of 1965. However, his term of office was increasingly proving to be a difficult period of transition. In 1965 Erhard himself spoke in a policy statement of the end of the postwar era. Old problems, which had either receded into the background or been pushed aside, re-emerged and a number of fundamental new problems arose.
As far as relations between the two superpowers were concerned, a clear change was discernible after the Cuba crisis and Khrushchev's fall from power. The Cold War was followed by a period of détente in which the United States and the Soviet Union, while respecting each other's spheres of interest and the status quo, tried to come to an arrangement. The Federal Republic found it particularly difficult to adjust to this changed situation, since such an arrangement threatened to cement the status quo in Central Europe.
Moreover, the development of the economy created serious domestic problems. As had long been apparent from the slowdown in economic growth, the exceptional postwar boom, which had been sustained by the need for reconstruction, was coming to an end in the mid-1960s. In 1966 first the Ruhr, which faced structural problems, and subsequently the entire Federal Republic experienced an economic downturn. Erhard's basically conservative economic policy instruments proved incapable of overcoming this crisis, which soon developed into a government crisis. Not least because of the surprising electoral successes of a neo-Nazi party, the NPD, increasing doubts were expressed about the ability of the Federal Republic's political system – until then much praised for its stability – to withstand crises. By the autumn of 1966 the economic and political problems were considered so serious that the formation of a Grand Coalition consisting of the CDU/CSU and the SPD was considered the only possible solution.

VII/301 Demonstration sparked off by the Spiegel Affair, October 1962

VII/302 Konrad Adenauer's resignation as Federal Chancellor, Bundestag, 15 October 1963

VII/303 Coal stacks in the Ruhr, 1965

VII/304 Demonstration against Chancellor Erhard's economic policy in Moers, June 1966

The origins of the economic crisis

In the early 1960s the economy of the Federal Republic was booming. In 1964 high growth rates were again achieved and for the first time the number of foreign workers exceeded one million. However, the crisis was already looming. In particular, the Ruhr coal industry was no longer able to compete with oil and imported coal. At the end of 1965 a recession set in. Even so, the Government's economic policy was largely confined to appeals by the Chancellor for moderation and restraint, and the Government failed to take countermeasures in good time. Thus, unemployment rose rapidly after the autumn of 1966 and reached a peak of 673,572 jobless in February 1967. After the long years of economic prosperity, the first recession since the establishment of the Federal Republic aroused greater fears than the actual situation warranted.

Shadows of the past

Two events in the mid-1960s focused attention on the burden of the National Socialist past, which had only partly been dealt with during the Adenauer era: the trial of SS guards from Auschwitz concentration camp, and the stormy parliamentary and public debate on the question of extending the statute of limitations for Nazi crimes, which was eventually supported by a majority in the Bundestag. These events did not really play a very significant role until the NPD, founded in 1964, was able to score surprising electoral successes, which were also due to the economic crisis. The rise of neo-Nazi forces aroused, especially abroad, memories of the final years of the Weimar Republic.

Stagnation in German-German relations and foreign policy

The Erhard Government tried to adjust to the improvement in East-West relations by cautiously relaxing its earlier stance. In 1963/64 trade missions were established in several Eastern European countries, and in March 1966 the Federal Republic offered for the first time to sign treaties providing for mutual renunciation of the threat or use of force. However, the basic principles of its policy – the refusal to recognize the GDR and the status quo in Europe, the claim to be the sole representative of Germany, and the Hallstein Doctrine – remained unchanged. The Federal Republic's freedom of action in the realm of foreign policy thus remained limited. At the same time, a serious crisis arose with regard to its policy on Europe. In contrast to the "Gaullists", Adenauer and Strauss, the "Atlanticists", Erhard and his Foreign Minister, Gerhard Schröder, rejected the establishment of any special links with France.

The crisis facing Erhard

From the beginning of his chancellorship, Erhard faced severe criticism, especially from among the ranks of his own party, on account of his policy towards France and his qualities as a leader. The Chancellor's authority was gradually eroded. This trend accelerated following the state election in North Rhine-Westphalia in July 1966, in which the SPD came close to achieving an absolute majority. When the CDU/CSU and the FDP failed to reach agreement in the course of the budget deliberations on covering the budget deficit caused by the economic crisis, the four FDP ministers resigned on 27 October 1966. Erhard remained in office for more than a month but he was not actively involved in finding a solution to the government crisis, which eventually led to the formation of the Grand Coalition.

2. The Grand Coalition

Both the CDU/CSU and the SPD intended the alliance which they formed on 1 December 1966 to exist for only a limited period of time in order to solve a number of specific problems. Apart from the need to overcome the economic crisis, one such problem was legislation for which it had previously been impossible to find the necessary majorities in Parliament, such as the constitutional rules applicable in a state of emergency. Moreover, introduction of the British first-past-the-post electoral system was proposed in order not only to ensure that the Grand Coalition would come to an end but

VII/305 NPD rally on 17 June 1968 to mark the uprising in the GDR on 17 June 1953

VII/306 Visitors having their passes checked at the border control point in East Berlin, October 1964

VII/307 Kurt Georg Kiesinger and Willy Brandt shaking hands after agreeing to form a Grand Coalition

VII/308 Economics Minister Karl Schiller and Finance Minister Franz Josef Strauss, February 1967

also to make coalition governments entirely superfluous in the future.
In the years of the Grand Coalition, the constitution, the Basic Law, was amended more often than at any other time. The recession was rapidly overcome, partly with the help of a fundamental reform of economic policy instruments. In the same way, the constitutional rules governing public finances were amended in such a way that they met the demands of modern economic management. Moreover, the relationship between the Federation and the Laender was modified in many areas that were of significance for the future; this applied, for example, to the entire field of education, the financing of hospitals, and structural economic policy. It is this comprehensive adjustment of the government apparatus to the requirements of an advanced industrial society which must be regarded as the Grand Coalition's main achievement.
The CDU/CSU and the SPD were less successful in the foreign policy field, even though many attempts were made to initiate new policies, because they disagreed violently over the speed and the limits of a reorientation of their policy towards the GDR and Eastern Europe. In the run-up to the 1969 elections to the Bundestag, differences of opinion surfaced in other areas too and made the task of governing increasingly difficult. However, from the moment it took office, the Grand Coalition was criticized above all for one thing – its overwhelming parliamentary majority over the FDP opposition. Many people, including members of the SPD, felt that the absence of any genuine political competition posed a threat to parliamentary democracy. The younger generation in particular gained the impression that there was a closed political and economic establishment which only used democracy to consolidate its rule and block all change, an impression which contributed to the protest activities of those years.

An alliance formed for a limited period of time

On 10 November 1966, after the fall of the Erhard Government, the CDU/CSU parliamentary group in the German Bundestag nominated Kurt Georg Kiesinger, Minister-President of Baden-Württemberg, for the office of Chancellor. The CDU/CSU took up negotiations with both the FDP and the SPD on forming a coalition. For a brief time, a Social-Liberal coalition was considered, but these plans were soon abandoned because such a coalition would not have been able to rely on a solid parliamentary majority. The likelihood of a Grand Coalition being formed increased in the light of the NPD's electoral successes in Hesse and Bavaria. Not least because the SPD, after 17 years in opposition, wanted to prove its ability to govern, the advocates of a Grand Coalition prevailed, also in the party's executive bodies.

Economic and financial reforms

The new government's efforts centred on economic and financial policy. In planning their reforms, Economics Minister Karl Schiller (SPD) and Finance Minister Franz Josef Strauss (CSU) were guided by the belief that the increasingly complex economic environment made it necessary carefully to plan economic and budgetary developments and to ensure cooperation between the major social groups. With the help of new economic policy instruments and specific measures aimed at stimulating the economy, they succeeded as early as 1968 in ensuring adequate growth, halting the rise in prices and restoring full employment. However, in 1969 the coalition partners failed to reach agreement on the hotly debated question of a revaluation of the Deutsche Mark.

Policy on Germany and foreign policy: between rigidity and a new departure

The Grand Coalition also introduced new elements into the Federal Republic's foreign policy and its policy towards the GDR. In 1967 diplomatic relations were established with Romania and Yugoslavia, which meant that the Hallstein Doctrine was abandoned. In May/June 1967 the Chairman of the Council of Ministers of the GDR, Willi Stoph, and Chancellor Kurt Georg Kiesinger exchanged letters for the first time. Exploratory talks were also held with the Soviet Union on the policy of renunciation of force initiated by Ludwig Erhard, which was later continued by the Social-Liberal coalition. Still, little progress was made in this area before 1969. In addition to differences of opinion between the CDU/CSU and the SPD, the international tension created by the Soviet invasion of Czechoslovakia proved a major stumbling block.

The domestic policy of the Grand Coalition

The domestic debate during the Grand Coalition focused on emergency legislation, which was adopted by a two-thirds majority of the Bundestag in May 1968 despite strong public protest. These amendments to the constitution put an end to the rights that had been retained by the Allies in this respect and introduced carefully defined legal rules governing the state of defence and other crises. By contrast, the originally planned introduction of a majority voting system, which would presumably have spelled the end of the FDP and led to a two-party system, eventually foundered, following vehement protest by the public, on the resistance of the SPD.

3. Youth protest

It was also during the Grand Coalition that a major protest movement emerged, which was mainly supported by students. While they originally sought to bring about a reform of the universities and the educational system, they very soon came to demand far-reaching changes and the democratization of all spheres of life. The protests were clearly fuelled by the alliance between the two major parties and by the absence of an effective parliamentary opposition, which made those involved perceive themselves to some extent as an extra-parliamentary substitute for such opposition. The real roots went deeper, however, as parallel developments in many modern industrialized countries showed.

The protest movement reflected a global crisis of the parliamentary democracies which had been simmering for a long time. It was no coincidence that the leading Western power, the United States, experienced a major crisis at the time as a result of its military commitment in Vietnam. Faced with the increasing rigidity and bureaucratization of democratic structures and the saturation of a society primarily concerned – in the view of its critics – with consumption and material improvements, a major proportion of the young generation called for a radical rejection of all traditional forms of authority and expressed a desire for a departure for new shores. The protest movement failed because its objectives remained vague and unclear and because it ultimately succeeded in attracting only minorities. However, it clearly had an effect, as was evident not only from the fact that a number of educational reforms were introduced very rapidly or that the two major parties were increasingly drifting apart, which was also due to their differing assessment of youth protest. Most importantly, the protest movement furthered a fundamental change in the values and attitudes of a society that appeared to be particularly stable in this respect or had, as its critics put it, become extraordinarily rigid. To some extent, this process had set in even before the protest movement emerged, and was one of its causes. However, the protest movement strengthened and accelerated it to a decisive degree.

The origins and causes of the protest movement

Initially, student criticism focused on the outdated, rigid university structures and the unsatisfactory conditions at the universities. Very soon, however, it developed into fundamental opposition to the structures of West German society as such. The protests were fuelled by demonstrations against the war which the United States was waging in Vietnam and against dictatorial regimes, particularly in the Third World. When, during a demonstration against the visit of Shah Reza Pahlavi to Berlin on 2 June 1967, a student was killed by the police, the protest movement spread from West Berlin to the entire Federal Republic.

Climax and manifestations

The protest movement reached its climax at Easter 1968 after an attempt had been made to assassinate one of the leaders of the Berlin student movement, Rudi Dutschke. The principal target of the demonstrations, which degenerated into street battles and were accompanied by violence, was the Springer

VII/309 Demonstration against the emergency legislation, May 1968

VII/310 The Bundestag adopting the emergency legislation, May 1968

VII/311 Student protest in Hamburg, 1967

VII/312 Vietnam demonstration on the Kurfürstendamm in Berlin, 18 February 1968

publishing house, whose newspapers were held partly responsible for the attempted assassination. When the emergency laws were adopted in May, large-scale demonstrations took place in numerous towns and cities. The movement then gradually subsided, as did similar movements in France and the United States in particular. At the same time, the established institutions increasingly became the place where such controversies were argued out.

Problems and consequences

Youth protest, which had initially developed and propagated special non-violent forms of action, became increasingly radical in the course of its confrontation with state authority, as one of its slogans – "violence against property" – showed. On a scale hitherto unknown in the postwar period, violence became a means of fighting out political controversies. Even so, there were only a few isolated individuals who were prepared to resort to acts of terrorism in pursuit of their aims. The vast majority of young people, to the extent that they later continued to be politically active at all, relied on what was called the "march through the established institutions". Still, their protest continued to have an effect because almost all traditional life styles and patterns were radically called into question.

IV 1969–1982: The Social-Liberal coalition

From the Grand Coalition to the Social-Liberal coalition

The election of the Federal President – one element of the change of power

As a result of increasing tension between the parties making up the Grand Coalition, they did not succeed in proposing a joint candidate for the election of the Federal President in March 1969. The CDU/CSU nominated Defence Minister Gerhard Schröder, the SPD's candidate was Minister of Justice Gustav Heinemann – both had been chosen not least because each party hoped that its candidate would be supported by the FDP, whose votes were decisive. The Liberals, who had, while in opposition, undergone a process of renewal marked by a shift to left-wing liberalism, eventually voted for the Social Democratic candidate. When Gustav Heinemann was elected by a narrow majority in the third ballot, this was generally interpreted as a vote against the continuation of the Grand Coalition and for the formation of a Social-Liberal alliance after the Bundestag elections.

The formation of the Social-Liberal coalition

Even though neither the SPD nor the FDP committed themselves publicly, it was generally assumed that they might well form the next Federal Government. However, the result of the Bundestag elections of 28 September 1969 provided only a narrow basis for such co-operation, a narrower basis than in 1966. The CDU/CSU had lost votes and the NPD came close to clearing the 5-per-cent hurdle, but the ground gained by the SPD was more than offset by Liberal losses. Even so, Willy Brandt and Walter Scheel, the chairmen of the SPD and the FDP, agreed in principle on the night of the election to form a coalition. On 21 October 1969 Willy Brandt was elected Chancellor by 251 votes or, in other words, by a narrow majority of three votes. For the first time since the founding of the Federal Republic, a Social Democrat had become head of government.

VII/313 Scene of the attempted assassination of Rudi Dutschke in Berlin, 11 April 1968

VII/314 President Gustav Heinemann handing Chancellor Willy Brandt his letter of appointment, 21 October 1969

The second republic had proved its ability to bring about a change of government by democratic procedures.

1. The new Ostpolitik

From the very start, the Social-Liberal alliance was based above all on a determination to supplement the policy of Western integration by a policy of accommodation with the Federal Republic's Eastern neighbours. The new Ostpolitik was characterized by two major motives and objectives. For one thing, its supporters were convinced that the Federal Republic had to adjust to the steady improvement in East-West relations and they also hoped in this way to increase its room for manoeuvre in the foreign policy field. For another, they had the unity of the nation in mind and wanted to ensure that concrete improvements in the Federal Republic's relations with the GDR, in particular more intensive human contacts, would prevent the two German states from increasingly drifting apart, while at the same time keeping open the German question.
Both aspects of this policy were based on the assumption that the conditions which had been created in the wake of the Second World War had to be accepted as a reality before any progress could be made in relations with the Eastern European countries. It was above all against this assumption – as well as against the rapid pace of the negotiations – that the vehement criticism of the opposition was directed from the very start. To the extent that they were in any way prepared to abandon earlier legal claims and positions, most CDU/CSU politicians felt that the readiness to do so should be suitably rewarded in the negotiations. In their view, therefore, the treaties concluded in 1970 with the Soviet Union and with Poland, the Four-Power Agreement on Berlin signed in 1972 and the agreements concluded in the same year with the GDR failed to provide for a balanced give-and-take.
The new Ostpolitik gave rise to acrimonious domestic controversies, which can be compared only with the foreign policy debates of the early 1950s. They culminated in an abortive attempt to oust Chancellor Brandt by means of a constructive vote of no-confidence and subsided only after the early elections on 19 November 1972, from which the Social-Liberal coalition emerged as a clear victor.

On the basis of the Eastern treaties it was possible largely to normalize relations with the Eastern bloc. They also made a major contribution to the general process of détente, which entered a new phase in Helsinki in 1975 with the Conference on Security and Co-operation in Europe (CSCE). Despite a number of setbacks and even though expectations proved to have been too high in some respects, relations between the two German states improved in a way that was of direct benefit to the people. Last but not least, Ostpolitik increased the Federal Republic's room for manoeuvre in the foreign policy field and made it possible for the new Chancellor, Helmut Schmidt, to bring the Federal Republic's weight to bear more effectively in international politics, which, in the second half of the 1970s, were dominated by the problems of the world economy.

The opening towards the East

Upon taking office, Chancellor Brandt declared in his policy statement of 28 October 1969 that the new Federal Government was prepared, over and above the earlier offers of a mutual renunciation of force, to recognize the GDR and thus also to abandon the claim that the Federal Republic was the sole representative of Germany. His visit to Erfurt on 19 March 1970 aroused hopes, especially in the GDR, which proved to be premature, however, when Willi Stoph, the Chairman of the GDR Council of Ministers, made a return visit to Kassel two months later. The key to a solution of all further questions lay in an understanding with the Soviet Union, for which Brandt's closest foreign policy advisor, State Secretary Egon Bahr, had been preparing the ground in Moscow since January 1970.

The policy of treaties

The Treaty of Moscow, signed on 12 August 1970, was the centrepiece of the system of treaties which the Social-Liberal Government concluded with a number of Eastern European countries. Its clauses on the renunciation of the use or threat of force and on respect for the territorial integrity of all states in Europe within their existing borders were also included in the treaties later concluded with Poland, Czechoslovakia and the

VII/315 Signing of the Moscow Treaty, 12 August 1970

VII/316 Signing of the Warsaw Treaty, 7 December 1970

VII/317 Chancellor Brandt being awarded the Nobel Peace Prize, 10 December 1971

VII/318 Signing of the Four-Power Agreement on Berlin, 3 June 1972

VII/319 Foreign Minister Walter Scheel addressing the United Nations General Assembly, 19 September 1973

VII/320 Final meeting of the Conference on Security and Co-operation in Europe in Helsinki, 1 August 1975

VII/321 Demonstration in Bonn against the Eastern treaties, 1972

VII/322 Chancellor Brandt and Vice-Chancellor Scheel on the evening of the Bundestag elections of 19 November 1972

XXI Konrad Adenauer, oil painting by Oskar Kokoschka, 1966

XXII Bonn, the new City Hall – modern architecture in a historical setting

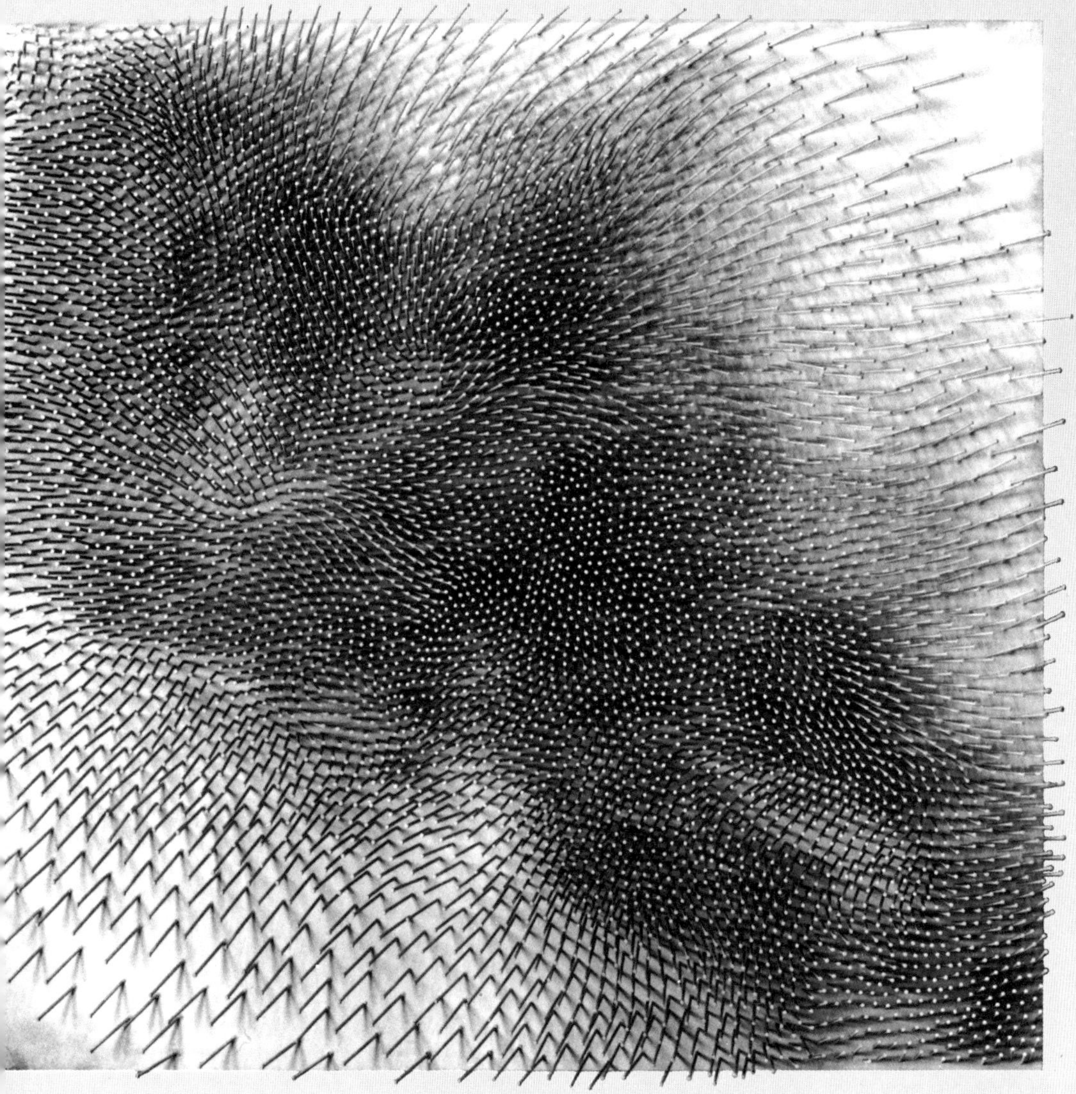

XXIII Günther Uecker, Relief in Nails, 1969

GDR. The Four-Power Agreement on Berlin should also be mentioned in this connection. While it left questions of status aside, it eased transit traffic to West Berlin, enabled West Berliners to visit the Eastern sector of the city, and confirmed West Berlin's ties with the Federal Republic.
In the so-called Basic Treaty, finally, the two German states established relations with each other on a basis of equality. The accession of the GDR and the Federal Republic to the United Nations in September 1973, which became possible as a result of this agreement, marked the end of the first phase of the new Ostpolitik.

Domestic disputes over the Eastern treaties

At the end of 1971, at the beginning of the parliamentary ratification process, the passionate debates about Ostpolitik entered a decisive phase. They became even more heated when a few members of the governing parties went over to the opposition, as a result of which the Social-Liberal coalition was in danger of losing its majoritiy. However, the attempt by the CDU/CSU to have its leader, Rainer Barzel, elected Chancellor by means of a constructive vote of no-confidence narrowly failed. Finally, the majority of the CDU/CSU decided to abstain in the vote on the Eastern treaties so as to make possible their passage through Parliament on 17 May 1972. Early elections were then called, from which, after a fiercely fought election campaign, the Social-Liberal coalition emerged considerably strengthened on 19 November 1972.

2. Internal reforms

XXIV (illustr. left) Berlin – a scene from Peter Stein's production of Kleist's "Prince of Homburg" at the Schaubühne am Halleschen Ufer, 1972/73

The change of government in 1969 perhaps aroused even greater expectations in the domestic than in the foreign policy field. In his policy statement, Chancellor Brandt summed up the principle that was to guide his new domestic policy as follows: "Courage for more democracy!" This slogan was based on the assumption that, after 20 years of Christian Democratic federal governments, there was an urgent need for reforms, which should above all aim to extend democratic structures beyond state institutions to all spheres of society.

The reform programme ranged from liberalizing and modernizing the legal system to extending the social system and strengthening employee participation. The principal aim, however, was to bring about qualitative and quantitative improvements in education.

The euphoric expectations placed in these reforms proved in many respects to be too high. During the first Brandt/Scheel Cabinet only a small proportion of the proposed legislation was in fact enacted, partly because of the heated controversies over the Eastern treaties. It was only in the two subsequent legislative terms that the reform programme drawn up in 1969 was gradually implemented, even though the original objectives were by no means fully achieved.

Apart from differences between the coalition partners, which made it difficult to hammer out compromise agreements in all cases, for example as regards employee participation, the attitude of the Christian Democrat-governed states and the Christian Democrat majority in the Bundesrat restricted the efforts to introduce such reforms. Moreover, several important reform laws were declared invalid by the Federal Constitutional Court either in whole or in part. However, it was not least the changed economic environment in the wake of the oil crisis of autumn 1973 which imposed major financial constraints on the reform plans and even led to a number of laws providing for new benefits being curtailed.

Still, during the years of the Social-Liberal coalition the Federal Republic changed considerably in the domestic policy field too. In addition to far-reaching legal policy measures, which had a profound effect on society, other successful reforms can be cited, such as a substantial increase in pensions and in the benefits provided by the health insurance scheme, the broadening of educational opportunities, and to a certain extent also the extension of employee participation.

Legal reforms

The Social-Liberal coalition continued the reforms which had been started during the years of the Grand Coalition by effecting a whole series of changes in the laws governing political and sexual offences. One of the most controversial issues was the amendment of Section 218 of the Penal Code concerning abortion. The law passed by the SPD and the FDP, which allowed termination of pregnancy within a specified period, was declared incompatible with the Basic Law by the Federal Constitutional Court, from which the CDU/CSU opposition had requested a ruling on this matter. In June 1976 it was replaced by a law allowing termination of pregnancy on a number of carefully defined grounds. In the same year an important law concerning marriage and the family was passed, one of the most significant features of which was abolition of the principle of guilt in cases of divorce.

Educational reforms

Partly because of the problems which it caused as regards the distribution of rights and responsibilities between the Federation and the Laender, the educational policy of the Social-Liberal coalition and the related reforms triggered the fiercest controversies of all; at the same time, there was a substantial discrepancy between the original intentions and the results that were ultimately achieved. This applies, for example, to changes in the curriculum and the restructuring of educational institutions (comprehensive schools, university reform), both of which were only partly realized. By contrast, the Social-Liberal coalition was successful in its efforts to provide a larger number of schools and educational institutions and thus to broaden educational opportunities – even though the situation on the labour market was beginning increasingly to call this achievement into question.

Extension of employee participation

The trade unions expected the SPD-led government to strengthen the rights of works' councils and extend employee participation on a parity basis beyond the iron, coal and steel industries. A new Law on Labour Relations at the Workplace was in fact passed as early as 1971, but the discussion on employee participation dragged on for years, mainly because of the differences on this issue between the SPD and the FDP. It was only in March 1976 that a new Co-Determination Law was passed by the Bundestag, which was also supported by the opposition. It provided for equal representation of employees on the supervisory boards of large companies, but gave shareholders' representatives a stronger position in the event of disputes or controversies.

Extension of the social state

The favourable economic situation in the early 1970s made it possible for the Social-Liberal coalition to extend and supplement the social security system in virtually all areas. The introduction of a flexible retirement age, financial assistance for students and pupils, improvements in the benefits provided by the health insurance scheme as well as a reform of child allowances and of the law governing tenancy were among the most significant measures. Following the crisis of 1974/75, however, the economic forecasts on which these improvements were based increasingly proved to be overoptimistic. Deficits in the pension funds and in the budget showed that the financing of the social security system had reached its limits.

The end of the Brandt/Scheel era

Even though the Social-Liberal coalition had been returned with a clear majority in the elections of November 1972, it faced increasing difficulties in the domestic field in 1973 and 1974. These were due to tension within the SPD, to disputes with the trade unions and to the deteriorating economic situation. When a close collaborator of the Federal Chancellor in the Chancellery, Günter Guillaume, was arrested on a charge of spying for the GDR, Willy Brandt announced his resignation on 6 May 1974. Foreign Minister Scheel had already announced his candidature for the office of Federal President and was elected on 15 May 1974. The Social-Liberal coalition continued under a new leadership: Helmut Schmidt, previously Finance Minister, became Federal Chancellor, and Scheel's successor as Federal Minister for Foreign Affairs and Chairman of the FDP was Hans-Dietrich Genscher.

VII/323 Demonstration against the law making abortion a punishable offence, 1975

VII/324 New university buildings in Constance, February 1982

VII/325 Otto Brenner, chairman of the Metalworkers' Union, speaking on employee participation, October 1968

VII/326 Ban on Sunday driving imposed in winter 1973 because of the oil crisis

3. Limits and strains

From the mid-1970s onwards, all advanced industrial nations faced a fundamental change in the economic and political environment. The deserted motorways – a consequence of the oil crisis in the autumn of 1973 – were generally perceived as an indication of bleak economic prospects. Still, the full impact of that crisis on economic growth and employment only became apparent years later. The "change in the underlying trend", as it was called in 1973/74, provoked a general change of attitude. Instead of reformist zeal and the expectation that the future could be mastered on the basis of specific plans, increasing complaints were voiced about the country being ungovernable and various constraints frustrating the plans and intentions of politicians.

One of the most urgent problems that had to be solved was the phenomenon of terrorism, which at times threatened to shake the very foundations of Western democracy. Other particularly serious problems were the dangers associated with increasing environmental pollution and the risks entailed by more extensive utilization of nuclear energy. This, as well as the deteriorating East-West climate and the resultant threat of a nuclear arms race between the superpowers, aroused fears and anxieties that the survival of mankind itself might be at stake. However, the world economic crisis loomed largest in people's minds. As a result of steeply rising energy costs, fundamental technological changes and the disruption of the world economic equilibrium, economic growth was stifled, unemployment reached a new postwar peak and the national debt assumed alarming proportions.

The crucial issue was whether the crisis was of a traditional nature and could thus be overcome by traditional means, or whether it was a result of the more deep-seated structural problems confronting developed economies, the solution of which called for new policies. In addition, there was the possibility that industrialized society had reached its limits, which would have required the adoption of a fundamentally new approach. The different answers which politicians and parties gave to these problems substantially changed the party landscape in the late 1970s. New political forces emerged and the differences within the Social-Liberal coalition became ever greater. Eventually, after 13 years of close collaboration, this resulted in the collapse of the Social-Liberal coalition on 17 September 1982.

Terrorism and preservation of the rule of law

Throughout the 1970s the Federal Republic was confronted with the international problem of terrorism. Terrorist attacks reached a climax in 1977 with the assassination of Federal Public Prosecutor Buback, the banker Ponto, and the President of the Employers' Association, Hanns Martin Schleyer, and the hijacking of a Lufthansa aircraft. The Government and the opposition worked together closely in this critical situation but found it difficult to agree on suitable measures for combating the terrorist threat. Some critics considered that the more stringent legal provisions introduced and some police measures violated the rule of law. Still, despite the grave threat faced by the state, the basic principles of the constitution remained intact. When in the autumn of 1977 the Federal Government refused to be blackmailed, this did not entirely banish the danger of new terrorist attacks, but the wave of terrorism subsided, as the subsequent years showed.

Environmental protection and nuclear power

During the Social-Liberal coalition, environmental protection became a dominant theme. An increasing number of people felt that pollution of the air and water, traffic noise and large-scale construction projects posed an elementary threat to the environment and to their lives. Although the Government's environmental policy achieved considerable successes, in many areas it failed to keep the growing problems under control. The construction of even more nuclear power stations and the issue of suitable nuclear waste disposal facilities provoked strong protest. A new grass-roots movement emerged and gradually developed into a party. The "Greens" demanded radical changes in environmental policy and, since 1979, have been elected first to a number of state parliaments and subsequently to the German Bundestag, thus calling the traditional three-party system of the Federal Republic into question.

VII/327 Chancellor Brandt and GDR spy Guillaume, April 1974

VII/328 The first Schmidt/Genscher Cabinet with Federal President Heinemann, 16 May 1974

VII/329 Scene of the kidnapping of Hanns Martin Schleyer, President of the Employers' Association, 5 September 1977

VII/330 Biblis nuclear power station

The end of détente

In the foreign policy field the Schmidt/Genscher Government was concerned above all to further the process of European union, harmonize the economic policies of the major industrial nations, intensify the dialogue with the developing world and, not least, continue the policy of détente. However, these efforts were increasingly overshadowed by a deterioration in East-West relations, which was due above all to the Soviet invasion of Afghanistan, the events in Poland, and the Soviet Union's arms build-up. The Federal Republic faced the difficult question of whether and to what extent it should fall in with the American change of course in response to Soviet policy. Moreover, it had to consider how the positive results of the policy of détente could be preserved and peace safeguarded. The passionate debates about these issues centred on NATO's dual-track decision of December 1979, which provided for the deployment of American intermediate-range nuclear missiles in Europe, should the Soviet Union not agree to dismantle its new SS-20 missiles.

Economic crisis and the limits of the social state

Not least because of the sharp increase in energy costs, the world economy experienced a sharp downturn in 1974/75. Although growth rates rose again in the following years, unemployment remained high and has reached new record levels since 1981. Increased international competition and radical structural change have led to large-scale job losses. The Federal Government's efforts to master the crisis by means of concerted international action and by programmes to stimulate economic activity, which were financed by loans, had some success but the price of this success was a substantial increase in the national debt. The growing deficits, which made it necessary to curtail benefits, particularly in the social field, triggered serious domestic controversies and made co-operation within the Social-Liberal coalition increasingly difficult.

The collapse of the Social-Liberal coalition

The CDU/CSU opposition scored successes in a number of local and state elections and, by virtue of its majority in the Federal Convention, it ensured that its candidate, Karl Carstens, was elected Federal President on 23 May 1979. However, in the Bundestag elections on 5 October 1980, the Schmidt/Genscher Government again obtained a clear majority, mainly because of gains made by the Liberals. However, the rapidly worsening economic crisis soon exacerbated the tension between the coalition partners. As in the previous year, the coalition partners had great problems agreeing on a draft budget for 1983. Amidst mutual recriminations, the Social-Liberal coalition collapsed on 17 September 1982. Chancellor Schmidt remained in office with a minority Social Democratic government until he was ousted by a vote of no-confidence on 1 October 1982.

VII/331 Chancellor Schmidt being welcomed by Mao Tse-tung in Peking, October 1975

VII/332 Peace demonstration in Bonn, 10 October 1981

VII/333 Since 1973 rising oil prices have made it necessary to save energy

VII/334 The first World Economic Summit in Rambouillet near Paris, 1975

V Developments leading to the present

The coalition government under Chancellor Helmut Kohl, which the CDU/CSU and the Free Democratic Party formed on 1 October 1982, is founded above all on a number of common objectives in the field of economic and financial policy. It was felt that the previous efforts to maintain economic growth and prevent mass unemployment through public programmes to stimulate economic activity had failed and that a radical change was needed: by consolidating the budget, making partial cuts in social expenditure, placing the pension scheme on a sound financial basis and providing for tax relief, the general conditions for growth were to be improved. As a result of an unusually high increase in exports, real economic growth of between 2 and 3 per cent has in fact been achieved and inflation has been brought down to below 2 per cent. The growth of mass unemployment has been halted, but with about 2 million jobless unemployment remains very high.

By contrast, the new government has maintained the continuity of foreign policy and policy with regard to intra-German relations, in spite of some reservations about the Ostpolitik that had been pursued by the Social-Liberal coalition. Thus, the Federal Republic's integration into the Western community and a policy towards Eastern Europe aimed at reconciling interests continued to be the basis of German foreign policy after 1982, too. Owing to the difficult international situation, which was characterized by the intensified arms race and increasing tension between the superpowers, there was only limited scope for progress as regards intra-German relations, however. Not until 1985, mainly as a result of the change in the Soviet leadership, was a new East-West dialogue on disarmament started, which has also given the Federal Republic more latitude in the field of foreign policy.

A new coalition and new elections

After the collapse of the Social-Liberal alliance, the CDU/CSU and the Free Democratic Party, the latter after fierce internal controversies, agreed to form a coalition. On 1 October 1982 Helmut Kohl, until then leader of the opposition, was elected Federal Chancellor. After taking a few decisions, especially with regard to the budget, the new coalition decided to call an early election and on 6 March 1983 was returned with a clear majority. The Greens cleared the five-per-cent hurdle. As a result, a fourth parliamentary group has been represented in Parliament for the first time since the 1950s.

Budgetary and financial reform

The Kohl/Genscher coalition government considers its main challenge to lie in the field of economic and financial policy. With a view to reducing the budget deficit, public spending and social security benefits have been cut. A tax reform has been introduced, which is to be implemented in stages and is designed above all to boost investment. However, the economic upswing has failed to solve the underlying structural problems, especially on the labour market. As a result, the Government's economic and financial plans have remained controversial.

Force modernization and the East-West relationship

The Government's willingness to allow new intermediate-range nuclear weapons to be stationed in the Federal Republic in the context of NATO's modernization programme gave rise to serious demonstrations and fierce internal debate. The unity shown by the Western nations and the Federal Republic's reliance on the United States in this matter strengthened the Alliance but placed a strain on relations with the Soviet Union and the German Democratic Republic. This development was viewed with concern by the opposition, but it has proved possible to limit the impact of international tensions on intra-German relations and to achieve further improvements in such matters as transport policy and travel opportunities for citizens of the GDR.

Structural change and unemployment

Although economic growth has picked up in real terms since 1983, there has been no marked reduction in the number of

VII/335 Helmut Kohl after his election as Federal Chancellor on 1 October 1982, with his predecessor, Helmut Schmidt

VII/336 Address by French President François Mitterrand to the German Bundestag on 20 January 1983 on the occasion of the 20th anniversary of the Franco-German Friendship Treaty

VII/337 The second Kohl/Genscher Cabinet with President Carstens, 30 March 1983

VII/338 Debate in the German Bundestag on NATO's force modernization and the deployment of intermediate-range nuclear weapons, 21 November 1983

VII/339 Demonstration by the Metalworkers' Union for the 35-hour week in Bonn, 28 May 1984

VII/340 Robots being used to weld car bodies

jobless. While new jobs have been created in the computer branch and in other high-tech industries, the crisis in a number of traditional sectors, especially shipping, coal and steel, has grown worse. The economic problems are concentrated primarily in the west and the north, with far-reaching consequences for the parties in these regions. The structural crisis is not least the result of changes in the world economy, the consequences of which have mostly not yet been mastered.

Reform and enlargement of the European Community

In December 1985 the Heads of State and Government of the European Community, after numerous abortive attempts, finally agreed on a revision of the Treaty of Rome which provides in particular for completion of the internal market, the development of economic and monetary union, and more extensive powers for the European institutions. With the accession of Spain and Portugal on 1 January 1986, the European Community increased its membership to twelve. The efforts of the Council of Ministers to cut surplus farm production and thus reduce the costs of the common agricultural policy have had drastic social consequences for farmers, particularly in the Federal Republic.

The disputes over the environment and nuclear energy

Low-emission car engines and unleaded petrol are among the measures that have been introduced above all with a view to improving the quality of the air. However, financial and technical constraints evidently restrict such endeavours, and it has proved difficult to secure the necessary consensus on environmental measures at Community level. The continuing controversy about the risks of nuclear energy was exacerbated by the serious accident in the Chernobyl nuclear reactor in April 1986. No agreement has yet been reached on new technologies in the field of nuclear energy, or on a concept for securing future energy supplies.

VII/341 Richard von Weizsäcker (CDU) before being sworn in as Federal President, 1 July 1984

VII/342 Meeting between Chancellor Kohl and the new Soviet leader, Mikhail Gorbachev, in Moscow, 12 March 1985

VII/343 Ceremony in the Bundestag to mark the 40th anniversary of the end of the Second World War

VII/344 US President Ronald Reagan visiting the historical exhibition in the Reichstag building, 12 June 1987

VII/345 Joschka Fischer, a member of the Greens, being sworn in as Minister of the Environment in Hesse, 12 December 1985

VII/346 The Soviet nuclear reactor at Chernobyl after the accident on 26 April 1986

VII/347 Erich Honecker, Chairman of the Council of State of the German Democratic Republic, being officially welcomed in Bonn, 7 September 1987

VII/348 The President of the German Bundestag, Prof. Dr. Rita Süssmuth, underlined the importance of the 40th anniversary of the founding of the German Bundestag in a speech on 7 September 1989

The changing party system

At the last elections to the German Bundestag on 25 January 1987, in which the CDU/CSU lost votes, while the FDP was able to increase its share of the vote, the coalition secured a new majority. With the SPD having suffered slight losses, the Greens were the only party to benefit from the opposition's gains and are again represented in the Bundestag. This election, like several state elections in which some new right-wing groups achieved their first successes, was a sign that the Federal Republic's three-party system may be about to come to an end.

Permanent
Special Exhibition

Parliamentary Berlin

The various parliaments and the parliamentary system were only gradually able to establish their place in the political and social life of Berlin alongside the Hohenzollern monarchy and the institutions on which it depended, primarily the bureaucracy and the military. The United Diet, an assembly of delegates from the provincial parliaments, which marked the beginning of parliamentary history in Berlin in the spring of 1847, was dissolved after only two months on account of its oppositional stance. Even the Prussian National Assembly, which was elected after the revolution of March 1848, failed in its efforts to give Prussia a liberal constitution. Following the successful counterrevolution, King Frederick William IV, acting on his own supreme authority, decreed the constitution. As was to be expected, it placed severe restrictions on the Lower House, the Chamber of Deputies, which was elected on the basis of the three-class electoral system. The Upper House, the Chamber of Peers, whose members were appointed by the King, provided an additional counterweight. It was not until after the founding of the Reich that the disputes between the parliamentary majority and the executive – its members were appointed by the King – which reached their climax in the Prussian constitutional conflict between 1862 and 1866, began to subside. The new Reichstag that had been elected by universal, equal suffrage, still had no real powers, but the growing responsibilities assigned to the state and the increasing volume of legislation to be dealt with slowly but surely strengthened Parliament's influence. Public interest focused increasingly on the Reichstag.

These political developments were clearly reflected in Berlin's parliamentary architecture. Whereas the early parliaments were housed in buildings designed for other purposes, such as halls in the Castle, in the Singakademie (Choral Society) or the Schauspielhaus (Theatre) at the Gendarmenmarkt, the two Prussian Chambers were provided with their own quarters in about 1850. However, both of these buildings, like the first domicile of the Reichstag in the Leipziger Strasse, were modified only to the extent necessary for parliamentary use and remained more or less inadequate temporary accommodation. Not until 1894 was the Reichstag able to move into the building designed by Paul Wallot in the Königsplatz. A few years later, the Chamber of Peers and the Chamber of Deputies moved into buildings in the Leipziger Strasse and the Prinz-Albrecht-

Strasse respectively. These monumental and representative buildings were unmistakable evidence that Parliament had established itself in Berlin.

However, it was not until the revolution of 1918/19, following defeat in World War I, that Parliament assumed full political responsibility. The Weimar Constitution made the Reichstag the focal point of the country's democratic system and made the Reich Government, too, dependent on enjoying the confidence of a parliamentary majority. The Prussia of the landed gentry, the Junker, had become "red" Prussia, a republican bulwark with a coalition government led by the Social Democrats. Virtually all social groups focused their expectations and demands on Parliament and the political parties. But the readiness to reconcile conflicting interests through parliamentary procedures, which had never been very strong at the best of times, was weakened still further in the final crisis-ridden years of the Weimar Republic. From 1930 onwards the Cabinet was appointed by the Reich President and the Reichstag was frequently dissolved, which increasingly undermined Parliament's authority. When the Reichstag building went up in flames, this symbolized the end of parliamentary democracy in the Weimar Republic. Under the Nazi dictatorship, the Reichstag ceased to have anything in common with a democratic parliament.

When the war ended in 1945, Berlin's parliamentary buildings and large parts of the capital and of the German Reich lay in ruins. The red flag of the Soviet Union was flying on top of the Reichstag. Parliamentary democracy had to be completely rebuilt in Germany. From the very start, the Western sectors of Berlin were included in this process of reconstruction in the three Western occupation zones. Under the Basic Law, the Federal Republic's constitution, Berlin is represented by its own Members in the German Bundestag, though they have only limited voting rights. However, the division of Germany has deprived Berlin of its status as the capital and parliamentary centre of Germany. The Reichstag building, which has been reconstructed and is the seat of the German Bundestag in Berlin, stands for national unity and the continuation of the city's parliamentary and democratic tradition.

I 1847–1870: Parliaments in opposition to the Crown

A. The first parliaments

The United Diet of 1847

Prussia's, and hence Berlin's, parliamentary history began on 11 April 1847 with the formal opening of the United Diet in Berlin Castle. King Frederick William IV had agreed to convene the Diet in response to increasingly vocal demands for an assembly representing the whole of Prussia. However, it merely had the power to approve the levying of taxes. It was dissolved after only two months when the majority of the assembly attempted to extend the Diet's powers and make it a true parliament.

The Prussian National Assembly of 1848

The temporary success of the March 1848 revolution also led to the election of a Prussian constituent National Assembly based on universal suffrage. This election was held simultaneously with the elections to the Frankfurt National Assembly on 1 May 1848. However, the deliberations on a new constitution failed to lead to an agreement between King and Parliament. When the counterrevolutionary forces gained the upper hand in the autumn of 1848, the Prussian National Assembly was dissolved by force. Acting on his own supreme authority, Frederick William IV gave the country a constitution by royal decree.

The Prussian Chamber of Deputies

The constitution, which was later unilaterally revised several times by the King, provided for the election of a Lower House, the Chamber of Deputies, which had only limited powers in respect of the levying of taxes and the passage of legislation. For decisions to be legally valid, the consent of the Crown and both Chambers was required. The inferior status of Parliament in the eyes of the executive was also apparent from the

1 Up to 1918 the solemn opening of Parliament took place in Berlin Castle

2 Sitting of the United Diet in the White Hall of the Castle, spring 1847

3 The Singakademie (Choral Society) designed by Schinkel and built between 1825 and 1827

4 In spring and summer 1848 the Prussian National Assembly met in the Singakademie

5 From 1848 the National Assembly met in the Schauspielhaus (Theatre) at the Gendarmenmarkt

6 In the course of the counterrevolution the National Assembly was driven out of the Schauspielhaus on 11 November and dissolved on 5 December 1848

7 The Prussian Chamber of Deputies in the Dönhoffplatz, Leipziger Strasse 75

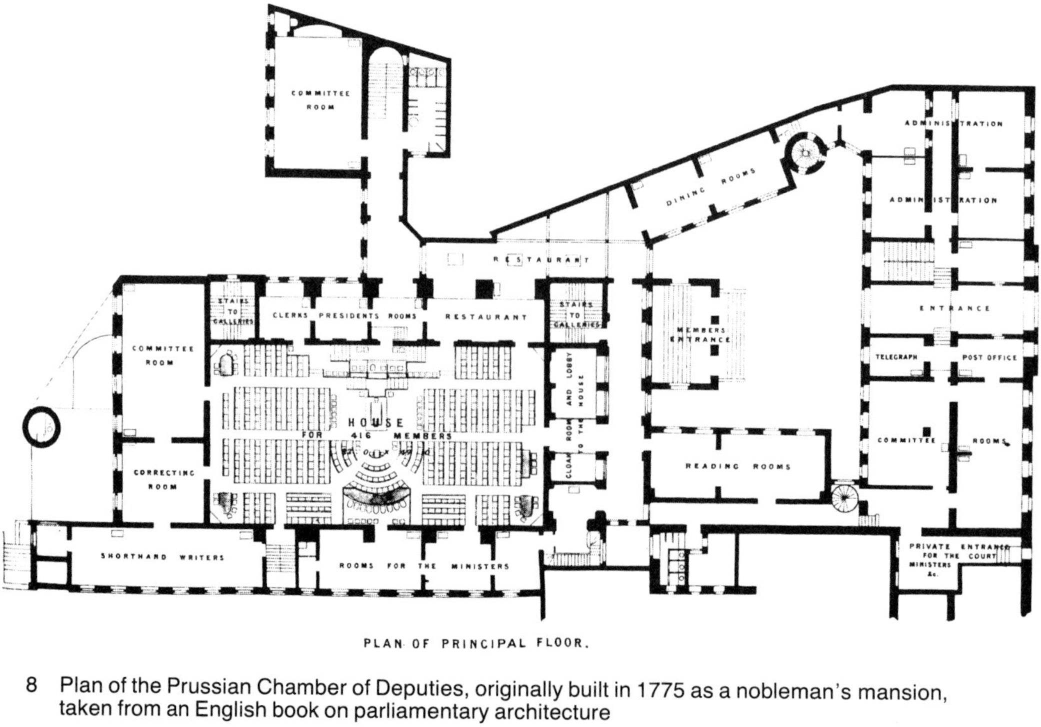

8 Plan of the Prussian Chamber of Deputies, originally built in 1775 as a nobleman's mansion, taken from an English book on parliamentary architecture

cramped and inhospitable buildings in which the Chamber of Deputies was accommodated almost until the turn of the century.

The Prussian Chamber of Peers

Under the Prussian constitution, the Upper House, the Chamber of Peers, was mainly conceived as a counterweight to the Chamber of Deputies. This explains why originally half, and later all, of its members were appointed by the King. The majority of the conservative Junker proved to be reliable supporters of the executive, which was accountable only to the King and protected above all the interests of the aristocracy.

B. The parliamentary system under the Prussian monarchy

The three-class electoral system

The Chamber of Deputies was elected indirectly by universal, but unequal suffrage and there was no secret ballot. The voters were divided into three classes according to the amount of taxes they paid. The small number of people with large incomes (4% of the population) were thus able to nominate as many members of the electoral college and deputies as the large majority of small taxpayers (80% of the population). For decades, though, this electoral system was largely responsible for the liberal majorities in the Chamber as the middle class in particular became increasingly affluent.

The people and its representatives

The deputies enjoyed increasing popular support. By 1862 the turnout at elections had increased to 34%, which, considering the three-class electoral system, was remarkable. A large proportion of the parliamentarians came from the educated middle class. The liberal opposition was primarily made up of civil servants, especially those with a legal background. In the early stages of the constitutional conflict over a reform and

9 The Prussian Chamber of Peers moved to Leipziger Strasse 3, formerly a nobleman's mansion

10 Between 1867 and 1870 the Diet of the North German Confederation met in the plenary chamber of the Chamber of Peers

expansion of the army, they formed the German Progress Party, which could always rely on the support of the Berlin constituencies.

Opposition and conflict

After the abortive revolution of 1848/49 the tension between Crown and Parliament subsided only briefly. In the late 1850s the Liberal opposition began to reorganize itself and redoubled its efforts to assert and extend parliamentary rights. A serious conflict arose between Parliament and the King's executive over the constitutional implications of Bismarck's plans to reform the army. It was not resolved until 1866/67, when, for the sake of national unity, the National Liberal forces and Bismarck reached a compromise.

II 1871–1918: Consolidation of the parliamentary system

A. Parliament under the Empire

The Reichstag and its precursors

Under the constitution of the North German Confederation of 1867, which, four years later, was adopted largely unchanged for the newly founded German Reich, the Reichstag was the main constitutional organ alongside the Prussian King, the hereditary head of the Confederation. However, its political influence was limited for the most part to legislation, which included the power of the purse, whereas the government was almost exclusively dependent on the monarch. As a result, a strong Chancellor like Bismarck was able to exert decisive influence on the policies of the German Reich. The Reichstag was elected directly by universal, equal suffrage and in a secret ballot. Bismarck had opted for this system as a means of fighting the Liberals. The candidates obtaining an absolute majority of the votes – if necessary, a second ballot was held – were elected. This system favoured parties with regional strongholds but disadvantaged the Social Democrats, especially since the constituency boundaries had not been redrawn

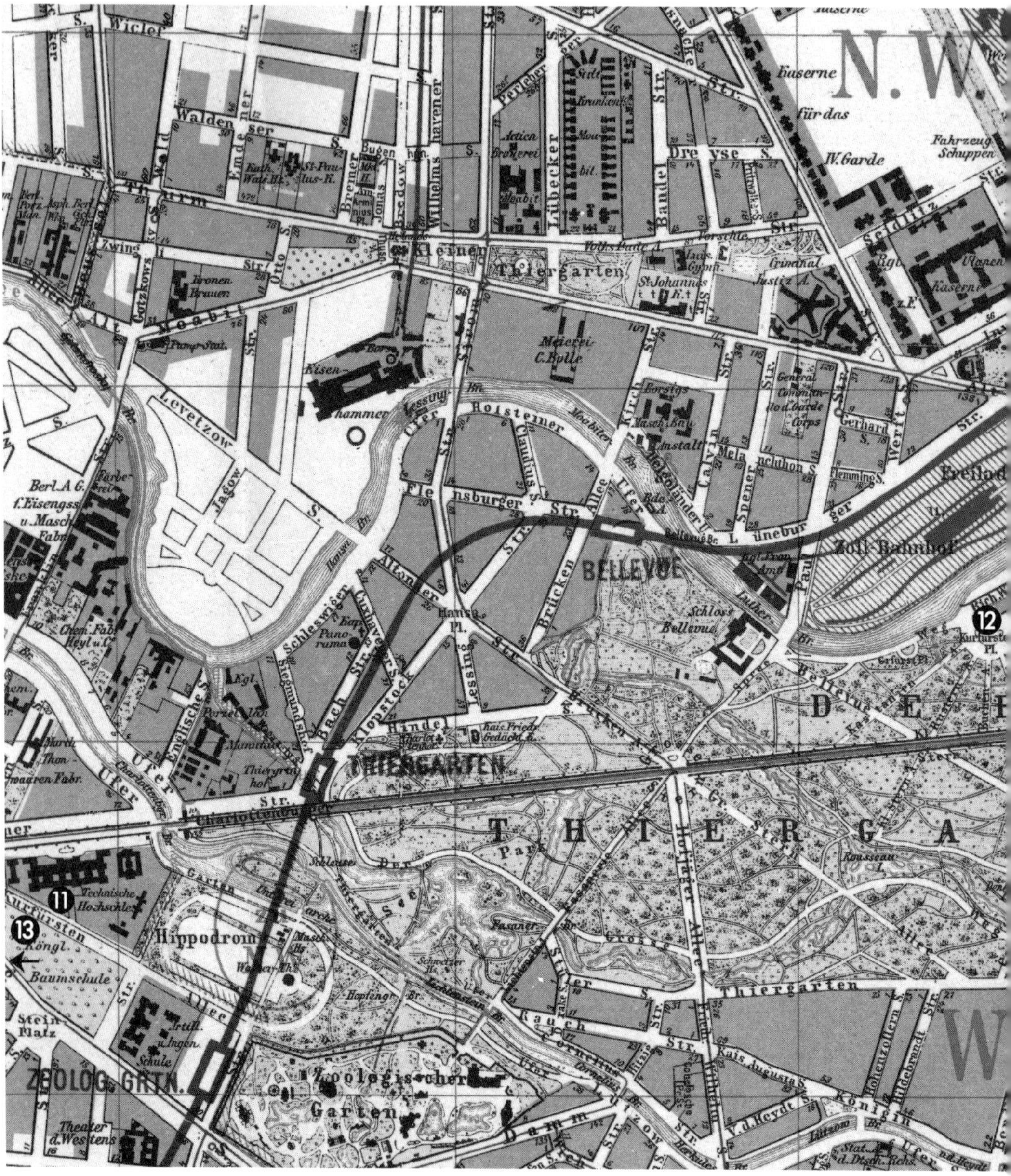

11 The parliament buildings in Berlin (map of 1896)

1. Berlin Castle
2. The Singakademie (Choral Society)
3. The Schauspielhaus (Theatre), Gendarmenmarkt
4. The Prussian Chamber of Deputies, Leipziger Strasse 75
5. The Prussian Chamber of Peers, Leipziger Strasse 3
6. The provisional Reichstag building, Leipziger Strasse 4
7. The Reichstag building, Königsplatz

❽ The new Prussian Chamber of Deputies, Prinz-Albrecht-Strasse 5
❾ The new Prussian Chamber of Peers, Leipziger Strasse 3–4
❿ The Kroll Opera House, Königsplatz
⓫ The main building of the Technical University
⓬ The Congress Hall
⓭ The Ostpreussenhalle beneath the Radio Tower

12 In the summer of 1871 the Reichstag moved into temporary accommodation at Leipziger Strasse 4

13 Sitting of the Reichstag in the provisional Reichstag building, the former Royal Prussian Porcelain Manufactory, about 1872

to allow for the process of urbanization and the growth of densely populated industrial centres.

Parliamentary work

The Reichstag did not meet in permanent session. It was convened by the Emperor only once or twice a year for sessions which lasted several weeks. Although, formally, it was subdivided into seven groups determined by lot, from the very start the conduct of parliamentary business was mainly in the hands of the parliamentary groups. They mostly nominated the speakers for plenary debates and the members of the committees and commissions, which play such an important role in the legislative process. In practice, therefore, the Reichstag was an instrument of modern party democracy and it increasingly became the focal point of public interest.

Parliament's increasing powers under the Empire

During the years of the Empire, the executive slowly but surely became increasingly dependent on the Reichstag and its majority. Parliament's influence increased above all as a result of the ever greater responsibilities assigned to the state and the – consequently – ever broader scope of legislation. However, parliamentarians were excluded from real power until the hour of Germany's defeat in the First World War. The continuing split between Parliament and Government was a major obstacle to the development of parliamentary democracy in Germany.

B. Parliament buildings

Provisional accommodation

Following its early sessions in the building of the Prussian Chamber of Deputies, the Reichstag met for more than 20 years in a provisional building, the former Royal Prussian Porcelain Manufactory, which had been hastily converted for this purpose in the summer of 1871. All plans for new and

14 The Reichstag building in the Königsplatz was completed in 1894

15 Georg Michaelis delivering his first speech as Reich Chancellor in the Reichstag, 19 July 1917

permanent parliament buildings were delayed for many years as a result of the tense relationship between Government and Parliament and because the site proposed in 1871, on the eastern side of the Königsplatz, was initially not available.

The Reichstag building

After protracted negotiations for the plot of land and two competitions to find the best design, work on the new Reichstag building began at long last in 1884. The winning entry was submitted by the Frankfurt architect Paul Wallot, who, departing from the traditional, classical type of building, developed a modern style which reflected the aspirations of the Reich. The Reichstag took ten years to build and was completed on 5 December 1894. Parliament was given a monumental, representative building which was not, however, suited in every way for the conduct of parliamentary business by parliamentary groups and committees.

New buildings for the Prussian Parliament

The two Prussian Chambers, too, were able to move into new quarters in the 1890s. New parliament buildings were constructed on a double plot between the Leipziger Strasse and the Prinz-Albrecht-Strasse, part of which had previously been occupied by the Chamber of Peers and the provisional Reichstag building. They replaced the totally inadequate accomodation dating back to the middle of the century.

C. Parliament and parliamentarians in Berlin

The Hohenzollern monarchy and Parliament

Berlin's political and social life during the years of the Empire was dominated by the monarchy and the upper class, especially the military. The relative weight of the monarchy and of Parliament was most strikingly manifest in the annual solemn opening of the Reichstag. The ceremony was not held in Parliament itself, as in England for instance, but in the White

16 The new building of the Prussian Chamber of Deputies, Prinz-Albrecht-Strasse

17 After the Reichstag moved into its new building in the Königsplatz, the new Prussian Chamber of Peers was built on the site at Leipziger Strasse 3 and 4

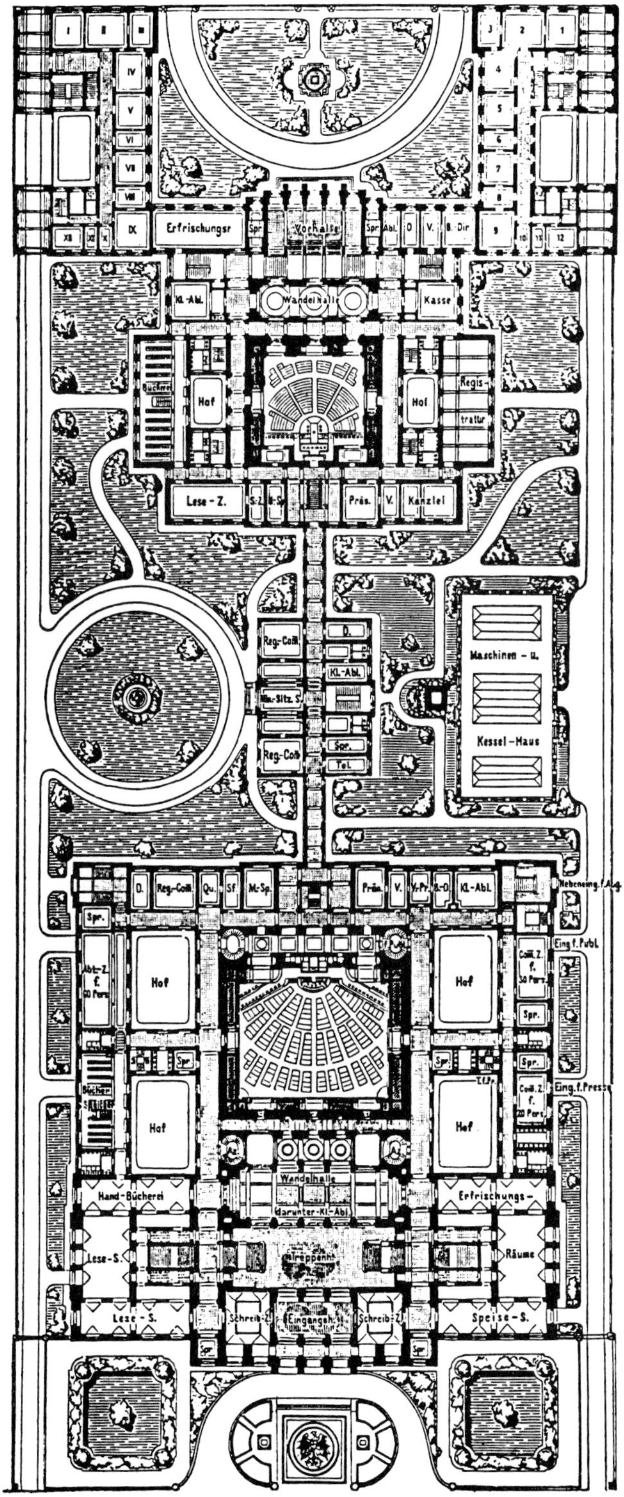

18 The double plot of land between the Leipziger Strasse and the Prinz-Albrecht-Strasse, showing the buildings of the Prussian Chamber of Peers (top) and of the Prussian Chamber of Deputies (bottom)

Hall of the Castle. Amidst the trappings of court ceremony and the many glittering uniforms, the deputies almost appeared to be mere supernumeraries.

The social life of parliamentarians in Berlin

The great majority of deputies came to Berlin only when the Reichstag was in session. The parliamentary groups met regularly in inns and restaurants in the vicinity of the Reichstag building. Sometimes receptions were given for them, with Bismarck's parliamentary "soirées" being particularly famous. Though the leading figures in the Reichstag of course belonged to Berlin's upper class, Parliament and its Members had very little impact on social life in the capital of the Reich.

The Berliners and Parliament under the Empire

Even after the founding of the Reich, Berlin's constituencies remained for many years firmly in the hands of the left-wing Liberals. By voting for the Liberals, large sections of Berlin's middle class expressed their political reservations about the Hohenzollern monarchy. However, the political scene changed as Berlin developed into an industrial metropolis with a growing working class and pronounced social disparities. First, the north and northeastern constituencies and then, from the mid-1890s onwards, all the constituencies in the capital switched their allegiance to the Social Democrats.

III 1919–1945: The heyday and decline of parliamentarianism

A. Parliament as the centre of democracy

Revolution and Parliament

After the collapse of the monarchy and the authoritarian state in the revolution of 1918, two alternatives were available for shaping the political order: a system of councils or parliamentary democracy. In December 1918 the National Congress of

Workers' and Soldiers Councils met for a time in the Prussian Chamber of Deputies. However, the leaders of the Social Democrats under Friedrich Ebert were able to assert themselves over the more radical groupings, with the result that elections were held for a constituent national assembly. The die had thus been cast for a system of parliamentary democracy.

The Prussian Diet

In the years of the Weimar Republic, the Prussia of the landed gentry, the Junker, who had been the mainstay of the Hohenzollern monarchy, became "red" Prussia, a republican bastion with an SPD-led coalition government formed by the Social Democratic Party, the Centre Party and the Liberals. The comparative political continuity in the Prussian Diet – there were no instances of early dissolution of Parliament or frequent changes of government – made a major contribution towards the temporary stabilization of the Republic.

The Reichstag

The Weimar Constitution made the Reichstag the centre of the country's democratic order. Its legislative powers were no longer circumscribed by the Reichsrat, which was made up of the representatives of the Laender, or states. Above all, however, the Government was now fully dependent on enjoying the confidence of a parliamentary majority. On the other hand, the strong position of the Reich President and the exceptional powers he was granted under the constitution reflected reservations about parliamentary democracy which had their roots in the tradition of the authoritarian state. In the final stages of the Weimar Republic this was to have fatal consequences.
By enfranchising women and introducing a system of proportional representation, the Weimar Constitution removed all the inequalities of the previous electoral system: henceforth, all votes were to have equal weight and determine the composition of Parliament. However, this form of electoral justice produced many small parties and made it difficult to form governments that could rely on stable majorities in Parliament.

19 The Kroll Opera House situated on the western side of the Königsplatz

20 Sitting of the Reichstag in the Kroll Opera House after the National Socialist seizure of power

B. Berlin society in the years of democracy

Berlin as the capital of the Reich

Berlin had become a European metropolis with four million inhabitants. It was an economically thriving city with hectic traffic, glittering facades, colourful advertisements and large department stores. Berlin's special urbane culture in the 1920s was manifest in the cafés and in the city's nightlife, in the theatre, literature and art, and in the abundance of modern buildings. However, to a far greater extent than before the First World War, life in the city was also marked by political conflicts and controversies.

Parliament, society and mass democracy

During the Weimar Republic, the political expectations and demands of nearly all social groups focused on Parliament and the parties. In Berlin itself, the elections to the Reichstag and to the Prussian Diet continued to be dominated by the workers' parties. Indeed, from 1930 onwards the Social Democrats were even overtaken by the German Communist Party. However, the parties were still not fully committed to reconciling their conflicting interests through parliamentary procedures, and they were even less prepared to do so in times of crisis.

The Republic's open society and its enemies

The young Republic was vehemently attacked by extreme left and right-wing groups who consistently exploited all the freedoms and possibilities afforded by a pluralistic democratic order. Right-wing extremists, in particular, did not even shrink from assassinating leading democratic politicians. Manifold emotional and political reservations about the Weimar Republic weakened the ranks of its supporters.

C. Political crisis and the end of parliamentary democracy

Parliamentary conflicts and confrontations

The grave political and social conflicts besetting the Weimar Republic were exacerbated by the world economic crisis of 1929. Instead of being settled in Parliament, they were increasingly fought out in the street. In the elections of 1930 and 1932, left-wing and above all right-wing, anti-democratic forces polled more votes than the parties which supported the Republic. Conservative circles around President von Hindenburg sought to exploit the crisis in order to reshape the political order along anti-parliamentary, authoritarian lines.

The eclipse of Parliament

From 1930 onwards the country was ruled by cabinets appointed by the Reich President, which increasingly restricted the Reichstag's possibilities of influencing the composition and policies of the Government. Normal legislative procedure was in many instances replaced by emergency decrees issued by the Reich President. If the Reichstag objected it was dissolved. On 22 July 1932 Reich Chancellor von Papen deposed the Prussian Government by decree, thus removing one of the last republican bulwarks of democracy and in effect depriving the Prussian Diet of its political powers.

The Reichstag aflame

On the night of 27 February 1933 the Reichstag went up in flames. The plenary chamber and parts of the cupola burnt down. The question of whether the Nazis were responsible for setting the blaze has still not been conclusively answered. However, the burning down of the Reichstag building symbolized the end of parliamentary democracy and of the Weimar Republic. The emergency decree issued on 28 February "to protect the people and the state", in which the most important basic rights were suspended, marked the beginning of the years of Nazi terror and the National Socialist dictatorship.

Dictatorship with a mock parliament

The deputies, who, following the burning down of the Reichstag, held their few remaining meetings in the Kroll Opera House opposite the parliament building, excluded themselves once and for all from the legislative process by voting for the Enabling Law of 23 March 1933. So-called elections to the Reichstag continued to be held in the one-party Nazi state, but the Reichstag's uniformed members were mere parliamentary decoration for the dictator, Adolf Hitler.

IV After 1945: The second democracy

A. A capital without a Reich

Parliamentary democracy in ruins

At the end of the war Berlin's parliament buildings, like many parts of the capital and of the German Reich, lay in ruins. The Reichstag in particular was severely damaged by bombs and artillery fire in the last years of the war, and on its dome there flew the Soviet flag. After the Nazi dictatorship parliamentary democracy in Germany had to be completely rebuilt.

A divided city and a divided nation

The sectoral boundary which, following Germany's division into two states with different political and social systems, also divides Berlin, cuts through the old government quarter, which had already undergone considerable changes under National Socialism. The larger part of that area, including the building of the Prussian Diet, lies just across the border in East Berlin. Only the Reichstag building and the part of the city where foreign missions used to be located are in West Berlin.

21 The main building of the Technical University during reconstruction

22 Plenary sitting of the German Bundestag on 19 October 1955 in the lecture theatre of the Physics Institute of the Technical University

23 In 1957 and 1965 the German Bundestag met in the newly built Congress Hall

24 Between 1954 and 1969 the Federal Convention met to elect the Federal President in the Ostpreussenhalle beneath the Radio Tower

B. Reconstruction and renewal

The German Bundestag and Berlin

From the very start, the Western sectors of Berlin were included in the process of democratic reconstruction. Under the Basic Law, Berlin is represented by its own Members of Parliament in the Bundestag, even though, on account of certain rights retained by the Allies, they only have limited voting rights. Between 1955 and 1965 the Bundestag also held several plenary sittings in Berlin. Until the Berlin crisis of 1958, neither the GDR nor the Soviet Union protested against these sittings. Since the conclusion of the Four-Power Agreement in 1971, however, the presence of the German Bundestag in Berlin has been limited to meetings of committees and parliamentary groups.

The reconstruction of the Reichstag building

After long discussions and debates, the reconstruction of the Reichstag began in 1961. The German Bundestag decided that it should again serve as a parliament building and therefore also have a new plenary chamber. At the same time it was decided not to restore the dome or all parts of the building. The Berlin architect Paul Baumgarten submitted a modern design, on the basis of which construction work was completed in 1971. As the seat of the German Bundestag in Berlin, the renovated Reichstag building is a symbol both of the tradition of parliamentary democracy in Germany and of national unity.

25 The Reichstag building, rebuilt between 1961 and 1971

26 The redesigned plenary chamber of the Reichstag building

Paula Abraham, Berlin
Konrad-Adenauer-Stiftung, Bonn
AEG-Telefunken, Berlin
Wolfgang Albrecht, Berlin
Jörg P. Anders, Berlin
Archiv der Deutschen Burschenschaft, Frankfurt/Main
Archiv Gerstenberg, Wietze
Archiv der sozialen Demokratie (AdsD), Bonn-Bad Godesberg
Associated Press GmbH, Frankfurt/Main
Augustinermuseum der Stadt Freiburg i. Breisgau

Badisches Generallandesarchiv, Karlsruhe
Heinrich Bauer-Verlag
Fred Bayer, Berlin
Bayer AG, Leverkusen
Bayerisches Hauptstaatsarchiv, München
Berliner Kindl Brauerei AG, Berlin
Berliner Kraft- und Licht (BEWAG) AG, Berlin
Berliner Morgenpost, Berlin
Berliner Post- und Fernmeldemuseum
Berliner Verkehrs-Betriebe (BVG)
Siegfried Bewersdorff, Berlin
Bezirksamt Tiergarten, Abt. Bauwesen, Berlin
Herbert Bode, Bonn
Robert Bosch GmbH, Stuttgart
Robert Bosch-Hausgeräte GmbH, Berlin
Bayerisches Hauptstaatsarchiv, München
Karl-Heinz Buller, Berlin
Bundesarchiv, Außenstelle Frankfurt/Main
Bundesarchiv Koblenz
Bundeskriminalamt Wiesbaden
Bundesministerium für Verteidigung, Bonn
Bundesministerium für Wirtschaft, Bonn
Bundespostmuseum, Frankfurt/Main
Bundespräsidialamt, Bonn
Burda-Verlag
Burschenschaft Teutonia zu Jena in Berlin

CDU, Bonn
Collection, The Museum of Modern Art, New York

Der Polizeipräsident in Berlin
Kurt Desch Verlag, München
Gerd Deutsch, Berlin
Deutsche Bank AG, Frankfurt/Main
Deutsche Presse-Agentur, Bildarchiv Berlin
Deutscher Bundestag
Deutsches Bergbau-Museum, Bochum
Deutsches Museum, München
Deutsches Rundfunkmuseum e. V., Berlin

Friedrich-Ebert-Stiftung, Bonn
EUROPA GmbH.

FDP, Bonn
Margarete Feist, Berlin
Focke-Museum, Bremen
Frankfurter Allgemeine, Frankfurt/Main

Geheimes Staatsarchiv Preußischer Kulturbesitz, Berlin
Generallandesarchiv Karlsruhe
v. Gerlach-Parsow, Hohenstein
Germanisches Nationalmuseum, Nürnberg
Karl Greiser
Claus-Peter Groß, Tegernsee
Großherzogliche Privatsammlungen, Darmstadt
Gruner und Jahr AG + Co, Hamburg

Horst Haitzinger
Irmin Hammelbacher, München
Wilma Hauck, Berlin
Hauptstaatsarchiv Stuttgart
Hilde Havel, Berlin
Brigitte Hellgoth
Colorfoto Hans Hinz, Basel
Historisches Museum der Stadt Frankfurt/Main
Hoesch Werke AG, Dortmund
Hanns Hubmann, Kröning
Burghard Hüdig

Imperial War Museum London
Industriegewerkschaft Metall, Frankfurt/Main
Institut für Zeitgeschichte, München
Institut für Zeitungsforschung, Dortmund
Interfoto Friedrich Rauch, München
Internationaal Instituut voor Siciale Geschiedenis, Amsterdam
Internationales Zeitungsmuseum der Stadt Aachen

Elfriede Kante, Berlin
Hilde Kaspar, Berlin
Keystone-Pressedienst
Barbara Klemm
Helga Kneidl, Hamburg
Kladderadatsch
Stefan Kresin, Heidelberg
Fritz Krüger, Berlin
Friedrich Krupp GmbH, Essen
Kunstbibliothek der Staatlichen Museen Preußischer Kulturbesitz, Berlin
Kunstgewerbemuseum, Staatliche Museen Preußischer Kulturbesitz, Berlin
Martin Kupke, Berlin
Kurpfälzisches Museum der Stadt Heidelberg

Landesarchiv Berlin
Landesbildstelle Baden
Landesbildstelle Berlin
Landesbildstelle Karlsruhe
Landeshauptstadt München
Leipziger Illustrierte

Marineschule Mürwik, Historische Sammlung, Flensburg-Mürwik
Maschinenfabrik Augsburg-Nürnberg (MAN), Augsburg
Wilfried Matthias, Bronzekunstwerkstatt, Berlin
Museum der Grafschaft Mark auf Burg Altena
Museum der Stadt Regensburg
Museum für deutsche Volkskunde Preußischer Kulturbesitz, Berlin

Neue Theaterkunst, Berlin
Herbert Nitert, Berlin

Ilsemarie Ollk, Berlin
Olympia Werke AG, Wilhelmshaven

Parlamentsarchiv Bundeshaus, Bonn
Willi Peiter, Diez
Pix-Features
Poddig Automobilmuseum, Berlin
Politisches Archiv des Auswärtigen Amtes, Bonn
Pressedienst Glaser, Berlin
Pressefoto Lehnartz
Presse- und Informationsamt der Bundesregierung, Bundesbildstelle, Bonn
Preußischer Kulturbesitz, Berlin
Propyläen Verlag, Berlin
Prof. Hubertus Protz, Berlin

Sophie Reimann, Berlin
Rheinisches Landesmuseum, Trier
Ringier Dokumentationszentrum, Zürich
Klaus Rose, Iserlohn
Ruhrland- und Heimatmuseum der Stadt Essen

Elisabeth Saier, Berlin
Alfred Schaefer, Berlin
Elisabeth von Schlegell, Berlin
Margret Schmitt, Berlin
Wolf Schöne
Margarete Schuppmann, Berlin
Dr. Erich Schwan, Darmstadt
Senatsbibliothek Berlin
Sven Simon, Hamburg
Spiegel-Verlag, Hamburg
Axel-Springer-Verlag
Staatliche Graphische Sammlungen, München
Staatsbibliothek Preußischer Kulturbesitz, Berlin
Staatsbibliothek Preußischer Kulturbesitz, Bildarchiv, Berlin
Staats- und Universitätsbibliothek Hamburg
Stadtarchiv Frankfurt/Main
Stadtarchiv Heidelberg
Stadtarchiv Konstanz
Stadtarchiv München

Städtisches Museum und Lottehaus Wetzlar
Städtisches Reiss-Museum
Stiftung Bundeskanzler-Adenauer-Haus, Rhöndorf
Stuttgarter Nachrichten
Süddeutscher Verlag, Bilderdienst München

Ullstein Bilderdienst, Berlin
Universitätsbibliothek der Freien Universität Berlin
Universitätsbibliothek der Technischen Universität Berlin

Verkehrsmuseum Nürnberg
Verwaltung der Staatlichen Schlösser und Gärten, Berlin
Volkswagenwerk AG, Wolfsburg

Wehrgeschichtliches Museum Rastatt
Gertrud Weinhold, Berlin
Detlef Weiß, Berlin
Werner-von-Siemens-Institut, München

Wolfgang Zierau, Berlin
Günter Zint

AEG-Telefunken, Zentralbibliothek
Berlin
XVI (color)

Jörg P. Anders, Berlin
XXIII (color)

Archiv der Deutschen Burschenschaft, Frankfurt/Main
27

Archiv Gerstenberg, Wietze
IX (color)
1, 5, 6, 10, 13, 15, 16, 17, 22, 23, 26, 28, 30, 33, 34, 38, 39, 40, 43, 44, 45, 46, 51, 52, 53, 54, 55, 56, 57, 65, 66, 68, 70, 76, 77, 83, 85, 86, 96, 98, 104, 113, 114, 115, 116, 124, 125, 126, 127, 133, 145, 147, 148, 150, 151, 155, 157, 163, 165, 184, 185, 222, 276

Archiv der sozialen Demokratie (AdsD), Bonn-Bad Godesberg
149, 186, 191, 197, 198, 228, 266, 300

Badisches Generallandesarchiv, Karlsruhe
42

Bayerisches Hauptstaatsarchiv, München
94

Bundesarchiv, Außenstelle Frankfurt/Main
X (color)
14, 24, 79, 82

Bundesarchiv, Koblenz
171, 175, 179, 181, 182, 183, 190, 194, 204, 212, 214, 228, 242, 256, 260, 298

Bundespostmuseum, Frankfurt/Main
4

Collection, The Museum of Modern Art, New York
XVII (color)

Kurt Desch Verlag, München
159, 213

Deutsche Presse-Agentur, Bildarchiv Berlin
173, 261, 264, 268, 270, 273, 290, 301, 313, 322, 325, 326, 329

Deutscher Bundestag
XIV, XV (color)
XIX, XX, XXI (color)

Deutsches Museum, München
32, 154

EUROPA GmbH
316

Geheimes Staatsarchiv Preußischer Kulturbesitz, Berlin
102, 131

v. Gerlach-Parsow, Hohenstein
119

Germanisches Nationalmuseum, Nürnberg
III, V (color)
9, 18, 19, 20, 58, 74, 91

Claus-Peter Groß, Tegernsee
158, 277

Herbert Bode, Bonn
XXII (color)

Historisches Museum der Stadt Frankfurt/Main
XI (color)
81, 122

Hanns Hubmann
292

Colorfoto Hans Hinz, Basel
XVIII (color)

Imperial War Museum London
263

Institut für Zeitgeschichte, München
236

Institut für Zeitungsforschung, Dortmund
196

Interfoto Friedrich Rauch, München
215

Internationaal Instituut voor Sociale Geschiedenis, Amsterdam
117

Helga Kneidl, Hamburg
XXIV (color)

Kladderadatsch
123

Stefan Kresin
330

Kunstbibliothek der Staatlichen Museen Preußischer Kulturbesitz, Berlin
I (color)

Kurpfälzisches Museum der Stadt Heidelberg
47, 48, 49

Landesarchiv Berlin
88

Landesbildstelle Baden
272

Landesbildstelle Berlin
110, 153, 164, 167, 168, 169, 172, 174, 176, 177, 180, 188, 199, 202, 217, 221, 257, 258, 262, 278, 279, 293, 306, 312, 318

Leipziger Illustrierte
31, 50, 62, 63, 64, 67, 71, 72, 75, 78, 87, 89, 90, 95, 97, 100, 101, 111, 112

Maschinenfabrik Augsburg-Nürnberg AG (MAN), Augsburg
108

Museum der Grafschaft Mark auf Burg Altena
8

Museum der Stadt Regensburg
2

Museum für deutsche Volkskunde Preußischer Kulturbesitz, Berlin
7

Politisches Archiv des Auswärtigen Amtes, Bonn
132, 156

Presse- und Informationsamt der Bundesregierung, Bundesbildstelle, Bonn
201, 216, 283, 289, 291, 307, 308, 310, 315, 317, 324, 328, 331, 336, 337, 338

Propyläen Verlag, Berlin
12

Rheinisches Landesmuseum, Trier
35, 36

Klaus Rose
323

Dr. Erich Schwan, Darmstadt
135

Senatsbibliothek Berlin
219, 222

Staatliche Graphische Sammlungen, München
11

Staatsbibliothek Preußischer Kulturbesitz, Berlin
146

Staatsbibliothek Preußischer Kulturbesitz, Bildarchiv, Berlin
II, IV, VI, VII, XIII (color)
37, 41, 59, 80, 84, 92, 93, 99, 105, 106, 107, 118, 120, 121, 128, 129, 130, 134, 136, 137, 138, 140, 141, 142, 143, 144, 152, 160, 161, 162, 166, 170, 178, 189, 208, 209, 218, 232, 234, 237, 238, 244, 245, 246, 247, 248, 249, 250

Stadtarchiv Frankfurt/Main
69

Stadtarchiv Heidelberg
61

Stadtarchiv Konstanz
60

Stadtarchiv München
VIII (color)
73

Städtisches Museum und Lottehaus
Wetzlar
3

Städtisches Reiss-Museum
21

Stiftung Bundeskanzler Adenauer
299

Süddeutscher Verlag, Bilderdienst
München
193, 206, 229, 274, 284

Ullstein Bilderdienst, Berlin
187, 192, 195, 200, 203, 205, 207, 210, 211, 223, 226, 227, 233, 235, 241, 243, 251, 253, 254, 256, 259, 265, 282, 287, 303, 319, 333, 334, 335

Universitätsbibliothek der Freien
Universität Berlin
25, 29

Universitätsbibliothek der
Technischen Universität Berlin
103, 109

Volkswagenwerk AG, Wolfsburg
294

Wehrgeschichtliches Museum Rastatt
XII (color)

Plan of the Exhibition Rooms in the Reichstag

I **1800–1815:**

Political Awakening and Congress of Vienna

The Old Empire
The effects of the French Revolution
The German Confederation

II **1815–1848:**

Pre-1848

The German Student Associations
Economic and Social Development prior to 1848
Manifestations of the national movement and national precedents in Europe
Grouping of the political forces

III **1848/49:**

The Revolution of 1848/49

The March Revolution of 1848
The National Assembly and the Second Wave of Revolution
The struggle for unity
The campaign for the Imperial constitution in the early Summer of 1849
The Reaction

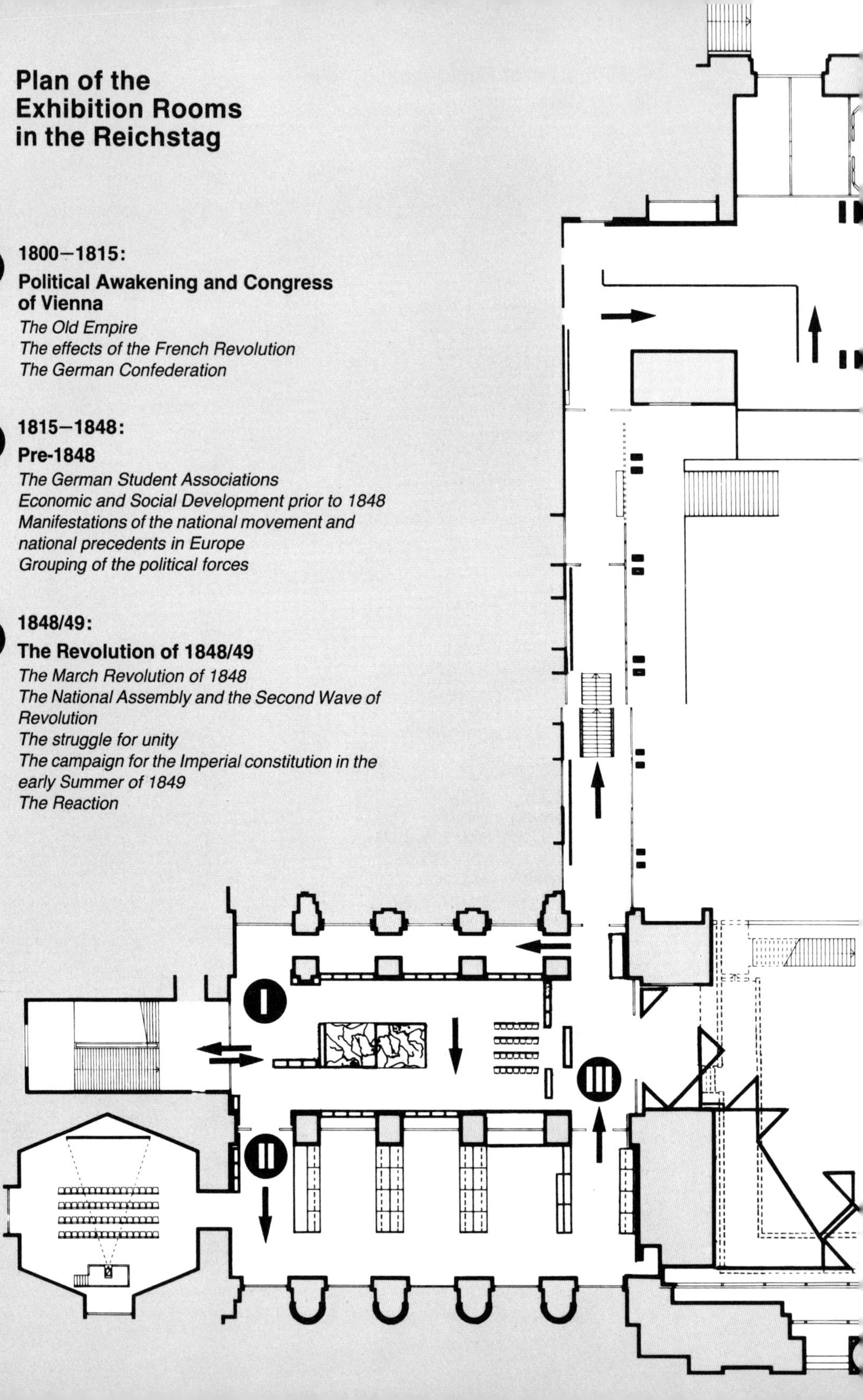

IV 1850–1918:

Industrial Revolution and the Establishment of the Empire – Imperial Germany

The Industrial Revolution – its social and political consequences
Parties and Associations
The Establishment of the Empire
The Little-German Nation State: Institutions, Parties, Problems
The Reich under Bismarck
Wilhelminian Germany
German Foreign Policy 1871–1914
The First World War

V 1919–1933:

The Weimar Republic

The Revolution of 1918/1919
The Development of the Weimar Republic
The Collapse of the Republic

VI 1933–1945:

The Third Reich

The Path to the 30th January 1933
The Consolidation of National Socialist Dominance
The National Socialist State
Power Politics and Resistance
The Second World War

VII 1945 to the Present Day

Establishment and Development of the Federal Republic of Germany

1945–1949: The Years of Fundamental Decisions
1949–1963: The Adenauer Era
1963–1969: The Years of Transition
1969–1982: The Social-Liberal Coalition

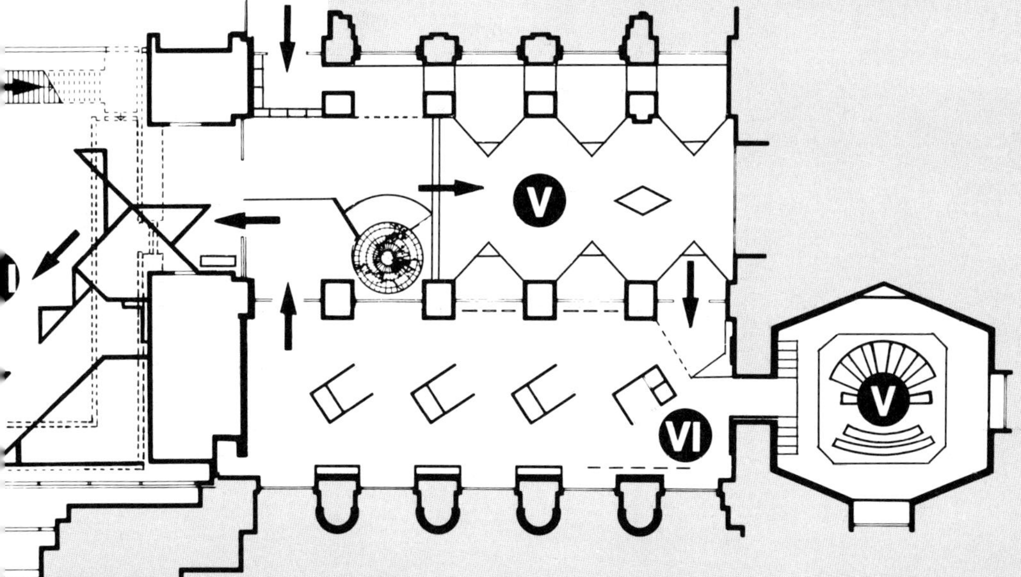

Expert Planning
and Catalogue:
Prof. Dr. Lothar Gall

Staff:
Jochen Bussmann
(constitution tables)
Dieter Hein
Ulrike Helbich
Dr. Rainer Koch
Jörg Riegel
Peter Scholz
Wolfgang Zierau

with the assistance of
the statt of the
German Bundestag
and the Federal Archive,
Koblenz

Organisers:
German Bundestag,
Historic Exhibition
in the Reichstag,
1000 Berlin 21

Creation and Visual
Conception:
Claus-Peter Gross

Graphic-Design:
Bernd Hildebrandt
Margret Schmitt
Wieland Schütz
Detlef Weiss

Production:
Quadriga, Design and Information
Claus-Peter Gross
Berlin/Tegernsee

Stage design:
Karl-Heinz Buller, Berlin
Waltraut Mau, Berlin

Production:
H. Jürg Steiner Museumstechnik,
Berlin

Catalogue Translator:
Dr. Peter J. Halstead

Films and Slides:
R. C. F. Film GmbH, Berlin
CHRONOS-Film, Berlin

Photographic Reproduction:
Wolfgang Schackla, Berlin

Printing of the Catalogue:
W. Kohlhammer Printers
GmbH + Co. Stuttgart

Chronological Table of the Catalogue

Around 1800		Fundamental challenges to the old political and social structure in middle Europe by the French Revolution.
1803	25.2	Decree of the Reich Deputation, Secularisation of all clerical principalities.
1806	11.7	Founding of the Confederation of the Rhine.
	6.8	Abdication of Kaiser Franz II.
	14.10	Battles of Jena and Auerstedt.
1807	7.7	Peace of Tilsit between France and Prussia.
	30.9	Freiherr vom Stein leading minister in Prussia, start of the Reformation.
1809	12.10	Metternich leading minister in Austria.
1813	28.2	Prussian-Russian Military pact signed at Kalisch.
	16–19.10	Battle of Leipzig.
1814	30.3	Occupation of Paris by allied troops, Napoleon goes into exile on Elba.
	18.9	Opening of the Congress of Vienna.
1815	1.3	Landing of Napoleon in France.
	8.6	Signing of the Federal Acts, Founding of the German Confederation.
	18.6	Defeat of Napoleon at Waterloo, sent into exile on St. Helena.
	26.9	Signing of the Holy Alliance between Russia, Prussia and Austria.
1816	6.11	Opening of the Federal Assembly in Frankfurt am Main.
1817	18.10	Wartburg Festival of the German Student Associations.
1818/1820		Modern Constitutions in Bavaria, Baden, Württemberg and Hessen-Darmstadt.

1819	23.3	Murder of the conservative author von Kotzebue by student representatives.
	6–31.8	Carlsbad Conference, suppression of liberal and national movements.
1820	24.5	Signing of the Acts of Vienna, extension of the Federal Acts of 1815.
1830	27–29.7	July Revolution in France, spreading of unrest to Brunswick, Hannover, Kurhessen and Saxony.
1832	27–30.5	Hambach Festival.
1833	4.4	Storming of the Frankfurt Guard by students and citizens.
1834	1.1	The Treaty setting up the German Customs' Union comes into force.
1835	7.12	Opening of the first German railway between Nuremberg and Fürth.
1837	1.11	Repealing of the state constitution in Hannover protest and dismissal of seven Göttingen professors.
1844		June uprising of Silesian weavers.
1847	3.2	Convocation of the United Landtag in Prussia. Establishment in June of the League of Communists in London led by Karl Marx and Friedrich Engels.
	12.9	Meeting of South German democrats in Offenburg.
	10.10	Meeting of moderate West and South German liberals in Heppenheim.
1848	24.2	Revolutionary unrest in Paris, abdication of King Louis Philippe.
	27.2	A People's Assembly in Baden, meeting near Mannheim, drafts the "March Demands".
	7.3	First revolutionary meetings in Berlin.
	13–15.3	Uprisings in Vienna; resignation of Metternich.
	18.3	Unrest and street-riots in Berlin.
	21.3	Proclamation by King Friedrich Wilhelm IV of Prussia "To my People and to the German nation."

1848	29.3	Appointment of the liberal minister Camphausen-Hansemann in Prussia.
	31.3–3.4	Assembly of the Vorparlament in the Paulskirche in Frankfurt, decision taken on the setting up of a German National Assembly.
	April	Republican uprising in Baden, led by von Hecker and Struve.
	15.5	A second uprising in Vienna forces the setting up of a Reichstag.
	18.5	Meeting of the German National Assembly in the Paulskirche in Frankfurt.
	29.6	Creation of a temporary central authority, election of Arch-duke Johann of Austria to the post of Imperial Administrator.
	26.8–16.9	Under pressure from the great powers. Prussia signed the ceasefire of Malmö which settled the conflict with Denmark over Schleswig-Holstein, which was initially rejected by the National Assembly in Frankfurt but eventually had to be accepted.
	6/7.10	Third Uprising in Vienna.
	31.10	Reconquest of Vienna by Imperial troops.
	2.11	Appointment of the conservative Brandenburg ministry in Prussia.
	21.11	Prince of Schwarzenberg became head of the Imperial Ministry in the Habsburg Monarchy.
	2.12	Abdication of the Austrian Kaiser Ferdinand I, accession to the throne of his nephew Franz Joseph I.
	5.12	Dissolution of the Prussian National Assembly, granting of a constitution.
	21.12	Passing of the law concerning the basic rights of the German People by the Frankfurt National Assembly.
1849	4.3	Dissolution of the Austrian Reichstag, granting of a constitution.
	27/28.3	Passing of a constitution for the German Reich in the Paulskirche in Frankfurt, election of Friedrich Wilhelm IV of Prussia as German Kaiser.
	28.4	Rejection of the German Kaiser's crown by the Prussian King.

1849	May–July	Campaign for a constitution for the Reich, uprisings in Saxony, Breslau and Baden were violently repressed.
	26.5	Three Kings' Alliance between Prussia, Saxony and Hannover; passing of the "Erfurt Reich Constitution" based on the Prussian Policy of union.
	6–18.6	Meeting of the Rump Parliament in Stuttgart.
	20.12	Resignation of the Imperial Administrator, Arch-Duke Johann.
1850	31.1	Implementation of the granted Prussian Constitution.
	1.9	Reopening of the Frankfurt Bundestag.
	29.11	Treaty of Olmütz: End of the Prussian Policy of union.
1854/1856		Crimean War between England, France and Russia; Austria and Prussia remained neutral.
1858	7.10	Wilhelm I of Prussia takes over the regency for his mentally-ill brother Friedrich Wilhelm IV; Beginning of the "New Era".
1859	3.5–11.7	Piedmont and France's war against Austria.
	16.9	Founding of the German National Association as an organisation for the supporters of a Little-German Nation-State under Prussian leadership.
1861	2.1	Death of Friedrich Wilhelm IV, accession to the throne of Wilhelm I.
	26.2	Patent-Act for the Constitution of the Austrian Monarchy.
	6.6	Founding of the German Progress Party.
1862	29.3	Signing of the Franco-Prussian Trade Treaty.
	24.9	Appointment of Bismarck as the Prussian Prime Minister; the constitutional conflict over the reform of the army became more serious.
	28.10	Founding of the German Reform Association as an organisation for the proponents of a Great-German Nation-State solution.

1863	23.5	Founding of the General Association of German Workers in Leipzig under the leadership of Ferdinand Lassalle.
	16.8–1.9	Princes' Convention in Frankfurt.
1864		Prussian-Austrian War against Denmark over Schleswig-Holstein.
1865	14.8	Treaty of Gastein between Prussia and Austria over the administration of Schleswig-Holstein.
1866	21.6–26.7	German War
	3.7	Battle of Königgrätz/Sadowa.
	23.8	Peace Treaty of Prague: Dissolution of the German Confederation, recognition of Prussia's dominant position in Germany.
	3.9	Passing of the Indemnity Bill by the Prussian Lower House, settling of the constitutional conflict.
	17.11	Founding of the National Liberal Party.
1867	12.2	Elections for the Constituent Reichstag of the North German Confederation.
	12.6	Austro-Hungarian settlement.
	21.12	"December Laws" in Austria, beginning of a liberal era.
1869	7–9.8	Founding of the Social Democratic Workers' Party in Eisenach, led by August Bebel and Wilhelm Liebknecht.
1870	13.7	Ems Telegram.
	18.7	Proclamation of the doctrine of papal infallibility by the First Vatican Council.
	19.7	France declared war on Prussia.
	2.9	Surrender of a French army at Sedan and imprisonment of Emperor Napoleon III.
	19.9	Start of the Siege of Paris.
1871	18.1	Proclamation of the German Empire in Versailles.

1871	10.25	Peace Treaty of Frankfurt am Main: ceding Alsace-Lorraine to Germany and payment of war-reparations of five thousand million francs. Start of the Cultural struggle in Prussia and in the German Empire.
1873	9.5	Collapse of the Vienna Stock Exchange, start of the period of the "Great Depression".
	22.10	Triple Alliance between Austria-Hungary, Russia and the German Empire.
1875	April–May	"War in Sight"-crisis.
	22–27.5	Supporters of Lassalle and Marx join forces in Gotha to form the "Socialist Workers Party".
1876	15.2	Founding of the Central Association of German Industrialists.
1878		Kaiser Wilhelm was seriously wounded in an assassination attempt.
	13.6–13.7	Berlin Conference.
	18.10	Passing of the Anti-Socialist Laws by the Reichstag.
1879	12.7	Passing of the Protectionist Laws by the Reichstag.
	7.10	Dual Alliance between the German Empire and Austria-Hungary.
1880	14.7	The passing of the first mitigating law heralded the end of the cultural struggle in Germany.
1883	15.6	Acceptance by the German Reichstag of the Law governing sickness benefits.
1884	27.6	Introduction of accident insurance in Germany. Acquisition of German colonies in South-West Africa, Togo and Cameroon.
1885		Acquisition of German East Africa.
1887	18.6	Signing of the Reinsurance Treaty between Russia and the German Empire.
1888	9.3	Death of Kaiser Wilhelm I; accession to the throne of his terminally ill son Friedrich III.
	15.6	Death of Friedrich III; accession to the throne of his eldest son Wilhelm II.

1890	25.1	The Reichstag rejected any extension of the Anti-Socialist Law; it expired on 30. 9. 1890.
	20.3	Resignation of Bismarck as Reich Chancellor and Prussian Prime Minister; under his successor, General Leo von Caprivi, a "New Course" in social and customs' policies.
	27.3	No extension of the German-Russian Reinsurance Treaty.
	1.7	Helgoland-Zansibar Treaty, settlement of Anglo-German colonial interests.
1891	1.7	Founding of the Pan German Association in Berlin.
1893	18.2	Founding of the League of Agriculturalists as the organisation of large landowners east of the Elbe.
1894	26.10	In connection with the "Overthrow Proposal" against the S.P.D., resignation of Chancellor von Caprivi; successor Chlodwig, Prince of Hohenlohe-Schillingfürst.
1895	21.6	Opening of the Kaiser Wilhelm Canal (North Sea-Baltic Canal).
1896	1.7	Granting of the Citizens' Law Book (B.G.B.) by the Reichstag; it came into force on 1. 1. 1900.
1900	17.10	As successor to the Prince Hohenlohe, Foreign Secretary Bülow became new Reich Chancellor.
1905/1906		First Moroccan Crisis between France and the German Empire.
1908	Oct./Nov.	Daily Telegraph Affair, strengthening of the Reichstag's position.
1909	14.7	As successor to the retired Reich Chancellor Bülow, Theobald von Bethmann Hollweg became new head of government.
1911		Second Moroccan Crisis.

1912	12.1	For the first time in Reichstag elections the Social Democrats were the strongest Party, even in terms of distribution of seats.
1914	28.6	Assassination of the heir to the Austrian Throne, Arch-Duke Franz Ferdinand, by Serbian Nationalists in Sarajeivo.
	28.7	Austria-Hungary declared war on Serbia.
	30.7	General mobilisation by Russia.
	1.8	German mobilisation; Germany declared war on Russia.
	3.8	Germany declared war on France.
	4.8	Great Britain responded to the violation of Belgian neutrality by German troops by declaring war on the German Empire.
	26–31.8	Battle of Tannenberg, slaughtering of the Second Russian Army.
1916	21.2–July	Battle of Verdun.
	29.8	von Hindenburg and Ludendorff assumed supreme command of the armed forces.
1917	9.1	German Headquarters agreed to unrestricted submarine warfare.
	8.3	Outbreak of revolution in Russia, abdication of Czar Nicholas II.
	6.4	U.S.A. declared war on the German Empire.
	6–8.4	Inaugural party meeting of the Independend Social Democratic Party in Gotha.
	14.7	Resignation of Reich Chancellor Bethmann Hollweg under pressure from the supreme army command.
	19.7	Passing of the "Peace Resolution" in the Reichstag with the demand for a conciliatory peace, formation of an inter-party committee from members of the Centre Party, S.P.D. and left wing liberals.
	6–7.11	October Revolution in Russia, Bolshevik uprising.
	15.12	Ceasefire between Russia and the German Empire.
1918	28.1	Mass strikes in Berlin and other German cities.

1918	3.3	Peace Treaty of Brest-Litowsk.
	29.9	Final demand made by the supreme army command for the offer of a ceasefire.
	3.10	Establishment of a new Reich government under Prince Max von Baden which also included representatives of the majority parties.
	24–28.10	Constitutional reform, the Reich Executive became responsible to Parliament.
	28.10	Outbreak of German Naval Mutiny.
	3–4.11	Sailors' mutiny in Kiel.
	6–8.11	The revolutionary movement spread to the rest of the Empire.
	9.11	Declaration of a republic by the Social Democrat Scheidemann.
	10.11	Establishment of the Peoples' Council from the ranks of the S.P.D. and U.S.P.D.
	15.11	Stinnes-Legien Agreement between employees and employers.
	16–20.12	Reich Congress of Workers' and Soldiers' Councils in Berlin.
	23.12	Mutiny of the Peoples' Naval Division in Berlin.
	29.12	The U.S.P.D. representatives walked out of the Peoples' Council.
	31.12	Founding of the K.P.D.
1919	5–12.1	Spartacus Rising in Berlin.
	15.1	Murder of Rosa Luxemburg and Karl Liebknecht.
	19.1	Election of a National Assembly.
	11.2	Social Democrat Friedrich Ebert was elected as Reich President by the National Assembly in Weimar.
	13.2	Formation of the Scheidemann Government, Weimar coalition of S.P.D., Centre Party and D.D.P.
	1–3.5	Defeat of the Munich Republic of Councils.
	6.6	Ultimatum to the German government demanding their acceptance of the Peace Treaty.
	28.6	Signing of the Treaty of Versailles.

1919	11.8	Announcement of the Weimar Constitution.
1920	13–17.3	Kapp-Lüttwitz Putsch in Berlin.
	March/April	Communist uprising in the Ruhr and in central Germany.
	6.6	Reichstag election; the parties of the Weimar coalition lost their majority.
1921	20.3	Plebiscite in Upper Silesia.
	26.8	Assassination of Centre Party politician Erzberger by right wing radicals.
1922	16.4	Treaty of Rapallo between U.S.S.R. and the German Empire.
	24.6	Assassination of Reich Foreign Minister Rathenau by right wing radicals.
1923	11.1	Occupation of the Ruhr by French and Belgian troops.
	13.1	Announcement of passive resistance against the Ruhr occupation.
	26.9	Abandonment of the Ruhr struggle by the Stresemann government, declaration of martial law in Bavaria, answered by the declaration of a state of emergency in the Reich by the government.
	19.10–18.2.1924	Conflict between Bavaria and the Reich.
	22–23.10	Attempted communist uprising in Hamburg.
	29.10	Action taken by the Reich against the S.P.D./K.P.D. in Saxony.
	8–9.11	Hitler Putsch in Munich.
	15.11	New currency. End of inflation.
	23.11	Collapse of the Stresemann government.
1924	July/August	Acceptance of the Dawes Plan by the London Reparation Conference and by the Reichstag.
	7.12	Reichstag election: gains made by the S.P.D. and the middle-class centre, start of a period of relative stability in the Weimar Republic.

1925	28.2	Death of Reich President Ebert, election of General Field Marshall von Hindenburg as his successor.
	1.12	Signing of the Locarno Treaty.
1926	24.4	Signing of the Treaty of Friendship and Neutrality with the Soviet Union in Berlin.
	10.9	Entry of Germany into the League of Nations.
1928	28.6	Formation of the Grand Coalition between the S.P.D., Centre, D.D.P. and D.V.P. under the Social Democratic Chancellor Müller.
1929	7.6	Young Plan finally settled the reparation problem.
	3.10	Death of Foreign Minister Stresemann.
	25.10	"Black Friday" in New York; beginning of the world economic crisis.
1930	27.3	Collapse of the Müller government over the question of financing unemployment benefits.
	30.3	Appointment of Centre Party politician Brüning to the post of Chancellor, with a minority government.
	30.6	French troops left the Rhineland ahead of schedule.
	16.7	First Emergency Decree by the Reich President in the interest of "economic and financial security".
	14.9	Reichstag election: N.S.D.A.P. landslide.
1931	11.10	Formation of the Harzburg Front from the ranks of the N.S.D.A.P., D.N.V.P. and Stahlhelm.
1932	10.4	Re-election of Reich President von Hindenburg.
	30.5	Resignation of the Brüning Government.
	1.6	Formation of a right wing cabinet under Franz von Papen.
	20.7	Action taken by the Reich against Prussia; the government, headed by the Social Democrats, was overthrown.
	31.7	Reichstag elections: N.S.D.A.P. became the strongest party.
	6.11	Renewed Reichstag elections: loss of support for the National Socialists.

1932	17.11	Resignation of the von Papen cabinet.
	3.12	General von Schleicher was appointed Reich Chancellor.
1933	28.1	Resignation of Chancellor von Schleicher.
	30.1	Hitler was appointed Reich Chancellor.
	27.2	Burning of the Reichstag.
	28.2	"Reich President's Decree to protect the people and the state."
	5.3	Reichstag election: majority for the N.S.D.A.P. and their coalition partner the D.N.V.P.
	23.3	The Reichstag accepted the Enabling Act, despite the opposition of the S.P.D.
	31.3	First law directed at aligning the Länder.
	1.4	Organised boycott of Jewish Businesses.
	7.4	Second law directed at aligning the Länder.
	2.5	Disbanding of Trade Unions.
	June/July	Disbanding of all parties with the exception of the N.S.D.A.P.
	20.7	Concordat between the German Reich and the Vatican.
	14.10	Germany left the League of Nations.
1934	30.6	"Röhm-Putsch", elimination of the S.A. leadership, assassination of General von Schleicher.
	2.8	Death of Hindenburg, swearing of the Oath of Allegiance by the Wehrmacht to the "Führer and Reich Chancellor" Hitler.
1935	13.1	Plebiscite in the Saarland on the issue of its return to the Reich.
	16.3	Reintroduction of mandatory national service.
	15.9	"Nuremberg Laws", Jewish population were deprived of their rights.
1936	7.3	German troops marched into the demilitarised Rhineland.
	1.8	Opening of the Olympic Games in Berlin.

1936	25.10	German-Italian Treaty, "Berlin-Rome Axis".
	25.11	Anticomintern Pact between Germany and Japan.
1938	12.3	German troops marched into Austria.
	29.9	Munich Treaty agreeing the ceding of the Sudetenland to the German Empire.
	9.11	"Reichskristallnacht", organised riots aimed against the German Jews.
1939	15.3	German troops invaded Czechoslovakia, the Reich Protectorates of Böhmen and Mähren were established.
	23.3	The Memel territories were given back to the German Reich.
	23.8	Signing of the German-Russian Non-Aggression Pact.
	1.9	Start of German attacks on Poland.
	3.9	Great Britain and France declared War on the German Empire.
1940	9.4	Occupation of Denmark, invasion of Norway.
	10.5	German attack on Belgium, the Netherlands, Luxembourg and France.
	22.6	Signing of the Franco-German ceasefire in Compiègne.
1941	22.6	Attack on the Soviet Union.
	11.12	Germany declared war on the U.S.A.
1942	20.1	"Wannsee Conference", announcement of the "final solution for the Jewish Question".
1943	14–25.1	Casablanca Conference between Roosevelt and Churchill, demand for "unconditional surrender".
	31.1–2.2	Surrender of the Sixth German Army in Stalingrad.
1944	6.6	Allied landing in North-Western France.
	20.7	Assassination attempt on Hitler by von Stauffenberg; attempted coups d'etat in Berlin and Paris.
1945	4–11.2	Yalta Conference.
	12.4	Death of American President Roosevelt.

1945	25.4	Meeting of American and Soviet troops near Torgau on the Elbe.
	30.4	Hitler's suicide.
	7–9.5	Signing of the German Surrender in Reims and Berlin-Karlshorst.
	10.6	Command No. 2 of the S.M.A.D.; licensing of parties and trade unions.
	11.6–5.7	Founding of the K.P.D., S.P.D., C.D.U. and L.D.P. in Berlin.
	1–4.7	Withdrawal of British and American troops from Saxony, Thuringia and Mecklenburg; Western troops entered Berlin.
	17.7–2.8	Potsdam Conference.
	Aug./Sept.	Start of party licensing in the western zones of occupation.
1946	20–27.1	First local elections in the American zone.
	21/22.4	Amalgamation of the K.P.D. and S.P.D. to form the S.E.D. in the Soviet zone of occupation and East Berlin.
	6.9	Speech by U.S. Foreign Minister Byrnes in Stuttgart.
	1.10	Passing of the sentences in the Nuremberg War Crime Trials.
	2.12	Washington Treaty on the economic unification of the British and American zones.
1947	25.2	Formal dissolution of the state of Prussia by the Control Commission.
	10.3–24.4	Moscow Foreign Ministers' conference of the four victorious allies.
	5.6	Announcement of a programme for the economic reconstruction of Europe by U.S. Foreign Minister Marshall.
	6–7.6	Munich Prime Ministers' Conference.
	10.6	Setting up of the Economic Council of the Bizone in Frankfurt am Main.
	25.11–15.12	London Foreign Ministers' Conference of the four victorious allies.

1948	23.2–6.3 and 20.4–2.6	Sic Powers' Conference in London, passing of the London recommendations on the founding of a West German state.
	20.3	Last session of the Allied Control Commission.
	20/21.6	Currency reform in the western zones.
	24.6	Start of the Berlin Airlift.
	1.7	Handing over of the "Frankfurt Documents" to the West German prime ministers.
	10–23.8	Constitutional conference on Lake Herrenchiem.
	1.9	Setting up of the Parliamentary Council in Bonn.
1949	4.5	Jessup-Malik Agreement on the lifting of the Berlin Blockade on 12. 5. 1949.
	23.5	Announcement of the Basic Law for West Germany.
	14.8	Election of the first Bundestag.
	12.9	Election of Theodor Heuss (F.D.P.) to the post of Federal President.
	15.9	Election of Konrad Adenauer (C.D.U.) as Federal Chancellor.
	21.9	Occupied status came into effect.
	7.10	Establishment of the German Democratic Republic.
	22.11	Petersberg Treaty which ended the dismantling process.
1950	6.1	End of food rationing in West Germany.
	15.6	Bundestag decree in favour of West German accession to the Council of Europe.
	25.6	Start of the Korean War.
1951	10.4	Passing of the Law, by the Reichstag, on equal worker-management status in decisionmaking in the steel-coalmining industries.
	18.4	Signing of the European Coal and Steel Community Treaty in Paris.
1952	26.5	Signing of the Germany Treaty in Bonn.
	27.5	Signing of the European Defence Community (E.D.C.) Treaty in Paris.

1952	10.9	Signing of the Reconciliation Treaty between Israel and West Germany.
1953	5.3	Death of Stalin.
	17.6	Uprising in East Berlin and East Germany.
	27.7	Cease fire in Korea.
1954	23.10	Signing of the Treaty of Paris allowing West Germany to join N.A.T.O. and permitting West German rearmament, following the rejection of the E.D.C. Treaty by the French National Assembly.
1955	5.5	Paris Treaty came into force, sovereignty for West Germany.
	14.5	Founding of the Warsaw Pact, including the D.D.R.
	9–13.9	Visit by Chancellor Adenauer to Moscow.
	23.10	Plebiscite in the Saarland, rejection of plans to form a European territory.
1956	20/23.2	F.D.P. forced the collapse of the Arnold government in North Rhine Westphalia, division in the F.D.P. group, F.D.P. left the Federal Government.
1957	1.1	Incorporation of the Saarland into the Federal Republic.
	22.1	Bundestag passed the Pension Reform Law.
	25.3	Signing of the Treaty of Rome establishing the European Economic Community.
	15.9	Bundestag election, absolute majority for the C.D.U./C.S.U.
1958	27.11	"Berlin Ultimatum" issued by the Soviet Union.
1959	1.7	Election of Heinrich Lübke as Federal President.
	13–15.11	S.P.D. Godesberg Conference, passing of a new programme.
1960	30.6	Bundestag speech by Herbert Wehner, acceptance by the S.P.D. of rearming and Western integration.
1961	13.8	Building of the Berlin Wall.

1962	14–28.10	Cuba Crisis.
	Oct./Nov.	Spiegel Affair, resignation of Federal Defence Minister, Strauss.
1963	22.1	Signing of the Franco-German Friendship Treaty in Paris.
	15/16.10	Resignation of Chancellor Adenauer, election of Economic Minister as his successor.
	17.12	First agreement on transborder travel between East Germany and the West Berlin Senate.
1966	26.10	F.D.P. ministers resign from the Erhard Cabinet.
	1.12	Forming of a Grand Coalition between C.D.U./C.S.U. and S.P.D. under Chancellor Kiesinger.
1967	31.1	Establishment of diplomatic relations between West Germany and Rumania, relaxation of the Hallstein Doctrine.
	14.2	Start of the process of "concerted action" chaired by Economic's Minister Schiller.
	8.6	Passing of the Stability Law by the Bundestag.
1968	11–17.4	Murder of student leader Dutschke, "Easter Riots" in Berlin and other West German cities.
	30.5	Bundestag passed Emergency Decree.
	21.8	Troops of the Warsaw Pact invaded Czechoslovakia.
1969	5.3	Election of Gustav Heinemann (S.P.D.) as Federal President.
	28.9	Bundestag election, considerable gains made by the S.P.D.
	21/22.10	S.P.D. Chairman Brandt elected Chancellor, formation of an S.P.D./F.D.P. Federal Government.
	28.11	Signing of Treaty blocking production of atomic weapons by West Germany.
1970	19.3	Meeting between Chairman of the D.D.R. Council of Ministers Stoph and Federal Chancellor Brandt in Erfurt.
	21.5	Return visit by Stoph to Kassel.

1970	12.8	Signing of the German-Soviet Non-Aggression Pact in Moscow.
	7.12	Signing of the German-Polish Treaty in Warsaw.
1971	3.9	Signing of the Four Powers' Agreement on Berlin.
	10.12	Chancellor Brandt received the Nobel Peace Prize.
1972	27.4	C.D.U./C.S.U. failed in an attempted vote of "No Confidence" against Chancellor Brandt.
	17.5	Ratification of the Moscow and Warsaw Treaties by the Bundestag.
	19.11	Bundestag elections: S.P.D. and F.D.P. gain a clear majority.
	21.12	Signing of the Basic Treaty between the D.D.R. and West Germany in East Berlin.
1973	18.9	West Germany and the D.D.R. became members of the United Nations.
	October	Start of a World oil crisis, Arab oil-producing nations restricted deliveries and increased prices.
1974	6.5	Resignation of Chancellor Brandt.
	15.5	Election of Foreign Minister Scheel (F.D.P.) as Federal President.
	16/17.5	Election of Finance Minister Schmidt (S.P.D.) as Chancellor, renewal of the S.P.D./F.D.P. Coalition.
1975	1.8	Signing of the Council for Security and Cooperation in Europe agreements in Helsinki.
1976	3.10	Bundestag election: a narrow victory for the S.P.D./ F.D.P. Coalition.
1977	7.4	Murder of Federal Attorny General Buback.
	30.7	Murder of the banker, Ponto.
	5.9–19.10	Kidnap and murder of Employers' President Schleyer, hijack of a Lufthansa plane, liberation of the hostages in Mogadishu, suicide of the terrorists Baader, Ensslin and Raspe.
1978	16/17.7	World Economic Summit of the seven most important western industrialised states in Bonn.

1979	23.5	Election of Carstens (C.D.U.) as Federal President.
	7–10.6	First European Parliamentary direct elections.
	12.12	Decision to increase deployment of nuclear missiles taken by N.A.T.O. Council of Ministers.
1980	30.6/1.7	Visit by Chancellor Schmidt to Moscow.
	5.10	Bundestag election: S.P.D. and F.D.P. strengthened their majority.
1981	10.10	Peace demonstration in Bonn.
	11–13.2	Visit by Chancellor Schmidt to East Germany.
1982	17.9	Collapse of the S.P.D./F.D.P. Coalition, resignation of F.D.P. ministers.
	1.10	Replacement of Chancellor Schmidt and the S.P.D. minority government by a C.D.U./C.S.U./F.D.P. Coalition under Chancellor Kohl.
1983	7.1	President Karl Carstens dissolves the German Bundestag in accordance with Article 68 of the Basic Law and orders new elections to be held on 6 March.
	6.3	Bundestag elections: the CDU/CSU and the FDP obtain an absolute majority, together polling 55% of the second votes, and are able to continue their coalition. The Greens win 28 seats and are represented in the Bundestag for the first time.
	29.3	The German Bundestag re-elects Helmut Kohl Federal Chancellor.
	21/22.11	Bundestag debate on NATO's dual-track decision and force modernization.
1984	May/July	Strikes for the 35-hour week in the metal and printing industries.
	23.5	Richard von Weizsäcker, Governing Mayor of Berlin, is elected Federal President.
1985	2/5.5	World Economic Summit in Bonn.
	5.5	US President Reagan visits Bergen-Belsen and Bitburg.
	2/3.12	EC summit on reform of the European Community and the accession of Spain and Portugal.

1986	January	The Neue Heimat scandal, involving a co-operative building association owned by the trade unions, reaches its climax.
	26.4	Accident at the Chernobyl nuclear reactor in the Soviet Union.
1987	25.1	Bundestag elections: the CDU/CSU and the FDP retain their majority and again form the Federal Government.
	7./11.9	Erich Honecker, Chairman of the Council of State of the GDR, visits the Federal Republic of Germany.